Understanding Cognitive Science

Understanding
Cognitive Science

Michael R. W. Dawson

Copyright © Michael R. W. Dawson 1998

The right of Michael R. W. Dawson to be identified as author of this work has been asserted in accordance with the Copyright, Designs and Patents Act 1988.

First published 1998

2 4 6 8 10 9 7 5 3 1

Blackwell Publishers Inc.
350 Main Street
Malden, Massachusetts 02148
USA

Blackwell Publishers Ltd
108 Cowley Road
Oxford OX4 1JF
UK

Library of Congress Cataloging-in-Publication Data

Dawson, Michael R. W., 1959–
    Understanding cognitive science / Michael R. W. Dawson.
      p. cm.
    Includes bibliographical references and index.
    ISBN 0-631-20894-1 (hardcover : alk. paper). — ISBN 0-631-20895-X (pbk. : alk. paper)
    1. Cognition. 2. Cognitive science. 3. Human information processing. I. Title.
    BF311.D35 1998
    153—dc21   98–13849
                                             CIP

British Library Cataloguing in Publication Data

A CIP catalogue record for this book is available from the British Library.

Typeset in 10 on 12½pt Sabon
by York House Typographic Ltd
Printed in Great Britain by M.P.G. Books, Bodmin, Cornwall

This book is printed on acid-free paper

Contents

Figures

Tables

1

The Coffee Room and Cognitive Science

Conversation

The psychology department at the University of Western Ontario has a coffee room on the seventh floor of the Social Sciences and Humanities Center that offers an attractive view of the deciduous forest northwest of the campus. When I was a graduate student in the department, the room was maintained by Jim Webster, whose voice was as gruff as his coffee. Jim has retired now, and has been replaced by an impressive-looking vending machine. The machine may make better coffee, but it can't replace the chat with Jim that was part of the coffee room ritual.

Conversation is what the coffee room was all about. At any time of the day, you could go there and find a handful of department members talking to one another. Of course, much of the time the topics discussed were the same as those discussed in any coffee room in any organization: gossip, politics, and sports. In addition, though, there was a generous amount of "shop talk." Faculty would test research ideas out on each other, would describe some of their latest results, and would discuss problems that were arising with one project or another. As a student, you could learn a lot by buying the occasional cup of Jim Webster's coffee.

Psychology students quickly learn from coffee-room chatter, lectures, and textbooks that their discipline is extremely fractured – a "large, sprawling, confusing human undertaking" (Leahey, 1987, p. 3). Psychologists have basic disagreements about fundamental issues like the existence of free will, the use of mentalistic terms in explanations, and the ability to translate psychological theories into neurophysiological ones. "There is no normal science, in Kuhn's sense, no universally accepted way of conceptualizing theory and experiment in psychology. It is as though opposing armies were fighting battles in order to win the right to define the nature of the war" (Boden, 1981, p. 71).

Indeed, scientific psychology changes paradigms almost as frequently as Paris changes fashions. Wilhelm Wundt established the first experimental psychology laboratory in 1879. The century hadn't even ended before Wundt's original *Ganzheit* psychology had been adapted into structuralism by Wundt's student Titchener, and had been attacked on separate fronts by Kulpe's Wurzburg school and by James's (1890) functionalism. Freud's *The Interpretation of Dreams* was first published in 1900; Watson launched behaviorism with a 1913 paper in *Psychological Review*. A variety of behaviorist schools dominated psychology from the mid-1920s through the 1950s, a period which also saw strong challenges to behaviorism arising from Gestalt psychologists (e.g., Koffka, 1935; Kohler, 1947/1975), from humanistic psychologists (e.g., Rogers, 1961), and from cognitivists (e.g., Bruner, Goodnow, & Austin, 1956; Chomsky, 1959; Miller, Galantner, & Pribram, 1960).

Given this mottled past, it is instructive to consider the kind of conversations that one might hear in a mythical coffee room. Imagine, for instance, that Sigmund Freud and B. F. Skinner were both members of the same psychology department. Would they have enough in common to engage in "shop talk" ? For Freud, the mind was a vortex of conflicting unconscious desires, and psychoanalysis was a tool to bring these unconscious forces under scientific scrutiny. In contrast, Skinner claimed that a scientific psychology should not include the study of mental states that could not be directly observed. Skinner reinvented the mind as a repertoire of overt responses under the control of (observable) environmental stimuli and a (putatively observable) reinforcement history. My suspicion is that in view of their wildly different worldviews, and in the interest of our imaginary department's peace, Freud and Skinner would arrange their coffee-room visits to occur at different times.

Really, what properties do Freud and Skinner share that even make us confident that both can be described with the term *psychologist*? When I ask my students this question, they usually find that their best answer is no deeper than "Freud and Skinner were both interested in human behavior," and begin to see that psychology is (at best) very broadly defined or (at worst) incoherent. Indeed, there are few, if any, foundational assumptions that are shared by all psychologists. Koch (1976) has argued that psychology must, in principle, divide into a diverse range of small "search cells," with researchers who belong to one cell unable to understand the language of another.

Hull (1935) complained that "we all know only too well that among psychologists there is not only a bewilderingly large diversity of opinion, but that we are divided into sects, too many of which show emotional and other signs of religious fervor." Little has changed in psychology over sixty years after this declaration. However, other approaches to mental phenomena have emerged in recent decades to provide some hope for a more unified view of mind.

Cognitive Science

Cognitive Science: a Multidisciplinary Journal of Artificial Intelligence, Psychology, and Language first appeared in January 1977. The purpose of this journal was to serve the needs of "a community of people from different disciplines, who find themselves tackling a common set of problems in natural and artificial intelligence" (Collins, 1977, p. 1). However, by the time this journal first appeared, cognitive science had been in existence as a distinct field of study for over twenty years: there is some consensus that it was born on September 11, 1956 at the Symposium on Information Theory held at MIT (Gardner, 1984).

Who made up the community of people that *Cognitive Science* wished to foster? Table 1.1 presents some excerpts from recent descriptions of cognitive science programs at various North American universities. These descriptions provide a compelling sense of cognitive science's interdisciplinary nature, noting that it includes (in alphabetical order) anthropology, computer science, history of science, linguistics, neuroscience, operations research, philosophy, psychology, and sociology. In my darker moments, I have the strong sense that being a cognitive scientist requires me to be a jack of all academic trades, and condemns me to being master of none.

What common set of problems did the members of this community find themselves tackling? Another glance at table 1.1 reveals a large, intimidating list. "The most immediate problem areas are representation of knowledge, language understanding, image understanding, question answering, inference, learning, problem solving, and planning" (Collins, 1977, p. 1). It seems that cognitive science's scope rivals psychology's breadth.

Now, theorists like Koch (1976) believe that different psychologists will have difficulty communicating with each other because of psychology's diversity. Given this, what kinds of "shop talk" could we even hope to hear between, for instance, a psychologist, a philosopher, and a computer scientist? Surprisingly, cognitive scientists coming from quite different research areas can fill coffee rooms with detailed, technical conversations. The community served by *Cognitive Science* is held together by a common language (e.g., Lachman, Lachman, & Butterfield, 1979, chaps 1–4), which it discovered in the conferences and writings that began to emerge in the 1950s.

The discovery of new groups of researchers with whom to communicate was exhilarating. Gardner (1984, p. 29) quotes George Miller's reaction to the 1956 Symposium on Information Theory: "I went away from the symposium with a strong conviction, more intuitive than rational, that human experimental psychology, theoretical linguistics, and computer simulation of cognitive processes were all pieces of a larger whole, and that the future would see progressive elaboration of their shared concerns." Such inspiration, fueled by early empirical successes, led researchers to make brash forecasts about what this future would look like, and about when it would arrive. For example, Simon and Newell (1958) made several bold predictions, including "that within ten years most theories in psychology will take the form of computer programs." One possible measure of cognitive science's success is the fact that Dreyfus (1992), a noted critic of artificial intelligence research, concedes that this particular prediction has been partially fulfilled.

Table 1.1   Some university calendar descriptions of what cognitive science is.

Institution	Definition of Cognitive Science
University of Toronto, Scarborough Campus	"Cognitive science is the name for a field of academic inquiry that has become popular since the late 1950s. The topic of the field is how people come to have, represent, and communicate knowledge; in general, how people come to be intelligent. It includes many aspects of perception, memory, and communication. It is concerned with the representation of knowledge in many forms, including literal and metaphoric representation. It tackles the relations between mechanical computation and human knowing and problem solving. It discusses robot vision as well as human vision and animal vision. The field is inherently interdisciplinary; it includes parts of philosophy, psychology, computer science, and linguistics. To a lesser degree, neuroscience and anthropology are involved."
Carleton University	"Cognitive science is a multi-disciplinary approach to the study of cognition: learning, language, perception, memory, consciousness, reasoning, attention, and so on. Cognitive Science grew out of Psychology, Computer Science, Philosophy, and Linguistics, with the various neurosciences joining in more recently."
UCSD	"Cognitive science is the scientific study of the mind, the brain, and intelligent behavior, whether in humans, animals, machines, or the abstract . . . It is a multidisciplinary approach to the study of cognition that blends anthropology, computer science, psychology, neuroscience, linguistics, sociology and philosophy."
University of Rochester	"Cognitive Science is the study of cognitive processes – reasoning, remembering, perceiving, learning, and language understanding. It is an interdisciplinary field that combines work done in cognitive psychology, artificial intelligence, computer science, and parts of linguistics and philosophy."
Princeton University	"Cognitive Science is the interdisciplinary study of cognitive processes involved in the acquisition, representation and use of human knowledge, particularly including the study of natural language, memory, problem solving, learning, vision, and reasoning . . . It includes work done in anthropology, philosophy, psychology, operations research, computer science, linguistics, and history of science."

Another measure of its success is the growing number of cognitive science programs that have been formally established. For example, a 1995 proposal for establishing Ph.D. studies in cognitive science at a Canadian university noted that various types of cognitive science programs exist in at least 200 universities and research centers around the world. The language that was being discovered, created, and defended by the pioneers of the 1950s has become conventional enough to be handed directly down to many new generations of cognitive scientists.

A Foundational Assumption

There is an important asymmetry in the interdisciplinary characterization of cognitive science. For instance, just because cognitive science includes psychology, this does not mean that every psychologist is a cognitive scientist. Indeed, cognitive science is not an umbrella organization that encompasses all of the disciplines mentioned in table 1.1, but is instead a specialized domain that emerges at the *intersection* of these various fields.

Researchers found at this intersection of disciplines belong to a community bonded together by a common language. Where does this common language originate? What do psychologists, computer scientists, linguists, neuroscientists, and philosophers share that even makes conversation possible? The descriptions in table 1.1 emphasize the kinds of content areas that students might encounter in cognitive science programs. What these descriptions fail to note is that cognitive scientists share a fundamental assumption that allows them to communicate with one another, even though their particular fields of training might be very different.

This assumption is that *cognition is information processing*. The modern lineage of this assumption can be traced to K. J. M. Craik (1943, p. 57): "My hypothesis then is that thought models, or parallels, reality – that its essential feature is not 'the mind,' 'the self,' 'sense-data,' nor propositions but symbolism, and that this symbolism is largely of the same kind as that which is familiar to us in mechanical devices which aid thought and calculation." In the 1950s, a select group of psychologists (e.g., Miller, Galantner, & Pribram, 1960), computer scientists (e.g., Newell, Shaw, & Simon, 1958), and linguists (e.g., Chomsky, 1959), were attacking specific problems in their field from this representational perspective. They were able to communicate with one another because they were all immersed in the information-processing vocabulary of the day. More importantly, they realized that the integration of parts of several disciplines was possible and desirable, because each of these disciplines had research problems that could be addressed by designing "symbolisms." Cognitive science is the result of striving towards this integration.

Implications of the Assumption

The central assumption for cognitive science can be phrased as follows: "The human mind is a complex system that receives, stores, retrieves, transforms, and transmits information" (Stillings *et al.*, 1987, p. 1). In short, the mind is assumed to be an information processor. This statement, which served as a revolutionary hypothesis for Craik (1943), is rather mundane these days to psychology students immersed in a curriculum that includes courses in cognitive psychology, cognitive development, social cognition, animal cognition, and cognitive neuroscience. A central theme of this book is that this assumption, once adopted, has profound effects on the basic questions, the research methods, and the explanatory status of cognitive science.

For now, let us merely observe how this assumption begins to lead us towards a unified cognitive science. Koch (1976, p. 515) argued that "the subject matter of psychology is such that every significant meaning that can be conveyed in a natural language must, in principle, constitute potential data for our discipline." Furthermore, this is potential data that psychology must attempt to explain. The sheer breadth of this task forces Koch to conclude that psychology, in principle, will never be a coherent science.

In contrast, the assumption that the mind is an information processor narrows cognitive science's focus considerably. In the end, cognitive science will only be able to provide explanations of those phenomena that will yield to the representational approach. "The set of phenomena that constitute cognition, in this technical sense, is a long-term empirical question: we have no right to stipulate in advance which phenomena will succumb to the set of principles and mechanisms that we develop in studying what appear pretheoretically to be clear cases of cognition" (Pylyshyn, 1991, pp. 189–90). While scientific psychology is a set of phenomena looking for a paradigm, cognitive science is a paradigm looking for a set of phenomena. This latter approach appears to be more pragmatic, as cognitive science has provided insights into an interesting and important subset of mental abilities (for example, see table 1.1). In comparison, "theory in a field as immature as psychology cannot be expected to amount to much – and it doesn't" (Royce, 1970, p. 17).

What can Cognitive Scientists Say?

Neils Bohr said that "it is wrong to think that the task of physics is to find out how nature is. Physics concerns only what we can say about nature" (Gleick, 1992, p. 244). This is true for any science, because science is in the business of developing a vocabulary that describes certain regularities, but which necessarily ignores others (see also Pylyshyn, 1984).

The information-processing assumption makes conversation possible in the cognitive science coffee room by providing a scientific etiquette which tells the kinds of sentences that are sensible, as well as the kinds of sentences that are not. (Note that this is only a matter of etiquette, because the assumption doesn't tell us which sentences are *true*!) When we claim that "the mind is an information processor," we are saying that minds have particular properties that are also properties of information processors. So, if we overhear a sentence that says "the mind has property x," and we know that this property is not true of information processors, then we also know that this is not a meaningful sentence in cognitive science.

To say that the information-processing assumption provides some guidelines as to what cognitive science can talk about isn't to say that cognitive science conversation is limited by this assumption. The reason for this is that explanations of information processors require many different kinds of descriptions. Neuroscientists, computer scientists, psychologists, and philosophers can have good talks about cognitive science, because each has something crucially important to contribute to the conversation.

From Conversations to Arguments, and Back Again

One of the main themes of this book is to describe a framework for the "language" of cognitive science, and to demonstrate how this framework makes interdisciplinary conversation possible. Given this theme, one might think that cognitive science is a friendly discipline. However, few of my students are willing to accept such a neighborly view. They have witnessed, within fields related to cognitive science, harsh arguments between researchers who share similar foundational assumptions.

Indeed, it often seems that cognitive science is an angry science, and that interactions between cognitive scientists may be better described as arguments than as conversations. To a certain extent, this might be the result of having a shared language, which allows researchers to be more adept at communicating the problems and inadequacies that they perceive in their opponents' models, experiments, or theories. Unfortunately, when these arguments get very heated, some of the parties involved break off the conversation. Sometimes, they even go so far as to make this break permanent, by claiming that they have invented a new (and better) language.

It used to be the case that when cognitive scientists presumed that "cognition is information processing," they were really postulating that cognition involves step-by-step processes of the type that are carried out by a digital computer. As will be detailed in the next chapter, it is instructive to think about these digital processes in the context of a very simple computing device called a *Turing machine*. These days, researchers who use the Turing machine as a metaphor for cognition are called *classical* or symbolic cognitive scientists.

In the early days of artificial intelligence and cognitive science, the Turing machine metaphor was highly productive. By viewing cognition as the manipulation of symbols according to a set of rules – and thus bringing Craik's (1943) notion of symbolism to life – classical researchers were able to provide many examples of how computers could be programmed to deal with problems whose solutions appeared to require intelligence. These problems included playing games at expert levels of ability, proving mathematical theorems, answering questions about complex domains, and general problem-solving. An excellent overview of this early work can be found in the collection of papers compiled by Feigenbaum and Feldman (1995).

These early successes were very encouraging, but in recent years there has been a growing disenchantment with classical research (see, for example, various articles in Born, 1987, and in Graubard, 1988). This is because over the last few decades, while there has been great success in producing computers that can do very well on tasks that give trouble to people, at the same time there has been much less success in producing computers that can do well on tasks that people find very easy – like seeing the world, or learning a language.

Today, many researchers have abandoned the Turing machine metaphor of classical cognitive science because they believe that the brain is quite unlike a digital computer. "In our view, people are smarter than today's computers because the brain employs a basic computational architecture that is more suited to deal with a central aspect of the natural information processing tasks that people are so good at" (McClelland, Rumelhart, & Hinton, 1986, p. 3). They have replaced classical models with computer programs that have a "brainlike" appearance. Such programs are often called *artificial* neural networks, and cognitive scientists who believe that these networks provide a better architecture for cognition are called *connectionists*.

The rise of connectionism in cognitive science has not been a friendly event. On the one hand, connectionists seem to view the Turing machine metaphor as original sin; they argue that many of the problems facing cognitive science could be solved if a different, brainlike architecture was adopted (e.g., McClelland, Rumelhart, and the PDP Group, 1986; Rumelhart, McClelland, and the PDP Group, 1986). This position has blown new life into old arguments against classical cognitive science (e.g., Dreyfus, 1992, pp. xiii–xv; Searle, 1992, p. 246). On the other hand, proponents of classical cognitive science have argued that connectionist networks do not have sufficient computational power to be seriously considered as a theoretical or modeling medium for cognitive science (e.g., Fodor & Pylyshyn, 1988; Minsky & Papert, 1969/1988; Pinker & Prince, 1988). " 'Voodoo,' remarks Zenon Pylyshyn, a professor of cognitive science at Rutgers University. 'People are fascinated by the prospect of getting intelligence by mysterious Frankenstein-like means – by voodoo! And there have been few attempts to do this as successful as neural nets' " (Stix, 1994, p. 44).

The growing popularity of connectionist modeling gives the appearance that cognitive science is in the midst of a dramatic split. Schneider (1987) has described connectionism as a paradigm shift for cognitive psychology. Two decades after *Cognitive Science* was created as a forum for classical researchers, one now finds new journals dedicated to a community engaged in connectionist research (e.g., *Connection Science, IEEE Transactions On Neural Networks, Neural Computation, Neural Networks*). The putative differences between classical and connectionist architectures, along with their relative advantages and disadvantages, are frequently debated in the literature (e.g., Clark, 1989; Dawson & Shamanski, 1994; Dennett, 1991; Graubard, 1988; Ramsey, Stich, & Rumelhart, 1991; VanLehn, 1991).

It is clear that tension exists between classical and connectionist schools of cognitive science. What is a student to do in this situation, particularly if they begin their training in one tradition instead of the other? Fortunately, while there are important technical differences between symbolic models and connectionist networks, one's choice of one architecture over another does not affect the basic questions that cognitive scientists have to answer, nor the ability to communicate with other cognitive scientists – even those who have chosen an alternative architecture. Throughout this book, I hope to show that while classical and connectionist researchers can have important arguments about what trees they are looking at, they can still agree that they are both in the same forest.

What is this Book About?

To summarize some of the main points that were made above, cognitive science involves researchers from many different disciplines who are able to talk constructively to one another because they share the information-processing assumption. As the book proceeds, I want to describe what the information-processing assumption is, and discuss how and why it shapes the kinds of questions that cognitive scientists are interested in answering. As we will see in the next chapter, when one assumes that a system is information processing, one must address three different questions in order to explain how the system works: What information-processing problem is the system solving? What information-processing steps are being used to solve the problem? How are these information-processing steps actually carried out by a physical device? These three questions define the tri-level hypothesis (e.g., Marr, 1982; Pylyshyn, 1984) that characterizes cognitive science. A major purpose of this book is to present an overview of the tri-level hypothesis, showing how it provides the unifying glue that keeps the different disciplines within cognitive science working productively together.

This is not to say that the tri-level hypothesis is accepted universally. Many researchers have strong disagreement with it. Edelman (e.g., 1987, 1988, 1989, 1992) is concerned that the approach to cognitive science that I will be describing is too far removed from biological details. Churchland and Sejnowski have raised concerns about the adequacy of the tri-level hypothesis (Churchland, Koch, & Sejnowski, 1990; Churchland & Sejnowski, 1989, 1992). Searle (e.g., 1980, 1984, 1990) has argued that any approach based on the information-processing hypothesis cannot provide a complete account of the semantic nature of human mentality. All of these criticisms are important, and their implications should be considered. But in my view, it is premature to do this before getting some sense about what cognitive science is, and about the kinds of questions (and answers) that are encountered when the information-processing hypothesis is adopted. We have to learn quite a bit about the language of cognitive science before we can adequately assess the kinds of things that can and cannot be said with it!

A second purpose of this book is to use the tension between classical and connectionist cognitive science as a case study of the unifying power of the tri-level hypothesis. Let me state my biases on this matter right now: I do not believe that there is a marked qualitative difference between these two approaches, and I am very concerned by the tendency of some researchers to argue otherwise. For instance, Schneider's (1987) suggestion that connectionism is a paradigm shift disturbs me. Kuhn (1970) has argued that one of the defining characteristics of different paradigms is their inability to communicate with one another. However, when I look at connectionism, I don't see such an inability, because connectionists are speaking the same language as classical cognitive science, a language that depends upon the tri-level hypothesis. One of the threads running through this text will be my attempt to convince you of this position.

This is not to say that classical cognitive science and connectionist cognitive science are identical. There are interesting technical differences between the two approaches that have to be seriously considered by someone deciding on what architecture to use to model a cognitive phenomenon. However, these differences are often very subtle. This will become clearer in later chapters when the two approaches are compared as they should be – at each level of the tri-level hypothesis.

Why did I Write this Book?

For the last several years, I have been involved in teaching cognitive science courses to undergraduate and graduate students from psychology, linguistics, computer science, philosophy, business, and mathematics. Most texts available for these courses (e.g., Green, 1996; Posner, 1991; Osherson, 1995; Stillings *et al.*, 1987) are surveys of research in the many different content areas of cognitive science, with each chapter reflecting a different research area (e.g., concepts and categorization, mental imagery, deductive reasoning, etc.), and with each chapter written by different specialists. Such books provide excellent surveys of many of the technical details of cognitive science, and give a good overview of the kinds of experimental and theoretical "facts" that are part of this new discipline. However, often times these books emphasize the finer details of cognitive science at the expense of giving students a sense of the "big picture."

This book represents an attempt to reverse this tradition, by emphasizing what I take to be the "big picture" of cognitive science. Rather than trying to exhaustively catalogue cognitive scientists' current views of memory, language, vision, and so on, I am more intent on giving students a sense of what kinds of questions cognitive scientists are interested in, as well as why they are interested in them. My experience has been that after students acquire this kind of knowledge, they are comfortable with the general language of cognitive science, and have a theoretical framework that enables them to better understand the more technical and specific details to be found in survey texts or in journals.

Who is this Book Written For?

The students that I am used to seeing on a day-to-day basis in my classes are the intended audience for this book. In general, these students are one of two different types. The first type of student is a senior undergraduate who has already been exposed to a survey course in one of the core disciplines related to cognitive science. These students have a background in some specific facts and particular methods related to this discipline, and have an interest in finding out how this knowledge is related to cognitive science in general. After going through the material in this book, this kind of student should have a broader framework that can be used to elaborate their understanding of the core discipline. This student should also have an appreciation of the different kinds of methodologies and expertise offered by other disciplines that could be brought to bear on the study of phenomena that this student finds of interest. For such students as these, I would spend an entire term going over the material presented in this book.

The second type of student that this book is intended to reach is a graduate student with a deeper exposure to one of the core disciplines. The student could be doing graduate work in the core discipline, or embarking on graduate studies in a bona fide cognitive science program. For this type of student, the purpose of this book is make explicit some themes that they might have already inferred from the literature. When I teach the material in this book to such a student, I usually spend half a term on it (viewing it as either an accelerated introduction or as a review of basics), and then go to other sources, such as primary journal articles, to find additional case studies that illustrate the important issues.

While addressing the issue of the book's audience, I'll own up to the fact that my training in psychology sometimes biases the kind of examples that I choose to illustrate my points. (The current chapter is one instance of this bias rearing its head.) However, this book is not intended exclusively for psychology students. In my own lab, I supervise Ph.D. students from philosophy and computer science as well as from psychology, so I am sympathetic to the perspectives of other disciplines. In later chapters, when illustrating my main points, I have tried to choose a variety of examples that would be of interest to students with backgrounds in different disciplines. I have also tried to describe these examples in plain enough terms that they can be easily understood by those unfamiliar with the discipline they have been selected from.

A Look Ahead

How are we going to proceed from here? In order to get a sense of the "big picture" for cognitive science, we have to get some understanding of what an information processor is. After all, the assumption "cognition is information processing" is pretty empty if we don't have something interesting to say about what information processing is! The next two chapters do this. Chapter 2 describes information processing from the perspective of classical cognitive science, and introduces the kinds of questions that are raised by the tri-level hypothesis. Chapter 3 describes information processing from the perspective of connectionist cognitive science, and examines the relationship between connectionism and the tri-level hypothesis.

The chapters that follow these general accounts of information processing are all organized around the framework of the tri-level hypothesis. Chapter 4 looks at the computational level of analysis, and the kinds of issues that arise when cognitive scientists ask, "What information-processing problem is the system solving?" Chapter 5 looks at the algorithmic level of analysis, which is involved when cognitive scientists ask "What information-processing steps are being carried out to solve this problem?" Information-processing steps are typically thought of as being a program for accomplishing some task, and a program is written in a particular programming language. Cognitive scientists have to pay attention to this fact, and search for the "programming language of the mind," as is detailed in chapter 6 on the functional architecture. Chapter 7 looks at the implementational level of analysis, which is the center of attention when researchers ask, "What kind of machine is carrying out these information-processing steps?" Chapter 8 offers a brief case study of one specific area of research in cognitive science, my own work on apparent motion (e.g., Dawson, 1991), to illustrate how all of these different levels might be coordinated in a single research program. Finally, chapter 9 tries to summarize the structure of cognitive science as I see it, putting classical and connectionist cognitive science into the context of the tri-level hypothesis.

2

The Classical View of Information Processing

In chapter 1, I argued that the information-processing hypothesis provided a unifying framework for cognitive science which permits different cognitive scientists to communicate with one another, even if they are trained in different disciplines. The purpose of this chapter is to describe in more detail what the information-processing hypothesis is, and how it affects the practice of cognitive science.

This will be done as follows: First, I am going to describe the properties of a very simple (but extremely powerful) information processor called a Turing machine. I am going to do this to give you a sense of what the fundamental properties of an information processor might be. Second, I am going to spend some time talking about what one might say if asked to explain how a Turing machine was actually working. I will argue that there are three very different kinds of explanations that one could give, each representing an answer to a fundamentally different kind of question. One explanation answers questions like "What information-processing problem is the Turing machine solving?" Another answers questions like "What steps is the Turing machine carrying out to solve this problem?" The third answers questions like "How are these information-processing steps actually implemented on a physical machine?" I will also argue that all three of these types of questions must be answered if one is going to have a complete explanation of a cognitive phenomenon.

The view that cognitive explanations must provide answers to all three of these questions is called the *tri-level* hypothesis, because each type of question involves looking at a system at a different level of abstraction. The most explicit treatment of the tri-level hypothesis was provided by David Marr (e.g., 1982), and the current chapter has been heavily influenced by Marr's approach.

Before proceeding, it is critical to point out that the specific view detailed below – that is, that information processing is the kind of thing that Turing machines do – is consistent with what we will be calling "classical" cognitive science, and is not accepted by all cognitive scientists. As was noted in chapter 1, a new brand of cognitive science called "connectionism" has been experiencing an explosion of popularity. I am going to delay writing about the connectionist view of information processing until the next chapter. By the end of this chapter and the next, though, I hope that you will be of the opinion that whether a researcher buys into the classical or the connectionist approach, he or she is still assuming that cognition is information processing, and is still committed to the tri-level hypothesis.

Part I   Turing Machines and Cognitive Science

From Mathematics to Cognitive Science

At the turn of the nineteenth century, the German mathematical giant David Hilbert defined a research program to establish the absolute foundations of mathematics. Hilbert proposed a number of precise questions about the fundamental nature of mathematics, and believed that the answer to all of his questions would be "yes." Thus for Hilbert, these questions represented a few loose ends for the field to tie up. For other mathematicians, these questions represented a challenging puzzle whose solution would validate the entire discipline. Unfortunately for the Hilbert program, by the early 1930s mathematicians had shown that the answers to many of Hilbert's questions were actually "no," and as a result an absolute basis for mathematics was not possible.

Interestingly, the negative answer to one of Hilbert's questions, the *Entscheidungsproblem*, had enormous positive consequences in nonmathematical arenas, and eventually led to the development of cognitive science. The *Entscheidungsproblem* was this: Is mathematics decidable? If mathematics was decidable, then there would exist a "definite method" that would work as follows: One could write down any mathematical expression, and then give this expression to the definite method. The method would be guaranteed to decide whether the expression was true or false. In short, the definite method would be a mechanism for determining the truth of any mathematical claim.

To answer the *Entscheidungsproblem*, two very contradictory conditions had to be met. On the one hand, the definite method had to be extraordinarily general and powerful. This is because it had to be capable of dealing with any mathematical expression. On the other hand, the method had to be exceptionally simple, so that mathematicians would agree about its suitability for claims about decidability. In other words, to solve this problem, a mathematician would have to propose an extremely simple information-processing mechanism capable (in spite of its simplicity) of resolving exceptionally complicated mathematical expressions. To prove that no such method could exist for all expressions, the British mathematician Alan Turing had to invent the basis for modern computers (Turing, 1936).

The Supertypewriter

Cognitive science may have become possible in part because Alan Turing had terrible handwriting. From his early days in school, Alan Turing had been plagued with horrible handwriting. His teachers' wrote that "I can forgive his writing, though it is the worst I have ever seen, and I try to view tolerantly his inexactitude and dirty, slipshod work" (Hodges, 1983, p. 30). Even as a child, though, Turing fought back against this liability. In April of 1923 (when he was only 11) he wrote a letter using a less-than-successful fountain pen that he had invented, and a few months later another of his letters "described an exceedingly crude idea for a typewriter" (p. 14).

This childhood fascination with writing machines may have played an important role in an older Turing's thoughts about a definite method for resolving the decidability question (for a detailed development of this view, see Hodges, 1983, pp. 90–102). Turing realized that a typewriter had many of the characteristics that would be required of a general purpose information processor. First, it essentially had an infinite memory. Its continually replaced sheet of paper was reconceived by Turing as an infinitely long ticker tape. Second, it could move back and forth along this paper, at any time pointing to a particular location on the sheet. Turing proposed that the ticker tape of his machine was divided into small cells, and that at any particular time, only one of these cells would be processed. Third, the typewriter could write a symbol to its memory. Fourth, this writing was a definite act that depended upon a machine configuration. For instance, in the regular physical state of the typewriter, if one pressed a specific key the symbol "q" was written. However, if the physical state of the typewriter was changed by pressing the "CAPS LOCK" key down, pressing the same key would produce a different symbol, "Q."

With the addition of three more properties, Turing envisioned a "supertypewriter" that defined his definite method. First, he gave it the ability to read the symbol in the memory cell that it was processing. Second, he gave it the ability to erase the symbol in the current cell (i.e., by writing a special BLANK symbol). Third, he allowed it to have many different physical configurations – it was not just limited to two (i.e., CAPS LOCK down or up!).

The resulting device is now known as the Turing machine, and figure 2.1 presents one manner in which such a machine can be illustrated. The machine itself is separated into two different components: an infinitely long ticker tape which serves as a memory and a machine head which manipulates the contents of memory. The tape is divided into a series of cells, any one of which can only contain a single symbol. The head includes mechanisms for moving left or right along the tape (one cell at a time), for reading the symbol in the current cell, and for writing a symbol into the current cell. The head also includes a register to indicate its current physical configuration or machine state. Finally, the head includes a set of basic instructions, the machine table, which precisely defines the operations that the head will carry out.

Figure 2.2 illustrates an example machine table for a particular Turing

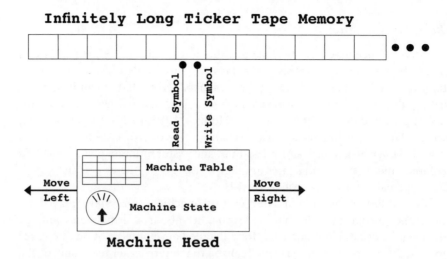

Figure 2.1 The basic properties of a Turing machine.

machine. The table has six different rows, because this particular machine will at any time be in one of six possible machine states. The table has three columns, because at any particular time it will be reading only one of three possible symbols on the tape: a blank ("B"), a "0," or a "1." Each entry in the table consists of a simple instruction to be carried out when the Turing machine is in a specific state and is reading a specific symbol. Most of the instructions involve either writing a particular symbol to the tape, or moving one cell to the right or to the left. All of these instructions also involve adopting a specific machine state. There are a couple of other instructions of note on the table as well. For instance, at row 4 and column 0 the table says "Eh?" This simply means that some mistake has been made, because this particular machine should under normal circumstances be in state 4 while reading the symbol "0." At row 6 and column 0 the table says "Stop." When the machine carries this instruction, it simply stops processing, because it has completed the task that it was programmed to do.

How does a Turing machine actually work? Essentially, a programmer writes a particular question on the tape in symbols that the machine recognizes. Then, the programmer places the Turing machine at a particular cell on the tape in a starting machine state (usually state 1). Then the machine begins to follow its machine table, moving back and forth along the tape, usually rewriting it as it goes. Finally, the machine executes its "Stop" instruction, and quits moving. At this point, the symbols written on the tape represent the machine's answer to the original question.

For example, imagine that the Turing machine described in figure 2.2 was placed in machine state 1 on the tape drawn in figure 2.3a. The really interested reader could pretend to be that machine, working along the tape following the instructions in the table. To do this, it would be useful to have available a little

Symbol Read From Tape

		B	0	1
Current Machine State	**1**	Write 1 to tape. Adopt State 6	Write B to tape. Adopt State 2	Move 1 cell left Adopt State 6
	2	More 1 cell left. Adopt State 2	Write B to tape. Adopt State 3	Eh?
	3	Move 1 cell left. Adopt State 3	Write B to tape. Adopt State 4	Write B to tape. Adopt State 5
	4	Move 1 cell right. Adopt State 4	Eh?	Move 1 cell left. Adopt State 6
	5	Move 1 cell right. Adopt State 5	Eh?	Move 1 cell left. Adopt State 1
	6	Write 0 to tape. Adopt State 6	STOP?	Move 1 cell left Adopt State 3

Figure 2.2 An example machine table.

scratchpad to keep track of the current machine state. At the end of this exercise, the machine will "Stop," and the answer to figure 2.3a's question is the tape illustrated in figure 2.3b. (Before reading on, stop to consider this: there is no doubt that you would have no difficulty in pretending to be this particular Turing machine, and that by following your figure 2.2 program you could generate the correct answer to the question in figure 2.3a. But can you tell me right now what this answer means, or even what you think the original question is?)

In general, Turing machines can be built to answer a diversity of questions. For example, a Turing machine can compute functions from integers to integers. So, if you were to write an integer value down in some notation on the tape, a Turing machine computing a particular function would write the function's value for that integer on the tape and then halt. Such a function is called a "partial recursive function." If the Turing machine is guaranteed to halt for any input when it computes its function (i.e., if it is guaranteed to keep out of an infinite loop of moving back and forth along the tape), then it is computing a total recursive function. All common arithmetic operations on integers are total recursive functions. As another example, a Turing machine can accept or reject a string of symbols as representing a sentence belonging to a language. Such a language is called recursively enumerable. If the Turing machine is

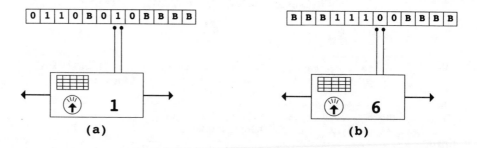

Figure 2.3 The machine starts in State 1 at the location of the tape specified in (a). When the "Stop" instruction is executed, the tape has been rewritten by the machine to appear as in (b).

guaranteed to halt for the language that it "knows," then the language is said to be recursive. The set of recursive languages includes context-free grammars, which have been used to model the syntactic structure of natural human languages.

The Universal Machine

Any reader who took the trouble to pretend to be the Turing machine in figure 2.2 should realize that he or she is a particularly powerful computing device. This is because they would have absolutely no difficulty simulating any machine table that I could have decided to put in this figure. In short, the reader can be thought of as a universal machine, capable of carrying out the operations that define any Turing machine.

Amazingly, it is possible to build special Turing machines that are themselves universal machines. This is accomplished by creating an important qualitative distinction in the machine's tape between data that is to be manipulated and a program that is to do the manipulating. Figure 2.4a illustrates this kind of distinction. For a Universal Turing Machine (UTM), the first part of the tape provides a description of some Turing machine T that is to operate on some data. This description is essentially the stringing out of machine T's table (see figure 2.4b) in a format that can be read by the UTM's tape head (for one sample notation, see Minsky, 1972, section 7.2). The next part of the tape provides a small number of cells to be used as a scratch pad. The final part of the tape is the actual data, representing the question that machine T is supposed to answer.

A UTM works in a fashion very analogous to the reader simulating the machine in figure 2.3, moving back and forth between the machine description and the data, keeping track of important information (like the current machine state) in the scratchpad. Essentially, the UTM reads a data symbol, goes back to the machine description to find out what machine T (in its current state) would do after reading that symbol, and then goes back to the data tape and performs this operation. The UTM itself is defined as a machine table capable of reading

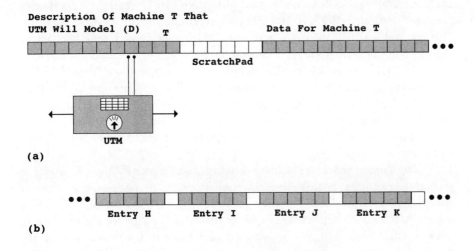

Figure 2.4 The components of a Universal Turing Machine. (a) The machine itself is similar to the one in figure 2.1, but with a more elaborate set of distinctions in how one describes the tape being manipulated. (b) The machine description is essentially the table of entries of the to-be-modeled machine written in a form that can be acted upon by the UTM when it reads these entries on the tape.

and acting out machine T's description, and need not be a particularly complicated looking device.

Why is Cognitive Science Interested in Turing Machines?

To summarize a few things to this point, we have described a Turing machine as a device that uses a machine table to answer questions written on a data tape (essentially by rewriting the tape). In addition, special Turing machines (UTM's) have the ability to pretend to be any possible Turing machine. Thus a single UTM can answer any question that can be answered by a Turing machine. An important question remains: Why in the world would cognitive science be interested in these kinds of machines? The answer to this question really depends on the answers to three related issues.

1) *How well do Turing machines describe information processing?* Cognitive science is extremely serious about its view that cognition is information processing. "For me, the notion of computation stands in the same relation to cognition as geometry does to mechanics: It is not a metaphor but part of a literal description of cognitive activity" (Pylyshyn, 1979, p. 435). Given this view, we can ask the extent to which a Turing machine provides a faithful account of what information processing is all about. The answer to this question is surprisingly strong: a Turing machine gives a complete account of what information processing is all about.

According to what we will call the Church-Turing thesis, "Any process which could naturally be called an effective procedure can be realized by a Turing machine" (Minsky, 1972, p. 108). This thesis cannot be proven because of the intrinsic ambiguity of the term "naturally." However, most researchers accept this thesis as being true. This is because it has been shown that all other accounts of what an effective procedure (or an information processor) is, though at first glance often quite different in appearance from Turing's proposal, have been shown to be formally equivalent to a Universal Turing Machine. In short, a Universal Turing Machine is the most powerful description of information processing we have, because anything that can be computed could be computed by this device.

2) *Can Turing machines answer psychologically interesting questions?* A second question that must be answered in order to understand cognitive science's interest in Turing's work concerns the competence of a Universal Turing Machine – when we write queries on the ticker tape for the machine to answer, what kinds of questions can we ask? More to the point, is there any reason to believe that the kinds of questions that a Turing machine can answer might be of psychological interest? Again, the answer to this question is far from univocal – if we had a definite answer, either cognitive science would be complete (because we would have found a way to make a thinking machine) or abandoned (because we would have found that the information-processing hypothesis is wrong). Nevertheless, there are many indications that the Turing machine's competence is sufficiently powerful to be of psychological interest. For instance, let us briefly consider how the power of a Turing machine is relevant to the study of language.

One of the kinds of questions that can be given to computing devices concerns the acceptability of sentences. For this type of question, you write a sentence in some language (usually an artificial one) on the machine's tape, and then start the machine running. At the end, the machine is supposed to tell the user whether the sentence is a valid or grammatical example of a specific language.

Bever, Fodor, and Garrett (1968) were concerned with an extremely simple-looking artificial grammar, whose sentences were made entirely from the following two "words" : "a" or "b." Here are some valid sentences created from this grammar: "a," "bab," "bbabb," and so on. Here are some ungrammatical sentences that are inconsistent with this grammar: "ab," "babb," "bbb," and "bbabbb." From this information, would you agree that "bbbbbabbbbb" is a grammatical sentence in this language? It is, because this string can be generated by the rule that defines this "mirror image" language, $b^{N}ab^{N}$ where N is the number of "b's" in the string.

Bever, Fodor, and Garrett (1968) were able to show that a particular computational device, called a finite state automaton, could not correctly decide whether strings of "a's" and "b's" were acceptable according to their simple grammar. A finite state automaton is similar to a Turing machine, but has less computational power. This is because it can only move in one direction along a tape, and can only read tape symbols. It doesn't write to the tape – it only stops at the end of a sentence, finishing in a physical state that means (for our example) either "yes it's grammatical" or "no it's not grammatical." Because it can't go backwards along the tape, it can't deal with languages (like the artificial mirror-image one) that have embedded clausal structure.

The reason that this proof is so powerful is because Bever, Fodor, and Garrett (1968) argued that the finite state automaton had essentially the same computational power of a device guided by the principles underlying associationism (not to mention radical stimulus–response behaviorism). Their message was clear: associationism wasn't powerful enough to deal with the embedded clauses of natural human language, because a finite state automaton wasn't powerful enough to deal with even an extremely simple language in which clauses could be embedded. As a result, associationism should be abandoned as a theory of mind. The impact of this proof is measured by the lengthy responses to this argument by memory researchers with strong associationistic tendencies (for examples see the responses to the so-called "terminal metapostulate" in Anderson (J. R.) & Bower, 1973; Paivio, 1986).

In contrast, Turing machines can decide the acceptability of sentences created from grammars that can generate embedded clauses. So, a Turing machine could (like the reader) make the correct judgment about the string "bbbbbbabbbbbb" for the artificial language that was described earlier (for additional discussion, see Johnson-Laird, 1983, ch. 12). This suggests that Turing machines provide a framework for cognitive science that may be sufficiently rich to explain human cognition. Turing himself was convinced about the inevitability of machine intelligence, and in one extremely influential paper he described an empirical method for identifying it (Turing, 1950).

3) *From the finite to the infinite.* There is one final note to make about cognitive science's interest in Turing machines before we move on to other issues. Like the decidability question, the notion of human intelligence appears to pull us in competing directions. On the one hand, we have a strong intuitive sense that human intelligence is unlimited; as far as we are concerned, it has no bounds, and is capable of producing an infinity of products (sentences, ideas, works of art, and so on). On the other hand, we also have a strong belief that, mechanically speaking, human intelligence is quite limited. In general, most people would agree with Searle's (e.g., 1980, 1984, 1990) proposal that brains cause minds, and recognize that brains are not infinite or magical devices. How is it possible for three pounds of flesh and blood to instantiate human intelligence?

A Universal Turing Machine provides one approach to resolving this conundrum because it is inherently componential in nature. On the one hand, such a machine is definitely finite in structure. On the other hand, the machine has an incredibly large potential repertoire of behaviors. This is possible because the machine does not have to understand any question written on the ticker tape as a whole. Instead, the machine breaks the question down into meaningful chunks or components – the individual symbols written on the tape – which it does "understand," at least to the extent that it will carry out a specific operation according to its machine table. The power of the Turing machine comes from the fact that if you take a small number of simple, basic, information-processing operations (i.e., machine table actions) and string them together in a specific sequence, very complicated behaviors can emerge.

Human language can be viewed as another example of the computational power that can emerge from componential systems. Human language appears to have limitless novelty. We apparently have no problem whatsoever producing novel sentences, utterances which have never before been seen or heard on this planet. (Sentences like "My dog would make a fine mascot for the Montreal Canadiens hockey team.") Not only is the production of such sentences fairly straightforward, but the amazing thing is that when they are heard or read by others, they are easily understood in spite of their novelty. However, this may be the result of the fact that with a finite number of words (the documentation for my wordprocessor says that its spellchecker contains about 140,000) and a finite number of rules for putting them together sensibly, there is essentially no restriction on the number of different sentences that the human race can produce. Furthermore, if someone reading or hearing a novel sentence knows something about the meanings of the components of the sentence, as well about the rules for putting these components together, it becomes a little less surprising that they can understand what was being said.

Is the Brain Really a Turing Machine?

The previous section provided us with three general reasons why Turing machines are of interest to classical cognitive scientists: a) they provide a complete description of what information processing is all about; b) they are in principle capable of answering psychologically interesting questions; and c) they provide an example of how a finite device is capable of generating an infinite variety of behavior. Turing machines give the appearance of being central to cognitive science.

However, while a Turing machine provides a powerful and complete *theoretical* description of what information processing is all about, if you went and built such a machine you would find that it was not very *practical*. The Turing machine is just too simple to be very fast or efficient. For example, when moving from one point on the tape to another, the Turing machine has to pass through all of the intermediate cells – Turing machines don't have random access memory! As a result of such practical problems, classical cognitive scientists do not believe that if you open up the brain and peer inside, you will find a Turing machine (e.g., part of the brain corresponding to a ticker tape, another part corresponding to a machine head that moves back and forth along this ticker tape). Instead, they would expect that you would find an architecture that shares many properties with Turing machines, but which has additional features that make it more efficient and practical. This architecture would be no more powerful than a Universal Turing Machine, in terms of the questions that it could answer, but it would be more powerful in the practical sense that it could give answers to these questions much faster.

One generic example of such an architecture is called a *physical symbol system* (e.g., Newell, 1980, 1990). A physical symbol system consists of a memory, a set of operators, a controller, receptors, and a motor output. In general terms, the behavior of such a system is very much like a Turing machine – the controller calls one of the operators which processes the symbols stored in memory (i.e., reads/rewrites memory structures). Only one operator can process memory at a time, which is similar to a Turing machine's ability to execute only one machine table instruction at a time. The efficiency of the physical symbol system comes from the fact that its memory and operators are far more sophisticated than those of a Turing machine. For example, a physical symbol system's memory can consist of structured symbolic expressions (e.g., sentences), which can be accessed as entire wholes. Furthermore, the memory is random access – the controller can direct an operation immediately to any symbol structure in memory. Similarly, the operations are far more powerful. For example, the specific system that Newell (1980) describes has an operation that can copy an entire symbolic expression, and has logical operators that determine what action to take on the basis of a test of memory conditions, in addition to the standard kinds of operations that we saw earlier in the Turing machine (i.e., write to memory, read memory, delete from memory). However, even these standard operations are more powerful in the physical symbol system, because this system can write, read, or delete entire symbolic expressions (instead of a single symbol located at a specific memory location).

Importantly, all of the sophistication that has been added to the physical symbol system improves its efficiency and speed, but does not improve its power where power is defined in terms of the kinds of questions that the system can answer. Newell (1980, pp. 151–4) proves that his physical symbol system can simulate any specific Turing machine, and thus has exactly the same power as a Universal Turing Machine. He does this by taking the basic operations of the physical symbol system, and creating from them a program that makes the physical symbol system behave exactly like a Turing machine. In order to do this, some of the symbol structures in memory correspond to cells on the Turing machine's ticker tape, and other symbol structures represent the Turing machine that is being simulated. Newell's program uses the basic components of the physical symbol system to read the current cell, look up what the simulated Turing machine would do on the basis of this information, and then act on symbol structures in memory accordingly.

In summary, classical cognitive scientists are *not* committed to the notion that the brain is *really* a Turing machine. Instead, they adopt the more general assumption that the brain is a physical symbol system. "Our situation is one of defining a symbol system to be a universal machine, and then taking as a hypothesis that this notion of a symbol system will prove adequate to all of the symbolic activity this physical universe of ours can exhibit, and in particular all the symbolic activities of the human mind" (Newell, 1980, p. 155). Importantly, physical symbol systems and Turing machines are both universal machines, as Newell demonstrated with his proof that a physical symbol system (in spite of its efficiencies) is functionally equivalent to a Universal Turing Machine. As a result, we can continue in this chapter to explore the foundations of classical cognitive science using the Turing machine metaphor. But as we do this, it is important to keep in mind that as far as classical cognitive science is concerned, this is *only* a metaphor. Classical cognitive scientists really believe that while the brain manipulates symbols in a way that can be translated into a Turing machine description, the brain will have many features that make it a practical information-processing device.

Part II   What Can You Say about a Turing Machine?

To this point in this chapter, we have described some of the basic properties of information processing from the Turing machine perspective. We have also briefly considered why cognitive science is interested in Turing machines. What we have not covered yet, though, is how viewing information processing from this perspective affects basic research in cognitive science. It turns out that by considering briefly the different ways in which we can explain the behavior of a Turing machine, we can begin to see a number of fundamental properties of cognitive science, and to understand where these properties come from.

The remainder of this chapter is going to argue that as soon as you take seriously the hypothesis that the mind is an information processor, then you also have to take seriously several other claims. First, in order to have a complete explanation of mental processes, you will be forced to describe them using several qualitatively different vocabularies, each of which captures different (but important) regularities. This is the essence of Marr's (1982) tri-level hypothesis. Second, in addition to coming up with these qualitatively different descriptions, you will have to come up with some relationships between them – after all, they are all describing the same system. Third, for complex systems (like biological organisms), these vocabularies are going to be so different, and so difficult, that it is unlikely that one researcher will be technically competent to deal with them all. As a result, a number of different researchers, each with quite different kinds of expertise, will be required to provide these different descriptive accounts and to provide the links between them. In short, the interdisciplinary nature of cognitive science is a necessary consequence of adopting the information-processing hypothesis!

To begin, imagine that our goal is to provide some account of a Turing machine. What different kinds of things might we say about it? How are these different accounts related to one another? Let's start at the most concrete level, and then work our way up to more abstract descriptions.

Physical Descriptions

In order to make claims pertaining to the decidability problem, Turing did not have to actually build his "supertypewriter." One reason for this was the astonishing simplicity of the machine, which permitted Turing to make claims about its ability without requiring them to be defended empirically. A second reason was the fact that Turing was doing mathematics, not computer science. What was important was an abstract description of what an effective procedure was, not a piece of hardware capable of performing such a procedure. A third reason was the obvious inefficiency of the device – Turing machines are remarkably slow, even for very simple computational tasks. Interestingly, this was also true of the first electronic computers. For instance, Turing was a key figure in the development of working computers in the United Kingdom, and was also the author of some of the first chess-playing programs. However, Turing did not test these programs on the machines that he was developing because they were too limited in speed and memory. "Alan had all the rules written out on bits of paper, and found himself very torn between executing the rules that his algorithm demanded, and doing what was obviously a better move" (Hodges, 1983, p. 440).

All of this aside, if we wanted to, we certainly could build a Turing machine. This would be a mechanical device that would process a ticker tape memory in a manner consistent with a particular machine table. We could give it some sample problems on a ticker tape, watch it process the tape, and then check its answers to ensure that this particular physical device was functioning according to its design.

After building this machine, if someone asked how it worked, then one perfectly valid answer would be a physical description of the thing that we had built. We could describe the mechanical processes involved in moving along the tape, involved in reading symbols, and in writing new symbols to the tape. We could explain the mechanisms for switching from one machine state to another. We could provide some physical measurements of the machine – how much it weighed, how long it took to move from one tape cell to the next, how much heat it generated as it worked. Thus it seems pretty plain that one kind of vocabulary that can be applied to information processors is a description of their physical or mechanical characteristics.

This kind of vocabulary has several advantages. For instance, when you describe things physically, you can make certain predictions about their performance that you would likely not be able to make had you used any other kind of description. For example, if our physical Turing machine was powered by alkaline batteries, then physical descriptions would allow us to predict that its performance would decrease over time because of a decrease in terminal voltage of the battery (e.g., Boylestad, 1990, fig. 2.16) and to predict that its performance would be poorer in colder temperatures because of a temperature-related decrease in battery capacity (e.g., Boylestad, 1990, fig. 2.15b).

From psychology's standpoint, physical descriptions are particularly alluring because they give a strong sense of grounding relatively weak psychological theory in the established foundations of harder and more respected sciences. Recent advances in the neurosciences make biological accounts of psychological processes particularly seductive. For instance, it is amazing these days the extent to which researchers can relate behaviorally interesting claims about memory to underlying neural circuitry, not to mention mechanisms described quite literally at the molecular level (e.g., Alkon, 1987; Lynch, 1986). It is small wonder that some philosophers are of the opinion that as neuroscience develops, the folk psychology that we use everyday to predict the behavior of others will evolve into a more precise and effective folk physiology (e.g., Churchland, 1988, pp. 43–5). For our purposes, though, it is critically important to realize that physical descriptions, while extremely powerful, are not complete.

Limitations of Physical Descriptions

One kind of incompleteness involves what philosophers call the multiple realization argument. Essentially, what this means is that you could build many qualitatively different physical devices that all instantiated the same information-processing device (e.g., the same Turing machine). A physical description of one of these devices would tell you nothing about any of the others. A very nice real world example of this has recently come to light. Researchers in the United Kingdom have successfully built Charles Babbage's analytic engine (Swade, 1993). This device is a machine that, like modern computers built from silicon technology, has the same computational power as a UTM (Haugeland, 1985). However, unlike modern computers, the analytic engine is like a beautiful clock, with rotating cylinders used to represent floating point numbers, and with computation carried out by physically turning a crank which rotates these cylinders via a system of gears. Obviously, information-processing devices share certain abstract properties that are not captured in purely physical descriptions.

Physical accounts of information-processing systems are limited by another consideration as well. Consider this beautiful story provided by Arbib (1972, pp. 11–12): In December 1966, the computer science department at Stanford University installed a new computer. Unfortunately, the computer arrived without its instruction manuals. Undaunted, a group of graduate students decided that they didn't need these manuals, and attempted to deduce enough information about the computer's structure to write meaningful programs. Given that these students knew that this device was a digital computer, and had loads of experience with other computers, they quickly located the power switch, the data entry switches, and some important control push buttons. They were soon able to enter and execute some basic instruction words – but that was about it. "In several hours of experimentation we completely failed to deduce such simple items as the format of the instruction word (or even the location of the op-code). We were unable to program the addition of two numbers or the simplest input–output." These difficulties were assumed by the students to be due to the fact that this new machine was quite perverse; dramatically different in structure from machines that they had worked with in the past. However, when the instruction manuals arrived, this turned out not to be the case: the new machine was very much like the others that the students had used.

Why did the students fail in their attempt to program this computer? One reason is that the physical states of the computer did not themselves provide any obvious organizational principles for determining how this machine would behave as an information processor. This is because very few of the physical states of a computer are relevant to the kind of information processing that the machine is actually carrying out. "In a given computer, only a minuscule subset of physically discriminable states are computationally discriminable" (Pylyshyn, 1984, p. 56). Churchland and Churchland (1990, p. 37) make a similar point in their reply to Searle's (e.g., 1990) claim that any system capable of causing minds would have to have the causal power of the brain: "We presume that Searle is not claiming that a successful artificial mind must have all the causal powers of the brain, such as the power to smell bad when rotting, to harbor slow viruses such as kuru, to stain yellow with horseradish peroxidase and so forth. Requiring perfect parity would be like requiring that an artificial flying device lay eggs."

In short, while physical descriptions of information-processing devices are going to be extremely useful, they will not be complete. First, the physical description of one device may not tell us anything about another information processor that is just as powerful, but is built from different stuff. Second, if you start with a physical description, you may have extreme difficulty getting a handle on information processing because only a small number of physical properties are germane to computing, and nature hasn't been kind enough to tell us exactly what these properties are.

Procedural Descriptions

Arbib (1972) argues for the necessity of organizational principles to guide the analysis of any complex information processor. What kinds of organizational principles were contained in the computer manuals that the Stanford graduate students failed to do without? One important set of principles would be some (nonphysical) description of the information-processing steps that could be carried out by the computer. To be more specific, we could provide a very different explanation of how our Turing machine worked if we described the program or procedure that it was carrying out instead of describing its physical mechanism.

For a Turing machine, it turns out that there are two different kinds of procedural descriptions that we could provide. I'll call the first of these the *architectural description*, because in many respects it provides the most basic nonphysical account of the device. An architectural description of a Turing machine would be a description of that device's machine table. Note that all the machine table does is describe exactly the basic set of information-processing steps (symbolic transformations of the tape) that characterize the device. It does not tell you anything about what the machine is built of – indeed, the machine described in this vocabulary may never have been built at all! Nevertheless, this kind of description is very powerful. For example, if we know a Turing machine's table, and know a little bit more information about the machine (i.e., its current state and the current symbol that it is reading from the ticker tape) then we can predict exactly what the machine will do next. This ability allowed us to pretend to be the machine described in figure 2.2.

However, architectural terms are not the only procedural ones that could be used to describe a particular Turing machine. This is because of the existence of the UTM. To provide a complete step-by-step account of a UTM's behavior, we would also have to describe the program that it was running (i.e., the particular Turing machine that the UTM was pretending to be). I'll call this the *programming description*. This is kind of description is going to be very useful because when the program is changed, the UTM will be doing something completely different, even though its architectural description remains the same.

For the time being, I'm not going to make too much of the distinction between the architectural description and the programming description. I will, however, point the way to two related themes that are going to be fleshed out in greater detail in later chapters. First, the architectural description of a UTM is more fundamental than its programming description. If you wanted to build a UTM, your goal would be to create a physical device that implemented the UTM's machine table, not a physical device that implemented the UTM's programming description. As a result, when looking for relationships between different vocabularies, we would expect that stronger relationships should be found between physical descriptions and architectural descriptions than between physical descriptions and programming descriptions. Second (and related to the first), as far as cognitive science is concerned, programming descriptions are going to be very powerful predictors of behavior. However, they are not going to suffice as explanations of behavior. To actually explain what might be going on in, say, a cognitive psychology experiment, some sort of architectural vocabulary is going to have to be employed.

Limitations of Procedural Descriptions

One might think that if you had two types of descriptions of a Turing machine – say, a physical description and an architectural description – then you would be in a position to provide a precise explanation of this device to some other interested party. Unfortunately, this isn't going to be the case. While procedural descriptions capture regularities that physical descriptions don't, they themselves can't capture everything.

For example, let's go back to the question that I asked earlier about figure 2.3 – after following the machine table in figure 2.2 to transform the tape in figure 2.3a into the tape in figure 2.3b, what exactly have you done? What question was the Turing machine that you simulated answering? What was the answer to

Programmer's Question

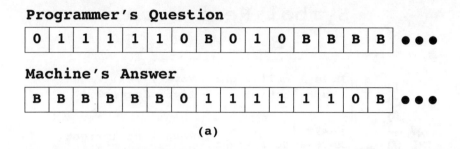

Machine's Answer

(a)

Machine Answer

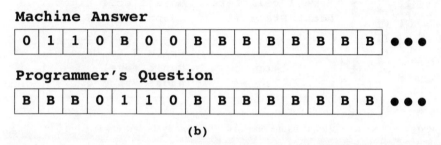

Programmer's Question

(b)

Figure 2.5 Two more examples of the answers generated by the machine described in figure 2.2.

this question that you produced? It turns out that to answer these two questions, you actually have to produce some interpretation of the tapes, as well as of the general procedure carried out by the Turing machine.

Figure 2.5 is an attempt to help you come up with an answer to the question of what your simulation of the figure 2.2 Turing machine actually meant. It provides some other examples of tapes as they would appear at the start of the machine's processing, and how the tapes would appear when the machine executed its "Stop" instruction. By looking at these tapes, as well as the pair illustrated in figure 2.3, do you have a better idea about the meaning of the machine's actions?

It turns out that the Turing machine table in figure 2.2 is an architectural description of a device that takes any two integers and computes their sum (Adler, 1961, p. 24). Integers are represented in a slightly idiosyncratic unary notation. In this notation, the symbol "0" is used to mark the beginning or the end of an integer quantity. The number of times the symbol "1" is duplicated between these punctuation marks gives the integer value being represented. So, the string "011110" represents the integer 4, and the string "011111111110" represents the integer 10. For this particular Turing machine, two integers are written on the tape and are separated by a blank. So, the tape "010B0110BBB ..." represents the question "What is the sum of the integers 1 and 2?" At the end of processing, the machine's answer 3 is written as "01110."

Symbol Read From Tape

		B	1
Current Machine State	1	Move 1 cell right Adopt State 1.	Move 1 cell right Adopt State 2.
	2	Write 1 to tape Move 1 cell right Adopt State 3.	Move 1 cell right Adopt State 2.
	3	Move 1 cell left. Adopt State 4.	Move 1 cell right Adopt State 3.
	4	Stop.	Write B to tape. Don't move! Adopt State 4.

Figure 2.6 Another Turing machine table. Is it the same as the one described in figure 2.2?

The fantastic thing about information-processing devices is that they are purely formal: they can carry out sophisticated computations by paying attention to the identity (or shape, or form) of the symbol on the tape without requiring to know what that particular symbol actually means, or requiring to know the meaning of what they are doing. This is due to the componential nature of the devices. Instead of requiring them to be extremely intelligent, understanding complex, whole strings of symbols, you simply require them to recognize a component of this string and respond to this symbol in a simple and definite way.

Unfortunately, a purely formal account of an information processor (i.e., either an architectural or a programming description) doesn't make it obvious how one should interpret a machine's actions or the symbols that the machine is processing. As a result, this descriptive vocabulary fails to capture some interesting regularities about information processors. To get a concrete sense of this, consider the architectural description of another Turing machine that is provided in figure 2.6. At first glance, this description appears to be quite a bit different than the description of the other Turing machine in figure 2.2, because the machines have different numbers of physical states, and because the machines respond to different numbers of symbols. Nevertheless, these machines are identical at a more abstract level, because both machine tables describe how a Turing machine can compute the sum of two integers. The difference between the two machines is that for the second one, "0's" are not used as punctuation marks in the unary notation for integer values.

Computational Descriptions

In order to capture the equivalence between the architectural descriptions provided by figures 2.2 and 2.6, a third and even more abstract description of the Turing machine is required. This computational description would tell someone what kind of information-processing problem is being solved by the machine without telling anything about the processing steps being used, or about how these processing steps are carried out by mechanical or physical processes. In very general terms, a computational description is an interpretation of what the system is computing. For instance, a computational description of the Turing machine in figure 2.2 would simply say "this is an information processor that computes the sum of two integers."

In certain respects, computational descriptions appear to be relatively weak. However, they can capture generalizations that the other kinds of descriptions that we have discussed do not, and as a result, give a different kind of predictive power. For example, let me tell you that I have a Turing machine that uses the unary notation from figure 2.3 and that computes the product of two integers. If the machine is given the tape "0110B01110BBB . . . ", what will the tape look like after the "Stop" instruction is executed? Notice that you can predict the behavior of this machine without building it, and without even knowing what its machine table would look like. All you need to know to predict the behavior is the scheme for interpreting the tape, and the knowledge that this particular machine is going to obey a particular semantic rule (i.e., multiplication).

Figure 2.7 provides another example of the predictive power of computational descriptions. Imagine that I have a system that can be described computationally as a chess player. Thus, all you know about this system is that whatever it does, it will never violate the rules of chess. Let us imagine that the machine is playing black. Given the board position in the figure, what is Black's next move? If you know how to play chess, you will recognize this as an instance of "Zugzwang" : "the right of moving in Chess is at the same time an obligation" (Lasker, 1947, p. 17). As a result, by knowing what is going on computationally (i.e., that the laws of chess are being followed), you can predict that Black will move his King to KB2. No other move is possible.

Computational descriptions are generally formulated in some logical or mathematical notation, and as a result they provide extremely powerful non-experimental methodologies for making discoveries about cognitive science. "The power of this type of analysis resides in the fact that the discovery of valid, sufficiently universal [computational] constraints leads to conclusions . . . that have the same permanence as conclusions in other branches of science" (Marr, 1982, p. 331). Bever, Fodor, and Garrett's (1968) proof of the limitations of associationism is an example of a computational account. So are proofs that there must exist some functions that even Turing machines can't compute, meaning that the answer to Hilbert's *Entscheidungsproblem* is "no" (for one example of this proof, see Minsky, 1972). We will see several other examples of computational analyses in later chapters.

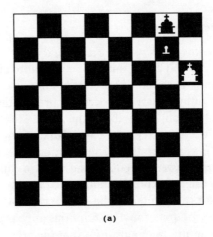

(a)

(b)

Figure 2.7 Given the position of the black king, white king, and white pawn in (a), a computational account – the laws of chess – dictate black's only move, which results in the board looking as it does in (b).

Limitations of Computational Descriptions

As I attempted to show with the proof above, computational descriptions can be extremely useful. We were able to show how one could make an enormously powerful claim about what Turing machines can't do without building a machine, without writing a program, and without running an experiment. In cognitive science, though, by themselves computational descriptions may not be particularly powerful, as was the case with both physical and procedural descriptions. For example, with figure 2.7, if all you know is that white and black pieces are being moved according to the rules of chess, then you can't predict with certainty that Black's forced move will result in a lost game. You can only make this prediction if you know a little bit more about how White chooses its next move, which is something that computational descriptions have nothing to say about, while procedural descriptions do. Similarly, you couldn't make any predictions about which addition machine (figure 2.2 or 2.6) is faster without knowing the machine tables as well as the physical characteristics of the two devices.

The Tri-Level Hypothesis

To summarize our discussion of what you can say about Turing machines, I have argued that there are three very general vocabularies that can be used to describe these devices (physical, procedural, computational). Each of these vocabularies describes certain things (or makes certain predictions) that the other two vocabularies do not. However, none of these vocabularies provide a complete account of information processors. This is the essence of Marr's (1982) tri-level hypothesis.

Some researchers (e.g., Dennett, 1978), while in agreement about the applicability of these three different descriptive vocabularies, would argue that their use has only heuristic value. From this perspective, there is no obligation to use all three vocabularies to describe a single system. Other researchers (e.g., Churchland, 1988) would argue that the goal of cognitive science should be to eliminate computational and procedural terms, reducing them to purely physical concepts. I do not believe that either of these approaches are correct. I've tried to use some informal examples above to show that if you are missing one or more of the descriptions, then you are literally saying less about information processing, because there are certain predictions that you cannot make without using all three types of vocabularies.

This sense that a complete explanation of information processing will require physical, procedural, and computational descriptions is in fact characteristic of cognitive science. "There is a natural theoretical domain within psychology which corresponds roughly to what we pretheoretically call cognition, in which the principal generalizations covering behavior occur at three autonomous levels of description, each conforming to different principles" (Pylyshyn, 1984, p. 259). Without all three vocabularies, explanation vanishes into incomplete description. Furthermore, the need for these three vocabularies is necessitated by the fundamental, complicated nature of information processors. I would strongly argue that if you can omit one of the vocabularies without losing any predictive or explanatory power, then the system that you are explaining is not an information processor. For example, while it is perfectly appropriate for philosophers to ascribe beliefs to thermostats to make particular points, it is important to realize that assuming that your thermostat believes that the room is hot doesn't tell us anything more about it that we didn't already know from a physical description. For similar reasons, we don't purchase any new explanatory power by claiming that falling rocks are actively computing their trajectories.

I think that we are now in a position to state the tri-level hypothesis as a piece of cognitive science dogma: Cognitive scientists believe that the mind is an information processor. As a result, a cognitive phenomenon must be explained by (1) describing it using a physical vocabulary, a procedural vocabulary, and a computational vocabulary, and (2) finding principled relationships between these three qualitatively different accounts.

Conversations and Cognitive Science

In the previous chapter, I argued that the information-processing assumption provided some common ground that permitted cognitive scientists to have fruitful conversations with one another, even if different individuals had widely different research backgrounds. Now that we have talked at length about a particular view of what information processing is, we can strengthen this thread a little bit by suggesting why in addition to being possible, these conversations are going to be necessary.

To this point, this chapter has been an extended argument that when a cognitive scientist starts with the assumption that cognition is information processing, then he or she must apply the tri-level hypothesis. Consider what that means for explaining human cognition. We are going to require a mature neuroscience to provide the physical account. We are going to require many technical results from psychology and linguistics to provide enough empirical details in which to ground procedural descriptions. We are going to require computer scientists and philosophers to provide adequate computational descriptions of the information processing that is being carried out. Finally, we are going to require conversations among all of these different researchers in order to put all of this together in a complete package in which all of the relationships among the vocabularies are spelled out. A successful cognitive science is going to require a lot of teamwork.

In short, the assumption that cognition is information processing forces the tri-level hypothesis upon us, and this in turn requires cognitive science to be interdisciplinary. In my opinion, this is why I find cognitive science such an exciting and attractive field. Its basic assumptions force you to look at one problem from a number of completely different angles, allow you to use an enormous variety of methodologies to solve these problems, and require you to start talking about these problems and methodologies with colleagues from a variety of disciplines.

Classical Cognitive Science

One idea that will receive more detailed treatment in the next chapter is that the tri-level hypothesis is true of all cognitive science. However, within cognitive science different traditions have emerged which can be differentiated with respect to the extent that other properties of the Turing machine have been incorporated into cognitive theory. Classical cognitive science not only assumes that the tri-level hypothesis is valid, but it uses this hypothesis in a particular methodological manner. Let's imagine that, like the the Stanford graduate students, a classical cognitive scientist is presented with the task of explaining an unknown information processor. How will this task be approached? In general, classical cognitive scientists adopt a very specific top-down strategy (Marr, 1982). First, they attempt to describe the system with the computational vocabulary. Second, they attempt to use the programming vocabulary, working their way towards the architectural description. Finally, they attempt a physical description. There are a number of reasons for adopting this top-down strategy.

First, with this approach a more abstract vocabulary provides Arbib's (1972) organizational principles, which guide the analysis with the less abstract vocabulary. Second, basically restating the first, this approach defines a particular methodological practice called functional analysis (e.g., Cummins, 1983) which has been enormously productive in cognitive science. Third, moving from more to less abstract descriptive vocabularies is viewed by classical cognitive scientists as providing deeper understanding. "It is not that one gains precision in descending the explanatory reduction hierarchy. What one gains is a deeper, more general, and therefore more complete, explanation" (Pylyshyn, 1979, p. 428). Finally, as one moves in this direction, one proceeds from computational claims that should be true of all information processors to physical claims that are likely to only be true of a small number of information processors, one of which is the system under study.

Classical cognitive scientists also take to heart some additional distinctions that are made explicit in the Turing machine formulation of information processing. In general, they endorse a sharp distinction between the processes or rules that are manipulating information, and the symbols that actually represent the information being manipulated. This is the distinction between the tape and the head of the Turing machine. As well, they also endorse the sharp distinction between a program that can be represented in memory and data that can be manipulated by this program. This is the distinction between a machine description and other symbol strings that are processed by the UTM.

However, not all cognitive scientists are so eager to adopt a view of information processing that is inspired by the Turing machine. In particular, connectionist cognitive scientists argue that the brain is capable of cognitive activity because it processes information in a fashion that is markedly different from that which we have described above. Let us now turn to a description of the connectionist view of information processing.

3

The Connectionist View of Information Processing

The previous chapter described information processing from the perspective of classical cognitive science. In this chapter, I am going to describe information processing from an alternative perspective – connectionism. At the end of this chapter, you should have a sense that the kind of information processing performed by artificial neural networks is quite different from the kind that is carried out by Turing machines. However, you should also agree that such networks are still information processors, and as a result the tri-level hypothesis is just as fundamental to a connectionist as it is to a classical cognitive scientist.

The main points of this chapter will proceed as follows: First, I will provide a brief overview of some problems that emerge when one attempts to model cognitive processes with a classical architecture (i.e., a physical symbol system). Second, I will introduce the connectionist architecture by relating it to some "simplifying features of the brain" that neuroscientists have discovered, and I will show how this biologically inspired architecture might deal with the problems faced by classical systems. Third, I will make the general case that the tri-level hypothesis that was introduced last chapter can be fruitfully applied to connectionist research. Finally, I will try to spell out some very general properties of connectionist cognitive science, and compare these with the characteristics of classical cognitive science that were introduced last chapter.

Part I Problems with the Classical Architecture

The Trouble with Turing

The pioneers of cognitive science made some bold claims and some aggressive predictions. For example, in 1956 Herbert Simon announced to a mathematical modeling class that "Over Christmas Allen Newell and I invented a thinking machine" (McCorduck, 1979, p. 116). In 1957, Simon further predicted that by 1967 computer programs would be the world chess champion, would discover an important new mathematical theorem, and would be the medium in which psychological theories would be expressed (see Dreyfus, 1992 for a discussion).

Unfortunately, these predictions have never been completely satisfied, and have come back to haunt computer modelers. "An overall pattern had begun to take shape [...]: an early, dramatic success based on the easy performance of simple tasks, or low-quality work on complex tasks, and then diminishing returns, disenchantment, and, in some cases, pessimism" (Dreyfus, 1992, p. 99). In short, several decades of research on artificial intelligence appears to have shown that it is easy to program a computer to do something that people do poorly, but it is not easy to program a computer to do something that people do well. As a result, many researchers question the appropriateness of the classical architecture for the study of cognition. Their concern is that this kind of architecture is too slow, too brittle, and too inflexible to provide an adequate account of the complex information-processing tasks that people do naturally (e.g., vision, language acquisition, locomotion). Let's consider some of these potential problems in more detail.

1) *Serial processing is too slow*. As we saw in the previous chapter, the Turing machine processes information in a serial, or one-step-at-a-time, manner. It can only execute a single instruction from the machine table at any given time, and this instruction will only affect a single cell on the tape. Connectionist researchers argue that such serial processing is simply too slow to be of interest to cognitive science.

One instance of this argument is Feldman and Ballard's (1982) hundred-step constraint. They point out that an active neuron will be generating an action potential every 1 to 3 milliseconds. Furthermore, chronometric studies of human information processing (e.g., Posner, 1978) have shown that people can perform very complicated tasks in only a few hundred milliseconds. Feldman and Ballard argue that the speed of these tasks coupled with the speed of neurons implies that some complex behaviors can be carried out using only around a hundred information-processing steps. They go on to point out, though, that classical simulations of complex behaviors typically involve millions of operations. As the brain could not carry out these millions of operations in a few hundred milliseconds if it were a serial processor, the implication is that classical models are simply too slow for cognitive science.

2) *The structure/process distinction leads to brittleness*. The Turing machine exhibits a marked distinction between structure and process. That is, the data being manipulated (the structure) exists on one part of the machine (the tape), while the rules doing the manipulating (the process) exist in another part of the machine (the machine head). Furthermore, both structure and process are represented locally – a single symbol is encoded at each tape location, while the machine head is really just a list of individual rules. As a result, this architecture is extremely brittle in the sense that it can be easily damaged, and this damage can have catastrophic effects.

For instance, imagine that the tape was "lesioned" by replacing one symbol with some other symbol that the machine head could not recognize. When the machine head encountered this "damaged" symbol, it would not have an instruction to carry out, so processing would "crash." Similarly, damage to one cell in the machine table (e.g., the erasure of a single instruction) would be a fatal blow to machine function. This is a problem for classical cognitive science, because research has shown that the brain is not brittle – damage to part of the brain often only affects parts of its ability to process information, and in some cases large amounts of damage may lead to no noticeable deficits in information processing at all (e.g., Lorber, 1968; Sperry, 1958).

3) *Digital processing produces inflexibility*. The Turing machine is a digital computing device. The machine head holds a set of formal rules that are activated on the basis of what kind of symbol has been identified on the tape. It is the act of identifying symbols that makes the Turing machine digital. As is described in more detail by Haugeland (1985), a digital system is a set of positive and reliable techniques for identifying (or writing) symbols from some prespecified types. The word "positive" means that when identification occurs, it succeeds totally. On the one hand, the enormous complexity of the kinds of computations that Turing machines can carry out depends on such positive and reliable methods. On the other hand, the digital nature of the Turing machine can make it inflexible and unable to cope with noisy or novel input.

For example, we will see in the next chapter that many information-processing problems require that appropriate constraints be applied in order to find a solution. In some instances, these constraints are best applied in a "soft" fashion – one constraint might be relaxed, or even ignored, if a better solution can be obtained with respect to other constraints. However, the digital nature of a Turing machine makes the application of "soft" constraints difficult, because either a rule is activated or not. Rules can't be applied in some "relaxed" manner. As a result, Turing machines are better seen as applying "hard" constraints, which may not lead to the best solution to a problem.

Related to this is the notion that the performance of Turing machines does not degrade gracefully. That is, as more and more noise is introduced to the system (e.g., by adding more and more random dots to the tape to make the symbols on it less legible), there will be an abrupt transition from the machine working perfectly (because it is still able to apply its rules positively) to the machine failing totally (because symbols cannot be identified at all). There will *not* be a gradual decrease in the machine's performance that is proportional to the amount of noise that has been added. This is problematic because many cognitive systems appear to degrade gracefully. For example, when the lights in a room are gradually dimmed, our visual system does not see perfectly for a while, and then suddenly become blind. Our visual system degrades gracefully, delivering a poorer and poorer visual image of the world as the room gets dimmer and dimmer.

4) *Some miscellaneous problems*. For the three types of problems that were introduced above, one can make a plausible case that each is the result of a

fundamental property of the Turing machine. Other problems have also been discussed by connectionists as well. To my mind, many of these concerns do not appear to be "in principle" limitations of the classical architecture. This is because I can see how, in general terms, a device like the Turing machine could address these issues. However, I would agree that such solutions might be more difficult to find and implement in a classical architecture than in a connectionist network. Let's briefly discuss some of these miscellaneous problems, if only to reinforce the notion that connectionists are very, very unhappy with classical cognitive science.

First, connectionist researchers are much more focused on developing general learning rules that are capable of teaching networks to do one of any number of tasks, depending upon environmental input. The idea here is that by changing the environment, and applying a general-purpose learning rule, one network (i.e., a fixed set of input, hidden, and output units) can learn to do many different kinds of things. In contrast, classical researchers have traditionally placed less emphasis on general-purpose learning, and instead have focused on programming (instead of teaching) specific systems to solve specific tasks (for an alternative, though, see Gallistel, 1996). This is not to say that learning is impossible for classical systems. For instance, one could imagine a UTM that learns by using environmental input on the "data" part of its tape to change symbols on the "program" part of its tape, effectively changing what the machine will do later on. However, it is fair to say that connectionist researchers have a much stronger emphasis on learning than do classical researchers.

Second, as we will see below, connectionist researchers argue that their systems are much more biologically plausible than those developed by classical researchers. What this means is that when a researcher is faced with explaining, at the physical level, how the brain is actually working as a specific kind of information processor, the explanation will be easier to formulate for a connectionist because a network looks more "brainlike." I have found that this kind of argument is frequently very convincing to my students, who find the idea of intelligent machines bizarre when presented in a classical context, but are much more receptive to the idea when the machine is described as an artificial neural network. Nevertheless, there are a number of reasons to be wary of this argument. On the one hand, we saw in the previous chapter that physical accounts are not sufficient for cognitive science, and there is no reason in principle not to assume that the brain is a physical device that is best described in classical terms. On the other hand, many neuroscientists are highly skeptical of the biological plausibility of connectionist networks. (For instance, Douglas and Martin (1991, p. 292) dismiss such networks as "stick and ball models.") Just the same, biological plausibility is frequently raised as an argument in favor of connectionism, generally because of a tendency of classical cognitive scientists to ignore neuroscience. For example, Clark (1989, p. 61) argues that "no serious study of mind (including philosophical ones) can, I believe, be conducted in the kind of biological vacuum to which cognitive scientists have become accustomed."

Problems with Classical Architectures

In the preceding section, I have tried to illustrate the concerns that connectionists have raised using one information-processing system that we
became familiar with in the previous chapter (i.e., the Turing machine). However, other kinds of classical architectures exist which are far more efficient than
Turing machines. It is important to realize that they are still subject to the
problems that we have been describing.

One example of such an architecture is the von Neumann machine (e.g., von
Neumann, 1958; Wiener, 1948), which is the basis for almost all modern
computers. The central processing unit (CPU) of a von Neumann machine
serves pretty much the same function as the machine head of a Turing machine,
and the memory chips of a von Neumann machine serve the same function as a
Turing machine's tape. However, a von Neumann machine does not have to
scroll cell-by-cell through lots of memory locations to retrieve some desired
information – it can go immediately to any memory location in its random
access memory (RAM). A von Neumann machine is like a Turing machine with
a random access tape. This design feature, coupled with its being built out of
electronic components, makes a von Neumann machine incredibly fast. However, it is still a serial machine. As a result, it is still subject to all of the problems
that we have been discussing in the preceding paragraphs.

For instance, Hillis (1985) points out that no matter how fast the CPU of a
von Neumann machine is, computation time is dominated by the amount of
time taken to shift data from RAM to the CPU. This problem increases with the
size of the machine (i.e., the amount of RAM that can be addressed), resulting
in what Hillis calls "the von Neumann bottleneck," in which "the bigger we
build machines, the worse it gets." As a result, the most advanced von Neumann
computers that are known to man would take days to solve information-
processing problems that humans solve effortlessly in a few hundred
milliseconds. In other words, the problems that we introduced earlier are not
just faced by Turing machines in particular, but arise for classical physical
symbol systems in general.

Part II   Information Processing in the
Connectionist Architecture

One of the goals of connectionism is to provide an alternative to the physical
symbol system hypothesis. Connectionists assume that the architecture of
cognition is more like that of the brain, and less like that of a von Neumann or
a Turing machine. The properties of this alternative architecture are intended to
offer a solution to the general types of problems that we have been discussing
above. In the following sections, the properties of this alternative architecture
are introduced.

Simplifying the Features of the Brain

Why is the brain so smart? Connectionists believe that the architecture of the brain is qualitatively different from the architecture of digital computers and Turing machines. Furthermore, these qualitative differences are such that brains are currently much more capable of solving many "natural" information-processing problems than are computers. In order to understand this position, we have to get some sense of how the brain might process information.

However, trying to describe neural information processing is a particularly daunting task because of the brain's enormous complexity. Churchland and Churchland (1990, p. 35) note that "the brain is the most complicated and sophisticated thing on the planet," a view that is shared by many neuroscientists (e.g., Kolb & Whishaw, 1990; McGeer, Eccles, & McGeer, 1987; Shepherd, 1988). In many respects, the sheer complexity of the brain should make neuroscience impossible. Fortunately, researchers have discovered a great degree of order in the brain's structure. Kolb and Whishaw (1990, p. 4) note that "if there were no order in [the brain's] complexity, it would be incomprehensible." To the relief of Nicholls, Martin, and Wallace (1992, p. 2), "there are many simplifying features in the nervous system," and one theme of their neuroscience text is the exploitation of these features to make sense of brain function.

One example of a simplifying feature is the notion that with respect to processing mechanisms, the components of the brain are relatively uniform (for a competing view, though, see Getting, 1989). For example, electrical signals are virtually identical in all nerve cells in the human body, not to mention the nerve cells of other organisms. Similarly, the neurotransmitters released at synapses to send chemical signals from one neuron to another are also common to many different species of animals. "In this sense, nerve impulses can be considered to be stereotyped units. They are the universal coins for the exchange of communication in all nervous systems that have been investigated" (Nicholls, Martin, & Wallace, 1992, p. 2).

Neuroscientists have also discovered simplifying features concerning the organization of neurons into functioning systems or networks. The pioneering work of Hubel and Wiesel in the 1950s and 1960s led to the realization that there is a marked hierarchy in neural connections, in which the receptive field of one neuron can be understood completely by considering the receptive fields of those cells from which it receives input. Furthermore, cells that are physically near one another in the visual cortex respond to very similar properties, as well as to neighboring locations in the visual field.

The Connectionist Architecture

The search for simplifying features of the brain appears to have led to at least two central assumptions in modern neuroscience: (i) that the building blocks of the nervous system are relatively uniform with respect to their mechanics, and (ii) that patterns of connections among neurons are central to determining how the brain instantiates phenomena of interest. One fruitful way to think about the parallel distributed processing (PDP) or connectionist architecture is that it is a computer simulation of the simplified brain features identified by neuroscientists.

In other words, connectionism is a description of a very small set of brain properties that might be crucially related to the brain's ability to process information. Typically, the basic building blocks of a PDP network are a number of processing units, which almost always are of the same type. By connecting these processing units in a particular way, a specific task of interest can be accomplished. As a result of this "neuronal inspiration," connectionist networks appear to process information in a very different fashion from a Turing machine. This is why connectionists believe that this will lead to models whose performance is more like humans, and less like computers, on those "natural" tasks that people find easy.

A PDP network is a computer simulation of a "brainlike" system of interconnected processing units (see figure 3.1). In general, such a network can be viewed as a multiple-layer system that generates a desired response to an input stimulus. The stimulus is provided by the environment, and is encoded as a pattern of activity in a set of *input units*. The response of the system is represented as a pattern of activity in the network's *output units*. Intervening layers of processors in the system, called *hidden units*, detect features in the input stimulus that allow the network to make a correct or appropriate response.

Each *processing unit* in a PDP network is analogous to a neuron. The behavior of a single processing unit in this system can be characterized as follows: First, the unit computes the total signal being sent to it by other processors in the network. Second, the unit adopts a particular level of internal activation on the basis of this computed signal. Third, the unit generates its own signal which is based on its level of internal activity, and sends this signal on to other processors. These three activities are illustrated in figure 3.2, and are described in more detail in the following three paragraphs.

A *net input function* is used to define how a processing unit computes the signal that it is receiving. In most PDP networks, a processor's net input function is simply the sum of all of the incoming signals. However, some connectionist architectures use slightly different net input functions. For example, radial basis function networks (e.g., Moody & Darken, 1989) use a distance function instead of a summation, and sigma-pi networks (e.g., Rumelhart, Hinton, & Williams, 1986b) use multiplication instead of addition.

Once a processing unit has computed its net input, it is in a position to calculate its internal level of activity, which is defined by an *activation function*. The value of the unit's net input is passed into the activation function, which outputs a number representing the unit's internal activity. A variety of different activation functions are used in different types of PDP networks. Regardless of

Output units

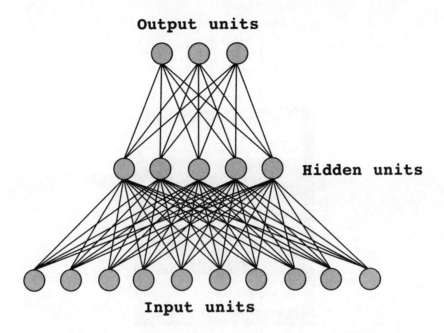

Hidden units

Input units

Figure 3.1 An example of a modern connectionist network called the multilayer perceptron. Input units receive stimuli from the environment. Hidden units detect (possibly complex) features in the input pattern, which in turn enable an appropriate response to be made by the network. This response is encoded in the output units. The lines in this figure represent weighted connections, through which a signal is sent from one unit to another. In this kind of network, the signal travels in a "feedforward" direction, from the input units to the hidden units, and from the hidden units to the output units.

the specific equation used, though, the activation function is used to approximate the "all or none" law used by neuroscientists, where a neuron is either "on" or "off" depending on its input. As a result, activation functions usually return a value between 0 and 1, where near-zero values represent "off," and near-one values represent "on."

After the activation function has been used to convert net input into internal activity, the processing unit is able to send a signal elsewhere. This is done by passing internal activation through an *output function*. In most PDP networks, this is accomplished with the identity function, which means that the processing unit simply sends its internal activity out as a signal. However, in some cases more complex functions might be used to convert internal activity into some other number.

The signal that one processor sends to another is transmitted through a *weighted connection*, which is typically described as being analogous to a synapse. The connection serves as a communication channel that amplifies or attenuates a numerical signal being sent through it. This is done by multiplying the signal by the weight associated with the connection. The weight defines the nature and strength of the connection. For example, inhibitory connections are

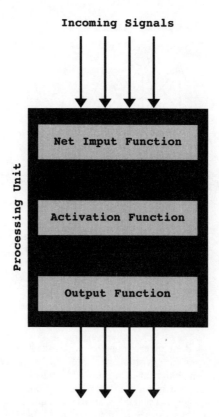

Figure 3.2 The basic properties of a processing unit.

defined with negative weights, and excitatory connections are defined with positive weights. Strong connections have strong weights (i.e., the absolute value of the weight is large), while weak connections have near-zero weights.

The pattern of connectivity in a PDP network (i.e., the network's entire set of connection weights) defines how signals flow between the processors. Different families of PDP networks are defined, in part, by what kinds of information flow are possible in the network. In turn, the kinds of problems that a connectionist network is well-suited to solve depends on how information can flow within it. For example, in *feedforward networks* information can only flow in the direction from input units to output units. Such networks are excellent for detecting visual regularities in patterns that are laid out in space. Another kind of connectivity is found in *recurrent networks*, which permit information to flow in the direction from input to output units and in the direction from output to input units. Such networks are excellent for detecting temporal regularities in patterns that are presented over some duration of time, because the backward flow of information permits these systems to have some memory of previous processing-unit activities.

Because the pattern of connectivity defines how signals can flow in a PDP network, it's connection weights are analogous to a program in a conventional computer (e.g., Smolensky, 1988). However, in contrast to a conventional computer, a PDP network is not given a step-by-step program to perform some desired task. Instead, the network is taught to do the task. For example, consider a popular learning procedure called the generalized delta rule (e.g., Rumelhart, Hinton, & Williams, 1986a, 1986b).

Figure 3.3 illustrates the steps involved in training a network with the generalized delta rule. One starts with a network that has small, randomly assigned connection weights. The network is then taught by presenting it a set of training patterns, each of which is associated with a known correct response. To train a network on one of these patterns, the pattern is presented to the network's input units, and (on the basis of its existing connection weights) the network generates a response to it. Early in training, this response will likely be incorrect. As a result, one can compute an error term for each output unit, where error is essentially the difference between the desired response of the output unit and its actual response. This error term can be used to modify the network's connections in such a way that the next time this pattern is presented to the network, the amount of error in the network's response will be smaller.

When using the generalized delta rule, error is used to modify connection weights by sending it backwards through the network, in the opposite direction of the feedforward signal. This is why this learning rule is often called back-propagation, or backprop for short. Once the error term for each output unit has been calculated, an equation specifies how the connections directly attached to each output unit can have their weights changed. Once this is done, the output units send their error as a signal – to be scaled by the new connection weights – to the next layer of hidden units. Each hidden unit computes its overall error by treating the incoming error signals as net input (i.e., a hidden unit's total error is the sum of the weighted error signals that it is receiving from each output unit). Once a hidden unit has computed its overall error, then it can use an equation to alter all of the connections that are directly attached to it. This process can be repeated, if necessary, to send error signals to the next layer of hidden units, and stops once all of the connections in the network have been modified.

By repeating this procedure a large number of times for each pattern in the training set, the network's response errors for each pattern can be reduced to near zero. At the end of this training, the network will have a very specific pattern of connectivity (in comparison to its random start), and will have learned to perform a particular stimulus–response pairing.

The properties that I have introduced in the preceding paragraphs do not do justice to the variety of systems that fall into the connectionist camp. There is a bewildering array of net input functions, activation functions, output functions, and learning rules available to connectionist researchers, and a complete discussion of these is impossible here. Fortunately, there are a number of excellent introductory texts available, several of which include software for

(A) Environment
activates input
Units

(B) Output from input
units activates hidden
units

(C) Output from hidden
units activates output
units

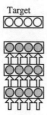

(D) Actual output of
network is compared
to desired or
"target" output

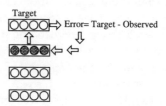

(E) Error is calculated for
output units

(F) Output unit error is
used to modify weights
of connections to output
units only

(G) Hidden unit error
is calculated by sending
output unit error as
signal backwards through
modified connections

(H) Hidden unit error
is used to modify the
weights of connections
to hidden units only

Figure 3.3 The steps involved in training a multilayer perceptron (see figure 3.1) with the generalized delta rule. The figure illustrates how learning proceeds when the network is given a single presentation of one stimulus; these steps would be repeated over and over again for this pattern and for any other patterns that the network was being trained on. At the end of modifying the connections (Step H), if this pattern were presented immediately to the network again, the total amount of error in the network's response to this pattern (calculated in Step E) should be smaller.

exploring connectionist simulations (e.g., Amit, 1989; Bechtel & Abrahamsen, 1991; Caudill & Butler, 1992a, 1992b; Gallant, 1993; Hecht-Nielsen, 1987; Hertz, Krogh, & Palmer, 1991; McClelland & Rumelhart, 1988; Muller &

Reinhardt, 1990; Wasserman, 1989; Zurada, 1992). For the time being, though, we are not interested in providing an exhaustive catalogue of connectionist architectures. We are instead interested in trying to get a general sense of how PDP networks process information in such a way that the problems that classical information-processing architectures face can be solved. To accomplish this goal, we can focus on the properties of an example system built from the components of the connectionist architecture.

An Example Network

These days, many cognitive neuroscientists are interested in identifying a method to provide an early diagnosis of Alzheimer's disease. One approach that has been explored is the use of imaging techniques that generate a three-dimensional picture of a patient's brain. One such technique is called SPECT, which stands for Single Photon Emission Computed Tomography. In SPECT, a mildly radioactive chemical is introduced to the blood flowing through the brain. As this chemical decays, it releases photons that are detected by cameras that are rotating about the subject's head. The pictures taken by these cameras can be used to create a three-dimensional image of brain function. This image can be used to locate brain regions that have normal blood flow (because large amounts of the tracer chemical are present) and brain regions that have less than normal blood flow (because very small amounts of the tracer chemical are present). For a more detailed introduction to SPECT, see Mettler and Guiberteau (1991, ch. 4).

SPECT has some advantages over other types of brain imaging methods, such as PET and MRI, because it is less expensive and more readily available. However, at the same time it has much less spatial resolution than these other techniques. As a result, there have been questions raised about the utility of SPECT for the early diagnosis of Alzheimer's. For example, in a review of the efficacy of various imaging techniques, Albert and Lafleche (1991) noted that while SPECT was highly accurate in diagnosing severe cases of Alzheimer's, it had accuracy rates as low as 25 percent for diagnosing mild to moderate cases. They concluded that other techniques should be preferred over SPECT for this particular diagnostic task.

Dawson, Dobbs, Hooper, McEwan, Triscott, and Cooney (1994) wondered whether the inability to use SPECT to diagnose mild cases of Alzheimer's disease was not an inherent limitation of the imaging technique, but was instead the result of using weak methods to interpret SPECT data. They tested this hypothesis by seeing whether a PDP network could be trained to distinguish Alzheimer's patients from healthy control subjects on the basis of input SPECT measures.

The database provided to the network was a summary of SPECT images obtained from 97 Alzheimer's patients (almost all in the early stages of the disease) and 64 healthy comparison subjects. In the Dawson *et al.* (1994) study, each subject's SPECT image was carved up into 14 different brain volumes (e.g., the left parietal cortex, the right frontal cortex, and so on), and the total number of photons detected from each of these volumes was tallied. As a result, the network had 14 input units – one for each brain region. During training, a patient was presented to the network by activating each input unit with a number that reflected the total number of photons detected in that region of the patient's brain. The network had a layer of 15 hidden units. The network also had two output units, and was trained to use these units to classify the two types of patients. If the patient was an Alzheimer's patient, then the network was trained to turn the first output unit "on," and to turn the second output unit "off." If the patient was a member of the control group, then the network was trained to turn the first output unit "off," and to turn the second output unit "on."

The network was trained with a variant of the generalized delta rule that was originally developed by Dawson and Schopflocher (1992a). After approximately 15,000 epochs (that is, after 15,000 presentations of each of the 161 patients' SPECT data, followed by modifying connections according to the learning rule), the network's error had been reduced to the extent that it had learned to use its output units to perfectly discriminate Alzheimer's patients from the controls, as is illustrated in figure 3.4. It would appear that SPECT can be used for the early diagnosis of Alzheimer's disease, provided that the SPECT data is analyzed in the proper manner.

For our purposes, though, the importance of this example comes from considering how this network does medical diagnosis, not *how well* it works. For instance, when the final performance of the network was being tested, what exactly was going on? First, an input was presented to the network, which was accomplished by setting the internal activations of all 14 input units to values that represented a single subject's data. Second, signals traveled from all of the input units through the first layer of connections, where they were scaled. Third, all 15 hidden units computed their net input, and on the basis of this net input adopted an internal level of activity. Fourth, signals traveled from all of the hidden units through the second layer of connections, where they were scaled. Finally, the two output units computed their net input, and adopted an internal level of activation, which was interpreted as the network's response to the presented stimulus. Note that a predominant feature of this processing is that lots of processing units are working simultaneously. This parallel processing is quite different from the serial processing that characterizes devices like the Turing machine.

We might also ask about where in the network would we find the knowledge or expertise that the network uses to distinguish an Alzheimer's patient. In a classical system, this would amount to generating a list of the rules that the system used to manipulate symbols. Unfortunately, in a connectionist network like the one for medical diagnosis, locating such rules is extremely difficult. One reason for this is because in this network there is no sharp boundary between structure and process – the network is what Hillis (1985) calls an active data structure, which both stores and manipulates information. A second reason is

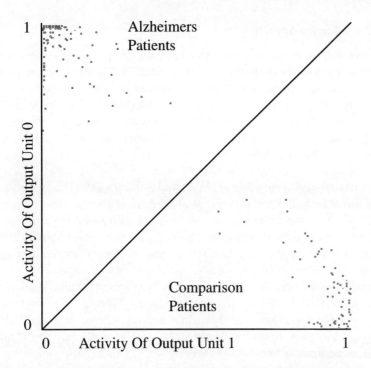

Figure 3.4 The response of the network to SPECT data at the end of training. One axis represents the activity of Output Unit 0 (which is trained to turn "ON" to Alzheimer's patients), and the other axis represents the activity of Output Unit 1 (which is trained to turn "ON" to control patients). As is indicated by the diagonal line, the network is able to perfectly distinguish the two groups of patients on the basis of SPECT data alone.

because the network's "knowledge" is smeared or distributed throughout its connection weights. As a result, connectionists often face what Lewandowsky (1993) calls Bonini's paradox, in which the model is as hard to understand as the thing that it models! Indeed, connectionists often have to resort to using multivariate analyses of their networks to uncover the network's algorithm (for a review see Hanson & Burr, 1990), and network interpretation is an active field of connectionist research (e.g., Berkeley, Dawson, Medler, Schopflocher, & Hornsby, 1995; Fu, 1994; Giles, Miller, Chen, Chen, Sun, & Lee, 1992; Omlin & Giles, 1996; Watrous & Kuhn, 1992).

In summary, by considering our example network we can see that it is a system that attempts to blur the distinction between structure and process, that it processes information in parallel, and that its knowledge is distributed throughout all its connection weights. These fundamental properties of parallel distributed processing are a reaction to the kind of information processing carried out by a classical architecture, and are presumed to offer solutions to the kind of problems that were introduced earlier in the chapter.

Why is the Brain So Smart?

To summarize our connectionist story so far, we have talked briefly about some simplifying features of the brain that have been identified by neuroscientists, we have introduced the connectionist architecture as an embodiment of these simplifying features, and we have seen a concrete example of one type of PDP network in action. We are now in a position to return to our original question – why is the brain so smart? – by considering how parallel distributed processing might solve the problems that we identified for devices like Turing machines.

First, recall that arguments like Feldman and Ballard's (1982) hundred-step constraint are claims that serial classical architectures are too slow to model cognition. The fact that a connectionist network processes information in parallel is intended to solve this problem. Indeed, parallel processing may be the most important reason that the brain can solve problems involving vision, language, and locomotion so effortlessly.

For example, at the time that I am writing this paragraph, Digital is advertising their Alpha AXP 21164 microprocessor as the "World's Fastest Chip," capable of speeds greater than one billion instructions per second (one BIPS). In comparison, an average brain has in the order of 10^{12} neurons. Individually, each of these neurons is very slow, carrying out a single "instruction" (i.e., generating an action potential) every millisecond. However, imagine a situation in which all of these neurons were spiking *simultaneously* (which is possible in a parallel architecture). In this case, the brain would be carrying out 10^{12} instructions per millisecond. By multiplying by 1,000, this figure converts to 10^{15} operations per second, meaning that in this situation the brain would be running at a speed of one million BIPS! In other words, parallel processing enables the brain (in principle) to be a million times faster than the world's fastest CPU. Parallel processing clearly provides a method for enormous speeding up of processing, and thus offers a solution to the hundred-(90)step constraint.

Second, it was noted earlier that the sharp distinction between structure and process can make the classical architecture very brittle or not very resistant to damage. The distributed nature of a connectionist network, in which the structure/process distinction is substantially blurred, can remedy this problem. This is because one consequence of distributing "knowledge" throughout a large number of connection weights is to produce redundancy in the system. As a result, one can damage the system (e.g., by cutting a connection weight or by lesioning a hidden unit) without completely destroying the network's ability to function. This is because redundant information can be used to compensate for information lost because of the damage.

One nice example of this is provided by McClelland and Rumelhart's (1988, ch. 2) famous Jets and Sharks model, which is a software demonstration of one type of connectionist network. In this demonstration, there are links between a processing unit representing an individual named Lance and a processing unit representing the fact that he is a burglar. If the network is started by activating Lance's "name" node, then after 500 cycles the "burglar" unit generates a high activity of 0.66, while units representing other professions ("pusher" and "bookie") both have low activities of −0.14. Now, if one follows McClelland and Rumelhart's (p. 45) instructions to sever the links from Lance's individual unit to the "burglar" unit, resets the network, and runs it for another 500 cycles, then the "burglar" unit achieves a lower activity of 0.57, while the other two profession units achieve activities of −0.13. So, the lesioned network generated a weaker answer to the question "What does Lance do for a living?" , but its outputs could still be used to correctly conclude that Lance is a burglar.

How is this possible with the link between Lance and his profession severed in the network? For this particular network, the answer is redundancy. When Lance's name node is activated, all of the units representing his properties (except his profession) grow in activity. These units in turn start activation units associated with other people who are very similar to Lance (Jim, John, and George). It turns out that one property that these three people have in common with Lance is that they are also burglars. Furthermore, their links to the "burglar" unit are still intact in the network. So, information from their units eventually allows the "burglar" unit to activate, albeit not quite as strongly as was the case for the intact system.

Third, it was noted that the digital nature of classical machines makes them less suitable for the application of "soft" constraints, and less likely to gracefully degrade their performance as input information degrades. In the next chapter, we will consider in detail an example of a network used to apply soft constraints to an information-processing problem. For the time being, let us consider the issue of graceful degradation as it relates to connectionism.

The activation function that is part of a connectionist processing unit is generally used to emulate the "all or none law" of neuroscience, which essentially stipulates that neurons will be adopting one of two states, "on" or "off" (e.g., Levitan & Kaczmarek, 1991, p. 38). Now, if a processing unit could only be "on" or "off," then it would certainly be behaving in a digital manner. However, in most PDP networks activation functions are not digital, but are instead analogue or continuous approximations of the all or none law. What this means is that while we might interpret a processing unit as being "on" or "off," in actuality it will have an internal activity that lies somewhere between these two states. This is apparent in the Jets and Sharks example above, where all of the activation values that I provided you are decimal values.

The analogue nature of activation functions allows connectionist networks to make responses that are "noisy," in the sense that they can lie somewhere between an "on" or "off" value. This allows graceful degradation to occur. That is, as the input to the system becomes noisier, so should the responses of the system. The system should not suddenly shift from performing perfectly to crashing completely, as one would expect with a digital system.

To illustrate this, I ran a simple experiment using the generalized delta rule (e.g., Rumelhart, Hinton, & Williams, 1986a, 1986b). I trained a network with

| Definition of XOR using four different input patterns | | | Actual output of trained XOR network when presented inputs in which new definitions of "On" and "Off" are used | | | | |
Pattern	Input 1	Input 2	Desired output	On = 1.0 Off = 0.0	On = 0.9 Off = 0.1	On = 0.8 Off = 0.2	On = 0.7 Off = 0.3	On = 0.6 Off = 0.4
1	Off	Off	0.0	0.036	0.119	0.043	0.041	0.040
2	On	Off	1.0	0.961	0.961	0.950	0.148	0.048
3	Off	On	1.0	0.961	0.961	0.961	0.233	0.072
4	On	On	0.0	0.050	0.111	0.038	0.039	0.040
			A	B	C	D	E	F

Table 3.1 Graceful degradation in an XOR network. In the XOR problem, there are four different input patterns. Each pattern is defined by turning two input units "on" or "off". A network trained to compute XOR is being trained to generate the output values given in column A. After training a network on the XOR problem with standard inputs, it generates the outputs given in column B. Columns C through F illustrate the graceful degradation of this network – the four outputs to the patterns become more and more similar as the input patterns are "dimmed" by decreasing the difference between "on" and "off" states.

two input units, two hidden units, and one output unit on the exclusive-or (XOR) problem. Typically with this problem the input units are turned "on" with a value of 1.0 or "off" with a value of 0.0, and the network is trained to turn its output unit "on" only for the two patterns that have only one "on" input unit. The network is supposed to turn its output unit "off" when both input units are "off," or when both input units are "on." Column A of table 3.1 illustrates the ideal responses of a network trained to make the XOR judgment on four patterns, and column B presents the actual responses of a typical network that has successfully learned this task.

To investigate graceful degradation, after successfully training a network on the traditional version of the problem, I presented some new patterns to it without giving it any more training. These patterns were intended to be analogous to presenting the XOR problem to the trained network after "placing" it in a "dimly lit room." I accomplished this by reducing the contrast between "on" and "off" input unit activities. In the first case, my "off" value became 0.1 and my "on" value became 0.9. As you can see from column C, the network gives slightly poorer responses to these "dimmer" inputs. In the next case, I reduced contrast even more by using 0.2 to represent an "off" input and 0.8 to represent an "on" input. Column D reveals a further decrease in performance. In the third case, I represented "off" with a value of 0.3 and "on" with a value of 0.7. The output unit reveals yet again a much poorer discrimination between types of patterns (column E). Finally, I represented "off" with a value of 0.4 and "on" with a value of 0.6. In this case, network performance is very poor, although it still generates slightly higher responses for patterns whose desired output is 1.0 than for those whose desired output is 0.0 (column F). The important point to be taken from all of these results is that as the contrast between "off" and "on" input activations is gradually reduced, there is a gradual reduction in the ability of the network to perform the XOR discrimination. The network does not suddenly shift from performing perfectly to not being able to perform at all. This graceful degradation is a consequence of the analogue nature of the processing units in the trained network.

Part III   Connectionism and the Tri-Level Hypothesis

We now have a sense of what connectionist information processing is all about, and we have seen how parallel distributed processing is intended to correct certain shortcomings that connectionists claim that classical architectures are subject to. For the remainder of this chapter, we are going to use this knowledge to consider the relationship between connectionism and the tri-level hypothesis. At this point, I am going to focus on only a couple of ideas. First, while connectionist networks process information in a fashion that is quite different from devices like Turing machines, they still process information. As a result, the tri-level hypothesis still applies to connectionism, and should guide the kinds of questions that connectionists must address. Second, because of this, connectionism does not necessarily represent a paradigm shift for cognitive science, as some have claimed (e.g., Schneider, 1987). In later chapters, when different aspects of the tri-level hypothesis are looked at in more detail, I will be trying to strengthen this perspective, and will argue that the connectionist and classical approaches are far more similar than their respective proponents are actually claiming.

What are Connectionist Models About?

When a connectionist researcher comes to you with a network, it is reasonable to ask what kinds of questions that model is supposed to address. Interestingly enough, a quick survey of the literature reveals that there is some confusion about the kinds of claims that connectionists are interested in making.

For instance, some of the arguments in favor of connectionism that we have already seen give the impression that PDP networks are intended to be viewed as implementational descriptions (i.e., as biological models). However, when connectionism is criticized as being *merely* implementational (e.g., Broadbent, 1985; Fodor & Pylyshyn, 1988), connectionists beg to differ. "Our primary concern is with the computations themselves, rather than the detailed neural implementations of these computations" (Rumelhart & McClelland, 1986, p. 138). Should connectionism thus be viewed as a computational account of cognition, primarily concerned with determining what kinds of information-(90)processing problems can be solved? Again, this does not appear to be the case. For example, Rumelhart and McClelland (1986, p. 122) claim that "PDP models are generally stated at the algorithmic level and are primarily aimed at specifying the representation of information and the processes involved in cognition." From these quotes, one gets the sense that connectionists themselves are not sure whether their theories are computational, algorithmic, or implementational in nature (for an elaborated discussion of this, see Dawson & Shamanski, 1994).

The fact of the matter, though, is that connectionist networks *must* be addressed at *all three* of these levels. This is because while connectionists wish to abandon the physical symbol system hypothesis, they do not want to abandon the assumption that cognition is information processing. After contrasting brains with von Neumann machines, Churchland, Koch, and Sejnowski (1990, p. 48, their italics) make this point quite nicely: "These dissimilarities do not imply that brains are not computers, but only that *brains are not serial digital computers*" In other words, brains – and neuronally inspired connectionist networks – are still information processors, and as a result the tri-level hypothesis continues to apply to them.

The following sections briefly consider connectionist networks at each of the levels of the tri-level hypothesis, and each section addresses three questions: 1) What does it mean to say that a network can be analyzed at that level? 2) How might addressing issues at that level aid or guide connectionist cognitive science? 3) How might answering questions at that level affect the debate between connectionist and classical camps? Introducing these questions here is meant to provide the reader with an overall sense of direction, because we will be considering these issues in more detail later in specific chapters devoted to each level of analysis.

Connectionism and the Computational Level

As we saw in the previous chapter, a computational description of an information processor is an account of the system's competence – it defines the *kinds* of functions that a system can compute. Such a description is usually expressed in mathematical or logical notation, because computational claims are usually expressed as formal proofs.

Computational descriptions of PDP models are important to connectionists, because they are used either to establish the adequacy of a particular network for a particular task, or to develop innovations for connectionist architectures, such as new learning rules. For example, in some instances recurrent networks change states as they process an input stimulus over time, and it is important to know whether the network will eventually stabilize into a constant state that represents a solution to the input problem. A convergence proof can show that such a network will indeed find a solution to the problem, and convergence proofs are common in the literature (for three different kinds of examples related to recurrent networks, see Anderson, Silverstein, Ritz, & Jones, 1977; Dawson, 1991; Hopfield, 1982, 1984). Similarly, the development of a new learning rule for a connectionist system usually involves mathematical proofs to ensure that the rule works. Typically this is done by defining the total error generated by output units, and then using calculus to define a method that guarantees that when connection weights are changed, this error term will decrease. Examples of such proofs can be found in Rumelhart, Hinton, and Williams (1986a, 1986b) and Ackley, Hinton, and Sejnowski (1985).

The keen interest that connectionists have about learning raises other computational issues when their models are being evaluated. For example, Elman (e.g., 1990) has proposed a recurrent PDP architecture that appears to be well-suited to analyze the structure of inputs strung out in time. However, this architecture has difficulty learning some problems. This raises an important question – are these difficulties due to the fact that the architecture is incapable of representing a solution to these problems, or is it the case that the architecture is powerful enough, but the learning rule could be improved? This question is important, because if it is the case that (regardless of the learning rule) the architecture is simply not adequate, then it would not be of much interest to cognitive science. However, if the architecture is powerful enough, but the learning rule is not the best, then this points the way to solving the problem (i.e., build a better learning rule). One of my former graduate students addressed this issue by using formal techniques. He was able to prove that an Elman-style network was sufficiently powerful to represent solutions to these stubborn problems (Kremer, 1995a), indicating that the problem was with the learning rule. He went on to suggest some methods to be used to improve learning in this architecture by placing constraints on how the network searched for connection weights that would provide solutions (Kremer, 1995b).

By now, we are well aware that within cognitive science there exists a certain tension between connectionist and classical camps. One arena in which this is evident concerns computational analyses of the different architectures. In particular, if a classical researcher could use computational methods to prove that connectionist networks were not sufficiently powerful to deal with many of the key information-processing problems in cognitive science, then this would provide a crippling blow to the connectionist cause. Indeed, such arguments have made up an important component of the literature. Many standard histories of connectionism cite the success of Minsky and Papert's (1969/1988) mathematical analysis of the limitations of an early kind of connectionist network (the perceptron) as a major reason for a decline in work on artificial neural networks in the 1970s. More recently, researchers have criticized modern connectionist networks on the grounds that such networks do not have the computational power of a UTM, and thus are not adequate of dealing with such phenomena as language (e.g., Fodor & Pylyshyn, 1988; Lachter & Bever, 1988). Not surprisingly, connectionists have responded with computational claims of their own.

In some of the earliest work on neural networks, McCulloch and Pitts (1943/1988) were able to prove that a UTM could be constructed from one of their artificial neural networks: "To psychology, however defined, specification of the net would contribute all that could be achieved in that field" (p. 25). More recently, researchers have developed many different kinds of computational proofs that have converged on the claim that connectionist networks are of sufficient computational power to be of keen interest to cognitive science (e.g., Cotter, 1990; Cybenko, 1989; Funahashi, 1989; Hartman, Keeler, & Kowalski, 1989; Hornik, Stinchcombe, & White, 1989; Lippmann, 1987). In other words, computational analyses are providing support for claims like "if we have the right connections from the input units to a large enough set of hidden units, we can always find a representation that will perform any mapping from input to output" (Rumelhart, Hinton, & Williams, 1986b, p. 319).

In summary, when connectionists concern themselves with the computational level, they are using formal methods to determine the limitations of their networks (by identifying what kinds of input/output mappings can or cannot be rendered by a network) and of their learning rules. Such methods provide a powerful tool for advancing and evaluating different varieties of connectionist architectures. Such methods are also required to deal with computational criticisms leveled at connectionists by their opponents.

Connectionism and the Procedural Level

In the previous chapter, we noted that a Universal Turing Machine could be described at the procedural level of analysis, and that such a description could take two different forms. First, it could involve a description of the machine on the tape that the UTM was pretending to be (the programming description). Second, it could involve a description of the machine table of the UTM (the architectural description). Not surprisingly, because PDP networks are information processors, both of these procedural-level descriptions can also be applied to them.

1) *Connectionism and programming descriptions*. Informally, an algorithm is a completely mechanical procedure for performing some computation – "an infallible, step-by-step recipe for obtaining a prespecified result" (Haugeland, 1985, p. 65). In PDP connectionism, a network can itself be described as an effective procedure for computing some function, or for categorizing some patterns. Indeed, a tremendous amount of enthusiasm for connectionism has been fueled by specific demonstrations that PDP networks offer practical algorithms for a diverse range of problems. A wide range of connectionist systems have been proposed to model aspects of memory (e.g., Anderson, 1972; Anderson, Silverstein, Ritz, & Jones, 1977; Eich, 1982; Grossberg, 1980; Knapp & Anderson, 1984; Murdock, 1982). Connectionist pattern recognition networks have a long history (e.g., Selfridge, 1959), have become benchmarks to which other methods are compared (e.g., Barnard & Casasent, 1989), and can outperform standard methods for such tasks as speech recognition (e.g., Bengio & de Mori, 1989). Connectionists have successfully used networks to solve problems related to locomotion (e.g., Brooks, 1989; Pomerleau, 1991), and have designed systems to mediate behaviors once thought to be exclusive to classical systems, such as logical inference (Bechtel & Abrahamsen, 1991, pp.

163–74) and sentence parsing (e.g., Jain, 1991; Lucas & Damper, 1990; Rager & Berg, 1990). Connectionist interests have ranged from classical learning theory (Kehoe, 1988) to dreaming (Antrobus, 1991). As Hanson and Olson (1991, p. 332) point out, "the neural network revolution has happened. We are living in the aftermath."

Why has the neural network revolution happened? With respect to programming-level descriptions, two major answers to this question emerge. First, connectionist networks permit researchers to explore algorithms of a very different sort than those found in classical models – namely, algorithms that depend upon massively parallel operations. Second, a great deal of connectionist research has been driven by powerful (and general) learning rules. As a result, connectionist researchers do not require a fully specified theory of a task before modeling begins. Instead, these researchers can think about different ways in which a task's inputs and outputs can be specified, design a training set, and finally let their learning rule discover a promising algorithm. In other words, procedures like the generalized delta rule can be thought of as powerful, general-purpose techniques for discovering new algorithms of interest to cognitive science. It is as though artificial neural networks allow "for the possibility of constructing intelligence without first understanding it" (Hillis, 1988, p. 176).

This possibility, however, is also the source of a current weakness with many connectionist models. At the programming level, connectionists want their models to "be considered as a competitor to other psychological models as a means of explaining psychological data" (Rumelhart & McClelland, 1985, p. 194). This makes perfect sense, because we will see in chapter 5 that a key theme in cognitive science is the validation of the algorithms that cognitive scientists produce. The problem, though, is that because of their parallel, distributed, and nonlinear nature, connectionist networks are extremely hard to understand – connectionists, after training their network, are hard pressed to describe how the network is actually working. "One thing that connectionist networks have in common with brains is that if you open them up and peer inside, all you can see is a big pile of goo" (Mozer & Smolensky, 1989, p. 3). McCloskey (1991) and Dawson and Shamanski (1994) have argued that the difficulty that connectionists have in describing their algorithms places a severe limit on connectionism's potential contributions to cognitive science.

Of course, connectionist cognitive scientists are acutely aware of such criticism. In response, there is a great deal of research aimed at developing techniques that can be used to extract programs from the networks that have discovered them. For example, one strategy is to perform graphical or statistical analyses of connection weights in an attempt to define the structure of a trained network (e.g., Hanson & Burr, 1990; Hinton, 1986). A second approach is to analyze network behavior in such a way that one can redescribe a network in more classical, rule-like terms (e.g., Gallant, 1993, ch. 17; Omlin & Giles, 1996). A third approach is to map out the response characteristics of units within the network in an attempt to identify the features to which these processors are sensitive (e.g., Berkeley, Dawson, Medler, Schopflocher, & Hornsby, 1995; Moorhead, Haig, & Clement, 1989).

In summary, entire connectionist networks can be viewed as algorithms for performing some mapping from input to output. The advantage of this is that networks can be trained to perform a variety of tasks, can be used to explore parallel information-processing algorithms, and can generate an algorithm in the absence of a completely specified theory. The chief disadvantage of this is that it is very difficult to look at a connectionist network and describe, in general terms, how the network actually works. As a result, at the programming level, many connectionist researchers are busy developing new techniques for interpreting network structure.

2) *Connectionism and architectural descriptions.* For a Turing machine, the distinction between a programming-level description and an architectural description was quite evident – the former was related to information written on the machine's tape, while the latter was related to properties of the machine's head. If an entire connectionist network is to be viewed as an algorithm, as was suggested above, then how can we describe the network at the architectural level?

As we will see in chapter 6, the architectural level of an information processor is used to specify its fundamental building blocks. It turns out that this approach serves us well with respect to PDP networks, because there is a staggering variety of different network architectures, each of which involves specifying different characteristics of the generic connectionist properties that were introduced earlier in this chapter.

For example, when connectionism was introduced above, we simply noted that an activation function was used to specify how a processing unit converted its net input into an internal level of activity. However, one can differentiate different kinds of connectionist building blocks – or, more correctly, different connectionist architectures – by taking note of the specific activation function that is used. For example, in early connectionist models (e.g., Rosenblatt, 1962), the activation function was a discontinuous function that was equal to 0 if the net input was below threshold, and was equal to 1 if it was above threshold. More modern backpropagation architectures approximate this kind of behavior with a continuous "squashing" function, such as the logistic equation (e.g., Rumelhart, Hinton, & Williams, 1986a, 1986b). A variation of backpropagation architectures use a particular form of the Gaussian equation as an activation function (e.g., Dawson & Schopflocher, 1992a). More complex activation functions are employed in so-called regularization networks (e.g., Poggio & Girosi, 1990), which include as a special case the popular radial basis function networks (e.g., Moody & Darken, 1989). Figure 3.5 illustrates some of the activation functions that have been used in different kinds of connectionist architectures.

Similarly, there are many learning rules that are available to researchers. A brief survey of the literature reveals a wide variety of training procedures that includes the Hebb rule (e.g., Hebb, 1949), the delta rule (e.g., Widrow & Hoff,

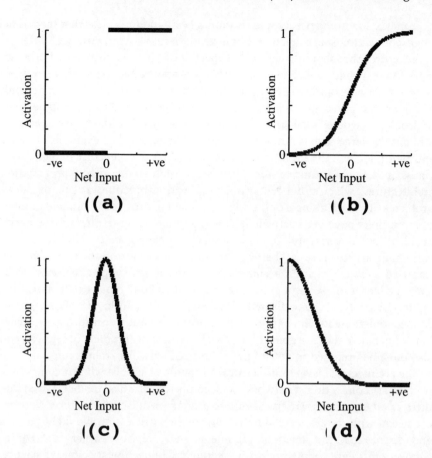

Figure 3.5 Graphs of activation functions from a variety of different Connectionist architectures. (a) The step function used in a simple perceptron. If the net input is greater than a threshold (which is 0 in this example), then activity is 1; otherwise, activity is 0. (b) The logistic activation function that is used in traditional backpropagation architectures. This particular function delivers an activation of 0.5 when the net input is equal to 0. (c) The Gaussian activation function used in networks of value units. This particular function has a standard deviation of 1, and achieves a maximum value of 1 when the net input is equal to 0. (d) The Gaussian activation function used in radial basis function networks. As these networks use a measure of distance as the net input, and as distances can never be negative, net input can never go below 0 for this activation function.

1960), the generalized delta rule (e.g., Rumelhart, Hinton, & Williams, 1986a, 1986b), simulated annealing (e.g., Ackley, Hinton, & Sejnowski, 1985), adaptive resonance theory (e.g., Grossberg, 1987), cascade correlation (Fahlman & Lebiere, 1990), and backpropagation through time (e.g., Rumelhart, Hinton, & Williams, 1986b). Amazingly, this list is quite incomplete. The June 1996 "frequently asked question" (FAQ) posting on the USENET group comp.ai.neural-nets listed 42 different learning rules to answer the question "How many learning methods for neural nets exist?" , and went on to note that new learning rules, or variations of existing ones, are invented every week!

From the foregoing paragraphs, it should be abundantly clear that there is no single connectionist architecture, but instead there is a wide variety of different architectures that share the general properties of "parallel distributed processing." As a result, one issue that affects connectionist research directly is choosing an appropriate network architecture for the job at hand. In general, one finds that one connectionist architecture is well-suited to solve some types of problems (where "well-suited" might mean something like "learns quickly"), but at the same time is not well-suited to solve others. For example, Dawson and Schopflocher (1992a) found that their value unit architecture (which uses a Gaussian activation function) is much better than standard backpropagation architectures (which use a "squashing" activation function) at solving parity problems, in which a single output unit is trained to turn "on" if an odd number of input units have been activated. This is an interesting result, because parity problems are notoriously difficult. However, it cannot be concluded that the value unit architecture is "better," because it has more difficulties than the standard backpropagation architectures on the much simpler majority problem, in which a single output unit is trained to turn "on" if more than half of the input units have been activated (Dawson & Shamanski, 1994). In short, connectionist researchers have to make important design decisions about what kind of network they are going to use to deal with some problem of interest, and also must be prepared to defend their choice of network architecture.

The architectural level is also critical to cognitive science when it comes time to compare connectionist networks with competing classical models. Given that there is an enormous variety of different connectionist architectures that are consistent with the generic claim that information processing should be parallel and distributed, the kinds of arguments that we saw earlier in favor of connectionism are simply not precise enough. Connectionist cognitive science, if it is to succeed, must at some point make the argument that a specific PDP architecture is the most appropriate for cognitive science. As a result, a detailed theoretical and empirical analysis of this architecture is going to be necessary. This analysis is not only going to have to compare the properties of this connectionist architecture to competing classical architectures, but also to the architectures of alternative PDP networks. We will see some examples of sticky connectionist architectural issues in chapter 6.

Connectionism and the Implementational Level

As we saw in chapter 2, an implementational description of an information-processing system attempts to relate its representational and formal properties to the causal laws governing its mechanical structure. We will see in chapters 5 and 6 that classical cognitive science has typically placed little emphasis on this type of description. Connectionism, however, is motivated by quite different considerations. Why has connectionism been so enthusiastically adopted by some cognitive scientists? One reason is that PDP models are claimed to be *biologically plausible* algorithms. In other words, when examining a diagram of a connectionist system, one could imagine that it illustrates a sufficient neural circuitry for accomplishing some task. In this sense, a PDP network not only represents a procedure for solving a problem, but also represents a (potential) physical device for carrying this procedure out.

In spite of connectionism's implementational intentions, neuroscientists are quite skeptical about the biological plausibility of the PDP architecture. A number of reasons are often cited for this skepticism. First, one can generate long lists of properties that are true of the PDP architecture, but are clearly not true of the brain (e.g., Crick & Asanuma, 1986; Smolensky, 1988, table 1). As a result, PDP models are often vilified as oversimplifications by neuroscientists; Douglas and Martin (1991, p. 292) refer to them as "stick and ball models." Second, researchers find it extremely unlikely that supervised learning rules like error backpropagation could be physiologically instantiated. This is because it is highly unlikely that the environment could specify a "training pattern" as accurately as is required by such rules (e.g., Barto, Sutton, & Anderson, 1983), and because there is no evidence at all for neural connections capable of feeding an error signal backwards to modify existing connections (e.g., Bechtel & Abrahamsen, 1991, p. 57; Kruschke, 1990).

However, such criticisms miss the mark. As we have already seen, PDP networks are designed to be extreme simplifications, glossing over many of the complex details true of neural systems (for an example, see Braham & Hamblen, 1990). This is because a PDP architecture attempts to capture just those properties of biological networks that are computationally relevant (e.g., Churchland & Churchland, 1990). The intent of this enterprise is to describe neural networks in a vocabulary that permits one to make rigorous claims about what they can do, or about why the brain might have the particular structure that it does. For example, why do different functions appear to be localized in different regions of the brain? Ballard (1986) argues that this type of organization is to be expected of a connectionist system that evolves to solve the so-called packing problem: how to pack an enormous variety of functions into a network (like the brain) with a finite number of processors. However, Ballard would not be in a position to make such a claim if he did not first use a connectionist vocabulary to abstract over neurophysiological details. In a related vein, connectionist researchers are now able to address some methodological issues that are pertinent to neuroscience by examining the behavior of lesioned networks (e.g., Farah, 1994). Again, this is only possible by viewing networks as simplified implementational models.

However, there are many factors working against realizing connectionism's potential to subsume cognitive theory. This is because connectionists often make design decisions about their architecture without justifying them as computationally relevant properties of neural circuits. Dawson and Shamanski (1994) have argued that this is because in some cases these design decisions are motivated more by engineering concerns (e.g., designing an architecture that will learn faster) than by cognitive science concerns (e.g., designing an architecture that is more closely related to brain function). Fortunately, this is not a problem in principle. Rather, this presents a research opportunity – connectionist networks provide an ideal medium in which the potential utility of a range of biological constraints can be explored.

For example, Moorhead, Haig, and Clement (1989) trained a standard backpropagation network on a simple vision task in an attempt to see whether the receptive fields of the hidden units in this network would resemble those found in the mammalian cortex. Unfortunately, they found that their trained network had few properties in common with the brain. However, a quick glance at their network reveals that many of the properties of their network were based on engineering principles instead of biological ones. For example, they used an extremely small number of hidden units, and each hidden unit was connected to every input unit in the network. Dawson, Kremer, and Gannon (1994) rebuilt this network using properties that were more characteristic of the visual system – they employed a large number of hidden units, and each of these units was connected to only a small "window" of input units. They found that after training, many of the hidden units in this more biological network had receptive fields that were analogous to those found in simple cells in the visual cortex. We will see other examples of how one can strengthen the implementational relevance of connectionism in chapter 7.

In summary, at first glance the neuronal inspiration of connectionist models appears to make them more relevant to the implementational concerns of cognitive science than classical models are. However, the biological plausibility of connectionist models is not completely established, because there are some concerns that connectionist architectures exclude some properties that neuroscientists view as being critical. As a result, connectionists who are concerned with relating their networks to the brain are currently exploring additional biological constraints on their network in an attempt to make them even more "brainlike."

Part IV   Connectionism and Cognitive Science

Connectionist Cognitive Science

In chapter 2, we saw that in addition to adopting the Turing machine metaphor, classical cognitive science uses the tri-level hypothesis to motivate a particular methodological approach. There is a strong tendency for classical cognitive scientists to move from the top of the tri-level hypothesis down, starting with abstract descriptions of phenomena at the computational level, moving to less abstract (and more finely detailed) descriptions at the programming level, with the ultimate aim of grounding these accounts in the vocabulary of the implementational level. Following Braitenberg's (1984) terminology, we might call this top-down approach to explaining cognitive phenomena *analytic psychology*.

In contrast, connectionists incorporate the tri-level hypothesis into a very different methodological approach. Like devotees of Edgar Allan Poe, who begins *Murders in the Rue Morgue* by writing that "the mental features discoursed of as the analytical, are, in themselves, but little susceptible of analysis," connectionists reject the analytic approach that classical cognitive scientists endorse.

Seidenberg (1993) provides an excellent overview of the alternative methodology employed by connectionist researchers. He argues that the goal of connectionism is to construct explanatory theories that use a small number of principles to account for a broad range of cognitive phenomena. These principles are "independently motivated" in the sense that they are general, and are not task- or phenomenon-specific. "If the principles are identified correctly, modeling should merely involve incorporating domain-specific variables such as different types of stimulus inputs, motoric responses, and learning experiences. The relevant generalizations about the domain in question should then fall out of the model. That is, it will develop the correct sorts of representations, obviating the need to build them in by hand" (p. 231). In other words, connectionists don't take complex cognitive phenomena and break them down into their parts. They start with a set of parts (the independently motivated principles), and see whether they can put these parts together and build complex cognitive phenomena. Connectionists don't analyze, they synthesize!

What are the general, independently motivated principles that form the starting point of this synthesis? They are those properties that define the particular architecture that a connectionist is using (i.e., a specific learning rule; processing units with particular net input, activation, and output functions; constraints on how units can be connected to one another). So instead of adopting a top-down research strategy in which a broadly defined phenomenon is decomposed along lines consistent with the tri-level hypothesis (i.e., from the computational level and downwards), connectionists practice bottom-up research. The question of interest to a connectionist is "What kinds of interesting phenomena can I construct from the building blocks that I have proposed?" Seidenberg (1993) calls this approach *explanatory connectionism*, because if an architecture is properly motivated, and can be used to construct models of lots of interesting cognitive phenomena, then it will have a great deal of explanatory force. Personally, I prefer to use Braitenberg's (1984) terminology, and say that the bottom-up methodology endorsed by connectionist cognitive scientists is an example of *synthetic psychology*.

The synthetic psychology practiced by connectionists requires them to start their investigations by proposing a particular architectural description. Does this mean that they have no interest in the other levels of the tri-level hypothesis? Of course not. Instead, their bottom-up strategy indicates that they will encounter these levels in a different order than a classical researcher who adopts a top-down approach. After proposing an architecture, and training a network, a connectionist is going to have to analyze the trained network to come up with its programming description in order to contribute to cognitive science (see

McCloskey, 1991 for a discussion of this point). After proposing an architecture, a connectionist is likely to perform computational analyses to try and
determine the kinds of problems that the architecture can (and cannot) solve
(see Minsky and Papert, 1969/1988 for an example of this). And after proposing an architecture, a connectionist must establish its "independent
motivation," which might involve making detailed arguments about how the
properties of the proposed architecture map onto the brain.

The Cognitive Science Debate

This chapter has introduced the connectionist view of information processing,
and has contrasted this view with the classical approach that was introduced in
chapter 2. We have seen a number of differences between the classical and
connectionist camps. However, we have also seen that because these approaches to cognitive science agree that cognition involves information processing,
the tri-level hypothesis is fundamental to both.

   Table 3.2 is an attempt to illustrate the applicability of the tri-level hypothesis
to both approaches to cognitive science. For each level in the tri-level hypothesis, the table indicates the general question of concern at that level, as well as
some example research questions that might be addressed at that level by both
classical and connectionist cognitive scientists. One point of the table is to
suggest that at each level both types of cognitive scientists are addressing very
similar questions – and as a result should be able to talk to one another about
their research program. This theme will be amplified in later chapters devoted to
each level of description.

Level Of Description	Main Question	Example Classical Questions	Example Connectionist Questions
Computational Level	What information processing is being solved, and why?	Is the proposed set of structures and processes powerful enough to solve the problem of interest? Can it be proven that the proposed system will always solve the problem?	Is the proposed network architecture powerful enough to solve the problem of interest? Can it be proven that the proposed network will converge to a problem solution during learning?
Programming Level	What general information-processing steps are being used to solve the problem?	What sequence of information-processing steps is being used to solve the problem? What evidence suggests that humans use this sequence as well?	How does the specific pattern of connectivity among network processors solve the problem? What evidence suggests that the network and humans solve the problem by attending to the same kind of input features?
Architectural Level (part of Programming Level)	What is the fundamental programming language being used to solve the problem?	What are the specific properties of the tokens or symbols being used by the system, and of the rules available to manipulate these symbols? What evidence suggests that humans use these tokens and symbols as well?	What are the specific properties of the network's processors, patterns of connectivity, and learning rule? What evidence suggests that these basic properties are true of the cognitive architecture?
Implementational Level	What physical properties are required to build the programming language into a physical device?	What physical properties (e.g., brainstates) are used to create the functional properties of tokens and rules?	What physical properties (e.g., brainstates) are used to create the functional properties of processors and connections?

Table 3.2 Applying the tri-level hypothesis to two approaches to cognitive science.

4

The Computational Level of Analysis

Cognitive scientists can communicate with one another because they share the foundational assumption that cognition is information processing. In chapters 2 and 3, I pointed out that one consequence of this assumption is that cognition must be described at three different levels of analysis: the computational level, the procedural level, and the implementational level. The purpose of the next few chapters is to characterize cognitive science in terms of the kinds of questions it asks, as well as the different methodologies that it uses to answer these questions, at each of these three levels. The current chapter focuses on the computational level of analysis, and looks at this kind of analysis in two different ways.

First, a computational analysis often involves translating a vague statement about a phenomenon of interest into a more precise statement about an information-processing problem that can be investigated using formal methods. For example, and as is described in more detail below, a general statement like "I am interested in finding out how children learn a language" might be converted to a much more specific form such as "I am interested in proving that if the grammar of a natural language has characteristic X, then such languages can be identified in the limit." After such translations, it often becomes apparent that in order for the (formally defined) information-processing problem to be solved, certain assumptions or properties must be built into the system that solves the problem. As a result, computational analyses can identify properties that are necessary components of information processors that generate phenomena of interest.

Second, a computational analysis often involves using formal methods to assess the general ability of a system to solve information-processing problems. For example, with the rise of connectionism in cognitive science, one might ask whether in principle connectionist networks are powerful enough to be of interest to cognitive scientists. In other words, it is important to know whether a connectionist network is capable of answering the same kinds of questions as a Universal Turing Machine. Computational analyses are capable of addressing this kind of issue.

In order to deal with these two aspects of computational analyses, this chapter proceeds as follows: First, I make some general comments on the need to translate general descriptions of cognitive phenomena into more technical definitions of information-processing problems. Second, I provide one example (language learning) that shows how this approach can lead to important discoveries about the underlying nature of cognitive systems. Third, I provide an example of how computational analyses are important for determining whether connectionist systems are powerful enough to be seriously considered by cognitive science. Finally, to motivate the next chapter on the procedural level of analysis, I consider ways in which a computational analysis is not by itself sufficiently powerful to count as a complete explanation for cognitive science.

Part I   What is the Computational Level?

Carving Nature at her Joints

Deep down, all scientists are taxonomists. They aim to carve Nature at her joints, assigning natural phenomena into a system of meaningful categories. For a scientist, a category's "meaning" is the set of properties that characterizes all its members. So, taking a single observed event and assigning it to a specific category is an attempt at explanation: the researcher is claiming that all of the regularities or laws that define the category also apply to the observed event.

What is cognitive science a science of? What natural set of generalizations does it attempt to capture using cognitive terms? To start to shed light on these questions, let's consider the primary categorization statement for cognitive scientists: cognition is information processing. One problem with this assumption is that it does not place any restrictions at all on the kind of information processing that is being done. In other words, it doesn't provide researchers much guidance about the specific sorts of things they should be looking for when they seek the "information processing" that underlies cognition. A related problem is that the assumption does not distinguish cognition from other types of noncognitive information processing. After all, while it may be the case that cognition is information processing, it is certainly the case that not all information processing is cognition. Otherwise, cognitive scientists would be committing themselves to the claim that pocket calculators, programmable VCRs, and electronic bicycle odometers (among other things) are cognate organisms.

What is needed is a more precise or technical sense of what cognitive scientists really are talking about when they use the term "information processing." For example, in the research program championed by Marr (e.g., 1977, 1982), when cognitive scientists make technical claims about "information process-ing," they are really proposing a theory of the computation that a cognitive system is performing. For Marr a theory of a computation provided an answer to two related questions. The first question was "What is being computed?" , and the answer to this question should specify what information-processing problem is being solved. The second question was "Why do we say this is being computed, and not say that something else is being computed?" , and its answer should specify why the system was solving a particular information-processing problem, and not some other problem. Such an answer would detail the set of constraints that were being placed on the potential operations of a problem-solving system. The idea would be to specify a set of constraints that (1) would be sufficient to solve a particular problem, and (2) would identify a system uniquely as one that is solving the problem.

Constraints on Information-Processing Problems

Importantly, the identification of constraints on solving information-processing problems turns out to be one of the major contributions of the computational level of analysis. This is because over the last couple of decades, when research-ers have translated vague descriptions of cognitive phenomena into technical descriptions of information-processing problems, they have found that these problems are ill-posed (e.g., Poggio & Girosi, 1990) or underdetermined. What this means is that there are many possible responses to the problem, only one of which is correct. The problem itself does not supply enough information to indicate which is the correct response to choose (this is often described as "poverty of the stimulus"). In order to solve the problem, there must be some assumptions that are already built into the information processor that can be used to choose the correct response from the many possible responses.

Before proceeding, let's illustrate an ill-posed problem with a noncognitive example. Pretend that you are doing a crossword puzzle, and are given the clue "the place where one lives." By itself, this clue isn't particularly helpful, because you could likely think of several different words that were consistent with it: "abode," "domicile," "dwelling," "habitation," "home," "house," and "resi-dence" for example. In other words, filling in this part of the crossword puzzle is an ill-posed problem. However, if additional constraining information is available to you, then this ill-posed problem can be solved. For instance, by looking at the puzzle you would note that the desired word must be made up of only eight letters. This leaves only "domicile" and "dwelling" as possible solutions. Furthermore, if you notice that from filling in another word on the puzzle that the fifth letter must be "l," then the only solution is "dwelling." The constraints that you have noticed on the problem (i.e., the length of the word, certain restrictions of possible letters) are sufficient to uniquely identify how you should fill the puzzle in.

In cognitive science, many of the information-processing problems that researchers have defined are ill-posed in exactly the same sense as the crossword puzzle example that I've just given. For example, in visual perception, it is almost always the case that the pattern of stimulation that activates light detectors at the back of our eyes does not provide enough information by itself to say what arrangement of objects in the world caused that activation (e.g., Marr, 1982). To solve such problems, additional constraining information is required – and computational analyses can be used to identify what this information is, and to prove that it is necessary and sufficient to solve the problem. However, unlike the crossword example, these constraints don't exist as separate clues in image. Instead, these constraints are best viewed as very general assumptions of the world that are built into the visual apparatus. For instance, it has long been known that if you watch the movement of an object's shadow cast on a two-dimensional screen, your visual system is able to use this movement to give you the impression of the three-dimensional structure of this moving object (e.g., Wallach & O'Connell, 1953). However, inferring this 3D structure from the 2D image is an ill-posed problem. Ullman (1979) demonstrated that this ill-posed problem could be solved if a very general assumption (that whole objects tend to be rigid structures) was already built into the visual system.

Summary

In a very broad sense, then, a computational-level analysis involves translating a general description of a phenomenon of interest into a very specific account of an information-processing problem that is being solved. Importantly, this translation will usually involve some formal description of the information-processing problem – that is, a logical or mathematical description of what the system is doing. Once this translation has been carried out, cognitive scientists will describe constraints that can be used to solve this problem. Crucially, because the information-processing problem is itself described in some formal language, formal methods (e.g., logical analysis, mathematical proofs) can be used to discover these constraints. Later, these proposed constraints can be used to defend claims that this particular information-processing problem is being solved, or to make predictions about the behaviors of some system that is solving this problem.

What is to be gained by translating a cognitive phenomenon into an information-processing problem? One advantage is that researchers have had a lot of experience in dealing with information-processing problems, and are armed with many formal techniques for finding solutions to them. In many cases, the biggest hurdle to be faced is identifying the information-processing problem to be solved. Once this hurdle has been passed, often times a variety of standard techniques can be then be employed in determining how the problem is to be solved. Let's illustrate this with a concrete example.

Part II   Language Learnability as a Classical Example

In a computational-level analysis, one provides insight into a very generally described phenomenon by translating it into a very specific information-processing problem. Gold (1967) has provided an interesting example of this approach as it relates to the study of language learning. Gold's goal was "to construct a precise model for the intuitive notion 'able to speak a language' in order to be able to investigate theoretically how it can be achieved artificially" (p. 448). He began with the classical assumption that a language is defined by a set of rules. He realized, however, that native speakers of languages are only implicitly aware of these rules: while they follow the rules, they are rarely able to explicitly state what the rules are. As a result, one could not expect that a programmer could write down a set of rules that would result in a system speaking, say, English. Instead, "an artificial intelligence which is designed to speak English will have to learn its rules from implicit information" (p. 448). Gold's contribution came from providing a formal specification of this kind of learning.

In order to describe Gold's (1967) paradigm, and the more recent research on language learning that it has inspired, three topics will be considered in order. First, I will briefly describe one example of how natural languages can be described as a system of rules. Second, I will introduce Gold's formal definition of language learning, and show the problems for language learning theorists that Gold raised by proving a number of theorems using his formal definition. Third, I will show how theorists invoke natural constraints on language to solve the problems revealed by Gold's theorems.

Formalizing Language (I)

We saw in chapter 2 that one of the major reasons for viewing cognition as information processing was to get a tremendous (possibly infinite) variety in behavior from a finite machine. Cognitive scientists attempt to account for the creativity and flexibility of human thought by assuming that cognition is the product of applying a number of rules sensitive to the componential structure of complex symbols. Recall that such sensitivity results in the tremendous computational power of a Universal Turing Machine.

Up until the late 1950s, linguistics was essentially based upon a taxonomy of physical sounds. "On the taxonomic conception of linguistics, there is nowhere from the beginning to the end of a linguistic investigation any appeal to mental capacities or mental processes" (Katz, 1964, p. 124). The rule-governed assumption – the foundational belief that cognition is information processing – was motivated by the cognitive revolution in linguistics that occurred because of the growing realization that taxonomic and behavioristic accounts were inadequate. "Lashley recognizes, as anyone must who seriously considers the data, that the composition and production of an utterance is not simply a matter of stringing together a sequence of responses under the control of outside stimulation and intraverbal association, and that the syntactic organization of an utterance is not something directly represented in any simple way in the physical structure of the utterance itself" (Chomsky, 1959).

Because of the cognitive revolution, linguistics was transformed from a discipline concerned with taxonomies of physical utterances to one concerned with identifying the system of rules (grammar) that characterize human language. "The theory of language can be regarded as a study of the formal properties of such grammars, and, with a precise enough formulation, this general theory can provide a uniform method for determining, from the process of generation of a given sentence, a structural description which can give a good deal of insight into how this sentence is used and understood" (Chomsky, 1959). One important proposal for the formal structure of natural languages was the *transformational grammar* (e.g., Chomsky, 1965).

In essence, a transformational grammar consists of two different systems of rules. The first is a set of phrase-structure rules that define the base grammar. Phrase-structure rules are used to construct the tree-like phrase markers that linguists use to represent the full structure of sentences (see figure 4.1). A phrase-structure rule is a rewrite rule that specifies how new nodes can be grown from existing nodes in the "tree." For example, the second layer of nodes from the top in figure 4.1 are produced by applying the rule S => NP Aux VP.

The second set of rules in a transformational grammar are called transformations. The purpose of a transformation is to produce a special phrase marker, called a surface structure, which can be operated on by phonological rules to produce speech. A transformation takes as input a phrase marker from the base grammar, and converts it into a surface structure phrase marker. For example, imagine that the phrase-structure rules in the base grammar have built the phrase marker that represents the sentence "The Montreal Canadiens won the Stanley cup in 1993." By applying a question-making transformation, one could convert this into the surface structure phrase marker that represents the sentence "Did the Montreal Canadiens win the Stanley cup in 1993?"

From all of this, it should be clear that one move in the computational study of language learning is to formalize the definition of language. For instance, it would be very natural for a learnability theorist to ask whether a transformational grammar could be learned. However, the answer to this kind of question requires that the theorist also formalize the definition of learning. This is the topic of the next section.

Formalizing Language Learning

Gold (1967) formally described the process of learning in terms of generating a hypothesized set of rules for the language (a grammar) on the basis of information provided about a to-be-learned language. The learning process was divided

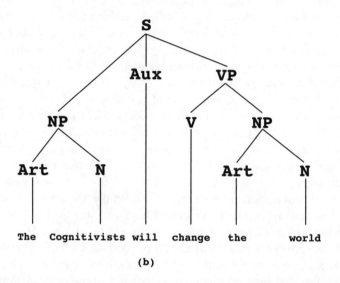

```
S  = >  NP Aux VP
NP = >  Art N
VP = >  V NP
PP = >  Prep NP
NP = >  Art N
```

(a)

(b)

Figure 4.1 (a) A set of phrase-structure rules that could define part of the base for a transformational grammar. The "node" on the left of the arrow is rewritten as the set of nodes on the right of the arrow when a rule is applied, resulting in the growing of a "tree-like" structure called a phrase marker. (b) An example phrase marker that could be created by successively applying some of the phrase-structure rules in (a).

into discrete units of time. At any discrete moment in time, Gold assumed that the learner would be presented a unit of information about the to-be-learned language. For Gold, a language was defined as a large set of possible sentences. For instance, the English language would be the set of meaningful (in English) finite strings that could be produced by arranging letters of the alphabet and punctuation marks. A unit of information about the to-be-learned language would be a sample string presented to the learner. Gold was concerned with two ways in which language instances could be presented.

  In *text learning*, the learner is only presented a valid instance of the language. (In the vocabulary of those who study language acquisition in children, text learning only involves the presentation of positive evidence.) For example, if I were teaching my children English via text learning, at time *t* I might present the instance "This is a ball," at time (*t* + 1) I might present the instance "Cognition is information processing," and so on. I would never present an instance that was not a valid English sentence.

This is not true of another approach to learning that Gold (1967) considered. In *informant learning*, the learner is presented either valid or invalid instances of the language, and is also told about the validity of the instance. If I were teaching my children English via informant learning, at time *t* I might say "Here is an example of an English sentence: 'This is a ball,' " at time (*t* + 1) I might say "Here is an example of a sentence that is not English: 'Ball this a is,' " and so on. In the parlance of researchers who study language development, informant learning involves the presentation of both positive and negative evidence.

Regardless of the method of instruction, after each presentation the learner generates (unconsciously) a hypothesis about the rules that define the language. Gold (1967) proposed that each hypothesis could be described as being a Turing machine that would either generate the (hypothesized) language, or would test it (i.e., when given a string, would indicate whether or not the string belonged to the hypothesized language). It has become common practice among formal learnability theorists to describe "learning a language" as selecting a Turing machine to represent the language's grammar (e.g., Osherson, Stob, & Weinstein, 1986, p. 13).

Given this description, when is a language learned? "A person does not know when he is speaking a language correctly: there is always the possibility that he will find that his grammar contains an error. But we can guarantee that a child will eventually learn a natural language, even if it will not know when it is correct" (Gold, 1967, p. 450). With this rationale, Gold formally defined "learning a language" as identification of the language in the limit. When a language is *identified in the limit*, then after some finite amount of time the learner has generated a particular hypothesis that generates a language, and never changes that hypothesis even as new examples of the language are presented. This is illustrated in figure 4.2.

What is the advantage of defining language learning in this formal manner? As is the case with any computational analysis, such descriptions allow the methods of formal proofs to be used to make powerful claims about the phenomenon. Gold's (1967) formalization revealed an extremely challenging research problem for those interested in explaining how children learn languages.

In computer science, a formal description of any class of languages (human or otherwise) relates its complexity to the complexity of a computing device that could generate or test it (e.g., Hopcroft & Ullman, 1979). Gold (1967) used formal methods to examine each class of language in terms of its learnability. Specifically, he worked out a number of proofs to determine the conditions under which each class of languages were identifiable in the limit. He was able to show that text learning was very weak; it could only be used to acquire the simplest of languages (finite cardinality languages).

Informant learning was much more powerful; Gold (1967) proved that with it much more complicated languages (including context-sensitive and context-

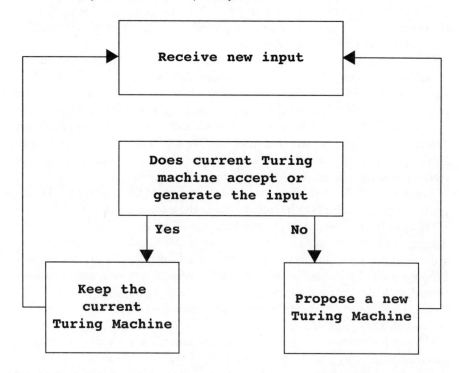

Figure 4.2 A simplified flowchart for text learning. A language is learnable – identifiable in the limit – if at some point in time the learner moves into the "Yes" loop on the left, and is then never forced out of this loop.

free grammars) were identifiable in the limit. The context-sensitive and context-free grammars are members of the so-called Chomsky hierarchy (e.g., Hopcroft & Ullman, 1979), and have been proposed as possible grammars for natural human languages (see also Johnson-Laird, 1983, pp. 267–76); the phrase-structure rules described earlier define a context-free grammar.

Gold's proofs provide an important theoretical view of language learning, and show that grammars complex enough to be considered as models of human languages are identifiable in the limit from informant learning, but not from text learning. Problems emerge, however, when empirical data is added to the mix. Specifically, all of the evidence indicates that children do not appear to acquire a language from informant learning, but rather acquire it from text learning (e.g., Pinker, 1979, 1990). For instance, Newport, Gleitman, and Gleitman (1977) estimated that 99.93 percent of the language that children are exposed to is grammatically well-formed. In addition, when children do receive feedback about the grammaticality of their utterances, this feedback does not appear to be systematic enough to reliably be used to pick out a correct grammar (Marcus, 1993). This is because different parents of a child often react to ungrammatical utterances in different ways, and some kinds of grammatical errors made by a child may not be corrected at all. Finally – perhaps because of the previous point! – children usually are insensitive to the small amount of negative evidence that they might be exposed to (e.g., Pinker, 1994, p. 281).

Now, why is this so interesting? Well, all of this evidence suggests that children learn language from positive evidence alone. But this is text learning – and Gold proved that text learning was not powerful enough to permit a system to learn something as complex as a natural human language! So, an intriguing question immediately arises: what enables children to be more powerful learners than Gold's proof permits? "Since children presumably do have a procedure whereby they learn the language of their community, there must be some feature of Gold's paradigm itself that precludes learnability" (Pinker, 1979, p. 228).

Theories about the learning of natural human languages have evolved by proposing restrictions on Gold's formalization. The goal has been to show that, in the restricted paradigm, more complex grammars can be acquired via text learning. Pinker (1979) points out that there are four general strategies for avoiding the limits of Gold's theorems. The first is to place restrictions on the order in which text samples are presented (e.g., by starting with simple sentences). The second is to make the definition of when a language is learned more liberal than the one used by Gold. The third is to assume that the learner has additional a priori information about the probability that a particular grammar is correct, and so can always guess the most probable grammar given the text information so far. The fourth is to assume that additional constraints are placed upon the hypotheses that the learner can generate. The next section briefly considers one approach to revising Gold's paradigm in an attempt to show that transformational grammars can be acquired via text learning.

Learnability of Transformational Grammars

Wexler and Culicover (1980) have proposed a reformulation of Gold's (1967) paradigm that has enabled them to prove that transformational grammars can be identified in the limit. In general, their approach is to place powerful constraints on the hypotheses that the learner can generate, and as such is very similar in spirit to the natural computation approach to vision that was described above. There are two versions of the theory that they describe. In the first, a single constraining hypothesis enables them to prove that transformational grammars are learnable, but this particular proof doesn't place realistic constraints on learning. For instance, the proof indicates that learning may require consideration of extraordinarily complicated sentences. In the second version of their theory, additional properties are assumed to constrain the nature of the grammar being learned. As a result, Wexler and Culicover were able to show that transformational grammars can be learned (via text learning) on the basis of relatively simple input.

The first learnability result for transformational grammars comes from adopting the extremely strong *universal base hypothesis*. According to this claim, all natural human languages are built upon the same base grammar. As a

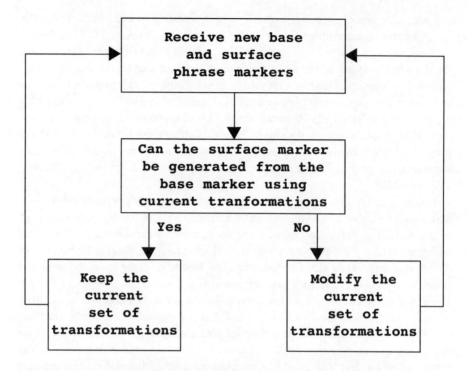

Figure 4.3 A simplified flowchart of Wexler and Culicover's (1980) algorithm for the text learning of a transformational grammar. By assuming that the universal base hypothesis can be used to elaborate the input, and by placing additional constraints on hypothesized transformations, Wexler and Culicover were able to prove that this algorithm could learn a transformational grammar: at some point in time, the learner does not exit the "Yes" loop on the left.

result, the only differences between languages are due to differences in their transformational rules. The universal base hypothesis figures into the learning paradigm as possible: it is assumed that during text learning, the learner not only receives the surface structure of the language sample, but the learner also receives the base structure from which the surface structure was created. In their formalization, this dual input is made explicit for the sake of notational simplicity (see figure 4.3). With respect to the actual circumstances surrounding a child learning a language, Wexler and Culicover (1980) note that the base structure would not be explicitly given. Instead, the child – by interpreting the intended semantics of the sentence that he or she was exposed to – would infer the base structure. "Suppose that the rules of translating between the base grammar and semantic interpretation are available to the child (as they will be if they are innate or if they are learned first). Then if the child has semantic interpretation of some sentences available, he will be able to reconstruct the base phrase-marker" (p. 83).

In the revised algorithm for learning (figure 4.3), the universal base hypothesis focuses attention on learning the correct set of transformational rules, because the base grammar is fixed. In the learning procedure, the learner takes the given base phrase marker and attempts to use his or her existing transformations to produce the (given) surface phrase marker. If this is successfully accomplished, then the existing grammar is unchanged. If this cannot be accomplished, then the existing grammar is changed by adding or deleting a single transformational rule. Successful learning of a language is defined in a fashion very similar to Gold (1967): it occurs when the learner has built a set of transformations that define the language, and when the set will not be changed as further inputs are received.

This (constrained) proposal for the learning of transformational grammars requires errors to occur in order for it to work. These errors must be such that not too many changes in the existing set of transformations need to be considered, and as a result there is a reasonable chance of correcting the existing transformations. Furthermore, such errors must occur sufficiently often for learning to occur. This entails that there is a limit on the complexity of phrase markers for which errors will occur. Wexler and Culicover (1980) were able to show that transformational grammars are learnable under the figure 4.3 paradigm by establishing a property that they called *boundedness of minimal degree of error* (BDE). Essentially, this property proves that if the learner is making errors, then these errors will be revealed in sufficiently simple phrase markers for learning to be possible.

However, BDE by itself does not impose particularly practical constraints on learning. This property essentially places an upper bound on the number of embedded clauses in a phrase marker that have to be considered in order to detect an error. The mere fact that a bound can be established lets the learnability of transformational grammars be established in principle. However, in practice, the bound established by BDE is very unrealistic: Wexler and Culicover (1980, p. 118) note that it restricts language learners to considering phrase markers with 400,000 embedded clauses or less!

The second approach that Wexler and Culicover considered further restricted the hypotheses generated by the learner. This was done by imposing five additional constraints on the possible nature of the transformation rules: the freezing principle, the binary principle, the raising principle, the principle of no bottom context, and the principle of the transparency of untransformable base structures. A full discussion of these principles is well beyond the scope of this chapter (for details, see Wexler & Culicover, 1980, Chap. 4). However, two general points can be made about these constraints. First, by assuming these five constraints, Wexler and Culicover were able to prove that transformational grammars could be learned using very simple inputs (i.e., phrase markers with no more than two embedded clauses). Second, in requiring these constraints to prove (realistic) learnability, Wexler and Culicover were in fact postulating new, structural characteristics for the grammar of human language. "The restrictions on grammar (and possibly on other aspects of the theory) might lead to constraining the learning theory in such a way that the theory constructs more descriptively adequate grammars for languages" (p. 91).

Formalizing Language (II)

The investigation of the learnability of transformational grammars, as descri-bed above, provides what I think is a very elegant example of the computational approach that cognitive scientists adopt. However, it is important to recognize that this example is quite dated. This is because there has been considerable change in how linguists formally describe language, and this in turn has affected formal investigations of language learning. In particular, the transformational grammar approach has, since the early 1980s, been replaced with what is now known as *principles and parameters theory*. Let us take a brief moment to consider some aspects of principles and parameters theory, and then examine how changes in the way that language is described affects computational analyses of language learning. A detailed account of principles and parameters theory is far beyond the scope of this text; I'm only interested in giving you the flavor of this approach. For the interested reader, an excellent introduction to the theory is provided by Cook and Newson (1996). A shorter (but much more technical) introduction can be found in Chomsky and Lasnik (1995).

Principles and parameters theory arose from the recognition that there were deeper similarities among different human languages than was evident from describing them as transformational grammars. In the transformational gram-mar approach, each human language would be described as a different set of transformational rules. In contrast, principles and parameters theory describes a smaller set of principles that are shared by all languages. Some of these principles are associated with a small number of parameters that can be thought of as "switches" that specify exactly how the principle is manifested. Variations from one language to another are accounted for in terms of variations of how the parameters are set.

The structural components of principles and parameters theory are illus-trated in figure 4.4. The *lexicon* is a set of entries for words in the language, and also includes information about syntactic regularities associated with these words. For example, the verb "like" might have an entry in the lexicon of the form "like: VERB, [__, NP]" indicating that this verb must always be followed by a noun phrase. So, this lexicon entry alone could be used to determine that the sentence "Mike likes the Habs" is grammatical, but the sentence "Mike likes" is not (because there is no noun phrase following "likes" in the second example).

The *D-structure* in figure 4.4 provides an underlying representation of the sentence. This structure is represented as a phrase marker similar to that of figure 4.1. However, in principles and parameters theory, it is presumed that one language universal is that all phrases (in all languages) have the same kind of structure. This structure is described by the *X-bar theory* of lexical phrases. In this theory, the generic phrase marker XP provides the generic structure for phrases in the language. By filling in a verb for X one gets the structure for a verb phrase, by filling in a noun for X one gets the structure for a noun phrase, and so on. This is illustrated in figure 4.5a. One noticeable difference between this

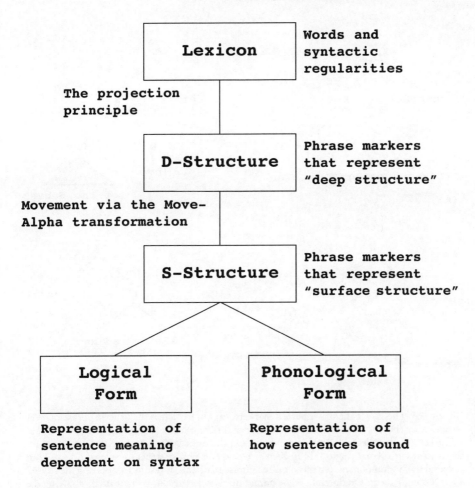

Figure 4.4 The main structural components of principles and parameter theory, in which S-structure is viewed as a computational bridge between the logical form and the phonological form of sentences. See text for details.

approach to phrase markers and older approaches is the inclusion of the constituent X', which functionally lies somewhere between the head of the phrase (whatever X is) and the phrase itself (XP in figure 4.5a). X-bar theory represents the recursive embedding of clauses by permitting these intermediate constituents X' to be expanded into adjunct components, as illustrated in figure 4.5b.

The *S-structure* in figure 4.4 provides another representation of the sentence, again using the representational apparatus of X-bar theory. The S-structure of a sentence is created by taking the sentence's D-structure and moving its constituents to other locations, which produces an alternative phrase marker. Whenever a constituent is moved to a new location in the phrase marker, a trace is also included in the phrase marker to indicate the old location of that

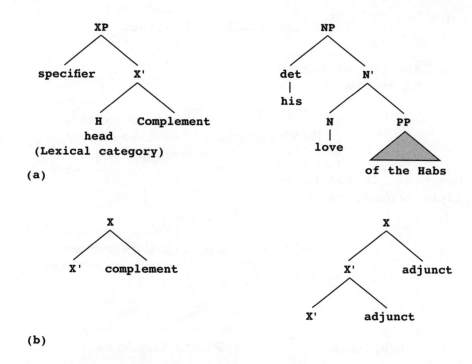

Figure 4.5 The X-bar theory of phrase markers. (a) On the left is the generic phrase marker from X-bar theory, where X can be a number of different lexical categories (e.g., N or noun, V or verb, A or adjective, P or preposition). On the right is the structure of a noun phrase consistent with X-bar theory. (b) In X-bar theory, two phrase structure rules can be used to expand the X' component. On the left is the phrase marker that results by applying the rule X' => X complement. On the right is the phrase marker that results by repeatedly applying the rule X' => X' adjunct. This latter rule enables X-bar theory to represent the embedded clausal structure of natural languages.

constituent. The presence of these traces can affect how the sentence is actually pronounced, or aspects of the sentence's meaning. This is important because in figure 4.4 the S-structure is intended to provide the necessary structure to bridge between the *phonological form* of the sentence (i.e., how the sentence is pronounced) and the *logical form* of the sentence (i.e., a representation of the semantic aspects of the sentence that depend crucially upon its syntactic structure).

   Importantly, the relationship between S-structure and D-structure in principles and parameters theory permits a dramatic simplification of the older transformational grammars. Under the old approach, each language was associated with a large number of specific transformations that were used to convert one phrase marker into another. Under principles and parameters theory, we still have a transformational grammar, because a transformation is required to convert a D-structure phrase marker into an S-structure phrase marker. However, only one transformational rule is required – the ubiquitous *move-alpha rule*. In general terms, by applying this one transformational rule, one can move any component of a phrase marker to another location – provided that this move does not violate any of the other principles that apply to the grammar!

A set of independent principles describe the internal organization of the grammar; that is, these principles determine the kinds of structures that can emerge in the components illustrated in figure 4.4. Each of these principles is often called a theory; as a result, major components of the grammar include such principles as "bounding theory," "government theory," "theta theory," "binding theory," "case theory," and "control theory." (Again, for more details on each of these principles, see Cook & Newson, 1996). Each of these principles represents an independent account of a particular type of regularity that manifests itself in the grammar. For example, binding theory concerns the relationships between anaphors (e.g., "himself") or pronouns (e.g., "him") and their antecedents. For example, binding theory would explain why in the sentence "Mike is talking to him, not himself," "Mike" and "him" refer to different individuals, while "Mike" and "himself" refer to the same individual.

Some of these principles have only one form. One example of this is the *projection principle*, which stipulates that the properties of entries in the lexicon project onto the syntax of the sentence. This means that if the lexicon has the entry "like: VERB, [__, NP]," then whenever the verb "like" is represented with a phrase marker (e.g., in D-structure or S-structure), then it must be associated with a noun phrase. Another example of a one-formed principle is structure dependency, which stipulates that operations on grammatical representations (e.g., movement) depend on structural relationships among words, and not just upon their linear order. This is why phrase markers are used in X-bar theory to represent sentence structure.

Other principles can take one of two (or more) forms, depending what setting is given a parameter. For instance, consider the X-bar representation of syntax. In figure 4.6, it is clear that in this representation, the head of the phrase could either come first or last. It turns out that this is an "option" governing human languages; some, like English, are head-first, while others, like Japanese, are head-last. The *head parameter* is a setting that determines which of these two options is selected. Importantly, once this parameter is set, it determines the structure of all of the phrases of the language (verb phrases, noun phrases, prepositional phrases, and so on!) – because it concerns the X-bar representation that is used for *all* of these phrases.

In principles and parameters theory, the description of a single sentence or phrase is the result of the combined action of all of the principles. This combined action depends upon all of the parameters being set in particular ways. "We may think of the system as a complex network associated with a switch box that contains a finite number of switches. The network is invariant, but each switch can be in one of several positions, perhaps two: on or off. Unless

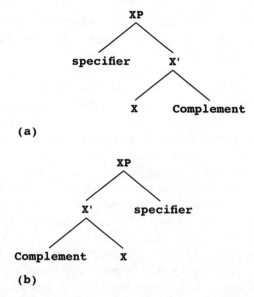

(a)

(b)

Figure 4.6 The exact form of a phrase marker depends on the setting of the head parameter. (a) In a language like English, which is head first, all phrases in the language will have this structure. (b) In a language like Japanese, which is head last, all phrases in the language will have this structure. Note that because X-bar theory describes all of the different kinds of phrases in a language, the head parameter will affect the structure of all of these phrases in the same way.

the switches are set, nothing happens. But when the switches are set in one of the permissible ways, the system functions, yielding the entire infinite array of interpretations for linguistic expressions" (Chomsky, 1993, p. 528).

Cook and Newson (1996) provide a nice example of how regularities in grammatical structure arise from interacting principles and parameters. They point out that some verbs are transitive and must be associated with a noun phrase (e.g., the verb "drinks" in the phrase "drinks coffee"), while others are intransitive and are not associated with a noun phrase (e.g., the verb "fainted"). In the transformational grammar approach, this would have been represented as the phrase-structure rule VP => V (NP), which means "A verb phrase consists of a verb followed by an optional noun phrase." In principles and parameters theory, such rules are not required; indeed "it appears that they may be completely superfluous" (Chomsky & Lasnik, 1995). This is because the regularities described by such rules are emergent properties of principles and parameters theory. Consider how principles and parameters theory does away with the need for the verb phrase rule given above. In the lexicon, there will be an entry for "drink" that will indicate that it requires a noun phrase. The projection principle stipulates that this in turn will require a noun phrase to be associated with "drink" in any phrase marker headed by that verb in D-structure or S-structure. Finally, setting for the head parameter of the language will indicate that the verb comes before the noun phrase. "Many aspects of language that earlier models dealt with as 'syntax' are now handled as idiosyncrasies of lexical items; the syntax itself is considerably simplified by the omission of many rules, at the cost of greatly increased lexical information" (Cook & Newson, 1996, p. 19).

Principles, Parameters, and Language Acquisition

How do the notions of principles and parameters theory impact computational studies of language learning? One major consequence is a marked change in defining what is learned. In the older approach, typified by Wexler and Culicover's (1980) research, the assumption was that the purpose of language learning was to acquire a set of rules (e.g., the set of transformational rules that were consistent with a particular language). However, we have seen rules do not make up a large part of principles and parameters theory – it uses only a single transformational rule (move-alpha, which converts D-structures into S-structures), and it has essentially eliminated the need for phrase-structure rules. It would appear, then, that with this new formal description of language, language acquisition is not rule acquisition. Instead, it is the acquisition of the set of parameter values that are consistent with the language being learned, and theories of language acquisition must become theories of how parameters are set. "The problem will be to determine how the switches are set and to discover the principles of learning, or maturation, or whatever is responsible for carrying out the transition from the initial state of the language faculty to the steady state of adult competence; that is, for setting the switches of the language faculty" (Chomsky, 1993, p. 529).

The view that language acquisition is the process of setting the parameters of grammatical principles has immediate consequences for formal claims about language learning. In particular, in principles and parameters theory, it is assumed that there is a finite number of parameters to be set, and that each of these parameters can only be set to one of a finite number of values. This immediately implies that there is only a finite set of human languages that can be learned! In other words, language acquisition can now be construed as a search through a finite set of possible languages (i.e., parameter settings) in order to find one set of parameters consistent with the positive evidence that has been provided to the learner. This is a critical move when we face Gold's (1967) paradox (i.e., his proof that languages complicated enough to be described with transformational grammars cannot be learned, contrasted with the observation that humans normally learn such grammars). We saw earlier that one approach to dealing with this paradox was to assume that additional constraints are placed upon the hypotheses that the learner can generate. Principles and parameters theory constrains accounts of what language is to such an extent that language learning is extremely tractable.

Indeed, this tractability of language learning within the principles and parameters framework is evident in new claims about the kind of evidence that a language learner must be exposed to. Wexler and Culicover's (1980) work using the older formalism was able to prove that natural languages had *degree-2 learnability*; in other words, that transformational grammars could be learned from phrase markers with no more than two embedded clauses. As we saw earlier, this proof was the result of assuming that several different constraining properties were true of transformational grammar. Principles and parameters theory appears to provide an even more strongly constrained account of the structure of language. With stronger constraints, one might predict that a language could be learned from being exposed to even simpler evidence. Indeed, some researchers have argued that this prediction is supported. For example, Lightfoot (1989) claimed that under principles and parameters theory, human languages exhibit *degree-0 learnability*. This means that the parameters of the language can be set correctly when the learner is exposed to phrases that do not contain any embedded clauses at all. This is consistent with Lightfoot's philosophy that children learn language on the basis of "a haphazard set of utterances made in an appropriate context, utterances of a type that any child hears frequently" (p. 323). Lightfoot supports this claim by considering several different analyses of grammatical structures that have been thought to be (at best) degree-2 learnable; for all of these cases, Lightfoot was able to describe degree-0 "triggers" that could be used to set parameters that in turn would produce the required structure within principles and parameters theory.

Summary

A lot of terrain has been covered in this subsection on language acquisition. Let's take a moment to summarize some key points before moving on to other computational issues. The computational analysis of a system arises from classifying it in a particular way: as solving a particular information-processing problem. This requires a rigorous and precise definition of what information-processing problem is being solved. We have seen one example of such a definition, in the translation of "learning to speak a language" to "identifying a grammar in the limit." Typically, the definition of the information-processing problem is so precise that it is done in some formal notation.

The benefits purchased from a computational analysis are primarily the result of the formal description of the information-processing problem. With this kind of description, the formal tools of mathematics, computer science, and logic are at our disposal, ready to be used to provide new insights into the phenomenon of interest. For example, we can use these techniques to prove that if a particular constraint is applied, then the information-processing problem can be solved. One way to think about this is to consider the above example in the following light: Let's imagine that someone asked you why the grammar of a human language is governed by a particular principle. One answer that follows from learnability theory is that when that principle is present, language is constrained in such a way that it can be learned. Furthermore, when that principle is absent, the language cannot be learned. In other words, learnability theory involves computational analyses that can identify general properties that languages must have in order to be learned (i.e., in order to circumvent Gold's (1967) paradox).

Importantly, discovering or proposing new properties like the freezing principle can be done in the absence of experiments. In my mind, that is one of the major attractions of full-blown cognitivism to a traditionally experimental discipline like psychology: it provides a completely new set of methodologies that can be used to explore research questions. Given the apparent complexity of the problems addressed in such fields as psychology, linguistics, and neuroscience, making new methodologies available is no minor accomplishment.

Part III   The Computational Power of Connectionist Networks

The previous part of the chapter examined one role that computational analysis plays in cognitive science: using formal methods to explore specific information-processing problems. Furthermore, it illustrated this role in the context of classical cognitive science: the symbolic representations used by linguists (e.g., phrase markers) and the rules that are used to manipulate them (e.g., transformations) are prototypical examples of the physical symbol system hypothesis in action.

This is not to say that connectionist research could not be used to illustrate the computational analysis of specific information-processing problems. Indeed, many problems of underdetermination in vision are solved by using connectionist networks to impose constraints on processing (e.g., Marr, 1982). One advantage of this – which contrasts markedly with the classical research that we have already covered – is that with such networks, the constraints can be imposed in a "soft" manner. This means that with a network, in some instances a constraint might be violated to a certain degree in order to better impose other constraints. A detailed example of this is provided in chapter 9, when I present a case study of my own work on the motion correspondence problem.

However, rather than using connectionism to further illustrate this theme, let us now turn to a more general computational issue. In many cases, when researchers propose a new computational system it becomes important not only to ask whether the system can solve a particular information-processing problem, but to determine in general the kinds of information-processing problems that it can solve. For example, if this new system cannot be proven to be able to answer the same kinds of questions that can be answered by a Universal Turing Machine, then this new system will likely not be of interest to cognitive scientists. This is because classical cognitive scientists believe that systems that are less powerful than Universal Turing Machines are not powerful enough to solve the kinds of problems that cognitive organisms solve all the time.

In this situation, computational analyses can be used to make strong claims about the general power of a computational system, and are not used to examine how that system deals with a specific information-processing problem.

For example, if one could prove that connectionist networks are in principle as powerful as Universal Turing Machines, then this would indicate that such networks are indeed worthy of serious consideration by cognitive scientists. However, if one could prove that connectionist networks are in principle less powerful than Universal Turing Machines, this would be good reason to abandon connectionist cognitive science.

How Powerful are Connectionist Networks?

Even a cursory look at connectionist theory indicates that it is very similar to classical associationism (e.g., Bechtel, 1985; Bechtel & Abrahamsen, 1991, pp. 101–3). However, this resemblance is also disconcerting. It can be strongly argued that associationist models are formally equivalent to finite state automata, and as a result are not powerful enough in principle to instantiate human cognition. Indeed, we have already seen one example of this when we considered Bever, Fodor, and Garrett's (1968) critique of associationism in chapter 2. Bever, Fodor, and Garrett were able to prove that because associationist models are formally equivalent to finite state automata, they are not of interest to cognitive science. This is because these models are not powerful enough, for instance, to deal with the embedded clausal structures of human languages. For this reason, classical researchers are interested in more powerful information-processing devices, and attempt to design models that are equivalent to Universal Turing Machines (UTMs). If connectionist systems were equivalent to classical associationist models, then they would only be as powerful as finite state automata. This limit on their computational power would make them extremely unattractive to cognitive science (see also Fodor & Pylyshyn, 1988; Lachter & Bever, 1988).

In order to deal with this kind of critique, connectionist researchers must be able to prove that their information-processing systems are just as powerful as those used by classical cognitive scientists. In particular, they must be able to show that their networks are capable of dealing with the same set of information-processing problems that can (in principle) be solved by a UTM. In the sections that follow, I am going to give you a sense of three different computational approaches that connectionists have used to make the claim that their networks are powerful enough to be taken very seriously by cognitive science.

Connectionist Networks as Pattern Classifiers

Connectionist networks are commonly used to classify patterns (for reviews, see Carpenter, 1989; Lippmann, 1987, 1989). Essentially, the set of input activities for a particular stimulus define the location of a point in a multidimensional *pattern space*. The network "carves" this pattern space into different *decision regions*, which (potentially) can have different and complex shapes. The network classifies the input pattern by generating the "name" (i.e., a unique pattern of output unit activity) of the decision region in which the stimulus pattern point is located.

Figure 4.7 illustrates this way of thinking about what connectionist networks do. Imagine that we have a network that has only two input units, and that these input units can only be "ON" or "OFF." This means that we could present only 4 different patterns to this network. If we used the number 1 to represent "ON," and the number 0 to represent "OFF," then these patterns would be (0,0), (0,1), (1,0), and (1,1). Figure 4.7a shows how we could draw a pattern space for this network by treating these numbers as coordinates of points on a two-dimensional graph. Now, classifying these patterns requires that this pattern space be carved up into decision regions that will be associated with different names. For instance, if we wanted a network to perform the logical operation AND on these inputs, we are really asking it to generate the name "1" to the pattern (1,1), and the name "0" to the patterns (0,0), (1,0), and (0,1). To do this, the network would have to carve the pattern space into different regions as illustrated in figure 4.7b. If we wanted the network to perform the logical operation XOR on these inputs, it would have to carve up the pattern space in a different way to assign a different set of names ("1" to the patterns (1,0) and (0,1), and "0" to the patterns (0,0) and (1,1)), as illustrated in figure 4.7c.

When we perform a computational-level analysis of a connectionist pattern classifier, we ultimately are interested in finding out about the kinds of decision regions that it can "carve," because this will define the complexity of the classifications that it can perform.

For example, let us ask the question "What kinds of pattern classifications can in principle be performed by a perceptron?" A perceptron (e.g., Rosenblatt, 1962) is a simple network that can have several input units, a single output unit, and no hidden units. The activation function for a perceptron's output unit is the threshold function: if the net input to the output processor exceeds a threshold, the unit generates a "1", otherwise it generates a "0". Now, because this system has no hidden units, and because it uses this simple kind of activation function, it can only "carve" a single cut through the pattern space. (Technically speaking, it can only carve a single hyperplane through a multi-dimensional pattern space.) This means that this kind of system can only solve problems that are described as being linearly separable. A linearly separable problem is one that can be solved by using a single cut to separate a pattern space into two different decision regions. The AND logical relation is linearly separable, because we can see from figure 4.7b that a single cut is all that is required to separate the "ON" patterns from the "OFF" patterns. However, the XOR logical relation is not linearly separable. From figure 4.7c, we can see that two cuts are required to separate the "ON" patterns from the "OFF" patterns. In other words, a perceptron cannot solve a problem like XOR, because it is not linearly separable.

Historically speaking, proving that perceptrons are limited to solving linearly separable problems was a severe blow to old connectionism. Minsky and Papert (1969/1988) used formal methods to show that many problems of interest to

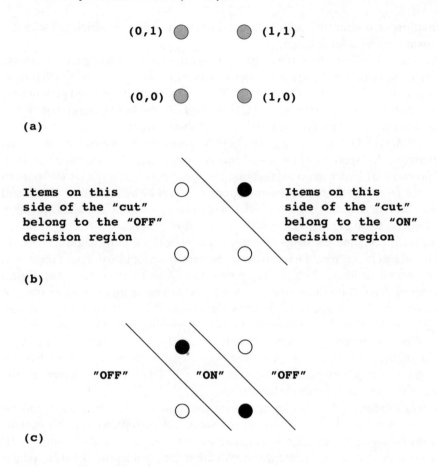

Figure 4.7 Pattern classification as the carving of a pattern space. (a) A pattern space is created by representing each pattern as a point in a multidimensional space. In this example, the four possible inputs to a network with two input units are represented as four points in a space. The coordinates of each point represent the value that each of the input units would be activated with when the pattern was presented. (b) To solve the logical function AND for these four points, a network would have to make a single cut through this pattern space (solid line) that separated the ON object (pattern (1,1)) from the other three objects, to which the network would turn off. This cut divides the pattern space into two decision regions. (c) To solve the more complex XOR problem, a network would have to make two parallel cuts in the decision region to separate the two "ON" objects from the two "OFF" objects. As two cuts are required, this problem is not linearly separable.

psychologists were *linearly nonseparable*, and as a result were beyond the ken of perceptrons. These old-style connectionist networks were simply not powerful enough to sustain the interest of cognitive science!

As we know from chapter 3, though, in the mid-1980s researchers discovered methods that could be used to train connectionist networks that were more powerful than perceptrons, because these new networks could have one or more layers of hidden units. These networks are more powerful because each hidden unit can be thought of as making a different cut through the pattern space. So, a network with hidden units at its disposal is capable of carving up a pattern space in a much more complicated fashion than is possible for a perceptron, enabling linearly nonseparable problems to be solved. For example, a multi-layer perceptron with two hidden units can solve the XOR problem of figure 4.7c, because each hidden unit could make one of the two cuts required to separate the "ON" patterns from the "OFF" patterns

Now, let us consider the most powerful classification device that is possible. This device would be capable of making any pattern classification that was of interest to us. This kind of power would mean that this system could partition a pattern space into arbitrary decision regions – any carving that we required would be a carving that this *arbitrary pattern classifier* could manage.

Could we use hidden units to give a connectionist network the power, in principle, to be an arbitrary pattern classifier? It turns out that there is an affirmative answer to this question. Lippmann (1987, p. 16), by considering the shape of decision regions created by each additional layer of hidden units in systems that use "squashing" activation functions, has shown that a network with only two layers of hidden units (i.e., a three-layer perceptron) is capable of "carving" a pattern space into arbitrary decision regions. "No more than three layers are required in perceptron-like feed-forward nets." In other words, modern connectionist networks have far superior computational power than older systems like perceptrons. Modern connectionist networks with no more than two layers of hidden units have the power to carve a pattern space into arbitrarily shaped decision regions, and thus perform any pattern classification task that we are interested in.

Connectionist Networks as Function Approximators

Historically, PDP networks have been most frequently described as pattern classifiers. Recently, however, with the advent of so-called radial basis function (RBF) networks (e.g., Girosi & Poggio, 1990; Hartman, Keeler, & Kowalski, 1989; Moody & Darken, 1989; Poggio & Girosi, 1989, 1990; Renals, 1989), connectionist systems are now often described as *function approximators*. Imagine, for example, a mathematical "surface" defined in N-dimensional space. At each location in this space this surface has a definite height. A function approximating network with N input units and one output unit would take as input the coordinates of a location in this space, and would output the height of the surface at this location.

An example of a function approximation problem faced by a connectionist network is illustrated by the crablike robot described by Churchland (1992), and studied further by Medler and Dawson (1994). Figure 4.8 illustrates the robot. The goal is to have it reach successfully toward an object placed in front of it. A connectionist network can be trained to become the control system that lets the robot achieve this goal. The inputs to the network are the two angles L and R, which represent the amount of rotation required for each robot eye to

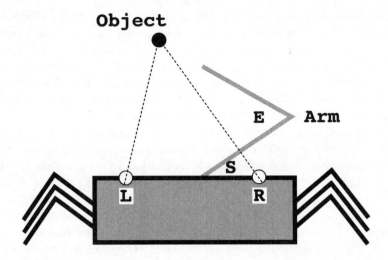

Figure 4.8 Churchland's (1992) crab-like robot. The robot rotates its left eye L radians and it rotates its right eye R radians in order for its eyes to fixate on an object in front of it. To reach out and grab the object with its arm, it must compute appropriate values for its shoulder angle S and its elbow angle E. This is a function approximation task that can be solved by a PDP network (e.g., Medler & Dawson, 1994).

fixate on the object. The network has two output units, which generate two continuous values S and E. These two numbers are angles which represent the amount of "bending" required at the shoulder and elbow joints respectively for the end of the arm to contact the object. In this problem, the network is not being asked to carve a pattern space into discrete decision regions. Instead, it is being asked to compute two continuous functions. The first, $S = h(L,R)$, determines the angle of the shoulder joint from the angles of the two eyes. The second, $E = f(L,R)$, determines the angle of the elbow joint from the angles of the two eyes. In other words, this network is not trained to be a pattern classifier, but is instead being trained to approximate two different continuous mathematical functions.

At the computational level of analysis, we are interested in determining how powerful a function approximator a connectionist network can be. What this boils down to is determining whether there are any limits to the kinds of functions that a PDP network can learn to approximate. Rumelhart, Hinton, and Williams (1986, p. 319) have claimed that "if we have the right connections from the input units to a large enough set of hidden units, we can always find a representation that will perform any mapping from input to output." In other words, they claimed that connectionist networks could approximate any function. What kind of computational results exist to support this bold claim?

Researchers have in fact proven that connectionist networks are *universal function approximators*. That is, if there are no restrictions on the number of hidden units in the network and if there are no restrictions on the size of the connection weights, then in principle a network can be created to approximate – over a finite interval – any continuous mathematical function to an *arbitrary* degree of precision.

The details of such a proof are beyond the scope of this book. However, we can get a general sense of how a network is treated in such a proof. In the 1950s, mathematician Andrei Komolgrov was competing against his colleague V. I. Arnol'd as they published articles concerning one of the problems from the Hilbert program (for more details, see Hecht-Nielsen, 1987, ch. 5). In 1957, Komolgrov won this competition hands down with a major result, the discovery of his "Mapping Neural Network Existence Theorem." From the mathematics of Fourier compositions, it is known that we can take any continuous function and describe it as the weighted sum of a number of different sine functions. Komolgrov's theorem treated neural networks as though they were composing functions in this way. Each hidden unit was viewed as computing a particular simple function (in this case, a logistic function instead of a sine function). The output unit was viewed as the mechanism that weighted all of these simple functions and then added them together to produce a more complicated function as the result. Komolgrov's theorem proved that this kind of system could *exactly* implement *any* continuous function. Furthermore, the theorem indicated the size of network that would be required to do this – a network with N input units would need no more than $(2N + 1)$ hidden units.

More modern research has extended Komolgrov's theorem to a variety of different networks. For instance, it has been proven that one can build a universal function approximator from networks with a single layer of hidden units whose activation function is a sigmoid-shaped "squashing" function (e.g., Cotter, 1990; Cybenko, 1989; Funahashi, 1989), from networks with hidden units that use multiple layers of such hidden units (e.g., Hornik, Stinchcombe, & White, 1989), and from RBF networks (e.g., Hartman, Keeler, & Kowalski, 1989).

Connectionist Networks as Turing Machines

The previous two sections have shown that connectionist researchers have established two very strong claims about the computational power of connectionist information processors. A PDP network is capable of being an arbitrary pattern classifier, and is also capable of being a universal function approximator. With such power, is there anything that a network cannot compute? In other words, these kinds of results give the strong suggestion that connectionist networks may be as powerful as a Universal Turing Machine (UTM). If this could be proven beyond a shadow of a doubt, then this would equate the power of connectionist networks to the power of the physical symbol systems touted by classical cognitive scientists. This would be a major result, because it would show that we could not dismiss connectionism from cognitive science by claiming that these networks are just not powerful enough (a move proposed by, for example, Fodor and Pylyshyn, 1988).

It turns out that the Turing equivalence of connectionist networks has been established for a long period of time. In some of the earliest work on neural networks, McCulloch and Pitts (1943/1988) examined finite networks whose components could perform simple logical operations like AND, OR, and NOT. They were able to prove that such systems could compute any function that required a finite number of these operations. From this perspective, the network was only a finite state automaton (see also Hopcroft & Ullman, 1979, p. 47; Minsky, 1972, ch. 3). However, McCulloch and Pitts went on to show that a UTM could be constructed from such a network, by providing the network the means to move along, sense, and rewrite an external "tape" or memory. "To psychology, however defined, specification of the net would contribute all that could be achieved in that field" (McCulloch & Pitts, 1943/1988, p. 25).

More modern results have validated and extended the pioneering research of McCulloch and Pitts (1943/1948). One common kind of recurrent connectionist network has been popularized by Elman (e.g., 1990). In this network, there is a bank of "context units" that are used to remember the current activations of the output units. As a result, network output at time $(t + 1)$ is a function of input at time $(t + 1)$ and the network's previous output at time t. Williams and Zipser (1989) used this kind of network to construct the machine head of a UTM. This network learned to use five different output neurons to perform the basic operations of a Turing machine (e.g., move left, no change, write "1", write "0", and move right) on a tape that was used to activate a single-input processor. Several formal analyses of this kind of network have also been performed. One theme of this work has been to determine whether or not in principle one could build a finite network to perform the computations of a UTM. Early work of Siegelman and Sontag (1991) developed a proof that such a network was possible in principle, but this proof limited the absolute size of the network to a relatively large value (a maximum of 10^5 processing units). In a follow-up paper (Siegelman & Sontag, 1992) refined this result, and proved that Minsky's (1967) well-known 4-symbol, 7-machine state UTM could be built from a recurrent network that used 1058 processing units. Kilian and Siegelman (1993) have developed a general proof that recurrent networks of the type used by Elman (e.g., 1990) are indeed equivalent to Turing machines. They have concluded that "Turing universality is a relatively common property of recurrent neural network modes" (p. 137).

Implications for the Cognitive Science Debate

The sections above have illustrated another role of computational analyses: investigating the "computational power" or "competence" of a class of information-processing systems. In other words, a computational analysis can be used to address the following issue: "In principle, what kinds of questions can we expect a particular type of information-processing system to be capable of answering?" We reviewed a number of results of this type of analysis of connectionist networks. This research has shown that in principle, such networks are extremely powerful – they are arbitrary pattern classifiers, universal function approximators, and functionally equivalent to Universal Turing Machines.

In chapter 1, I introduced you to the "cognitive science debate," in which classical cognitive science was under attack by a new connectionist school of thought. I indicated that one theme of this book was to show that these two approaches to cognitive science actually had much more in common than one might expect after a survey of the literature. However, by the end of chapter 3 it was also clear that an appropriate comparison of these two approaches must be done in the context of the tri-level hypothesis.

The results that were briefly reviewed above have offered our first point of comparison of classical and connectionist cognitive science in the context of the tri-level hypothesis. Specifically, in the previous sections we have been asking whether there are any significant differences between physical symbol systems and PDP networks at the computational level – are both types of information processors capable of answering the same kinds of questions? *At this point, we can conclude that there are no differences between classical and connectionist cognitive science at the computational level.* This is because both physical symbol systems and PDP networks are Turing-machine equivalent. This indicates that if there are interesting or substantial differences between these two approaches, they must emerge when we consider them at other levels of analysis.

Part IV   Computations and Semantics

The previous parts of this chapter have considered the methodological implications of computational analyses. In particular, we have been considering how certain research issues can be described at the computational level, and how formal methods can be used to address these issues. In the remainder of the chapter, I would like to change this emphasis somewhat, and examine some more general aspects of the computational level of analysis. In this part of the chapter, I want to briefly discuss potential relationships between the computational level as it has been described so far and what others might call the semantic or cognitive level of analysis. In the following part of the chapter, I want to illustrate why the computational level of analysis is not sufficient by itself to provide a complete cognitive science.

Computations and Semantics

Marr's (1982) notion of a computational theory is extremely abstract. Relating it to chapter 2's description of the Turing machine, it can be seen that all that a computational theory does is provide an interpretation of a system's behavior. For example, computational accounts of the Turing machines described in figures 2.2 and 2.6 would only specify (in some rigorous notation) that both of these machines compute the sum of pairs of integers. In other words, the computational theory would neither specify anything about the specific procedures being used to accomplish this task, nor describe any physical properties of the computing systems. Computational theories are purely semantic, in the sense that they account for what system states mean, but do not account for how these states come to be.

Indeed, this chapter has introduced the computational level in a less than typical fashion. It is much more common for cognitive scientists to present the most abstract level of their paradigm as the *semantic level* – the level at which the contents of representations are interpreted, and at which these contents play a causal role in the account of a system's behavior (e.g., Pylyshyn, 1984). This kind of description forms the basis of what is often called *folk psychology*. Every day we use folk psychology when we attempt to explain the behavior of others by appealing to the contents of their mental states.

For instance, moments ago I went downstairs to make myself some more coffee. How might a folk psychologist explain such behavior? They might tell the following story: "Well, Mike <u>realized</u> that he was not as alert as he <u>wanted</u> to be. Mike <u>believes</u> that drinking coffee makes him more alert, and he <u>recalled</u> that a new bag of coffee beans was in the kitchen. As a result, he <u>wanted</u> a fresh cup of coffee. He went down to the kitchen, where he brewed some coffee because he <u>remembered</u> how to make it." Cognitive scientists call each of the underlined words in this story an intentional term, because they refer to the content of a mental state: a belief, a desire, or a goal. Note that this story provides a perfectly plausible explanation of my behavior by appealing only to intentional terms; it does not require accounts of the specific procedures that I used (this explanation would still be valid whether I used a Bodum plunger pot or an old-fashioned percolator), nor does it require any physical account of what went on (such as a physiological account of why I was less alert). The success of folk psychology in everyday life has often been taken by cognitive psychologists as strong evidence that a semantic or cognitive vocabulary captures important psychological generalizations.

What is the relationship between the computational level, as I have been developing it in this chapter, and a semantic-level account that might be viewed as a rigorous folk psychology? My belief is that the two levels are one and the same. One reason for this is that ultimately the computational level amounts to providing an interpretation of a system's behavior; this interpretation is required if we are answering the question "What information-processing problem is being solved by the system?" The notion of "interpretation" strikes me as being identical to "semantic" in this context.

A second reason for this belief is that both computational analyses and semantic content appear to involve appeals to principles that are rooted in the world in which the information-processing system exists, and not principles that are confined to the system itself. It is quite common to construe semantic content as some sort of relationship between a representational state of an organism and some state of affairs "out there" in the world (e.g., Cummins, 1989). Importantly, many of the constraining principles that are discovered by computational analyses are also true of affairs "out there," and are assumed to be exploited by the system. This is elaborated in more detail in the case study of motion correspondence in chapter 9. For the time being, though, when we constrain the operations of mechanisms that solve problems related to visual motion by having them exploit the principle that objects in the world are rigid (e.g., Ullman, 1979), it is important to realize that this principle is a description of the world, not of the information processor. The natural constraints explored by those who have adopted Marr's (e.g., 1982) approach to vision can be plausibly viewed as semantic properties. The fact that they play a fundamental role in the computational analysis of visual processing simply adds weight to the notion that the computational level and the semantic level are highly similar.

A third reason for this belief is that the kinds of themes that arise frequently in computational analyses also emerge in accounts of semantics. In fact, these themes might be emerging because the answers to semantic questions might require computational analyses! For example, one view of semantics is that it is subject to specific constraints regarding the transition from one content to another; the *principle of rationality* is a constraint that specifies that there must be meaningful relationships between one's desires and one's actions (e.g., Pylyshyn, 1984). A computational account of semantics would involve elaboration of this kind of constraint, as well as the identification of other constraints on semantic content. Similarly, Jackendoff (1987) argues that an account of consciousness within cognitive science depends upon a qualitative analysis of experience. The purpose of such an analysis is to provide constraints upon a theory of representation. Specifically, the theory must be expressively adequate: the representational structures must be capable of making explicit exactly those distinctions that we can experience. Furthermore, evaluating the expressive adequacy of the representational structures is a job for computational theory: "The basic issue is to determine what categories, distinctions, and relations must be represented in mental information structures in order to account for human behavior and experience. ... A structural theory in the sense intended here is what Chomsky calls a 'theory of competence' and Marr calls a 'computational theory' " (Jackendoff, 1987, p. 38).

Now, I'm not in any position to offer a theory of semantics, nor to propose solutions to problems that have faced philosophers of mind for centuries (for more details see Cummins, 1989). However, if the computational level and the semantic level are one and the same, then this points researchers in a particular direction towards coming up with an account of representational content. This direction involves translating general statements about semantic content into more formal statements about information-processing problems that must be solved in order for one to claim that a particular symbol is associated with a particular meaning. One example of this approach in action is the work of Jackendoff (e.g., 1983, 1987), which is an attempt to show how the structure of a representational system might be constrained in a fashion that reflects the structure of the world, as well as the regularities that govern the "interface" between the world and semantic content – the visual system.

Computations and Consciousness

As soon as one proposes a semantic level on the basis of the predictive power of folk psychology (e.g., Pylyshyn, 1984), talk of consciousness cannot be far behind. This is because there is an important reflexive component to folk psychology – we believe that we act in particular ways because we ourselves are aware of the contents of our own representational states. As well, in a very generic sense, consciousness could be viewed as a special case of semantics. For example, if semantic content is a relationship between a representation and some state of affairs "out there," conscious content might be viewed as the same kind of relationship, but in this case one between a representation and *another* representation that has semantic content defined in the general way.

There is considerable debate today about whether consciousness can be studied scientifically (e.g., Horgan, 1994), and even about whether it has any role in cognitive science (e.g., Flanagan, 1992, ch. 2; Jackendoff, 1987, ch. 2). In recent years, attempts to explain the roots of consciousness have been highly visible (e.g., Chalmers, 1996; Crick, 1994; Dennett, 1991, 1995, 1996; Edelman, 1992; Gazzaniga, 1992; Penrose, 1989; Searle, 1992).

Although many of these recent books take very different approaches to explaining consciousness, one theme common to many of them is an attempt to portray consciousness as a natural phenomenon that can be studied scientifically. For instance, many authors describe consciousness as an emergent property of complicated biological properties, while some describe consciousness as the result of complex properties of subatomic particles. One consequence of this is the notion that further understanding of consciousness will only arise from a deeper understanding of biology or physics.

As will become clearer in later chapters, my perspective – which is typical of most modern cognitive science – is that it makes perfect sense to view consciousness as dependent, in some fashion, upon biological or physical processes. Most cognitive scientists are materialists. However, materialism doesn't commit one to reductionism, and because of this I'm not very sympathetic to the message that accounts of consciousness should await future revelations from biology or physics. The computational level is one at which important regularities and principles are discovered without requiring dependence upon less abstract accounts. If consciousness is deeply connected to semantics, and if semantics is conducive to computational-level analysis, then we should be concerned with examining consciousness as a computational problem. Is it possible to translate vague questions about the nature of consciousness into more specific computational statements? Might computational analyses shed some light on abstract (semantic?) principles that are necessary for consciousness to be present? Again, I'm personally not in any position to answer these questions – but I would be surprised if computational methods do not eventually turn out to be crucial to helping us understand the essential nature of consciousness.

Part V   Limitations of Computational Analyses

Not all empirically minded psychologists have expressed satisfaction with the formal offerings that computational analyses provide. For instance, Paivio (1986, p. 6) voices a typical concern: "a full-blown, top-down, wait-and-see strategy [in cognitive science] is risky, however, for it could lead to the most costly dead end of all, where the whole structure built from the top-down collapses for want of empirical support." In point of fact, there is a lot of merit in this kind of criticism. While computational analyses can yield information that other methodologies are not able to provide, it is also the case that computational analyses by themselves are not sufficient for a complete cognitive science. At some point, cognitive scientists will have to get their hands dirty, and provide empirical support for their formal analyses (see also Dawson, 1990b). One reason for this is sketched below.

The Computational Level and Weak Equivalence

When my daughter Michele was seven years old, she would watch me play chess against my computerized chess board, and she became interested in learning how to play the game. At her urging, I taught her the legal moves for each of the six different chess pieces. However, she found that she wasn't very interested in learning much more than this; she could move each piece legally, but she had no idea about chess strategy or tactics. So, if we were to play one another, we could both be described as chess players, because we both would be following the rules of the game. However, there would be a large discrepancy in our abilities, because while I would be attempting to choose the best legal move to apply, she would essentially be choosing legal moves randomly.

Now, how would the chess-playing abilities of my daughter and myself be described at the computational level of analysis? At this level one can only make claims about the information-processing problem being solved. To describe the information-processing problem that is being solved, one need only find an interpretation of the relationship between an information processor's inputs and outputs. For example, to say that a Turing machine is performing "addition," one need only show that the symbols on the starting tape represent two numbers, and that the symbols on the ending tape represent the sum of these two numbers, and that this relationship holds for any tape that can be given to this machine. From this perspective, a computational-level description of my daughter and myself would be identical – we would both be described as "chess-playing systems." The difference in our abilities would not be evident in this computational-level description.

The reason for this is that while a computational description defines the relationship between input and output, it does not define the specific steps or processes or mechanisms that an information processor uses to convert inputs to outputs. To relate this to Marr's (1982) view of cognitive science, a computational description tells us *what* is being computed, but it does not tell us *how* it is being computed. So, at the computational level chess players of widely different abilities would all be lumped together in a single category, because they are all following the rules for the same game. Let us introduce some terminology at this point. Imagine that we have two different systems that are solving the same information-processing problem, but are using different methods to solve this problem. Following Fodor (1968) and Pylyshyn (e.g., 1980, 1984) let us call these systems *weakly equivalent*.

Weak Equivalence and the Turing Test

How does the notion of weak equivalence impact cognitive science? To answer this question, let us consider one approach to evaluating computer simulations of cognitive abilities. In a famous paper, Turing (1950) proposed an empirical method for testing machine intelligence. This method, which has become known as the Turing test, is a version of an imitation game. For a definite period of time, a judge interacts (through a computer terminal) with two systems, one of which is human, the other of which is a computer program. In the most general case, the interaction takes the form of two separate conversations in which the judge engages with the two systems. At the end of the conversation, the judge must decide which system was the computer, and which system was the person. If this cannot be done reliably, then the computer program is deemed to be intelligent. Let us say that if this test is passed, then the computer simulation is *Turing equivalent* to the modeled organism.

Modern chess-playing programs can easily demonstrate Turing equivalence to highly skilled human chess players. For instance, the world's best chess-playing computer program, Deep Thought, has a chess rating of 2552, which places it at the grandmaster level (Hsu, Anantharaman, Campbell, & Nowatzyk, 1990). It held its own in a game against Anatoly Karpov (the world's second-ranked player, rated around 2710 in 1986), eventually losing because of a questionable decision on the 51st move of the game. In 1995 Deep Blue, a descendant of Deep Thought which incorporated a number of specialized chess-playing chips running in parallel, became the first computer program to win a game against the reigning world champion (Gary Kasparov) under tournament conditions.

Some researchers would argue that Turing equivalence is a satisfactory goal for cognitive science (e.g., Searle, 1990, p. 26). "The case for regarding the successful passing of a Turing test as a valid indication of the presence of thought, intelligence, understanding, or consciousness is actually quite a strong one. For how else do we normally form our judgments that people other than ourselves possess just such qualities, except by conversation?" (Penrose, 1989,

p. 11). But is Turing equivalence sufficiently powerful to be the ultimate goal of cognitive science? For instance, is the demonstration of the Turing equivalence of Deep Thought and Deep Blue a triumph for those interested in the cognitive science of chess? Unfortunately, while these programs are extremely adept at choosing the best legal chess move to apply in a game, they do not use the same processes to do so as would a human chess player. Deep Blue plays nearly as well as Kasparov, but this does not mean that it plays in the *same way* as Kasparov!

For instance, several experiments with expert human chess players have shown that they chunk the board into a relatively small number of meaningful units, and that the fashion in which they chunk the board leads them to consider a relatively small number of potential moves, each of which is of high quality (e.g., Bratko, Tancig, & Tancig, 1986; Chase & Simon, 1973). In contrast, most chess-playing programs consider an extremely large number of possible moves in a search for the best one. For instance, Deep Thought currently can consider 750,000 different positions per second (Hsu *et al.*, 1990). Deep Blue can consider approximately a billion moves per second! From this, it is quite clear that while both Deep Blue and Kasparov are extremely good chess players, the internal methods that they use to decide each move are markedly different. They may be Turing equivalent, but they do not play chess in the same way. Thus, there is no reason to believe that Deep Thought or its descendants are models of how humans play chess.

In short, Turing equivalence is not a sufficiently powerful goal for cognitive science, because such equivalence tells us that two systems (e.g., a computer simulation and a human) are solving the same problem, but does not tell us that they are solving the problem in the same way. In many cases, we are not only interested in finding out what information-processing problem is being solved, but we are also interested in finding out how it is being solved. Turing equivalence will help us achieve the former goal, but not the latter.

To relate all of this back to the computational level, Turing equivalence and weak equivalence are exactly the same thing. As a result, the limitations of computational analyses become evident – they do not tell us anything about *how* particular information-processing problems are being solved. Cognitive science requires that a stronger type of equivalence be established between a model and the system being modeled. The search for this stronger type of equivalence requires us to consider cognitive phenomena at levels other than the computational.

Towards Strong Equivalence

As we saw earlier, weak equivalence or Turing equivalence exists when two systems are solving the same information-processing problem, but are using different methods to do so. If one could defend the claim that two systems were both solving the same information-processing problem using identical procedures, then one could claim that the two systems were *strongly equivalent*.

Strongly equivalent systems choose the same rules to apply for the same reasons. "We can then say that a machine is strongly equivalent to an organism in some respect when it is weakly equivalent in that same respect and the processes upon which the behavior of the machine is contingent are of the same type as the processes upon which the behavior of the organism are contingent" (Fodor, 1968, p. 138). From this, it would appear that one approach for a cognitive scientist intent on explaining System A would be to create System B (a working simulation/theory) and then go on to show that System B was strongly equivalent to System A.

In my view, cognitive scientists should be exactly in the business of establishing the strong equivalence of their theories. However, in regards to the current chapter, note that this is not possible within a purely computational framework. In order to establish strong equivalence, researchers have to make forceful claims about the specific processes that underlie behavior. Yet we have seen that computational theory explicitly ignores such distinctions. A computational theory can be used to determine whether a theory has weak equivalence or Turing equivalence to an organism of interest, but it cannot be used to make stronger claims. Stronger claims must be made (and defended) by moving to a different level of analysis, which is the subject of the next chapter.

Chapter Summary

Cognitive science can be thought of as a discipline in which researchers are seeking a single category of entities. One member of this category is some system or organism that the cognitive scientist is interested in explaining. The other members of this category are theories (typically working computer simulations) that are equivalent in some way to the system of interest. The goal of the cognitive scientist is to restrict the size of this category as much as possible, in order that the theories that fall into the class count as explanations of the system of interest because they are strongly equivalent to it.

The computational level of description provides an important first step in restricting membership to this category. By translating a phenomenon of interest into a system that solves a particular information-processing problem, we can use the formal power of logic and mathematics to provide insights into the phenomenon. For instance, we can use these methods to examine the weak or formal equivalence of these proposals to the original phenomenon. We can also explore the kinds of questions in general that a particular type of information-processing system can solve. For example, we have seen that such investigations have shown that classical and connectionist systems are equally powerful when described at the computational level.

By themselves, though, computational constraints are not sufficient to restrict category membership so that it only contains explanations of the phenomenon. This is because computational accounts describe what is being computed, but not how it is being computed. As a result, important differences between information-processing systems are ignored at the computational level. By moving to finer levels of analysis (i.e., the algorithmic level and the implementational level), we can provide additional constraints on category membership in our search for explanations of cognitive processes (see also Newell, 1980; 1990, p. 17). The next chapter illustrates this, by considering how the algorithmic level of analysis guides research carried out by both classical and connectionist researchers.

5

The Algorithmic Level

The purpose of this chapter is to introduce the algorithmic level, and to describe how assuming the existence of this level affects the methodology of cognitive science. This will be accomplished as follows: First, I will introduce the notion of functionalism, and describe the role that it plays within cognitive science. Second, I will describe how cognitive scientists use empirical tests to move from a computational description of a system to a functional description, which is frequently realized as a computer simulation. Third, I will describe how connectionists create algorithmic accounts by analyzing the structure of their trained networks. Finally, I will consider how cognitive scientists attempt to validate their algorithmic descriptions by using a supplemented version of the Turing test. Underlying this discussion is my goal of providing some sense of how cognitive scientists view the algorithmic level, and to describe the kind of evidence that they collect at this level in their search for strongly equivalent models of cognition.

Part I   Methodological Functionalism

Why Classical Cognitive Science isn't Reverse Engineering

Imagine a situation in which you were presented some physical device (perhaps a brain), told that it is an information processor, and required to come up with the best explanation of how it works. Pretend that you could perform whatever tests you felt were required to help solve this problem. You might decide to tackle this challenge directly at the physical level. With the right set of physical measurements, perhaps you could obtain a rich enough physical description to explain how the device works. We will call this approach *reverse engineering*.

Classical cognitive scientists are extremely skeptical about the success of reverse engineering. One of the main reasons for this is because a precise, physical explanation of one information-processing system usually cannot be generalized to apply to other information processors. For example, imagine that you were presented with the beautiful brass gear assembly that comprises Babbage's "analytic engine" (Swade, 1993). One would presume that your successful account of this machine, via reverse engineering, would be essentially mechanical – accounts of gear ratios, interactions among moving parts, and so on. Clearly this account would *not* apply to other information-processing systems (e.g., electronic computers, brains) because they are governed by very different physical principles (e.g., electronics, neurophysiology) than the mechanical ones that govern Babbage's machine.

In other words, the class "information processor" is quite unlike the class "diamond" (for example), because information processors are not characterized by a set of unique, physical properties. With Rube Goldberg-like inspiration, one can build an information processor out of anything (e.g., Gardner, 1982). For instance, Stewart (1994) had described the work of Chalcraft and Greene, who were able to show how one could build a Turing machine out of a toy train set! As a result, a physical description of one information processor will not necessarily apply to another.

However, it could be argued that if cognitive scientists are ultimately interested in explaining human cognition, then we should restrict ourselves to biological information processors? Let us imagine that the physical device that you were presented was a brain, and that you were able to successfully reverse engineer it. Surely physical description that you produced would generalize nicely to other information processors of interest to cognitive scientists – that is, to other brains.

Importantly, this does *not* appear to be the case. First, consider the hydrocephalics studied by Lorber (1968). Because of unnaturally high pressure of cerebral spinal fluid in the ventricles of their brains at birth, these patients had severe tissue loss in their cerebral cortex. The cerebral mantle of Lorber's patients was 10 millimeters or less, where several centimeters would be a normal thickness. In spite of this striking absence of brain tissue, IQ tests revealed that 29 of 46 patients alive in 1968 had normal to good intelligence, while 5 were highly gifted. McGuigan (1994, p. 546) describes a later follow-up of one of these patients, who was a university student who had won honors in mathematics and had an IQ of 126. Clearly, these patients represent a sample of subjects who can pass any version of the Turing test, and are doing so with brains dramatically different and smaller than "normal." Physical accounts of the workings of normal brains clearly would not be applicable to Lorber's patients.

Lorber's (1968) hydrocephalics are not the only examples that radically different biological architectures can support human intelligence. While it would be generally expected that major brain lesions would lead to observable disruptions of observable behavior, this is not always the case. Sperry (1958) presented a number of examples in which multiple knife cuts or the insertion of multiple wires or mica plates into animal brains did not produce major functional disruptions. As well, the abnormal behavior of the famous split-brain patients studied by Sperry and Gazzaniga (e.g., Gazzaniga, 1978; Gazzaniga, Bogen, & Sperry, 1962) was not evident until extremely contrived laboratory conditions were used.

Perhaps these extreme cases are merely the exceptions that prove the rule. It could be that if a *normal* brain were reverse engineered, then the account of this brain would generalize well to other *normal* brains. Unfortunately, this again does not appear to be so. The brain of a human adult is an exceptionally complex organ, consisting of approximately 180 billion cells, about 50 billion of which are directly responsible for information processing (Kolb & Whishaw, 1990). Each of these information-processing cells has up to 15,000 connections to other cells. In general, patterns of connectivity are highly specialized, and to a large extent account for brain function (see Nicholls, Martin, & Wallace, 1992; for evidence that connectivity by itself is not enough to explain how the brain works, see Getting, 1989). So, brain function depends on the roughly 7×10^{14} connections among the 50 billion information-processing neurons.

Interestingly, while the complexity of the brain is reflected by the fact that more genes are devoted to nervous system proteins than are devoted to any other organ, the mammalian genome is only estimated to have in the order of 105 genes (Shepherd, 1988). This implies that even if all of the human genome was devoted to specifying brain structure, the amount of information directly encoded in human DNA is far too small to explicitly specify each neural connection. The immediate consequence of this is that the shear size and complexity of the brain, particularly in relation to the size of the human genome, precludes the possibility of physically identical brains. "Uniquely specific connections cannot exist. If one numbered the branches of a neuron and correspondingly numbered the neurons it touched, the numbers would not correspond in any two individuals of a species – not even in identical twins or in genetically identical animals" (Edelman, 1988, p. 182).

All of the examples that we have seen above can be used by a classical researcher to argue that cognitive science will not reduce to a discipline which depends solely on reverse engineering, because the results of this (physical) technology would not even be applicable to information processors of the same (physical) type. Does this mean that all cognitive scientists are against reverse engineering? Definitely not! In a later part of this chapter, we will see that an algorithmic-level account of connectionist cognitive science might go something like this: first, a network is trained to perform some task of interest, and second, the network is reverse engineered to find out how it actually works. However, let's postpone this discussion for a few pages, and instead consider what classical cognitive scientists use as an alternative to reverse engineering.

Functionalism as an Alternative

In chapter 4, I argued that a computational description of an information processor was not, by itself, sufficiently powerful to provide explanations for cognitive science. This was because all one can achieve at the computational level is weak equivalence to a system of interest; computational descriptions cannot be used by themselves to be strongly equivalent models. In the previous section, I have briefly reviewed some classical arguments that a purely physical approach (reverse engineering) will also fail. This leaves us somewhat in a pickle: if a direct physical assault on information processors cannot guarantee us strong equivalence, then what can?

Classical cognitive scientists almost always answer this question by appealing to a descriptive approach called *functionalism*. A functional description of a machine details what its parts do – what their functional role is in the system – and does not describe what these parts are built out of.

The realization that what parts do is quite independent from what they are made of has been extremely important in the applied sciences. In the latter half of the nineteenth century, one of the primary arenas for technological innovation was the telegraph industry. By the early 1870s, two major competitors were dominant in this field: Western Union and the Automatic Telegraph Company. The latter was the smaller firm, but had the advantage of being fronted by the infamous financier Jay Gould. Each company was funding applied research and as a result owned and controlled the patents for the latest developments in telegraphy.

In 1874, Western Union was poised to use patent control to provide a death blow to the Automatic Telegraph Company. Telegraphy consisted, essentially, of sending variable currents over long wires. One problem with this was the decay of the signal over very long distances. This was solved by using relays along the way. A relay was a device that took a weak signal from an incoming wire and used this signal to activate a switch which tapped out Morse code on an outgoing wire, renewing the strength of the signal. Western Union controlled the patent for a relay invented by Page, which used variable current through a magnet to activate the switch, and which was the only known method for enhancing telegraph signals over long distances. In 1874, after a long legal battle, the courts upheld the legality of this control and recognized that the Automatic Telegraph Company was illegally using the Page relay. Given this court decision, it appeared that Gould's telegraph company would be silenced for 17 years.

This desperate hour called for desperate measures. The Automatic Telegraph Company turned to Thomas Edison for salvation. "The loser in the Federal Court came to him in desperation and explained that some way must be found of relaying messages without the use of an electromagnet – an idea considered at the time as comparable to performing Hamlet without the Prince" (Clark, 1977, p. 55). In other words, Edison was being asked to invent something that had exactly the same function, but worked on the basis of completely different physical principles in order for the Page patent to be evaded.

Of course, Edison was up to the challenge. He recalled some of his early experiments in which he found that the friction between a rotating drum of chemically treated paper and a telegraph stylus was markedly reduced when an electrical current flowed from the stylus to the paper, and returned when the current was shut off. The effect was enhanced if moistened chalk was used. As a result, Edison was able to replace the magnet in the Page relay with a rotating drum of chalk, driven by a small electric motor. Josephson (1961, p. 118) relays an eyewitness account of the triumph of Edison's electromotograph: "First he detached the Page sounder from the instrument, an intensely interested crowd watching his every movement. From one of his pockets he took a pair of pliers and fitted [his own motograph relay] precisely where the Page sounder had been previously connected, and tapped the key. The clicking – and it was a joyful sound – could be heard all over the room. There was a general chorus of surprise. 'He's got it! He's got it!'"

The main point of this example is simply this: things that are extremely different physically (in particular, things recognized as being so different that they do not fall under some other inventor's patent!) can have exactly the same function. Thus one approach to describing and explaining a complicated system would be to describe its components in terms of the functions that they perform, and not in terms of their physical nature.

Are Connectionists Functionalists?

While we are developing the notion of functionalism in the context of classical cognitive science, it is instructive to keep connectionism in mind at the same time. For instance, is one of the possible differences between classical and connectionist cognitive science that the former is functionalist, while the latter (because of its neuronal inspiration) is not?

If we view functionalism as describing things in terms of the functions that they perform, and not in terms of their physical nature, then we must include that connectionists are functionalists too. In point of fact, the generic connectionist architecture that was introduced in chapter 3 is essentially a functional description of a neuron. It views neurons as performing three functions (compute an incoming signal, adopt internal activity, send an outgoing signal) and ignores the enormously complicated mechanisms that are responsible for doing all of this (e.g., connectionism ignores the physical and electrical accounts of voltage-gated ion channels, descriptions of which are available in Hille, 1990 for example). Because connectionists appear to be offering functional accounts of a very fine level of analysis (i.e., applying it to neural descriptions), Clark (1989) describes connectionism as a form of microfunctionalism!

Systems of Functions

The Edison example that was presented earlier illustrates functionalism with respect to a single component of a system. However, it is important to realize that when a functional account is applied to an entire, complicated system, it will be described as a set of functional subcomponents which typically are organized in a precise manner. The organization of the subcomponents produces the complicated behavior of the system viewed as a whole.

For example, a computer programming language can be thought of as a library of primitive functions or properties. The BASIC programming language built into the Commodore-64 has about 50 elementary properties that are available to a programmer. For instance, the PRINT property lets you print something to the computer display. The OPEN property lets you communicate with a peripheral device, like a disk drive or a printer. The POKE property lets you set the contents of a memory register. Note that as far as we are concerned, all of these properties are purely functional because we can understand what they do, and use them to build a computer program, without ever knowing (or caring) how they are physically built into the machine.

Now, by themselves the set of properties or functions that define Commodore BASIC (or any other programming language) are pretty uninteresting. However, when you start stringing them together in a particular order, complicated and interesting behavior can the result. For instance, if you start with some commands that read numbers in from a disk file, then have a series of commands that perform arithmetic on these numbers, and then finish with a series of commands that present the results of the arithmetic to the screen, the result might be a program that does statistics, or figures out your taxes, or balances your bank account. In short, complicated functions can be defined as an organized series of simple functions. Recall that this is one of the basic secrets to the power of the Universal Turing Machine.

The idea that complex information processing can be described as emerging from an *organized sequence of functions* or properties is one of the fundamental assumptions underlying classical cognitive science. From this perspective, the process of thinking is essentially equivalent to running a particular program on the "cognitive computer." This means that complicated thought processes are presumed to emerge when simpler (functionally described) thought processes are arranged or executed in a particular order. "Configuration is just as important a property of behavior as it is of perception" (Miller, Galanter, & Pribram, 1960, p. 12).

For example, in one of the pioneering works of cognitivism, *Plans and the Structure of Behavior*, Miller, Galanter, and Pribram (1960) explored the hypothesis that behavior could be explained by describing the "Plan" that controlled it. They helped herald the cognitive revolution by arguing that the instructions that were organized in a Plan were basic feedback loops that involved the processing of information, such as recurrently testing whether some predicate was true or false. As a result, "a Plan is, for an organism, essentially the same as a program for a computer" (p. 16). The elucidation of a plan required understanding the feedback loop components, the hierarchical organization of these components, and how control was passed from one component during another when the Plan was being executed.

The issue facing Miller, Galanter, and Pribram – and any cognitivist that followed in their footsteps – was trying to figure out the Plan or program controlling some behavior of interest. This is a thorny problem, because Plans or programs are theoretical constructs for cognitive scientists, and cannot be directly observed. How does one infer the nature of some internal program on the basis of behavioral observations? Realizing the limitations of reverse engineering, most classical cognitive scientists adopt a different methodology which is introduced in the next section.

Forward Engineering or Functional Analysis

In reverse engineering, by examining the physical properties of a system's components, one attempts to explain how the whole system works. Note, however, that most designers of complicated systems would rarely start with reverse engineering. Instead, they would start with a general notion of the desired behavior of the system that they wanted to construct, and carve this notion up into a set of required subsystems, which they would then attempt to build. In some cases, the design of the subsystems would require that this process be repeated. I will call this procedure *forward engineering*.

Most of us should be familiar with forward engineering, because it is a method that we apply quite naturally to a wide variety of problems. For instance, it is an extremely useful method for writing manuscripts. First, you decide on the general theme of a paper. Second, you decide on its basic structure – the basic points you need to make to convey the desired theme, as well as the order in which they are to be organized – by writing up an outline of the paper. For instance, in writing an experimental paper that has the major goal of presenting the results of new research, you might decide first to review the existing literature, to then highlight an important point that it does not address, to then use this point to motivate your study, to then describe your method and results, and finally describe the implications of your results in the context of the literature. Third, you might take the outline and elaborate it. This elaboration might include listing out the points in each section that you want to make, perhaps including a draft of the first sentence of each paragraph. Finally, your outline will be so detailed that you can quickly finish the manuscript by completing the paragraphs that the outline dictates.

Forward engineering is also used in the design and construction of physical devices. Interestingly, this kind of engineering can proceed functionally for a long time, waiting until the functional description becomes detailed enough that one can actually build a physical component that performs the function. Kidder (1981, pp. 121–2) provides an example of this in his description of the creation of a new computer by Data General Corporation: "West's decision to use the new chips called PALs gave the designers certain advantages. Certainly it helped some of them work swiftly. When Ken Holberger, for instance, came to a tricky part of a design, one that promised to take a long time to create, he could often just draw a box on his diagram and leave that box blank. A single pro-grammable PAL could be made to perform all the functions that the box had to do. 'PAL here,' he would write on his diagram, in effect. Later, he could come back and program the PAL."

When a researcher who holds the belief that "thinking is software" is confronted with the task of explaining some complicated cognitive behavior, it is natural for them to also engage in a form of forward engineering. A classical cognitive scientist will start by getting a good sense of what information-processing problem is being solved. This, of course, should entail a computational analysis of the system, as described in the previous chapter. However, the computational analysis will only tell what the system is doing; it will not tell how this is being accomplished. Forward engineering is used in an attempt to add this information. In the most generic sense, when a cognitive scientist performs forward engineering, he or she decomposes the to-be-explained behavior (i.e., the computationally described system) into a sequence of (functional) subcomponents, some of which may themselves require later decomposition. Cummins (1983) calls this approach *functional analysis*. The success of this approach depends largely on the ability of the researcher to ensure that each proposed subcomponent or subfunction is simpler to explain than the entire system. "Functional analysis consists in analyzing a disposition into a number of less problematic dispositions such that the programmed manifestation of these analyzing dispositions amounts to a manifestation of the analyzed disposition" (p. 28).

When a hardware or software designer is employing forward engineering or functional analysis, they are deciding upon a natural flow of operations that will result in the emergence of some intended behavior. The problem facing a cognitive scientist is slightly different. The "intended" behavior is already being exhibited by the system; the researcher is not interested in designing it. Instead, the researcher wishes to retrace the decisions of the "designer." In short, by watching the behavior of the to-be-explained system, a cognitive scientist tries to re-create the program that is producing its behavior. This is the essential goal of functional analysis.

Now, if cognitive scientists were only concerned with computers, this could turn out to be a trivial task. For instance, after loading a BASIC program into a Commodore-64, I could simply type the LIST command, and the entire program would be printed out on the computer's display. For better or worse (depending upon your perspective), cognitive organisms provide much more of a challenge. This is because cognitive systems are almost always boxes that are as black as the Tycho Monolith in Clarke's (1968) novel *2001: A Space Odyssey*. While a cognitive scientist can observe the external behavior of organisms, he or she has no direct access to their inner workings. There is no LIST command for the human computer!

Because internal cognitive processes cannot be directly observed, the only support for the forward engineering performed by a cognitive scientist are observations of external behaviors. As a result, two difficulties are constantly being faced. First, what methods does one use to carve up complicated behavior into an organized set of functions? In other words, how can observations of behavior be used to support decisions about functional decomposition? Second, after some functional decomposition has been decided upon, how does a researcher attempt to validate it?

The methods adopted by the experimentally-minded branches of cognitive science (in particular, cognitive psychology and psycholinguistics) are attempts to deal with both of these questions, because these components of cognitive science are primarily concerned with determining how particular information processing problems are being solved. The next two parts of this chapter will attempt to provide the general flavor of "how" questions are answered. First, we will use the literature on human memory as an example of how the results from memory experiments can be used to carve "memory" up into an organized set of subsystems. Second, we will use the literature on problem-solving to show how a careful analysis of what subjects say about what they are doing can be used to derive a description of the program that they are using to solve a problem. Importantly, I'm just using these as examples of how experiments can be used to flesh out the algorithmic level by providing the basis for forward engineering. The research reported below is just a sample from the tip of a very large iceberg. For a detailed survey of the experimental methods used to deal with these problems, the reader is referred to any current introductory text on cognitive psychology or psycholinguistics.

Part II   The Classical Analysis of Human Memory

Functional Dissociation and the Modal Memory Model

Many cognitive scientists use empirical methods to motivate or validate a particular functional decomposition. "Decomposing an empirical system into a set of hypothetical related components and then validating this decomposition through experiments is part of the goal of cognitive science" (Bower & Clapper, 1989, p. 255). How can one use experimental observations of behavior to carve a system into an organized set of subfunctions? One very general method is to search for a *functional dissociation*. In one type of a functional dissociation, different (but closely related) aspects of behavior are affected quite differently by the same independent variable. This provides strong evidence that these different aspects of behavior are being mediated by distinct functional components.

A very good example of this type of functional dissociation is provided by some of the early studies of human memory performed by cognitive psychologists. By the late 1950s, cognitive psychologists had used a very simple paradigm to demonstrate that relatively small amounts of information could be forgotten very quickly (Brown, 1958; Peterson & Peterson, 1959). In what became known as the Brown–Peterson paradigm, subjects were presented with a triplet of consonants (e.g., MRW) which was followed by a number. The subject was instructed to repeat the number, and to then count backwards from it in threes until the experimenter asked them to recall the initial triplet. Results from this paradigm typically demonstrated recall accuracy dropping to 30 percent or less after a 12 to 15 second delay before the recall signal was given.

At the time that these results were published, researchers were in general agreement that the forgetting of long-term information was due to new information interfering with the storage of old. Peterson and Peterson (1959) created quite a stir – and a long-lasting debate – by interpreting their results in terms of the quick decay of information in a short-term store. In other words, they assumed that the mechanism of forgetting that their experiment had revealed was qualitatively different from the mechanism that caused the forgetting of longer-term information. This raised the possibility that a relatively complicated behavior (memory) that could be studied experimentally by cognitive psychologists was mediated by two separate subsystems, a short-term store and a long-term store. As we shall see below, functional dissociation was an important weapon used by supporters of the two-memory view against their single-store antagonists.

A variety of different memory tasks have revealed that not all items in a list were equally likely to be remembered. For instance, a very common method used to study memory was the free recall experiment. In this kind of experiment, subjects are presented a list of to-be-remembered items, which could be digits, words, or nonsense syllables. At the end of the list, subjects are given a set period of time (e.g., two minutes) in which they write down as many of the presented items as they recall. They can write these items down in any order, which is why the method is called free recall. While the subject can recall items in any order that he or she pleases, the experimenter generally plots the probability that an item is correctly recalled as a function of its position in the list, producing what is known as a *serial position curve* (see figure 5.1). All things being equal, serial position curves routinely demonstrate, regardless of list length, a *primacy effect* in which the first three or four items in the list are better recalled than the middle items of the list. Serial position curves also typically reveal a *recency effect* in which the last three or four items in the list are also better recalled than the middle items (e.g., Craik, 1970; Glanzer & Cunitz, 1966, exp. 1; Postman & Phillips, 1965).

The proponents of the two-memory view made a strong case for their position by demonstrating a functional dissociation between the recency effect and the primacy effect. For instance, if free recall of the list was delayed as in the Brown–Peterson task, the recency effect would disappear, but the primacy effect would not be affected (e.g., Glanzer & Cunitz, 1966). In contrast, the primacy effect – but not the recency effect – could be eliminated by increasing the rate of presentation of list items or by constructing lists from low-frequency words (e.g., Glanzer, 1972). Similar dissociations were observed when Waugh and Norman's (1965) digit-probe paradigm was employed (e.g., Kintsch & Buschke, 1969), which provided converging evidence that the recency effect and the primacy effect were due to different mechanisms.

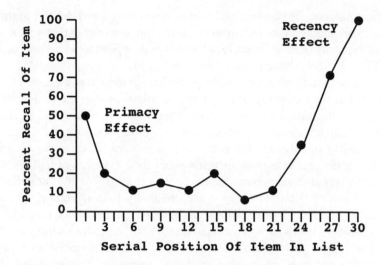

Figure 5.1 An idealized serial position curve, showing the percentage of times that a group of subjects will recall an item as a function of that item's position in a list. The primacy effect is the tail of the curve that indicates better recall for the first few items in the list. The recency effect is the tail of the curve that indicates better recall for the last few items in the list.

This functional dissociation between primacy and recency effects was in large part responsible for the development of what has become known as the *modal model of memory* (e.g., Baddeley, 1986). The basics of the modal model were proposed by Waugh and Norman (1965) and Atkinson and Shiffrin (1968), and are illustrated in figure 5.2. According to this model, to-be-remembered information is initially kept in primary memory, which has a small capacity, short duration, and codes items with respect to how they sound (e.g., Conrad, 1964). Without additional processing, items will quickly decay from *primary memory*. However, this can be prevented by using maintenance rehearsal, in which an item from memory is spoken aloud, and is thus fed back to the memory in renewed form. With enough rehearsal, or with additional strategies used to make rehearsed material more meaningful to the learner, some of the information in primary memory passes into *secondary memory*. Secondary memory has large capacity, long duration, and codes items with respect to what they mean.

Serial position effects are presumed to be an emergent property of the modal model. In a generic free recall study, subjects have lots of time to rehearse the first few items in the list before this process gets disrupted by later list items. Consequently, there is a much greater chance that these items will receive enough processing to make their way to secondary memory, producing the primacy effect. As well, the last few items in the list are the most likely ones to be undergoing maintenance rehearsal when the recall signal is given. Therefore, the subject is likely to recall these items first – writing them down as they are spoken aloud in the rehearsal loop – before attempting to recall other items.

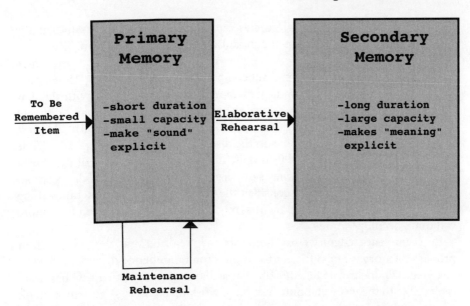

Figure 5.2 The modal memory model. To-be-learned items pass into a short duration primary memory, where they can be kept via maintenance rehearsal. With enough rehearsal, items can pass into a longer duration secondary memory.

This produces the recency effect. The middle items in the list don't last long in the rehearsal loop, and as a result are not likely to be present in either primary or secondary memory when subjects are asked to remember. As a result, the recall for middle serial position items is poor.

The functional dissociation of the two tails of the serial position curve can also be explained by noting that various manipulations will hurt one memory store, but not the other. For instance, if one increases the rate of presentation, the amount of maintenance rehearsal that can be performed decreases, as does the likelihood that items will receive enough processing to reach secondary memory. Also, if a researcher uses a list of low-frequency words, this decreases the likelihood of that subjects can use their familiarity with word meanings to perform elaborative rehearsal to place these items in secondary memory. It is not surprising that these manipulations reduce the primacy effect. Similarly, by delaying recall one allows the last items in the list to decay from primary memory by preventing their rehearsal. As well, lists of homophones increase the likelihood of interference during maintenance rehearsal. This accounts for why these types of manipulations reduce the recency effect.

Functional Dissociation and Working Memory

From the paragraphs above, the reader should be able to get some sense of one manner in which functional dissociation helped motivate the functional decomposition of memory into two qualitatively different subcomponents. However, modern results from memory studies have led researchers to substantially revise, elaborate, and redefine the modal model. The old notion of primary memory has been replaced with the new notion of working memory, which itself has a number of functional subcomponents (e.g., Baddeley, 1986). Similarly, the old notion of secondary memory has been replaced with the new notion of a semantic memory which also is viewed as having many different functional subcomponents (e.g., Paivio, 1971, 1986; Tulving, 1983). "Progress is the thing that puts most books in the discard" (Edison, 1948, p. 56). While the view of memory in the 1990s is quite different from the view of the 1960s, it should be stressed that both views owe a great deal to functional dissociation. To demonstrate this, let us consider the more modern notion of working memory, and how it is a componential model that has been derived from more elaborate decompositions.

In recent years, cognitive psychologists have realized that the old notion of primary memory is not sufficient to account for a number of different phenomena (e.g., Baddeley, 1986, 1990). These days, primary memory has been replaced with the more elaborate notion of working memory. One way to think about working memory is that it is the result of applying a further level of functional decomposition to primary memory, resulting in "primary memory" being the product of a number of organized subsystems.

Working memory is thought to consist of an organized system of storage and processing components. There are three major parts to working memory, as illustrated in figure 5.3. The *central executive* is a processing component that is responsible for operating on symbols stored in buffers, as well as for determining how attention will be allocated across a number of different tasks that might be going on in parallel. The *visualspatial buffer* is used for the storage of visual information. The *phonological loop* is responsible for storing verbal (or speech-like) information. In many respects, working memory is like a miniature Turing machine – the two buffers are analogous to two finite tapes for storing a small number of different kinds of symbols, and the central executive is very much like a machine head in the sense that it determines how these symbols are to be manipulated. However, this is a simplification, because the buffers themselves can be functionally decomposed. For example, the phonological loop (as indicated in the figure) consists of two different components. One of these is a phonological store that acts as a memory by holding symbols. The other is a rehearsal process that preserves items in the phonological store.

Details about the intricacies of working memory are beyond the scope of this chapter. For more information about this approach to memory, the reader is referred to Baddeley (1986). The only point that I want to make is that this elaborated version of primary memory has largely been the result of the discovery of additional functional dissociations in memory tasks. In other words, the old reliable methods used to pioneer the study of human memory are still being fruitfully applied by modern cognitive psychologists.

For example, what evidence can we use to claim that rehearsal is actually distinct from storage in working memory? This issue was tackled by Longoni,

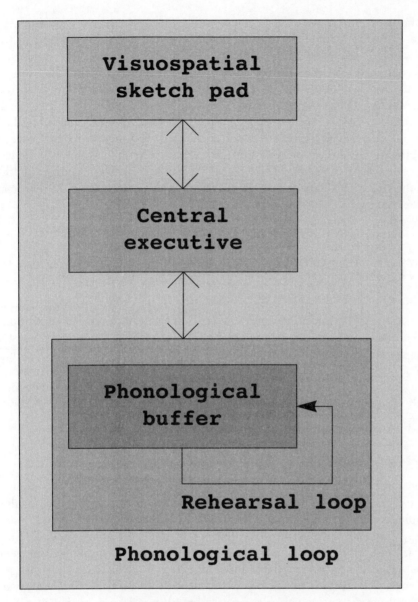

Figure 5.3 A modern view of working memory. A central executive controls processing of visual items stored in the visuospatial sketch pad, and of auditory items stored in the phonological loop. This entire system can be thought of as a functional decomposition of the primary memory system that was part of figure 5.2.

Richardson, and Aiello (1993). In a working-memory task, they manipulated three separate factors: the phonemic similarity of to-be-remembered items, word length, and whether the items could be rehearsed or not. One result that was obtained was that shorter words were remembered better than longer words. Another result was that different sounding items were remembered better than similar sounding items. The third result was a striking functional dissociation – when rehearsal was prevented, the effect of word length vanished but the phonemic similarity effect was unchanged. This indicated that the word length effect and the phonemic similarity effects were the product of different functional subcomponents. These results were interpreted as providing support for the functional dissociation between the phonological store and the rehearsal mechanism.

Part III   Protocol Analysis as a Classical Method

In the preceding part of the chapter, several examples were provided to show how functional dissociation can be used to motivate functional decompositions of behavior, and can also be used to evaluate alternative functional analyses. The search for functional dissociations is a key ingredient of cognitive science being pursued at the algorithmic level. However, this is not the only method that can be used to carve some complex behavior into functional components. This part of the chapter provides an overview of another important methodology.

Protocol Analysis

One of the characteristics of behaviorism's reign in psychology was the emphasis on studying objectively observable phenomena. One consequence of this emphasis was the view that certain kinds of measurements produced "hard data," and should be used, while other kinds of measurements produce "soft data," and should not be used. One example of the latter type of measurement was verbal reports from a subject about his or her own experiences or strategies when participating in a psychology experiment. "Ordinarily the simplest way to find out what a person is doing is to ask him. But psychologists have become very chary about asking people what they are doing because, they usually say, people really do not know what they are doing and it is just a waste of time to believe what they will tell you" (Miller, Galanter, & Pribram, 1960).

One key problem with this type of bias in psychology was its indiscriminate nature, treating many types of verbal data as being equally bad. "No distinctions are made among such diverse forms of verbalization as thinking-aloud protocols, retrospective responses to specific probes, and the classical introspective reports of trained observers. All are jointly and loosely condemned as 'introspection' " (Ericsson & Simon, 1984, p. 3). Another problem with this bias was that little justification was typically given to defend the claim that a limited class of verbal responses (e.g., saying "yes" or "no" to a query, or verbally recalling remembered items) could be used in a scientific psychology, but other verbal data could not be used.

Modern cognitivists have realized that the distinction between "hard" and "soft" data is unrelated to the distinction between nonverbal and verbal data (e.g., Ericsson & Simon, 1984). The hardness or softness of data is a function of the quality of the paradigm under which it is collected and analyzed, and is not a function of the data itself. For instance, what behaviorists might consider the "hardest," most objective measures possible in an experiment (e.g., bar presses in a Skinner box) would tell you nothing if the experiment was flawed in its design (because of a confound in the independent variable, sampling error, and so on). Data are only as hard as the inferences that they validly support.

Protocol analysis is an experimental paradigm that treats verbal reports seriously, and which specifies how one can collect and analyze these reports in a fashion that permits conclusions that are as "hard" as any others in experimental psychology. A deep discussion of protocol analysis is beyond the scope of this chapter; the interested reader should refer to Ericsson and Simon (1984) for a detailed treatment of the methodological and theoretical aspects of this paradigm. The purpose of this section is only to provide the reader with some sense of what protocol analysis involves by describing one of its earlier triumphs in cognitive science.

Human Problem Solving by Newell and Simon was published in 1972. This classic text was the culmination of 17 years of research, a program that had started with work in 1954 and 1955 on programming a computer to play good chess. The goal of the book was to describe a rigorous theory of human problem-solving from an information-processing perspective. Rather than focusing on very general characteristics of problem-solving, Newell and Simon aimed to generate explicit theories (in the form of computer simulation) of particular individuals solving particular problems. "Such a representation is no metaphor, but a precise symbolic model on the basis of which pertinent specific aspects of the man's problem-solving behavior can be calculated" (p. 5).

In the most general sense, Newell and Simon (1972) proceeded by collecting protocols of subjects as they thought aloud when solving a problem, and then by analyzing these protocols in such a way that a computer model of how a subject solved a particular problem could be developed. The problems that they studied included cryptarithmetic, in which subjects must decode a letter expression into numbers; logic, in which a subject is given a starting expression and a set of logical rules, and must use these to convert the starting expression into a goal expression; and chess, in which subjects must choose the best next move when presented a position from the middle of a chess game. These problems are all well-defined: they have a specific starting state, a solution that can be explicitly defined, and a set of explicit rules that a subject must follow when trying to go from the start of the problem to its solution. The problems that Newell and Simon studied were difficult enough to challenge subjects (i.e., to ensure that they actually engaged in problem-solving behavior), but were not so difficult that they could not be solved in a reasonable amount of time, or that they would produce a verbal protocol that was prohibitively long for later analysis.

To provide a more detailed sense of Newell and Simon's (1972) methodology, let us consider how they studied what might be the most famous problem in the problem-solving literature: the cryptarithmetic task DONALD + GERALD = ROBERT, D = 5. The subject's task is to figure out the digits represented by all of the other letters in the problem given this starting information. The first step in the analysis was to have a single subject solve the problem, speaking aloud at all times when the problem was being solved. The subject's session was tape recorded, providing the raw data for the analysis. (Indeed, the transcript of the protocol, which contains 2,186 words, is provided in their book!)

When the protocol was transcribed into written form, it was broken up into short phrases that were labeled for later reference. This labeling was the first processing of the raw data, for each phrase was assumed to represent a single task assertion or reference. However, the "phrasing" of the protocol was not presumed to explicitly affect later analysis. Furthermore, there was very little "cleaning up" of the protocol by removing variability and redundancy in what the subject is saying. This was because parts that were easy to code did not require this, and because Newell and Simon (1972) preferred to keep parts of the transcript that were difficult to code in their original form to extract any information that they did happen to contain.

The next step in the analysis was to take the transcribed protocol, and to infer from it the subject's problem space for the cryptarithmetic problem. A problem space defines the representational space in which a system's problem-solving activities take place. A human subject in their studies was presumed to "encode these problem components – defining goals, rules, and other aspects of the situation – in some kind of space that represents the initial situation presented to him, the desired goal situation, various intermediate states, imagined or experienced, as well as any concepts he uses to describe these situations to himself" (Newell & Simon, 1972, p. 59).

For instance, by examining the transcribed protocol for the cryptarithmetic subject, Newell and Simon (1972, pp. 166–8) recognized (among other things) that he assigned digits to letters, inferred relations from the columns of the problem, generated digits that satisfied certain relations, used relations like equality, inequality, and parity, and could consider disjunctive sets. Newell and Simon used the protocol to create a problem space that included approximately 25 states of knowledge and rules (see Newell & Simon, 1972, fig. 6.1).

The reason that Newell and Simon relied on the notion of a problem space was that they assumed that problem-solving was, in essence, a subject's search through this space to find a path (of rules that, when applied, produced intermediate states of knowledge) from the starting state for the problem to the goal state. Because of this assumption that problem-solving was a form of

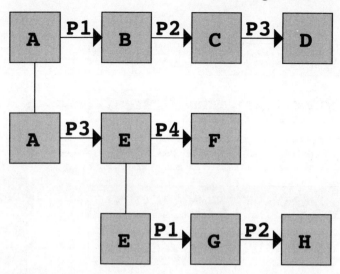

Figure 5.4 A simplified problem behavior graph. Each lettered box represents a knowledge state, and each labeled line represents the performance of an operation that moves from one state to another. Two back-tracks are illustrated in this figure, one from box D and one from box F.

search, their next step was to describe the full dynamics of the subject's search. The description that they produced was called a *problem behavior graph*.

A problem behavior graph consists of a set of nodes connected together by links. Each node represents some state of knowledge about the problem. Each link represents a rule in the problem space that, when applied to the state of knowledge to the left of the link, produces the state of knowledge to the right of the link (see figure 5.4). The dynamics of search are represented in two ways in a problem behavior graph. First, time increases from left to right across a single line in the problem behavior graph. Second, sometimes after pursuing a train of thought a subject reaches a dead end, and has to backtrack to some earlier point in their search. Newell and Simon represented this in the problem behavior graph by creating a new line. This line started with the node to which subjects had backtracked, drawn directly beneath its last location in the problem behavior graph. Newell and Simon showed how a detailed problem behavior graph could be constructed by examining the subject's protocol, and by adhering to the components in the problem space that had been derived for that subject (e.g., pp. 173–85).

The next step was to develop a computer simulation to account for the problem behavior graph that had been created from the subject's thinking-aloud protocol. The goal of the program was to make three things explicit: the processes for doing the arithmetic, the processes for deciding what to do next, and the information remembered by the subject as the problem is being solved (e.g., to permit backtracking). Newell and Simon decided that a *production system* was a programming language that was ideally suited to achieve these three goals.

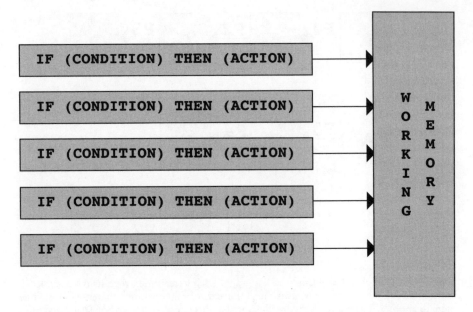

Figure 5.5 A schematic of a simple production system consisting of five different productions. Each of these productions would be seeking a particular condition in working memory, and would carry out a specific action once that condition was identified. See text for more details.

Production Systems

A production system is a prototypical information-processing architecture for classical cognitive science. It is essentially a set of operators that manipulate symbols stored in a working memory (see figure 5.5). Each operator can be thought of as a condition-action pair, or as an "if-then" rule. In general, all of the operators in a production system scan the working memory for the presence of their condition. When a particular operator finds its condition, it seizes control and prevents the other operators from working. It then performs its action, which usually involves rewriting some of the information in the working memory. In this sense, control – what to do next – is broadcast by the working memory, and is seized by one of the set of productions.

Newell and Simon were able to use the problem behavior graph to derive a production system that accounted for their subject's behavior. Each link between two nodes in the problem behavior graph represents the input and output for a particular operation. Newell and Simon examined the problem behavior graph to find evidence for the repetition of an operation's occurrence, viewing the operation as being a production. "Repetition of decision situations is the key issue, for if each situation called forth a unique process, then we could never verify that a proposed process was in fact the one used" (p. 191).

For example, the problem behavior graph for one subject solving the DONALD + GERALD = ROBERT problem consisted of 238 nodes. From this graph, Newell and Simon were able to find evidence for 14 different productions. "The total program, then, is the collection of these individual productions, plus the ordering of the productions that resolves conflict if serval conditions are satisfied concurrently" (p. 192). Amazingly, Newell and Simon were able to show that this production system accounted for approximately 80 percent of the subject's protocol! Furthermore, "most of the inadequacies of the model appear to be due either to the lack of a detailed account of attention and memory mechanisms or to missing data" (p. 227).

Summary

The description above doesn't really do justice to the Newell and Simon research program, which represents classical cognitive science in its purest and most successful form. Any serious student of cognitive science would do well to explore their work in more detail (for excellent compilations of papers, see Simon, 1979, 1989; for recent developments in the research program see Newell, 1990; for an intense survey of the protocol analysis methodology, see Ericsson & Simon, 1984). Nevertheless, four key points can still be drawn from what I have said above.

First, Newell and Simon (1972) viewed their work as an empirical investigation of a basic hypothesis: "that programmed computer and human problem solvers are both species belonging to the genus [information-processing system]" (p. 870). They were not concerned with judging the plausibility of this hypothesis directly, but rather intended to marshal objective evidence to either support or reject their assumption. Their ability to fruitfully describe problem-solving behavior with problem spaces and problem behavior graphs, coupled with their ability to emulate much of this behavior with computer models, demonstrated the plausibility of viewing an important aspect of human cognition as being the result of information processing.

Second, Newell and Simon demonstrated the utility of functional accounts of behavior. Note that the result of their detailed analysis of a subject's thinking-aloud protocol was a set of information-processing operations that described how a symbol was manipulated; they were not concerned with modeling physiological mechanisms of higher-order thought processes. For them, functionalism was profitable: "Perhaps the nonphysiological nature of the theory is not as disadvantageous as one might first believe, for the collection of mechanisms that are at present somewhat understood in neuropsychology is not at all adequate to the tasks dealt with in this book. We could not have proceeded to construct theories of human behavior in these tasks had we restricted ourselves to mechanisms that can today be provided with physiological bases" (p. 5). In point of fact, because Newell and Simon could propose working theories of problem-solving that were far more detailed than any competitor's, they were largely responsible for computer simulation's admission into psychology as a viable mainstream methodology.

Third, Newell and Simon were responsible for the introduction of the production system as a potential architecture for human cognition. In their historical addendum (1972, p. 889) they note that while this formalism had been introduced by Post in 1941, and was achieving wider acceptance in computer science in the late 1950s and early 1960s, it was unknown in psychology. "The production system was one of those happy events, though in minor key, that historians of science often talk about: a rather well-prepared formalism, sitting in wait for a scientific mission."

Fourth, Newell and Simon pioneered an important aspect of applied cognitive science, the development of expert systems. An expert system is a computer program that, in a typically narrow domain of interest, solves problems with an ability that is equal to, if not better than, a human expert in the field. Building expert systems is a big and growing business: it was a US$4 million industry in 1981, and a $800 million industry in 1990 (Kurzweil, 1990). Kurzweil has also noted that while the number of working expert systems was 700 at the end of 1986, it had grown to tens of thousands of systems by 1990. Expert systems are found in such diverse domains as finance, manufacturing control, fault detection, and medical diagnosis.

Protocol analysis plays a primary role in the development of expert systems (e.g., Feigenbaum & McCorduck, 1983, pp. 80–4). The typical expert system – which usually is based upon a production system architecture – is created by using thinking-aloud protocols to probe how experts solve problems in their field. This kind of knowledge engineering holds the promise of transporting diverse ranges of expertise to the nearest desktop computer. However, it can also have unexpected consequences. "One expert who gladly gave himself and his specialized knowledge over to a knowledge engineer suffered a severe blow to his ego on discovering that the expertise that he'd gleaned over the years, and was very well paid and honored for, could be expressed in a few hundred heuristics. At first he was disbelieving; then he was depressed. Eventually he departed his field, a chastened and moving figure in his bereavement" (pp. 85–6).

Part IV   Connectionism and Reverse Engineering

In the previous parts of this chapter, we have been concentrating on functionalism and forward engineering from the perspective of classical cognitive science. In this part of the chapter, we turn to algorithmic-level concerns that are faced by connectionist researchers. In particular, I am going to argue that in order to contribute to cognitive science, connectionists are going to have to extract an algorithmic account of how a trained network actually solves a particular task. In other words, connectionists are forced to reverse engineer their computer simulations in order to contribute algorithmic descriptions. It turns out that there are a number of potential techniques that are available to connectionists for doing this. I am going to describe one in particular that has been developed in my own laboratory, because some results that have been obtained with it raise some interesting questions about the putative differences between classical and connectionist models.

Bonini's Paradox

In cognitive science, computer simulations are supposed to offer rigorous accounts of cognitive phenomena. In considering simulation methods, Lewandowsky (1993) argues that they have several general advantages. First, they provide precise formulation for new ideas. Second, they permit the exploration of complex theories. Third, they are similar to traditional experimental methods in that they are subject to replication, inspection, and scrutiny. Fourth, they can reveal relationships between findings that at first glance appear to be unrelated. Fifth, they permit experimentation that may not be possible with human subjects.

At first glance, there would appear to be nothing about connectionist networks that prevents them from providing rigorous accounts of cognitive phenomena too. In point of fact, a trained PDP network can be viewed as an algorithm for accomplishing a specific task. This suggests that when we train a network to accomplish some task that is related to a cognitive phenomenon, we can gain further understanding of this phenomenon by taking a look and determining the processes that the network has discovered for solving the problem. These processes should constitute a connectionist, algorithmic theory of the cognitive phenomenon that we are interested in.

Unfortunately, things are not quite that simple. Lewandowsky (1993) has also noted that computer simulation methods are not without disadvantages. One disadvantage that is particularly relevant to connectionist models as algorithms has been called *Bonini's paradox* by Dutton and Starbuck (1971, p. 4). If a computer simulation falls into this trap, then this means that it is no easier (and perhaps is harder) to understand than the phenomenon that the simulation was supposed to illuminate. Dutton and Briggs (1971, p. 103) describe the problem quite plainly: "The computer simulation researcher needs to be particularly watchful of the complexity dilemma. If he hopes to understand complex behavior, he must construct complex models, but the more complex the model, the harder it is to understand. . . . As more than one user has realized while sadly contemplating his convoluted handiwork, he can easily construct a computer model that is more complicated than the real thing. Since science is to make things simpler, such results can be demoralizing as well as self-defeating."

As we saw briefly in chapter 3, connectionist researchers freely admit that in many cases it is extremely difficult to determine how their networks accomplish the tasks that they have been taught. "One thing that connectionist networks have in common with brains is that if you open them up and peer inside, all you can see is a big pile of goo" (Mozer & Smolensky, 1989, p. 3). Similarly, Seidenberg (1993, p. 229) states that "if the purpose of simulation modeling is to clarify existing theoretical constructs, connectionism looks like exactly the wrong way to go. Connectionist models do not clarify theoretical ideas, they obscure them." There are a number of reasons that PDP networks are difficult to understand as algorithms, and are thus plagued by Bonini's paradox.

First, connectionist networks are rarely developed a priori using forward engineering. Instead, they are the products of synthetic psychology – a generic learning rule is used to develop useful (algorithmic) structures in a network that is initially random. Thus, while one does not need a theoretical account of a to-be-learned task before a network is created to do it, one also does not have a theoretical account to fall back on to help figure out how the network is working. In other words, in order to interpret a network's structure, connectionists are confronted with the more difficult task of reverse engineering. This is exactly the same problem that faced the graduate students described by Arbib (1972) when they unsuccessfully attempted to reverse engineer the new computer before the manuals had arrived.

Second, general learning procedures can train networks that are extremely large; their sheer size and complexity makes them difficult to interpret. For example, Seidenberg and McClelland's (1989) network for computing a mapping between graphemic and phonemic word representations uses 400 input units, up to 400 hidden units, and 460 output units. Determining how such a large network maps a particular function is an intimidating task. This is particularly true because in many PDP networks, it is very difficult to consider the role that one processing unit plays independent from the role of the other processing units to which it is connected (see also Farah, 1994).

Third, as was pointed out in chapter 3, most PDP networks incorporate nonlinear activation functions. This nonlinearity makes these models more powerful than those that only incorporate linear activation functions (e.g. Jordan, 1986), but it also requires that descriptions of their behavior be particularly complex. Indeed, some researchers choose to ignore the non-linearities in a network, substituting a simplified (and often highly inaccurate) qualitative account of how it works (e.g., Moorehead, Haig, & Clement, 1989, p. 798).

Fourth, connectionist architectures offer too many degrees of freedom. One learning rule can create many different networks – for instance, containing different numbers of hidden units – that each compute the same function. Each of these systems can therefore be described as a different algorithm for computing that function. One does not have any a priori knowledge of which of these possible algorithms might be the most plausible as a psychological theory of the phenomenon being studied.

Given these four problems, one should not be surprised to find connectionists writing that "there is a growing suspicion that discovering [how a network does its job] may require an intellectual revolution in information processing as profound as that in physics brought about by the Copenhagen interpretation of quantum mechanics" (Hecht-Nielsen, 1987, p. 10).

Avoiding Bonini's Paradox

Difficulties in understanding how a particular connectionist network accomplishes the task that it has been trained to perform have given rise to serious doubts about the ability of connectionists to provide fruitful theories about cognitive processing. McCloskey (1991) suggested that "connectionist networks should not be viewed as theories of human cognitive functions, or as simulations of theories, or even as demonstrations of specific theoretical points" (p. 387). In a nutshell, this dismissal of connectionism was based largely on the view that PDP networks are generally uninterpretable (see also Dawson & Shamanski, 1994).

If connectionists want to contribute to cognitive science by providing algorithmic accounts of cognitive processing, some way must be found to avoid Bonini's paradox. This requires researchers to get their hands dirty, to divine the algorithmic structure of their networks. Fortunately, connectionist researchers are up to this kind of challenge. Several different approaches to interpreting the algorithmic structure of PDP networks – for reverse engineering – have been described in the literature.

One approach to interpreting a network's algorithm involves studying its connection weights. For example, Hanson and Burr (1990) review a number of techniques for doing this, including compiling frequency distributions of connection strengths, quantifying global patterns of connectivity with descriptive statistics, illustrating local patterns of connectivity with "star diagrams," and performing cluster analyses of hidden unit activations. Hinton (1986) provides an excellent example of how an examination of connection weights in a trained network can reveal the regularities that the network is using to solve a difficult pattern recognition task.

A second approach involves using algorithms to translate the pattern of connections in a network into a production rule that describes how the response of one processing unit depends on the responses of a subset of the processing units that feed into it (e.g., Gallant, 1993, ch. 17). In general, this is problematic, because as one increases the number of connection weights in the network, the number of possible productions encoded in a network increases exponentially. As a result, the researcher must use additional assumptions about the nature of the rules in order to help constrain the interpretation (i.e., to help limit the number of proposed productions).

A third strategy is to map out the response characteristics of each processor in the network. For example, Moorehead, Haig, and Clement (1989) used the generalized delta rule to train a PDP network to identify the orientation of line segments presented to an array of input units. Their primary research goal was to determine whether the hidden units in this system developed center-surround receptive fields analogous to those found in the primate lateral geniculate nucleus. They chose to answer this question by stimulating each input element individually, and plotting the resulting activation in each hidden unit.

A detailed discussion of any of the above methods, and their relevance to cognitive science, is well beyond the scope of this chapter. Instead, what I would like to do in the next section is describe in depth a technique that we have developed for interpreting the internal structure of the value unit architecture that was introduced in chapter 3. This technique is a variation of the response mapping technique used by Moorehead, Haig, and Clement (1989). The point of focusing on this particular example is that some recent results using this technique have begun to raise some interesting questions about the differences between connectionist and classical models.

Interpreting Value Unit Networks by Wiretapping

In the 1950s, researchers developed extracellular recording techniques to study the behavior of individual neurons in the brain (for a brief introduction, see Nicholls, Martin, & Wallace, 1992, pp. 7–8, pp. 138–9). In this technique, a very fine electrode is inserted into the brain, and is used to determine whether the cells near its tip are active by measuring their electrical activity. Extracellular recording can also be used to determine whether their rate of firing is increasing or decreasing, and on occasion it can be used to provide this information about individual neurons. Extracellular recording is sometimes known as "wiretapping" cells.

This methodology has been responsible for a great deal of our understanding of the biology of vision, as popularized by the pioneering (and Nobel prize winning) research of Hubel and Wiesel (e.g., 1959, 1962). For over half a century, neuroscientists have studied the visual system by mapping its receptive fields with extracellular recording (e.g., Barlow, 1972). This is done by presenting a number of different stimuli to the visual system of an animal, and by measuring the response of "wiretapped" neurons to determine the stimulus conditions that cause them to vigorously respond.

Because they are computer simulations, connectionist networks are very amenable to wiretapping (e.g., Moorehead, Haig, & Clement, 1989). Consider using a set of patterns to train a PDP network. After training, one could present each pattern once again to the network, and record the activity that each pattern produced in each hidden unit. This amounts to wiretapping each hidden unit while the stimulus set is being presented. One could use this information to create a *jittered density plot* for each hidden unit (see figure 5.6 for some example plots).

Each jittered density plot in figure 5.6 should be interpreted as summarizing the results of wiretapping a single hidden value unit in some trained network. In any one of these density plots, a single dot is used to represent the activity in one hidden unit produced by presenting one pattern to the network. So, if a network was trained on 500 different patterns, then one would expect to find 500 separate dots plotted in the density plot, one for each stimulus that was presented to the network. In a density plot for a hidden value unit, the *x*-axis ranges from a minimum of 0 to a maximum of 1 because the value unit activation function restricts a unit's internal activity to be in this range. So, by

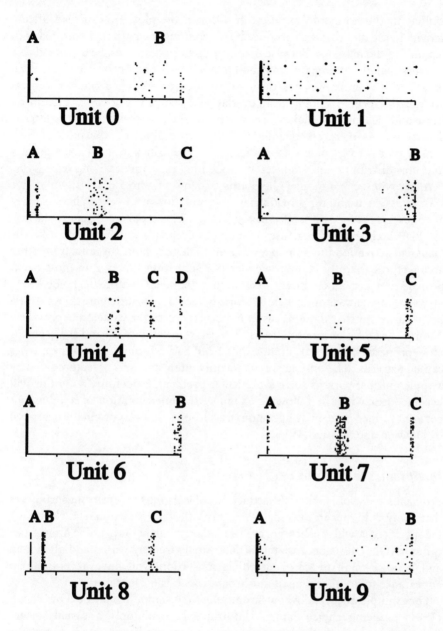

Figure 5.6 Density plots from a network of value units. All of these plots except for the density plot for Unit 1 show marked banding. These plots are from a network trained by Berkeley, Dawson, Medler, Schopflocher and Hornsby (1995), trained on a logic problem that is described in a bit more detail later in the chapter. Note that each dot in a density plot corresponds to a pattern presented to the network, and that by looking at the properties of patterns that fall into the same band, the algorithm that the network uses to solve the problem can be described.

looking at the horizontal position of a dot in the plot, we can read off the activity in the unit that was produced by presenting the pattern associated with that dot to the network. Because many different patterns can be presented to a network, many different plotted points might fall on top of each other. To prevent this from happening, the y-axis is used to provide a random vertical jittering that prevents points from overlapping as much as possible (Chambers, Cleveland, Kleiner, & Tukey, 1983, pp. 19–21). In reality, then, a jittered density plot is merely a one-dimensional scatterplot. The purpose of each density plot is to provide some indication of the distribution of activities in a unit; this distribution is produced by presenting the entire training set.

As we will see in a moment, and as is evident in figure 5.6, density plots for value units are useful for providing an interpretation of a network because they are often very striped or banded in appearance. This property appears to be true for PDP architectures that use nonmonotonic activation functions (like the Gaussian activation function in a value unit); density plots for units from other architectures (like the monotonic sigmoid activation function in most back-propagation networks) rarely exhibit this "banded" nature (e.g., Berkeley, Dawson, Medler, Schopflocher, & Hornsby, 1995). To anticipate things a little bit, it turns out that these bands in the density plots for value units provide a natural clustering of input patterns. Patterns that fall into a band share one or more properties. So, by examining each band and determining what properties caused patterns to fall into it, we can identify interesting sets of features used by a value unit network to solve a particular problem. Hopefully, all of this will become clear with the following example, the interpretation of a value unit network trained to identify poisonous mushrooms that was originally described by Dawson and Medler (1996).

Interpreting the Mushroom Network

Problem Definition. One of the attractions of learning to identify mushrooms is that many wild mushrooms make very tasty eating. Unfortunately, classifying the species of a wild mushroom, or even judging whether it is edible or inedible, is nontrivial. This is because mushrooms are extremely varied and abundant, and because in many cases an edible mushroom will have a very similar appearance to another type of mushroom which is poisonous.

For example, the meadow mushroom *Agaricus campestris* is noted by Lincoff (1981) as being choice eating. Unfortunately, with only a casual surface inspection, it looks essentially the same as *Amanita virosa*, more commonly known as the poisonous Destroying Angel mushroom. "Because the young, unexpanded caps [of *Amanita virosa*] resemble edible *Agaricus* mushrooms, an *Agaricus* must be carefully and completely removed from the ground to make certain no sheathing cup or remnant – indicating an *Amanita* – has been left or overlooked" (p. 552). The Destroying Angel is aptly named. Without treat-ment, it produces nausea, vomiting, diarrhea, and abdominal pain a few hours after being eaten. After a short remission from these symptoms, liver dysfunction, renal failure, coma, and death follow. Not surprisingly, Lincoff admonishes prospective mushroom hunters to take painstaking care in identifying field specimens.

Providing a biological classification of a mushroom (i.e., correctly identifying a mushroom's genus and species) requires paying attention to a wide variety of features, some of which are apparent from a casual inspection, others which are apparent only after microscopic examination. Lincoff (1981) provides a detailed description of these features. Dawson and Medler (1996) began to study a network's ability to use these features to classify a mushroom as edible or not after obtaining a copy of a data set originally compiled by Schlimmer (1987).

Schlimmer's (1987) data set consisted of the hypothetical description of 23 different species of mushrooms in the *Agricus* and *Lepiota* family (see Lincoff, 1981, pp. 500–25). Each mushroom was described as a set of 21 different features. Multiple featural descriptions of one species of mushroom were possible because one species might be found in several different habitats, have more than one possible odor, etc. The total data set consisted of 8,124 different instances: 4,208 of these patterns corresponded to edible mushrooms; the remaining 3,916 training patterns corresponded to inedible mushrooms (i.e., mushrooms that were definitely poisonous, or were of unknown edibility and therefore not recommended).

While each mushroom in Schlimmer's (1987) dataset was described as a set of 21 different features, it turns out that every instance can be correctly classified as being edible or not by examining five different features in order, as described in the algorithm for classifying edibility that is presented in table 5.1.

In training a value unit network to correctly classify all 8,124 mushrooms in this data set, we were interested in obtaining the answer to three different questions. First, could the network learn to accomplish this task? Second, if a network could learn to classify the mushrooms, then would its hidden units reveal density plots that were banded and interpretable? Third, if interpretable structure was discovered in the trained network, then what would the relationship be between this structure and the nested if-then statements in the algorithm described in table 5.1?

Network Architecture. In the version of the mushroom problem described below, only 16 of the 21 possible input features were used. The 5 features that were deleted were either constant across the entire training set, or were unrelated to classifying mushroom edibility. Each remaining feature was coded as an activation value in a single input unit, with each different activation value corresponding to a different value of that particular feature. The features that were presented to the network concerned bruises, odor, gill attachment, gill spacing, gill size, stalk shape, stalk surface above ring, stalk surface below ring, stalk color above ring, stalk color below ring, veil color, number of rings, ring type, spore print color, population, and habitat.

The network had 16 input units (one for each feature), 4 hidden value units, and one output value unit. The output value unit was trained to generate a

Step	Procedure Carried Out
Step 1	*What is the odor of the mushroom?* If it is almond or anise then the mushroom is edible. If it is creosote or fishy or foul or musty or pungent or spicy then the mushroom is poisonous. If it has no odor then go to Step 2.
Step 2	*Obtain the spore print of the mushroom.* If the spore print is black or brown or buff or chocolate or orange or yellow then the mushroom is edible. If the spore print is green or purple then the mushroom is poisonous. If the spore print is white than proceed to Step 3.
Step 3	*Examine the gill size of the mushroom.* If the gill size is broad, then the mushroom is edible. If the gill size is narrow, then proceed to Step 4.
Step 4	*Examine the stalk surface above the mushroom's ring.* If the surface is fibrous then the mushroom is edible. If the surface is silky or scaly then the mushroom is poisonous. If the surface is smooth then proceed to Step 5.
Step 5	*Examine the mushroom for bruises.* If it has no bruises, then the mushroom is edible. If it has bruises, then the mushroom is poisonous.

Table 5.1 A five-step algorithm for determining the edibility of mushrooms in the Schlimmer (1987) data set.

response of "1" to an edible mushroom, and a response of "0" to an inedible mushroom. The network was trained with the Dawson and Schopflocher (1992a) learning rule, which is a variation of the generalized delta rule (e.g., Rumelhart, Hinton, & Williams, 1986a) for value unit networks. The network learned to correctly classify all of the mushrooms after only 108 presentations of each training pattern. The fact that the network converged provided the answer to our first question – a value unit network could learn to classify mushrooms as being edible or inedible.

Interpretation of the Network. In order to interpret the internal structure of the mushroom network, Dawson and Medler (1996) presented all of the training patterns to the network once it had been trained while "wiretapping" each of its hidden units. The density plots that were obtained are presented in figure 5.7; all of these density plots revealed distinct banding.

Are these bands interpretable? This question can be answered by using simple descriptive statistics (means, variances, and correlations) on each band to determine the features shared by all of the input patterns that fall into the same band of activity in a hidden unit. (For more specific details on how simple descriptive statistics are used to extract the "definite features" from a band, see Berkeley, Dawson, Medler, Schopflocher, and Hornsby, 1995). Dawson and

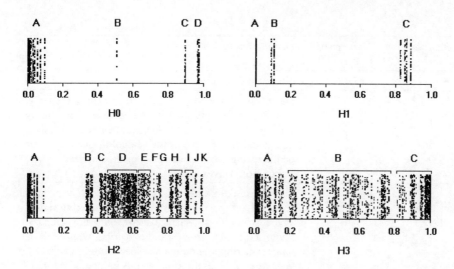

Figure 5.7 Density plots from the network of value units trained to determine whether mushrooms are poisonous or not, as reported by Dawson and Medler (1996).

Medler (1996) found that most of the bands were associated with definite features. Table 5.2 presents a sample of the features that were identified by listing the definite features for the bands found in hidden unit 0. Other units revealed this kind of detail when their bands were examined.

An examination of table 5.2 indicates that hidden unit 0 sends a strong signal when a member of a specific class of edible mushrooms is encountered. All of the mushrooms that fall into band C have almond or anise odor, which is characteristic of an edible mushroom (see table 5.1). Some of the mushrooms that fall into band D of hidden unit 0 are edible in virtue of having almond or anise odor. The others that fall into this band have no odor, but are edible because they pass all five questions in the table 5.1 algorithm. (Interestingly, all five steps in the algorithm must be applied to determine that these are indeed edible.) With respect to this latter set of mushrooms, mushrooms that fall into band B are nearly identical to them with one exception – the band B mushrooms have bruises. As a result, they pass the first four steps of the table 5.1 algorithm, but fail (i.e., are identified as poisonous) in the fifth step.

Analysis of the definite features for hidden unit 1 (not presented in the table) indicated that it detects inedible mushrooms on the basis of odor. In particular, all of the mushrooms in bands B and C of hidden unit 1 have foul odor, which the table 5.1 algorithm indicates is diagnostic of a poisonous mushroom.

An examination of definite features (again, not presented in table 5.2) revealed that hidden unit 2 captures different classes of mushrooms which are related to each other in terms of bruises, gill attachment, and number of rings (almost all of the mushrooms that produce high activity in this unit have no bruises, free gill attachment, and one ring). The classes diverge from one another with respect to combinations of other features, primarily odor and ring

Band label	Number of patterns	Definite features
A	7972	No definite features.
B	8	Has bruises, no odor, free gill attachment, crowded gill spacing, narrow gill size, enlarging stalk shape, smooth stalk surface above and below ring, white stalk color above and below ring, white veil color, one ring, pendant ring type, white spore print, clustered population, leaves habitat.
C	48	Has bruises, almond or anise odor, free gill attachment, crowded gill spacing, narrow gill size, tapering stalk shape, smooth stalk surface above and below ring, white stalk color above and below ring, white veil color, one ring, pendant ring type, spore print color not yellow, several population, woods habitat. If odor is almond, then spore print color is brown. If odor is anise then spore print color is purple.
D	96	Odor not spicy, free gill attachment, crowded gill spacing, narrow gill size, white stalk color above ring, stalk color below ring not yellow, white veil color, one ring, evanescent or pendant ring type, spore print color not yellow, several population. If odor is almond or anise, then has bruises, stalk shape is enlarging, stalk color below ring is white, ring type is pendant, habitat is woods. If odor is none then does not have bruises, stalk shape is tapering, stalk color below ring is brown, ring type is evanescent, habitat is leaves. Stalk surface above and below ring is either fibrous or smooth. If odor is almond or none then spore print color is purple or white. If odor is anise then spore print color is black or brown.

Table 5.2 Definite features for the four bands from hidden unit 0 of the mushroom network. Note that all of the features listed in the table above are true of every pattern that falls into that band.

type. As a result, this unit does not pick out features that are only definitive of poisonous (or edible) mushrooms. For example, band J in hidden unit 2 picks out edible mushrooms, while band K picks out some mushrooms that are poisonous (i.e., they have foul or musty odors) and some mushrooms that are edible (i.e., they have almond or anise odors). Interestingly, the reason that these two very different types of mushrooms appear to be grouped into the same band is that the edible features are the inverse of the poisonous features (i.e., one can move from a description of an edible mushroom to a poisonous mushroom in this band by flipping the values of a large number of bits, as is captured by the definite relational features for this band).

By studying its definite features, Dawson and Medler (1996) found that hidden unit 3 generates strong activity when it detects the presence of a combination of features that are characteristic of inedible mushrooms. Specifically all of the mushrooms that fall in bands B and C are inedible, and all of these mushrooms have free gill attachment, close gill spacing, stalk color above the ring that is not yellow, a white veil color, a spore print color that is not yellow, and a pendant ring type if it has no bruises, or a nonpendant ring type if it has bruises.

We can now summarize how the network determines that a mushroom is edible. For the most part, three of the hidden units in the network (hidden units 1, 2, and 3) detect features that are characteristic of poisonous mushrooms. As a result, the network defines a very large class of edible mushrooms as those that fail to produce activity in its hidden units. These mushrooms are classified as being edible because the network fails to find any poisonous features in them.

However, while this approach works for most of the mushrooms, it fails for a minority of them. A small percentage of edible mushrooms fall into the same (high activity) bands in hidden unit 2 as do a number of poisonous mushrooms. As a result, a different approach must be used to identify the edibility of these mushrooms. The network pools the activation of hidden units 0 and 2 to solve this problem, essentially by intersecting the features detected by the two units with an AND operation. The high activity bands of hidden unit 2 capture groups of mushrooms that are related, but include both poisonous and edible members. The high activity bands of hidden unit 0 capture groups of edible members. The intersection of the members of the high activity bands from both of these units define a set of edible mushrooms – this intersection picks out the edible mushrooms from the bands in hidden unit 2 that also contain poisonous mushrooms.

Summary

In this part of the paper, I have introduced a key algorithmic-level issue for connectionist cognitive science – the need to provide an account of how a network solves a particular problem by reverse engineering it. If this is not done, then connectionism is not going to be able to contribute very much to cognitive science at all (see also Dawson & Shamanski, 1994). Instead, it will be moving cognitive science from one unknown (e.g., how does a person perform a particular task?) to two unknowns (e.g., how does a person perform a particular task, and how does my network perform the same task?)!

I have also described one of several techniques available to connectionist researchers for extracting an algorithmic account from a network. This particular method, the "wiretapping" of hidden value units, coupled with plotting the results of this "wiretapping" with a jittered density plot, often reveals distinct bands in which hidden units group different input patterns together. By looking at the similarities between patterns that fall into the same group, one can identify the kinds of features to which that hidden unit is sensitive. An algorithmic account of the network then becomes a description of the kinds of features that the units are sensitive to, as well as how these features are combined to solve the problem of interest. We saw an example of this approach in the analysis of Dawson and Medler's (1996) mushroom network.

Part V   Classical vs. Connectionist Algorithms: A Case Study

The previous part of the chapter illustrated how "wiretapping" can permit value unit networks to be reverse engineered. In this part, we are going to expand upon this theme using an example much more relevant to cognitive science: training a PDP network to make judgments about logic problems. The theme that I want to flesh out with this example is that once you interpret the structure of a PDP network, it seems much more similar to a classical system than one might presume.

Finding Rules in the Logic Network

In this section, we will consider a logical inference problem originally studied by Bechtel and Abrahamsen (1991, pp. 163–71). The problem set consists of six different types of logical arguments. The task of a trained network is, when presented an argument, to identify its type and to classify it as being either valid or invalid. So, if the network is presented an example of a valid *modus ponens* problem, its output must indicate "valid *modus ponens*." Similarly, if the network is presented an example of an invalid *modus tollens* problem, its output must indicate "invalid *modus tollens*."

Bechtel and Abrahamsen's (1991) stimulus set consisted of 576 different logic problems. Each pattern in the training set was a logical argument consisting of two sentences and a conclusion. The first sentence was composed of a connective and two variables; the second sentence and the conclusion were each composed of a single variable. Each of the four variables in an argument could be negated or not negated. The problem set consisted of four classes of problem (*modus ponens* (MP), *modus tollens* (MT), *alternative syllogism* (AS), and *disjunctive syllogism* (DS)); there were two different versions of each AS and DS problem type. For each of these problem types, there were 48 examples of valid problems and 48 examples of invalid problems. Table 5.3 illustrates examples of valid arguments for each problem type, and also introduces the descriptive notation that Berkeley *et al.* (1995) adopted to aid network interpretation.

Bechtel and Abrahamsen (1991) were particularly interested in this problem because it involves stimuli that are propositional or sentence-like. The manipulation of propositional structures is a prototypical example of classical cognitive science's emphasis upon rules that manipulate symbols. For example, Fodor (1975, p. 156) hypothesized that the architecture of cognition was language-like in its structure: "The least that can be said in favor of this

Problem Type	Problem Example	Descriptive Notation
Modus Ponens (MP)	If A then B A ---------- Therefore B	Connective: IF ... THEN S1(V1): A, S1(V2): B S2: A Conclusion: B
Modus Tollens (MT)	If A then C Not C --------------- Therefore not A	Connective: IF ... THEN S1(V1): A, S1(V2): C S2: C, S2 is negated Conclusion: A, Conclusion is negated
Alternative Syllogism (AS) Type 1	D or A Not D ---------- Therefore A	Connective: OR S1(V1): D, S1(V2): A S2: D, S2 is negated Conclusion: A
Alternative Syllogism (AS) Type 2	B or C Not C ---------- Therefore B	Connective: OR S1(V1): B, S1(V2): C S2: C, S2 is negated Conclusion: B
Disjunctive Syllogism (DS) Type 1	Not both C and D C ---------------- Therefore not D	Connective: NOT BOTH ... AND S1(V1): C, S1(V2): D S2: C Conclusion: D, Conclusion is negated
Disjunctive Syllogism (DS) Type 2	Not both A and D D ---------------- Therefore Not A	Connective: NOT BOTH ... AND S1(V1): A, S1(V2): D S2: D Conclusion: A, Conclusion is negated

Table 5.3 Examples of valid instances of each of the argument types in the logic problem. The accompanying descriptive notation was used by Berkeley *et al.* (1995) as an aid for interpreting network structures. Note that in the problem set any of the variables [i.e., S1(V1), S1(V2), S2, C] could be negated. If two variables are both positive or are both negative, we say that they have the same sign. Otherwise we say that they are opposite in sign. In the problem set, valid MP and MT arguments were turned into invalid ones by interchanging the letter for S2 and the letter for the conclusion. For all other problem types, valid arguments were turned into invalid ones by interchanging the sign of S2 and the sign of the conclusion.

hypothesis is that, if it is true, it goes some way toward explaining why natural languages are so easy to learn and why sentences are so easy to understand: The languages we are able to learn are not so very different from the language we innately know, and the sentences we are able to understand are not so very different from the formulae which internally represent them."

For Bechtel and Abrahamsen (1991, p. 147), "connectionism represents a clear challenge to this way of representing knowledge, because connectionist networks encode knowledge without explicitly employing propositions." When they were able to successfully train a PDP network to perform the logic task, they used this as evidence to support the claim that "propositionally encoded knowledge might not be the most basic form of knowledge" (p. 174). But Bechtel and Abrahamsen based their conclusion on the assumption that propositions did not exist within the network, and did not examine the internal structure of the network to determine whether this assumption was valid or not. "Without a detailed analysis of the activities of the hidden units (which we have not performed), we cannot determine exactly how the network solved this problem" (p. 171).

Recently, Berkeley, Dawson, Medler, Schopflocher and Hornsby (1995) trained a network of value units on the Bechtel and Abrahamsen (1991) logic problem. The network used 14 input units to represent each problem as a string of 1s and 0s following Bechtel and Abrahamsen's coding scheme, 10 hidden units, and 3 output units. The three output units were used to indicate problem type and whether the presented problem was valid or not. Berkeley *et al.* then used the "wiretapping" technique to interpret the internal structure of this network. This analysis revealed distinct banding in 9 of these 10 hidden units; the definite features that were identified in these bands provided an extremely rich account of the kinds of features that this network was using to solve the problem.

Berkeley *et al.* (1995) then went one step further. Instead of describing the problem in terms of the 14 values that are used to represent it in the network's input units, the problem can be described in terms of which activity bands it falls into in the hidden units. For example, consider the *modus ponens* problem "If A then B; A; Therefore B." This problem would be presented to the network as the input unit activity pattern [0, 0, 1, 1, 1, 0, 1, 0, 0, 0, 1, 0, 1, 0]. In each hidden unit, this pattern would produce a certain amount of activity, and we could describe this activity in terms of which band that activity would fall in in each hidden unit. For instance, from this perspective the *modus ponens* problem "If A then B; A; Therefore B" would be described as [0-A, 1-A, 2-B, 3-A, 4-A, 5-A, 6-A, 7-B, 8-B, 9-A], where 0-A means "produced activity that fell into band A of hidden unit 0," 1-A means "produced activity that fell into band A of hidden unit 1," and so on. Let's call this new description of the input, in terms of the bands that it "falls into," the band pattern.

The advantage of representing stimuli as the set of hidden unit activity bands to which they belong is that these band patterns can be viewed as a "rule" that the network uses to make judgments about different types of logic problems (see below). This is because the band pattern represents a set of features which, when combined, dictate the network's response to the pattern. In short, the band pattern is like the set of conditions in production rules of the type that we discussed earlier in this chapter: if one band pattern is present, then the network will respond in one way. If another band pattern is present, then the network will respond in a different way.

For example, Berkeley *et al.* (1995) found that every valid *modus ponens* problem produced *exactly* the same band pattern in the network: [0-A, 1-A, 2-B, 3-A, 4-A, 5-A, 6-A, 7-B, 8-B, 9-A]. So, while describing the set of valid *modus ponens* problems at the level of the input units would require 48 different binary vectors (one for each problem), the same set of problems can be described at the level of the hidden units with exactly one band pattern! Furthermore, each band in this band pattern is associated with a specific interpretation, which came from identifying the definite features for the bands. In this particular example, by taking the definite features associated with the bands in the band pattern, Berkeley *et al.* defined the set of features that characterized a valid *modus ponens*. For the network, an input problem was a valid *modus ponens* if (in our notation), S1(V1) = S2, S1(V2) = C, SIGN S1(V1) = SIGN S2, and the connective is IF...THEN. Amazingly, this is essentially the rule for valid *modus ponens* that one might teach students in an introductory logic class (see table 5.4). In other words, in examining the internal structure of our network, we find something that Bechtel and Abrahamsen (1991) assumed could not exist in a PDP network: a rule for valid *modus ponens*!

Table 5.4 presents the rules of inference (in our notation) that Berkeley *et al.* (1995) discovered in their network for all of the valid problem types. There are several important points that arise from studying this table.

First, the network has a very small number of rules for identifying valid problem types: it has one rule for *modus ponens*, one rule for *modus tollens*, two rules for alternative syllogisms, and three rules for disjunctive syllogisms. Second, some of the rules in the network are equivalent to the traditional rules of inference used in natural deduction systems (cf. Bergmann, Moor, & Nelson, 1990). The network has learned the traditional rules of inference for *modus ponens, modus tollens*, and one version of alternative syllogism. Given this, we would expect that the network's performance would generalize well to patterns that it had not been trained on (e.g., by defining new variables by using continuous inputs to the relevant input units). Third, the network learned a number of rules of inference which are significantly different from the traditional ones. One of the rules for alternative syllogisms and one of the rules for disjunctive syllogisms are what might be termed default rules. Default rules work by identifying the main connective, and require that no other definite features are present. The other two rules for disjunctive syllogisms are similar to the traditional rules, but require in addition that S2 is not negated.

This last point is important for the psychological relevance of this type of model. It has long been known that the formal rules of inference do not always provide good accounts of how humans solve logic problems (e.g., Johnson-Laird, 1983). Instead, humans appear to deal with these problems by building *ad hoc* mental models that generally lead to correct solutions, though the models themselves have little resemblance to logical formalisms. Some of the

Table 5.4 Interpretation of the rules that the network uses to identify valid instances of each problem type. Grey shading is used to indicate the equivalence between network rules and traditional formal rules of inference. *Legend*: S1(V1) and S1(V2) are the first and second variables in sentence 1; S2 is the variable in sentence 2; C is the variable in the conclusion; SIGN refers to whether a variable is negated or not negated.

Problem Type	Formal Definition of Rule for Valid Problem Type	Network Rule Identified by the Interpretation	Notes About Network Rules
Valid *Modus Ponens* (MP)	S1(V1) = S2 S1(V2) = C SIGN S1(V1) = SIGN S2 SIGN S1(V2) = SIGN C CONNECTIVE: IF…THEN	S1(V1) = S2 S1(V2) = C SIGN S1(V1) = SIGN S2 CONNECTIVE: IF…THEN	The network rule is the same as the formal rule except that the network does not pay attention to the signs of S1(V2) and C. Due to the nature of the training set, though, this is not necessary.
Valid *Modus Tollens* (MT)	S1(V1) = C S1(V2) = S2 SIGN S1(V1) ≠ SIGN C SIGN S1(V2) ≠ SIGN S2 CONNECTIVE: IF…THEN	S1(V1) = C S1(V2) = S2 SIGN S1(V2) ≠ SIGN S2 CONNECTIVE: IF…THEN	Although the network does not pay attention to the signs of S1(V1) or C, this is not significant due to the nature of the training set.
Valid Alternative Syllogism (AS) [There are two versions of AS in the training set]	S1(V1) = S2 S1(V2) = C SIGN S1(V1) ≠ SIGN S2 SIGN S1(V2) = SIGN C CONNECTIVE: OR	CONNECTIVE: OR	This is a "default" rule. Provided the connective is OR and no other definite features are true of the pattern, then the problem must be a valid AS.
	S1(V1) = C S1(V2) = S2 SIGN S1(V1) = SIGN C SIGN S1(V2) ≠ SIGN S2 CONNECTIVE: OR	S1(V1) = C S1(V2) = S2 SIGN S1(V1) = SIGN C SIGN S1(V2) ≠ SIGN S2 CONNECTIVE: OR	Here the network employs exactly the classical rule.

Table 5.4 (continued)

Valid Disjunctive Syllogisms (DS) [There are two versions of DS in the training set]	S1(V1) = S2 S1(V2) = C SIGN S1(V1) = SIGN S2 SIGN S1(V2) ≠ SIGN S2 CONNECTIVE: NOT BOTH...AND S1(V1) = C S1(V2) = S2 SIGN S1(V1) ≠ SIGN C SIGN S1(V2) = SIGN S2 CONNECTIVE: NOT BOTH...AND	S2 IS NEGATED CONNECTIVE: NOT BOTH...AND	This is another default rule. Provided that S2 is negated, the connective is NOT BOTH...AND, and no other definite features are present, then the problem must be a valid DS.
		S1(V1) = C S1(V2) = S2 SIGN S1(V2) ≠ SIGN C SIGN S1(V2) = SIGN S2) S1(V2) IS NOT NEGATED S2 IS NOT NEGATED CONNECTIVE: NOT BOTH...AND	This network rule is the same as the second formal rule for DS apart from the additional stipulation that S2 and S1(V2) are not negated.
		S1(V1) = S2 S1(V2) = C SIGN S1(V1) = SIGN S2 SIGN S1(V2) ≠ SIGN C S1(V1) IS NOT NEGATED S2 IS NOT NEGATED CONNECTIVE: NOT BOTH...AND	This network rule is the same as the first formal rule for DS apart from the additional stipulation that S2 and S1(V2) are not negated.

rules learned by the network have this *ad hoc* appearance. For example, one of the rules for a valid alternative syllogism (the default rule) can be described as "If the connective is OR, and no other features that I know about are present, then it must be a valid AS." It is easy to imagine that this kind of rule might be used by a student who is learning about this type of problem, but is still unsure about its formal characterization.

In point of fact, the results in table 5.4 raise some interesting empirical questions that could be addressed by a cognitive psychologist. If human subjects were to learn to solve these logical questions, would they tend to develop *ad hoc* mental models for the AS and DS problems, but not to do so for MP and MT? Would human subjects treat DS problems with negated S2 differently than DS problems with nonnegated S2? Would human subjects develop a relatively small number of rules, paying attention to the same features as the model? Note that the fact that these questions can be raised depends on two things. The first is that unlike symbolic models of logic (e.g., Rips, 1994) in which the logical rules are programmed in, the connectionist network has to learn how to solve the problems, raising the possibility that surprising new rules will be discovered. The second is that the discovery of these rules in the network depends upon our ability to interpret its structure.

Implications for Connectionist Cognitive Science

Many connectionist claims about the role of PDP networks in cognitive science have depended upon the assumed qualitative differences between such networks and classical models (e.g., Bechtel & Abrahamsen, 1991; Schneider, 1987; Rumelhart & McClelland, 1985, 1986). One reason that I've gone into a fair amount of detail about the logic network is because the results of the Berkeley *et al.* (1995) interpretation of the logic network pose a strong challenge to this perspective. This is because these results indicate that abstract rules can indeed be found in a PDP network – if a researcher takes the trouble to look for them.

What might connectionists think of the search for such rules in their models? Bechtel (1994) admits that "it is reasonable to discuss whether some aspects of network processing can fruitfully be summarized by higher-level descriptions. However, it would be an exercise in futility to try to prove that all of the explicit activity generated by one of my networks in solving a problem corresponds exactly to a series of implicit symbolic operations. It is neither necessary nor desirable that this be the case" (p. 458).

Why is this neither necessary nor desirable? Bechtel (1994, p. 458) argues that it is because this approach would fail to reveal any unanticipated results: "We would all like to attain a better understanding of the internal operations of networks, but focusing our search on functional equivalents to symbolic operations could keep us from noticing what is most worth seeing." However, there is nothing in the interpretive analysis used by Berkeley *et al.* (1995) that biases a researcher towards one type of interpretation, and away from another.

For example, it led to the discovery of rules that are definitely not part of the formal definition of logical forms. The two default rules would certainly not be revealed by an analytic technique that only looked for rules that resembled traditional definitions of logic. For example, the default rule for a valid alternative syllogism can be described as "If the connective is OR, and no other features that I know about are present, then it must be a valid alternative syllogism." It is easy to imagine that this kind of rule might be used by a student who is learning about this type of problem, but is still unsure about its formal characterization.

From a psychological view, the discovery of these nontraditional rules provides a welcome surprise. It is the surprising (or at least nontraditional) nature of these rules that make them particularly worthy of additional experimental study. This is because it has long been known that the formal rules of inference do not always provide good accounts of how humans solve logic problems (e.g., Johnson-Laird, 1983). Instead, Johnson-Laird argues that humans deal with these problems by building *ad hoc* mental models that generally lead to correct solutions, though the models themselves have little resemblance to logical formalisms. The default rules revealed in the network have this *ad hoc* appearance. Furthermore, their existence raises questions that could be addressed by cognitive psychologists performing new experiments.

Implications for Classical Views of Connectionism

One standard classical criticism of connectionist networks is to say that they are "merely implementational." This amounts to the view that connectionist models are not cognitive theories, but are instead noncognitive implementational accounts. This dismissal of connectionism is well-established in classical cognitive science. Broadbent (1985) used this position to criticize the psychological relevance of PDP models. Pinker and Prince (1988) are quite comfortable with the possibility that connectionist models are implementational, as are Fodor and Pylyshyn (1988). Of course, the reason for all of this comfort is that if connectionist models are implementational, and not cognitive, then they cannot be viewed as alternatives to classical cognitive theories, because they are related to only one level of the tri-level hypothesis – the implementational level (see also Ramsey, Stich, & Garon, 1991). If PDP models are merely implementational, then the paradigm shift for cognitive science will have to be postponed, because from previous chapters we know that cognitive science requires that all levels of the tri-level hypothesis be explored.

Of course, connectionists are not eager to accept the position, so comfortable to classical researchers, that their networks are merely implementational descriptions. Instead, they propose that their networks are cognitive theories that can compete with those proposed by classical cognitive scientists (e.g., Smolensky, 1988). To compete with classical models, connectionist researchers are obligated to show that their networks are indeed cognitive theories. How is this to be done? One way to accomplish this is to follow Pylyshyn's (1991) lead, by showing that the network has semantic states, and by demonstrating that these states do figure in an account of its behavior.

The analysis of the logic problem provides a good example of how one can defend the cognitive nature of a connectionist theory. The analysis showed that particular network states – particular levels of activity in hidden units – were associated with specific semantic interpretations (see Berkeley *et al.*, 1995, table II). Berkeley *et al.* went on to show that mere knowledge of these semantic interpretations could be used to make very precise predictions about the network's behavior (1995, section 5.3). The upshot of all of this is that the logic network is a cognitive theory about how particular judgments about logical problems might be made. The essence of this theory is the set of seven rules discovered by Berkeley *et al.* that are presented in table 5.4.

Summary

In addition to providing another demonstration of the "wiretapping" technique for generating an algorithmic account of a network of value units, this example has generated some more evidence concerning one of the major themes of this book: the relationship between connectionist and classical cognitive science. The analysis of the internal structure of the logic network revealed regularities that make the network appear much more similar to a classical model than one might originally assume. While some connectionists might argue that their networks can perform logic without requiring classical rules, the Berkeley *et al.* (1995) analysis of their network indicated that such rules might indeed exist in these networks. Furthermore, the rules extracted from the network suggested some new experiments that could be performed by a cognitive psychologist interested in how human subjects draw logical inferences. This suggests that networks of this type cannot be dismissed as mere implementations by classical researchers. In short, when one interprets the internal structure of PDP networks, one can find evidence that suggests that connectionist and classical cognitive science are very similar – at the algorithmic level!

Part VI   Validating Algorithmic Descriptions

At the algorithmic level of analysis, researchers attempt to figure out a program, an algorithm, or a sequence of information-processing steps that are carried out when a system solves an information-processing problem. From the examples that we have seen above, it is clear that this kind of analysis is carried out by both classical and connectionist cognitive scientists. However, just being able to generate an algorithmic description of some cognitive phenomenon is not going to be enough for cognitive science. Researchers also have to be able to defend the claim that their algorithmic description is the right one. This aspect of algorithmic-level analyses is the subject of this final part of the chapter.

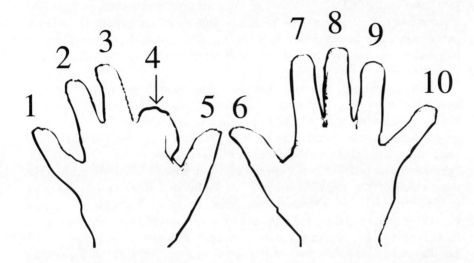

Figure 5.8 A "hands on" algorithm for multiplying 9 by any integer from 1 through 10. First, hold out your hands. Second, represent the problem by dropping the appropriate finger. The figure illustrates the problem "9 × 4" because finger 4 has been dropped. Third, count the number of fingers to the left and to the right of the dropped finger. As there are 3 to the left and 6 to the right in this example, 9 × 4 must equal 36.

Many Different Algorithms can Solve the Same Problem

We all know that there is more than one way to skin a dead cat. (Why we know this, or what good this specific piece of knowledge is to us, is a topic that I think we would all be more comfortable avoiding!) Similarly, there is more than one way to solve an information-processing problem.

Consider a very simple example of this. My long experience with computers and electronic calculators has caused me to forget the "9 times" multiplication table that I once was forced to learn. Let's imagine that in this sorry state of affairs, someone has asked me to compute "9 × 4" without the aid of a calculator. What procedures could I use to meet this challenge? Well, one technique (assuming that I can still do mental addition) might be to take the quantity "9" and add it to itself four times; that is to mentally figure out "9 + 9 + 9 + 9." A different procedure would be to mentally figure out a different sum, "4 + 4 + 4 + 4 + 4 + 4 + 4 + 4 + 4." Yet another procedure would be to use my "finger algorithm" for the "9 times" table as illustrated in figure 5.8. I believe that my weakness in mental arithmetic, and my subsequent reliance on calculating aids, can be traced back to when my father taught me that trick when I was still in elementary school.

Now, in the example above I described three different methods for solving a particular problem. Unfortunately, researchers concerned with formalizing our notion of what it means to compute a function can easily prove that there are an infinite number of possible procedures for computing any given function (e.g.,

Johnson-Laird, 1983, p. 7). "Most of them are trivial variations produced by inserting otiose evaluations of identities, but there are genuinely different procedures: e.g., in the lowly function of subtraction, 'borrowing' can be handled either by subtracting 1 from the upper digit or by adding 1 to the lower digit."

Pylyshyn (1981, p. 84) has noted that "the most frequent question that psychologists working in the computer simulation (or AI) tradition are asked goes something like this: 'Maybe your program can perform the same task as people can (in some domain), but how do you know whether it does it in the same way that people do?" If we assume (as cognitive scientists do) that "performing a task" means "computing a function," then we realize the importance of this question because we know that there is an infinity of different methods for solving the task. Why should we believe a researcher's claim that their method is the right one? Furthermore, because the result of a functional analysis is equivalent to a computer program even if computer simulation techniques are not used, it seems that psychologists who use computer simulations are not the only ones who must answer this question. Anyone who uses functional analysis – which means pretty much anyone who adopts cognitivism – has to defend their functional decomposition against others that are logically possible.

Of course, this point was raised in the previous chapter. If all that a researcher does is propose an algorithm for computing a function, then (at best) the most that they can say is that their algorithm is Turing equivalent to an organism of interest; (at worst) the most that they can say is that it is computationally equivalent. To get in the real business of cognitive science – establishing strong equivalence – the researcher has to provide additional evidence to say that their algorithm is the one that the organism of interest is actually using. Indeed, another major goal of empirical work at the algorithmic level is to validate the claim that a particular functional model of a cognitive phenomenon is the right one.

The Turing Test Revisited

Unfortunately, the need for empirical cognitive scientists to validate their model leads smack back into a major difficulty that was also discussed last chapter. Recall that the Turing test involved examining the external behavior of a system in an attempt to determine whether it was intelligent. However, it was noted that the Turing test could not distinguish between two systems that generated the same responses by using different underlying procedures. As a result, it is possible to create computer programs that solve interesting problems, but do so in a way that is irrelevant to someone interested in human intelligence.

The problem facing empirical cognitive scientists intent on validating their functional models is this: typically, the only information that they have direct access to is the overt behavior of the (human) subjects that they are modeling. In short, they are limited to performing the Turing test. Given that we have good reason to believe that the Turing test is not by itself powerful enough for cognitive science, doesn't this suggest that empirically based cognitive science is facing a dead end, and will be unable to establish the strong equivalence of the functional models that it proposes?

This conclusion, like the religion described in Hilton's *Lost Horizon*, is only moderately correct. By itself, the Turing test cannot provide an ultimate cognitive science. However, if one supplements the Turing test with some additional, weak assumptions about underlying processes, then substantial progress can be made towards establishing the strong equivalence of a functional model. While even this "supplemented" Turing test will not be sufficient to establish strong equivalence, it is a necessary step towards this ultimate goal.

What kinds of assumptions can be used to strengthen the Turing test? One can start by recognizing that not all of the observable behavior of an information processor is the result of explicit programming. In particular, certain types of behavior are not the product of the program *per se*, but are instead tacit properties of either the program or the particular machine on which the program is being run.

For instance, consider the Turing machine described way back in figure 2.2. The purpose of this machine is to compute the sum of the two integers represented on its tape when it begins processing. Now, some of the behavior of this machine is made explicit in its machine table. In particular, given the unary representation of some integer x and the unary representation of some integer y, this machine will write the unary representation of the integer $x + y$ on its tape because it has been programmed to do this. However, other aspects of this machine's behavior are very real, but can't be explained by appealing directly to the program. For example, this particular machine will compute its answers much slower for problems in which x and/or y are large integers than for problems in which x and/or y are small. This is because the integers are written on the tape in unary format (in which the quantity 554 would be represented as a string of five hundred and fifty-four "1s"), and because the Turing machine can only process one tape cell at a time, and because in order to move from one tape cell to another some distance away on the tape the machine head will have to process all of the intervening cells.

In the above example, the key point to make is that the time taken for the machine to solve a particular problem is a tacit consequence of the machine table (i.e., can be explained by talking about the kind of machine being used, and the procedures that it uses to solve its problem), but is not due to an explicit instruction in the machine table. To make this clear, let us imagine that we have some other architecture – the Dawson machine – that, no matter what x and y are, will compute their sum in exactly the same time (say, one millisecond) by using a built-in "PLUS (x,y)" function. Indeed, this machine is so fabulous that it will do this for unary-represented inputs, and will provide its answer in unary format as well. Furthermore, the Dawson machine has a built-in "WAIT (z)" function that, when called, will cause it to do nothing for exactly z milliseconds.

Now, I could use this machine to simulate (some of) the observable behavior of the figure 2.2 Turing machine by having it perform its "PLUS (x,y)" operation, and then by having it "WAIT (z)", where z was a carefully chosen function of the length of x and y represented in unary format. As a result, the Dawson machine would give the same answers as the Turing machine, and would also take exactly the same length of time to generate these answers.

However, the Dawson machine model of this Turing machine is intrinsically uninteresting. This is because computing time for the Dawson machine is not a tacit property. Instead, it is the result of an explicit instruction in the program. The time that the Turing machine takes to compute an answer should tell us something interesting about how the answer is being figured out (see below). The Dawson machine simulation ignores this and cheats by using "WAIT (z)" to provide a better fit to the behavioral data.

Varieties of Tacit Behavior

It seems reasonable to suppose that some of the regularities that can be observed by empirical cognitive scientists tell us something interesting about how information processing is being carried out, because these regularities are tacit consequences of this processing, and are not due to explicit instructions. For example, when people take longer to solve some problems than others, or when they make particular mistakes in solving a problem, it is sensible to think that this reflects something interesting in how they are solving the problem, and that this does not reflect the activity of explicit functions like "WAIT (z)" or "MAKE_MISTAKE_NOW ()" ! This section of the chapter briefly addresses two related questions. First, what general kinds of tacit behaviors might be measured by empirical cognitive scientists? Second, why might these behaviors tell us something interesting about the information processing that underlies these behaviors?

For Pylyshyn (1981), model validation requires establishing the strong equivalence of a computer model. So, before validation even begins, the model and the person being modeled are assumed to be computationally equivalent – they generate the same answers to the same questions. If the model is not strongly equivalent to the person, then it must be using a different set of procedures to generate the same answers. As a result, "there are differences between the processes in the human and in the machine which can be revealed by some types of observation, even though the two are indistinguishable with respect to other types of observation" (p. 86). From our perspective, if the two systems are not strongly equivalent, then their explicit behaviors will be the same, but their tacit behaviors will be different.

Pylyshyn (1981) argues that three general kinds of evidence can be used to test the strong equivalence of two systems: intermediate states, relative complexity, and component analysis. Each type of evidence involves measuring and comparing tacit behaviors of the system. In order to get a feel for these different kinds of observations, let us consider them in the context of a concrete example.

Children begin to learn early in elementary school how to add numbers together in their head. The Turing machine described in figure 2.2 is designed to add two integers together. Imagine that you are a practicing cognitive scientist, and that you are sometimes asked to review manuscripts before they are accepted for publication in academic journals. One day, a manuscript from a mad cognitive scientist lands on your desk. In this manuscript, this demented person claims that the figure 2.2 Turing machine is a strongly equivalent model of how children do mental addition. When you write your extremely negative review of this article, what kinds of evidence do you cite to indicate that this claim is wrong?

The first kind of evidence that you might cite is what Pylyshyn (1981) calls *intermediate state evidence*. This involves observations of the intermediate steps, and/or the intermediate states of knowledge, that the two systems pass through as they move from being given an addition problem to answering the problem. For the Turing machine model, one immediate source of intermediate state evidence would be what the machine does to its tape with each processing step. This is because the Turing machine does not sit idle in "thought," and then suddenly write down the correct answer to the question. Instead, it laboriously moves back and forth along the tape, all the while erasing existing information and replacing it with new symbols. (Note that the absence of such intermediate tape transitions would be excellent evidence that the Dawson machine descri-bed earlier is not a strongly equivalent model of this Turing machine.) For children who would be serving as subjects to compare the model to, inter-mediate states are not as easily accessible. However, one method that might provide some evidence about these intermediate states is protocol analysis, which was described above. We should expect that a thinking-aloud protocol would lead to a dramatically different view of how children do mental arithme-tic in comparison to the tape transitions that we record as the Turing machine processes.

A second type of evidence that you might cite in your negative review is what Pylyshyn (1981) calls *relative complexity evidence*. For any information-processing procedure, some of the problems that it is designed to solve might be harder than others. As was already noted, some problems will take longer (i.e., require more processing steps) than others on the adding Turing machine. This is because as the to-be-added integers become larger quantities, and because of their unary representation on the machine's tape, the machine's tape head will have to process many more tape cells before coming to an answer.

To collect relative complexity evidence, we could present a number of different addition problems to the Turing machine, and then rank order them in terms of the number of processing steps that each required. We could then present the same problems to a group of children, and rank order the difficulty they caused the children on the basis the reaction time taken to solve each problem. We would expect very different rank orderings for the two systems.

The only variable affecting processing difficulty for the Turing machine would be the length of the two integers when represented in a unary format. In contrast, because the children are assumed to use quite different operations on numbers represented in integer format, the time taken by the children would be unrelated to the unary properties of the digits. For example, Groen and Parkman (1972) found that the time taken for humans to do mental arithmetic depended on the size of the smaller digit! In addition, one would expect that the rank ordering would also reveal that problems that took longer to solve had multiple place values, required carrying quantities from one column of addition to the other, and so on.

Another kind of information that can provide relative complexity information is an analysis of the errors made by the two systems. One approach would be to rank order problem difficulty in terms of the number of errors that each problem produced in the two systems. Another, more detailed, approach would be to classify the nature of the errors that were made. On either of these accounts, we should find evidence that the Turing machine is not a strongly equivalent model of mental addition. First, under normal operating conditions, the Turing machine would never make a mistake, while we would assume that the children would. Second, the kinds of mistakes that the children are likely to make would be highly systematic – for instance, forgetting to carry quantities from one column to another, or forgetting some intermediate sum. In short, this would indicate that because the children were using a different method than the Turing machine, they would find different problems harder than would the simulation.

A third type of evidence that you could cite in your negative review is what Pylyshyn (1981) calls *componential analysis*. "If the problem can be resolved into a number of relatively independent subtasks, we can ask about how well the performance of each of these subtasks is modeled" (p. 89). In essence, componential analysis requires a researcher to functionally decompose a complex process, and then collect intermediate state and relative complexity evidence on specific components of this decomposition. This evidence is compared to the part of their functional model that implements these particular components.

The comparison of human and Turing machine addition using component analysis might focus on the subprocesses involved in reading parts of the addition problem after it has been represented. For instance, the "read" component of the Turing machine would involve the machine table instructions that are activated when the tape head reads a "1" . In contrast, the "read" component of human mental addition might reflect to a large extent processing of different columns; this time might increase dramatically as processing shifted from one column to another. Column-related changes in processing time would not be observed for the Turing machine (which does not use a columnar representation), which would again weigh against claims that these two systems were strongly equivalent.

More realistic examples require that the performance of part of a model be compared to human performance in which some component has been isolated for observation. In practice, this kind of isolation is very difficult to achieve, although it can be done. A good illustration of this is the use of nonsense stimuli by memory researchers. While this practice has often been maligned as having poor ecological validity (e.g., Miller, Galanter, & Pribram, 1960), it is typically intended to isolate aspects of memory that are insensitive to semantic content from those that are highly affected by it.

Many fine examples of using special stimuli to facilitate component analysis can also be found in the study of perception. For example, Sperry and Gazzaniga's (e.g., Gazzaniga, 1978) seminal work on split-brain patients relied on their ability to present stimuli to visual hemifields, so that visual information would be passed to only one cerebral hemisphere. Much of our modern understanding of motion perception has relied upon using stimuli that can isolate one motion perception system from another (e.g., Anstis, 1980; Petersik, 1989). Similarly, Julesz' (1971) important advances in the study of depth perception followed from his invention of the random-dot stereogram, which presents absolutely no depth information whatsoever to monocular systems, but provide pure measures of binocular processing.

Good Modelers Seek Surprises

To sum up the argument to this point, the Turing test can be supplemented by assuming that not all behaviors are created equal. Some behaviors are assumed to be due to explicit instructions in some mental program. Other behaviors are tacit; they emerge unintentionally from the nature of the program, as well as from the nature of the computer on which the program is being run. By measuring these tacit behaviors, empirical cognitive scientists can take important steps towards validating their functional models.

Now, the view that some behaviors are important indicators of the nature of underlying processing because they are tacit consequences of a running program has important implications for the computer modeling of cognitive phenomena. Some researchers have argued that computers can never surprise us, because the simulation would only do exactly what it was programmed to do (e.g., Lockhart, 1991; Reitman, 1965). However, experience has shown otherwise. In many cases, computer simulations produce unexpected behavior which in turn produce new insights into the phenomenon being studied (e.g., Lewandowsky, 1993 pp. 238–40). Accordingly, Lewandowsky cites the serendipity of discoveries from simulations as one of the advantages of computer modeling.

However, Pylyshyn's (1981) proposal that some behaviors can distinguish two systems even if the two systems are equivalent in other ways requires that a computer model necessarily offer surprises if it is to be considered valid. This is because tacit behavioral regularities cannot be captured by explicit program statements – they must be tacit properties of the simulation too! The mark of a good modeler would be to develop a functional description or simulation of some phenomenon of interest in which explicit instructions for generating behavioral regularities were kept to the minimum. One measure of the quality of the model would be the extent to which its tacit properties fit behavioral regularities that may not even have been considered or known when the original model was constructed. We can't "cheat" our way to validity by using kludges of the sort that the Dawson machine described earlier was guilty of.

Reprise: What is the Algorithmic Level?

A lot of material has been covered in this chapter in order to make a few very basic points about how cognitive scientists treat the algorithmic level. Let us take a moment to summarize this material:

1) A computational-level analysis is (by itself) too broad, and an implementational level analysis is (by itself) too specific to make interesting (and generalizable) claims about the nuts and bolts of cognitive processing. However, the algorithmic level seems just about right.

2) At the algorithmic level, the workings of a complex phenomenon are described as an organized system of functional components. Each of these components is described in terms of its role in the system; a physical account of how each component works is not provided at this level.

3) In order to describe a complex phenomenon as an organized system of functional subcomponents, a methodology called forward engineering or functional analysis is employed. When a cognitive scientist performs forward engineering, he or she decomposes the to-be-explained behavior (i.e., the computationally described system) into a sequence of (functional) subcomponents, some of which may themselves require later decomposition. Typically, this functional decomposition is motivated by empirical results. We reviewed two methodologies that can be used to aid in forward engineering: functional dissociation and protocol analysis. Connectionists are functionalists too, insofar as their architecture is viewed as a functional description of what neurons do, a description that glosses over many physical details. Connectionists are also required to generate algorithmic accounts for cognitive science. However, as they are more likely than not going to be creating a model without the aid of a analysis of behavior (because they practice synthetic psychology rather than analytic psychology), they are not forward engineers. Instead, they will use some technique to reverse engineer their network. Interestingly, though, techniques like the "wiretapping" method that was illustrated in this chapter have a strong analytic flavor to them. In certain respects, it might be fair to say that while classical cognitive scientists forward engineer their subjects to produce a model, connectionist cognitive scientists forward engineer (i.e., analyze) a network to explain their subjects.

4) For any given information-processing problem, there exists in principle an infinite number of different programs (i.e., functional decompositions) that could be used to solve it. As a result, once a researcher has proposed a particular model on the basis of forward engineering, he or she must then proceed to

collect evidence to show that this model is the correct one. For a cognitive scientist working at the algorithmic level, this requires the use of the Turing test supplemented by the assumption that some behavioral regularities are the tacit results of a program, and are not the result of explicit program instructions. Model validation requires comparing the tacit properties of a simulation to the (assumed) tacit behavioral regularities. We briefly considered three different kinds of evidence that could be obtained at the algorithmic level to do this: intermediate state evidence, relative complexity evidence, and componential analysis.

5) Because model validation at the algorithmic level requires paying special attention to tacit regularities, care must be taken in the construction of computer simulations. Specifically, what we assume to be systematic tacit behavior in our human subjects must also be realized as tacit behavior in our computer models. We can't simulate tacit behavior with explicit instructions if our goal is to build a strongly equivalent model.

There are two additional points to make before concluding the chapter.

First, the algorithmic level does not replace or obviate the need for a computational level of analysis. One reason for this is that the top-down view of functional analysis that has been described in this chapter requires that a computational account of a system has already been accomplished. In other words, the algorithmic level proceeds from the computational level. A second reason for this is that computational-level methodologies still let us make powerful claims about a system that cannot be made at the algorithmic level alone. For example, regardless of what functional model a researcher had come up with for solving an information-processing problem, it is still extremely useful to be able to prove that the system has (or does not have) certain limitations because of the kind of information processor it is, and not because of the steps that it takes. In the absence of a computational analysis, a researcher would have to run countless (and fruitless) simulations to empirically demonstrate that a model could not do certain things. The power of keeping the computational level is avoiding this messy and incomplete approach.

Second, as they have been described to this point, even a combination of the computational level and the algorithmic level cannot constitute a complete cognitive science. While this chapter has given a fair treatment to how empirical methodologies are related to functional analysis and model validation at the algorithmic level, it has carefully avoided one crucial issue: How does a classical cognitive scientist know when to stop his or her functional decomposition? For a connectionist, the same kind of question might be phrased in a different way: How does a connectionist know that their network building blocks are the right components for cognitive modeling?

The next chapter is devoted to this issue, because it is critical for cognitive science. Without having some principles for deciding that further functional decomposition is both unnecessary and impossible, cognitivists are incapable with providing explanations with foundations firm enough to satisfy behaviorists and positivistically minded philosophers of science. Furthermore, the properties of a completed functional decomposition have to include some appeal to natural, physical laws in order for cognitive scientists to have a coherent account of causation in their functional theories. The next chapter shows that cognitive scientists can have something interesting to say about causation in their theories – and also shows that many of the family squabbles within cognitive science have to do with deciding when forward engineering has been successfully completed.

6

The Functional Architecture

One of my favorite horror stories is H. P. Lovecraft's (1963) "The Dreams in the Witch-House." Its protagonist, the doomed Walter Gilman, uncovers intriguing links between mathematics and the magic of the Salem witches. For example, he learns that at her 1692 trial old Keziah Mason "told Judge Hathorne of lines and curves that could be made to point out directions leading through the walls of space to other spaces and beyond ... Then she had drawn those devices on the walls of her cell and vanished" (p. 297). Eventually, Gilman's tinkering with equations leads to his own gruesome death in another dimension. To truly enjoy this story, the reader must believe that the mere writing of mathematical equations can result in tangible, physical consequences. Once reality is suspended in this way, Lovecraft can terrify us with the view that a little mathematical knowledge is a very dangerous thing.

There is something dangerous about cognitive science as it has been described to this point in the book. I have been emphasizing the "cognitive" part of the discipline, focusing upon computational and algorithmic descriptions of mental phenomena. However, we haven't really considered in detail its "science," in spite of the fact that we have seen numerous examples of empirical research within cognitive science. My account of cognitive science has, to this point, begged the reader to suspend reality in exactly the same way as the Lovecraft story described above. In short, the preceding chapters have asked to reader to believe that abstract, nonphysical descriptions can be viewed as having causal consequences. If cognitive scientists don't attempt to ground their functional theories in physical principles, then these theories will have no more scientific import than dreams in the witch-house.

The purpose of this chapter is to introduce a level of analysis that serves as the bridge between algorithmic and implementational descriptions. This level, called the *functional architecture*, is required to tie the *functional* theories of cognitivism to the *physical*. One way to think about the functional architecture is that it is the fundamental programming language used to write the cognitive algorithms that were of interest to us last chapter. This programming language is fundamental in the sense that it must be built right into the cognitive computer. In other words, when we want to explain how complex cognitive algorithms work, all we need to do is to analyze them into their functional subcomponents, which will eventually bring us down to the level of the functional architecture. However, when we want to explain how a component of the functional architecture works, we are going to have to describe how it is built right into the machine!

This chapter proceeds as follows: First, I will introduce a deep problem, called Ryle's Regress, that is intrinsic to forward engineering of the type that was described in the previous chapter. Second, I will describe a basic strategy that classical cognitive scientists use to solve this problem. Third, I will consider the implications of this solution to classical cognitive science. Fourth, I will examine the role of the functional architecture in connectionist cognitive science. I will argue that even though connectionists are not forward engineers, they too have to pay strict attention to the properties of the functional architecture.

Part I   Escaping Ryle's Regress

Ryle's Regress

The work of Edward Tolman predated full-blown cognitive science by approximately three decades, but was important in blazing the trail that pioneering cognitivists would themselves follow. On the one hand, Tolman studied learning in animals, and kept rigidly to the methodology of behaviorism. On the other hand, Tolman recognized that the status quo vocabulary of behaviorism was not rich enough to account for the complex behavior that he was observing in the rats that he studied. As a result, Tolman found that he had to use theoretical terms that modern cognitive scientists would be very comfortable with (e.g., Tolman, 1932, 1948). For instance, Tolman suggested that his rats were constructing a "cognitive map" that helped them locate reinforcers, and he used intentional terms (e.g., expectancies, purposes, meanings) to describe their behavior. Furthermore, Tolman abandoned hard-line behaviorism by proposing that additional (and not directly observable) variables must intervene between overt stimuli and overt responses.

This last maneuver earned Tolman the wrath of his peers. For instance, consider this famous criticism of Tolman's work by Guthrie (1935, p. 172): "Signs, in Tolman's theory, occasion in the rat realization, or cognition, or judgment, or hypotheses, or abstraction, but they do not occasion action. In his concern with what goes on in the rat's mind, Tolman has neglected to predict what the rat will do. So far as the theory is concerned the rat is left buried in thought; if he gets to the food-box at the end that is his concern, not the concern of the theory." In other words, Guthrie found the same fault with Tolman that an unbelieving fiction reader would find with Lovecraft: formal or cognitive terms are bereft of physical causation. As a result, they do not provide adequate explanations. The philosophical underpinnings of this view can be attributed to the work of Gilbert Ryle (1949).

Ryle (1949) aimed a concerted attack against what he called the "intellectualist legend," which required intelligent acts to be the product of the conscious application of mental rules or criteria. Ryle argued that the intellectualist legend results in intelligent agents which, like Tolman's rats, are trapped in an infinite regress of thought: "According to the legend, whenever an agent does anything intelligently, his act is preceded and steered by another internal act of considering a regulative proposition appropriate to his practical problem. . . . Must we then say that for the hero's reflections how to act to be intelligent he must first reflect how best to reflect how to act?" (p. 31). Following Stillings *et al.* (1987), we will call this *Ryle's Regress*.

The problem, then, with using cognitive or functional terms to explain intelligent phenomena is that these terms assume some intelligence on their own behalf, which in turn must be explained. According to Ryle, this would lead into an infinite recursion of appeals to intelligence to account for intelligence. As far as functional analysis or forward engineering goes, Ryle's regress amounts to an infinite proliferation of unexplained functional subcomponents.

We can begin to appreciate Ryle's Regress by casting it into one of its equivalent forms, called the *homunculus problem* (for modern accounts of this problem and how it affects cognitive science, see Edelman, 1988, 1992). The homunculus problem arises when the processes used to explain a behavior are no less intelligent than the behavior itself. Imagine that one of my students tells me that they are from Crossfield, Alberta, and then asks me whether I know where in the province that is. One approach that I might take to answer this question would be to create a mental image of an Alberta map, scan this map with my "mind's eye," and "see" whether or not I can find Crossfield. Now, the issue becomes this: how does my "mind's eye" work?

A philosopher trying to illustrate the homunculus problem would suggest that it is as if in my mind there is a little man (hence the name of the problem) whose eyes serve as my "mind's eye." He can scan the image, find Crossfield on the map, and then answer my question (perhaps by whispering into my "mind's ear"). But the philosopher could then press the point further. How does the little man in my head see the map? Does he have his own "mind's eye" ? If so, then would he not too require another, tinier man in his head? Would not this second homunculus require a third to interpret the map? As you can see, by assuming something like a "mind's eye," one can get trapped into an infinite proliferation of tiny homunculi, each requiring another to interpret its mental images (see figure 6.1).

Unfortunately, unconstrained forward engineering leads into exactly the same problem. For instance, imagine that at the start of forward engineering, classical cognitive scientists wish to explain some mental phenomenon A. Now, the first pass at functional decomposition might result in researchers talking

Figure 6.1 The homunculus problem. When I claim that I scan the map of Alberta with my mind's eye, do I condemn myself to an infinity of little men within my mind?

about functions B and C instead of phenomenon A. However, B and C will not be any less mental (or more physical) than A: as an example, the terms "primary memory" and "secondary memory" are no more physical than the "memory" phenomenon from whence they were derived.

Now, because B and C are functional constructs, they themselves will require explanation (otherwise, we are back dreaming in the Witch-house!). It would be perfectly legitimate to apply forward engineering to each of these functions in turn. As a result, perhaps B could be decomposed into function D and E, and perhaps C could be decomposed into functions F, G, and H. However, each of these is a functional term too, begging for additional forward engineering. It would appear that functional analysis leads us directly into Ryle's Regress; each function that we propose to explain an earlier black box will rear its head as an ugly homunculus. We wind up with an infinite proliferation of unexplained functional terms.

"There is a concept which corrupts and upsets all others. I refer not to Evil, whose limited realm is that of ethics; I refer to the infinite" (Borges, 1962, p. 202). The philosophical argument of Ryle (1949), echoed by legions of behaviorist researchers in psychology, was that the infinite regresses that we have been describing above prevent cognitive terms from explaining behavioral regularities. Now, nearly 50 years after Ryle's landmark book, cognitivism is ascendant; the age of the behaviorists who adopted Ryle's position has, like the age of the dinosaurs, come and gone. Does this mean there was some intrinsic flaw in Ryle's argument against the intellectualist legend? I think not. Rather, classical cognitive scientists took strong measures to ensure that their functionalist theories can escape Ryle's infinite regress.

These strong measures include three general points. First, forward engineering must be constrained in such a way that each functional decomposition moves a researcher towards simpler functions. Second, classical cognitive scientists must have some principled reasons (as well as some empirical support) for claiming that a functional decomposition can stop. These principled reasons must argue not that further functional decomposition is unnecessary, nor that it is inconvenient, but rather that further functional decomposition is impossible. Third, a researcher must be able to say how the set of functions that exist at the end of forward engineering can be physically implemented. It is only with this third claim that a classical cognitive scientist can abolish the ghost from the machine.

The Functional Architecture

In very general terms, how does a computing device work? To answer this question, let us turn back to the Universal Turing Machine that we considered in chapter 2. Recall that for this machine, the symbols on the tape are divided into two qualitatively different classes. Some of these symbols represent the data that the UTM is to manipulate. The other symbols represent a program – a description of the specific Turing machine that the UTM is to emulate. So, in essence the UTM moves back and forth between these two types of symbols on the tape; reading a data symbol and then looking up how the emulated Turing machine would behave when presented that symbol.

Now, in describing or explaining this UTM at the algorithmic level, we noted in chapter 2 that there were two different approaches that could be taken. The *programming* description provides an account of the program that the UTM is running; namely, an account of the program on the data tape. In contrast, the *architectural description* is an account of a quite different, but extremely important, set of machine instructions: the machine table that defines the UTM. In chapter 2, we made very little of this distinction. The time has come to rectify this, because cognitive scientists can avoid Ryle's Regress by moving from a programming description of the system that they are interested in to an account that is analogous to the architectural description. Let us begin by considering important differences between the programming and the architectural descriptions.

First, changes to the program written on the tape are accomplished in quite a different manner than are changes to the program in the machine table. The programming description can simply be changed by writing new symbols on the tape. There is nothing special about these symbols as far as the UTM is concerned; to it, they are merely a set of data to be manipulated in accordance with the machine table instructions. However, the architectural description is not so easily changed. While it might look from figure 2.4 as if all that is required is writing a new set of symbols into the machine table, this is misleading. If the UTM were actually working, then it would be a physical device; the machine table simply describes some very basic behaviors of this device. In order to change these behaviors, one would actually have to go and change the physical structure of the machine head. In other words, while changing the programming description is a software problem, changing the architectural description is a hardware problem.

Second, the effects of changes in the programming description are quite different than the effects of changes in the architectural description. Let us assume that we replace one working program (which describes how to compute the function $f(x)$) on the data tape with another (which describes how to compute the function $g(x)$). This will cause us to change the description of the UTM's behavior, but it will not cause us to change the description of the UTM itself. We will change from saying "UTM A is computing $f(x)$" to saying "UTM A is computing $g(x)$," but we will still be talking about the same machine (i.e., UTM A). In contrast, if we proceed to physically alter the tape head in order to produce changes in the machine table, then we have to talk about a different device altogether. This is because we will be changing UTM A from one machine into another, different machine. If we are careful, it will be another UTM (e.g., UTM B). However, with careless changes to the machine table, we are likely to wind up with a new Turing machine that is not universal, and possibly a machine that won't do any useful computing for us at all.

Third, related to this point above, there is a striking asymmetry between the dependencies of the two descriptions on one another. Specifically, arbitrary changes to the programming description won't affect the ability of the machine table to process the data tape. The worst that can happen is that these arbitrary changes produce a nonsense program, or throw the machine head into an infinite loop. In short, the operations of the machine table do not depend upon the program written on the data tape. However, the reverse is not true. If we want to write a program for computing a specific function, then we must pay careful attention to the operations that are defined in the machine table. This is because for the machine to correctly compute the function, the algorithmic steps that we write on the data tape must be translated into a set of algorithmic steps that can be carried out by the machine – that is, a set of steps that represent successful operations as defined in the machine table. We can't just write any program on the data tape; we have to write one that will be successfully interpreted by the particular UTM that we are writing for. And if someone gives us a different UTM, then we are going to have to go back and rewrite our programs.

Fourth, if someone asked us to explain how our programming description actually works, then we would come up with a very different story than we would if asked to explain how our architectural description really works. To explain the programming description, we would likely talk about how the machine head moves back and forth between our program, the scratchpad, and the remaining data on the tape, all the while performing operations on the data that would be performed had our program been built directly into a tape head. In other words, to explain our programming account, we would functionally decompose it into an account of machine table operations! In contrast, our explanation of how each machine table instruction actually worked would not involve a decomposition into another functional account. Instead, we would probably move to a physical description of how the machine table instructions are actually built into the (physical) machine head.

We can summarize these observations as follows: for any information processor that works, and that physically exists, there will be a special set of functions that we will call *primitives*. Any program running on this information processor can be functionally decomposed into an algorithm in which every step involves calling one of these primitive operations. Indeed, this description would be a very plausible explanation of how the program works. However, explaining how each primitive works would not involve further functional decomposition. This is because the explanation of a primitive must be an account of how that operation is physically built into the information processor.

The set of all primitives for a particular information processor is called the *functional architecture*. Ultimately, any program running on an information processor can be completely described in terms of components from the functional architecture. "Specifying the functional architecture of a system is like providing a manual that defines some programming language. Indeed, defining a programming language is equivalent to specifying the functional architecture of a virtual machine" (Pylyshyn, 1984, p. 92). In other words, if we were to specify the functional architecture for human cognition, we would be providing an account of the mental programming language in which cognitive algorithms are written. This mental programming language would be analogous to the architectural description of a UTM, in the sense that the mental programming language would be built directly into the brain.

A component of the functional architecture has an interesting dual nature (see also Haugeland, 1985). On the one hand, it is an operation that has a symbolic, functional, or algorithmic role – complex programs can be created by stringing architectural operations together. From this perspective, the entities that comprise the functional architecture belong to the algorithmic level of analysis. On the other hand, an operation that is part of the functional architecture also has a physical description; as a matter of fact, to explain the operation, one must talk about its physical properties. "Being instantiated in the functional architecture merely means being explainable without appeal to principles and properties at the symbolic or the semantic level" (Pylyshyn, 1984, p. 132). Because architectural components are *both* algorithmic and implementational, I prefer to think of them as a bridge between algorithmic and implementational descriptions.

It is this last point that makes the information-processing assumption so enticing to cognitive scientists. Often times a computer programmer will describe their work at either the computational level (i.e., will describe what their program is computing) or at the algorithmic level (i.e., will describe the general steps executed by the program to solve the problem). However, a behaviorist would never be able to trap the programmer in Ryle's Regress. Computers are artifacts that we understand very well; it is this understanding that permits us to build them. The computer programmer is aware that at some level, his or her program is translated into a set of primitive statements that are carried out by physical operations of the computer. There is no ghost remaining in this machine.

Classical cognitive scientists want to take their functional theories of mental phenomena along exactly the same route. In order to stop Ryle's Regress, a classical cognitive scientist needs to decompose his or her functional theories in such a way that the only functions at the bottom of the decomposition are components of the functional architecture of cognition. When this is achieved, Ryle's infinite regress is avoided. This is because an explanation of these last functions does not require a further functional decomposition. Instead, it requires a detailed physical account of how these functions are actually carried out by a physical device; this account would be the goal of an implementational-level analysis. "Theories of human cognition are ultimately theories of physical, biological systems" (Newell, 1990, p. 42). *Cognitive science strives towards explanations by trying to identify the functional architecture!*

Functional Analysis and Functional Architecture

The sections above have suggested one way, in principle, for a functional theory to escape Ryle's Regress: decompose the theory into an organized set of components that belong to the functional architecture. What kind of method-ology can we practice that will take us from a computational account of a system to an algorithmic account grounded in the functional architecture? The general answer to this question is simply this: forward engineering of the type that was introduced in the previous chapter is a procedure that, if done properly, can save us from the homunculus problem. However, to borrow a phrase from G. K. Chesterton, like fire or the sea this is too simple to be trusted. Not surprisingly, the qualifier "done properly" needs elaboration.

Let us start by recalling the basic properties of functional analysis of the type detailed by Cummins (1975, 1983). The first step is to specify the function that the to-be-analyzed system is computing. In the previous chapter, it was argued that this step is equivalent to a computational analysis of a phenomenon of interest. The second step is what Cummins calls the analytic strategy. With this step, a researcher takes the specified function, and analyses it or decomposes it into an organized set of subfunctions. The analytic strategy can be performed iteratively; that is, we can take each of the subfunctions and decompose them into organized sets of sub-subfunctions. We are trapped in Ryle's Regress if we cannot stop the iterative application of the analytic strategy.

Cummins (1983) is fully aware of Ryle's regress. As a result, he notes that functional analysis as described in the previous paragraph (as well as the previous chapter) is not complete. "Analysis of the disposition (or any other property) is only a first step; instantiation is the second" (p. 31). What is meant here by instantiation?

To appreciate Cummins' (1983) notion of instantiation, two preliminary points must be made. First, Cummins notes that the most common explanatory move in science is an appeal to a causal law. A causal law (or a transition law) explains the transition from one physical state to another physical state; it "explains an effect by citing its cause" (p. 4). Second, Cummins views functional analysis as the decomposition of a special kind of property, called a disposition. A disposition is a regularity in which particular behaviors are exhibited under appropriate contexts. As a result, dispositions or functions imply transitions – the regularity is exhibited in some contexts, but not in others; "we have cause and effect, hence state transition" (p. 21). (For a related view, see Newell's (1990, ch. 2) general notion of how a machine performing a function relates to cognitive science.)

Given these points, instantiation can now be defined as follows: a function in a functional analysis is instantiated when one can cite a transition law that explains the input/output regularities of that function. Cummins (1975, 1983) calls this *causal subsumption*, and calls seeking such explanations of functions the *subsumption strategy*. This means that a complete functional analysis requires 1) the definition of a to-be-explained system function; 2) the decomposition of this function into an organized set of subfunctions via the iterative application of the analytic strategy; and 3) the end of this decomposition by successfully applying the subsumption strategy to the "bottom set" of functions proposed via the analytic strategy. "A functional analysis is complete when the program specifying it is explicable via instantiation – i.e., when we can show how the program is executed by the system whose capacities are being explained" (Cummins, 1983, p. 35). This is illustrated in figure 6.2.

In order for a functional analysis to be successfully completed, two general methodological points must be constantly kept in mind by a cognitive scientist. One is this: with each application of the analytic strategy, any new subfunctions that have been proposed should be simpler than the functions from which they were derived. This stands to reason from two different perspectives. First, if we believe, in accordance with the information-processing assumption, that the to-be-explained function is carried out by an algorithm built from component functions of the architecture, then it stands to reason that each of these component functions is less complicated and less powerful that the function that emerges from the program. Whether the whole is greater than or equal to the sum of its parts, it is still greater than each of the parts taken in isolation! Second, if the end of a functional analysis is a set of transition laws, the fact that we are carrying out a functional analysis in the first place suggests that we can't come up with a transition law for the to-be-explained function itself. (Otherwise, we would simply cite this transition law, and not require the functional analysis at all.) The whole point of the functional analysis is to carve up a complicated function into parts that are simple enough for us to discover their transition laws.

The second general methodological point that a classical cognitive scientist should keep in mind is this: whenever a subfunction is proposed in a functional decomposition, it should be asked whether this subfunction could be causally subsumed. One reason for this, of course, is that the application of the

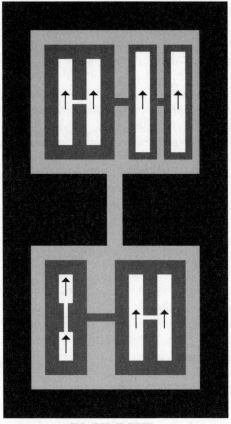

INPUT

Figure 6.2 Causal subsumption of a functional analysis. The big black box represents a to-be-explained input/output function. The first analysis decomposes it into two subfunctions (gray boxes). The second decomposition of these produces five sub-subfunctions (small dark boxes). The third analysis decomposes three of these five into two additional sub-sub-subfunctions; the other two resist decomposition (white boxes). The arrows in the white boxes represent transformation laws that explain how these functions can be instantiated in hardware.

subsumption strategy is the ultimate goal of a functional analysis. If we can support the claim that we have arrived at the functional architecture, then we can conclude that we have successfully explained a phenomenon of interest. Another reason to constantly question whether functions can be causally subsumed is a bit darker: there is always a danger that our functional decomposition is fundamentally wrong. It is often the case in cognitive psychology that there are two qualitatively different functional accounts of a mental phenomenon. These accounts represent competing theories, and are typically the source of heated debates in the literature. Imagine that, as far as functional decomposition is concerned, two different functional accounts are equally consistent with the empirical data. If this were the case, then there would be no way to decide which of the two theories was valid. However, if in addition we could show that the "bottom level" functions in one theory could be causally subsumed, but that this was not the case for the other theory, then we would have excellent reason for preferring the former. This is because the former theory would represent a functional explanation of the phenomenon, while the latter theory would merely be a functional description.

Subsumption: An Example

The reader might agree that the subsumption of a functional analysis sounds very nice in principle, but might also argue that it is impossible in practice. To allay these kinds of suspicions, let us consider one example of a subsumed functional analysis in psychology: the trichromatic theory of color vision.

In 1666, Sir Isaac Newton avoided the London plague by moving to Cambridge. There, for a few months, Newton performed all of his experiments with prisms and light that he would later publish in his book *Opticks*. One of Newton's major findings was that sunlight, when passed through a prism, is refracted into the full spectrum of the rainbow. A second major finding was that when this spectrum was brought into convergence by another lens, white light was again produced. A third major finding concerned laws governing the mixing of different components of the spectrum (for a detailed history, see Wasserman, 1978). Newton proposed that color vision was based upon the perception of seven primary colors (i.e., red, orange, yellow, green, blue, indigo, and violet). He argued that any other perceived color could be described as a weighted combination of these seven primary colors. He formalized this in his "barocentric" model of color vision. The barocentric model was a color disk; any point on the surface of this disk could be described as a weighted combination of the seven primary colors.

As far as color vision is concerned, Newton's seminal discovery was that some colors could be described as being constructed from combinations of others. His specific theory of color vision "was only a first approximation, and he did not take his own ideas as seriously as he might have" (Wasserman, 1978, p. 19). Consistent with this view, alternative accounts arose. For example, the poet Goethe was an ardent critic of Newton's theory, and proposed his own model in 1810, a two-color theory based on yellow and blue. Thomas Young proposed a trichromatic theory in 1801, and revised this theory in 1802; Helmholtz performed an important revision of Young's theory in 1852. Four-color theories were proposed by Hering in 1874 and by Ladd-Franklin in 1893.

It seems that one of the open questions with respect to Newton's theory was this: what is the minimum number of primary colors required in principle for a

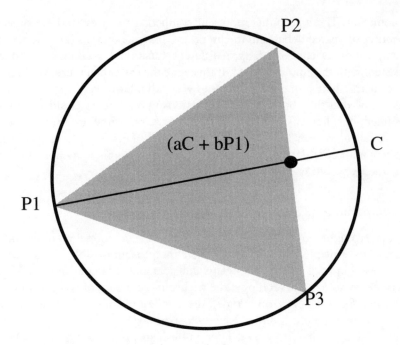

Figure 6.3 Maxwell's computational proof of trichromacy. The circle is Newton's baro-centric model; any point on its circumference is a pure color. Any point within the circle is a combination of colors. See the text for an explanation of Maxwell's proof.

complete theory of human color perception? The definitive answer to this question was provided in 1856 by the physicist James Clerk Maxwell in the form of a lovely computational proof (for more details, see Wasserman, 1978, pp. 31–5). Maxwell started with Newton's barocentric model, upon which he inscribed a triangle. Each vertex of the triangle represented a particular (pure) color; these are represented in figure 6.3 as the points P1, P2, and P3. Maxwell chose this triangular depiction to guarantee that the three colors were primary, in the sense that one of the colors could not be created by mixing the other two. This is because in Newton's model, linear combinations of two colors are represented as points on the straight line drawn between the points representing the two colors being mixed. The noncollinearity of the three vertices of a triangle therefore ensures that the three colors are primary.

Maxwell's next move was to choose a fourth point on the edge of the color disk, which is represented as point C in figure 6.3. This point stands for some other (nonprimary) color. Now, mixes of color C and primary color P1 lie on the line joining these two points. There is some point on this line – which we can call (aC + bP1), where a and b are two "weights" specifying how much of each color are being combined – which intersects the line connecting P2 and P3. Importantly, this second line represents all of the mixes of primary colors P2 and P3. This means that there must be some combination of P2 and P3 – let us call it (cP2 + dP3) – that produces exactly the same color as can be produced by a specific mix of colors C and P1. In short, by proving that there exist some constants a, b, c, and d for which aC + bP1 = cP2 + P3, Maxwell was able to show that any perceived color could be expressed in a relationship involving no more than three primary colors. This expresses the computational foundations of what we now call the trichromatic theory of human color perception.

Wasserman (1978, p. 37) observes that the trichromatic theory of color vision "should really be called the Newton–Maxwell theory because Newton provided the initial ideas (the barocentric rules and the first empirical observations) and then Maxwell provided the imaginary primary concept that yielded a workable approach to color vision." However, most students of perceptual psychology call the trichromatic theory the Young–Helmholtz theory. This is likely because Helmholtz was a physiologist who was popularizing the trichromatic theory in biological terms at a period in which the behavioral sciences were breaking away from physics.

In lectures given in 1873, Helmholtz presented Young's trichromatic theory as follows: "Dr Young supposes that there are in the eye three kinds of nerve-fibers, the first of which, when irritated in any way, produces the sensation of red, the second the sensation of green, and the third that of violet. He further assumes that the first are excited most strongly by the waves of ether of greatest length; the second, which are sensitive to green light, by the waves of middle length; while those which convey impressions of violet are acted upon only by the shortest vibrations of ether. ... Just as the difference of sensation of light and warmth depends demonstrably upon whether the rays of the sun fall upon nerves of sight or nerves of feeling, so it is supposed in Young's hypothesis that the difference of sensation of colors depends simply upon whether one or the other kind of nervous fibers are more strongly affected. When all three kinds are equally excited, the result is the sensation of white light" (Helmholtz, 1968, p. 95).

Helmholtz's important refinement to this theory was the added assumption that these three channels had overlapping color sensitivities. "Actual colored light does not produce sensations of absolutely pure color; that red, for instance, even when completely freed from all admixture of white light, still does not excite those nervous fibers which alone are sensitive to impressions of red, but also, to a very slight degree, those which are sensitive to green, and perhaps to a still smaller extent those which are sensitive to violet rays" (1968, p. 97). This added assumption provided an account of some failed experiments in which some spectral color could not be precisely matched by mixing the three primary colors in the Young–Helmholtz theory.

Let us now take a moment to consider the Young–Helmholtz theory in the context of the current chapter. In spite of all of this talk about "nerve fibers," the model that Helmholtz was so successfully championing was functional, not physical. Helmholtz himself was painfully aware of this in 1873: "It must be confessed that both in men and in quadrupeds we have at present no anatomical

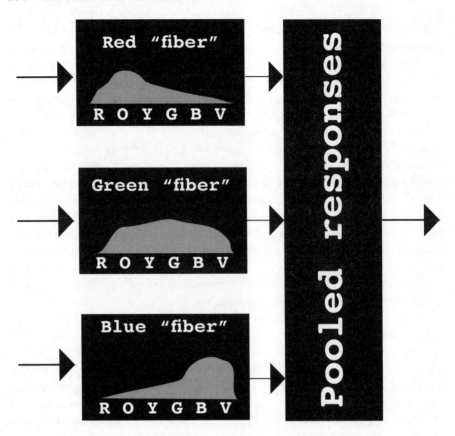

Figure 6.4 Black box depiction of the Young–Helmholtz theory. The sensitivity of each "fiber" to the various colors of light are shown in gray; these sensitivities were proposed by Helmholtz in 1860, and are adapted from Boring (1942, p. 200).

basis for this theory of colors" (Helmholtz, 1968, p. 95). The black-box version of the trichromatic theory is depicted in figure 6.4.

Given that this theory was not causally subsumed, then why was it so widely accepted? The major reason was that it provided a very elegant account of a variety of color vision phenomena. Since Le Blon's introduction of "printing paintings" in 1719, it was well known that one could produce a multitude of colors using trichromatic techniques (Mollon, 1982). More precise color mixing experiments performed by the likes of Helmholtz and Maxwell moored this general knowledge on firm theoretical and empirical foundations. Furthermore, the theory provided an account of why observers could judge that some colors were not primary. Finally, the theory could account for color blindness, which at Young's time was known as "Daltonism" because it afflicted the chemist John Dalton. Daltonism would result when one of the functional components of the system was absent.

Causal subsumption of the Young–Helmholtz theory had to wait for a century of methodological advances in neuroscience. As the reader is almost certainly aware, we now know that the "nerve fibers" hypothesized by Young and Helmholtz are more properly thought of as cone receptor cells in the retina. There are three different types of cones; each type contains a different photopigment. A technique called microspectrophotometry, in which a small beam of light is passed through individual receptors that have been dissected from a retina, has revealed that each photopigment is sensitive to (i.e., tends to absorb) different wavelengths or colors of light. For human cones, one pigment has peak absorption of light that is around 420 nm (blue); another has peak absorption at around 530 nm (green); the third has peak absorption around 560 nm (red) (e.g., Dartnall, Bowmaker, & Molino, 1983). These results have been replicated with a methodology that measures changes in action potentials of single receptors using suction electrodes (e.g., Schnapf, Nunn, Meister, & Baylor, 1990). Both types of methodologies have confirmed Helmholtz's hypothesis of overlapping sensitivities. Finally, at a biochemical level there is a reasonable understanding of how physical changes in the shape of a pigment molecule, induced by the absorption of light, can produce an action potential in a retinal receptor cell (e.g., Nicholls, Martin, & Wallace, 1992, pp. 567–82).

To summarize, a combination of theoretical analyses by Newton and Maxwell – analogous to computational-level analyses – indicated that human color vision could be accounted for in principle by a theory in which compound colors were built by mixing different amounts of three primaries. Empirical evidence – of the type familiar to researchers working at the algorithmic level – that included the results of color mixing experiments, known techniques for producing color prints, and observations of Daltonism, was used to support a functional model of color perception, the Young–Helmholtz theory, in which primitive red, green, and blue detectors mediated the perception of all other colors. Recent results from neuroscience have shown how the functional components of this model can be subsumed under causal laws of brain function: each channel in the Young–Helmholtz theory is instantiated as a cone receptor that is most sensitive to particular wavelengths of light (and signals this sensitivity as an action potential) because of the biochemical properties of a photopigment contained within the cell.

Multiple Levels are Still Necessary

Subsuming a functional analysis is not the same as reducing it to physical principles. Cognitive scientists who adopt forward engineering are materialists – they want to plant their theories firmly in physical principles – but they do not believe that once this is done they can throw away the computational and algorithmic analyses that we have discussed in previous chapters.

To understand why this is so, remember that an architectural description of an information processor will tell us what kind of machine it is, but it will not tell us what the machine is doing. A particular Universal Turing Machine will have a set architecture, as defined by its machine table. However, this one architecture can be used to do many different things. So, if we only know what the architecture is, then we will have an incomplete understanding of the machine. To know what specific problem the machine is solving, we will still require our computational analysis. To know how this machine is solving the problem, we will need our programming description. So, once we subsume the functional analysis, we still have to keep in mind all of the other results that we have obtained at higher levels of analysis!

To elaborate this point, think back to the trichromatic theory of color perception that was just described. Many of the fundamentally important aspects of this theory are rooted in functional accounts from the computational and algorithmic levels of analysis. For instance, if a neuroscientist was to throw away these accounts after identifying the color-sensitive pigments in the retina, he or she would be unable to answer questions like "Why are there only these three pigments?" Furthermore, merely identifying cells with different pigments doesn't point to the crucial fact that responses from these cells have to be integrated in some way to represent a spectral color. Finally, a scientific vocabulary at the implementational level (i.e., neuroscience) will simply not include words like "color," "red," "blue," or "green" – implementational words will talk about the chemicals that cells contain, but will not deal with the functions that these chemicals are actually subsuming.

Part II   Functional Architecture and Classical Theory

The sections above have described a problem that functional theories face before being viewed as explanations, and have described an approach for overcoming this problem. In this part of the chapter, we consider some additional implications of requiring that a functional analysis be "bottomed out" in a functional architecture. We now turn to consider how claims about the functional architecture can have important empirical consequences for classical cognitive scientists who are attempting to account for behavioral regularities.

Architectures for Cognition

The functional architecture is the primitive programming language – the basic set of operations available to an information processor. What is meant by the phrase "basic set of operations?" From the chapter 2 discussion of Turing machines, we know that the essence of information processing is symbol manipulation. Furthermore, our acquaintance with Turing machines suggests that "symbol manipulation" involves the discussion of two separate, physical entities: structure (i.e., the nature of the symbols being manipulated, as represented by the Turing machine's tape) and process (i.e., the legal rules for processing the symbols, as represented by the Turing machine's tape head). So, if one were to characterize the nature of the symbols that an information processor could manipulate, as well as the nature of the specific operations available to manipulate these symbols, then one would have taken large strides towards a complete specification of the architecture.

However, if one were to build an information processor from scratch, one could not specify structure and processes arbitrarily. This is because the physical nature of symbols determines the kinds of processes that can be easily applied to them. This in turn has a large impact on the tacit behavioral regularities of the system, because operations that can be applied easily are likely to be performed quickly and without error; operations that cannot be applied easily are likely to require that a more complex algorithm be employed.

For example, pretend that I am about to begin to write a final exam in a university course. The exam proctor waits until the digital clock in the room displays "9:00" , and then turns over a two-hour hourglass. Both the digital clock and the hourglass can be described as "dynamic symbols" that are both representing the same content: the passing of time during the writing of the exam. However, because these two symbols are of different formats, they permit different kinds of operations to be easily applied, and as a result permit different questions to be answered quickly. The digital clock is very well suited for me to answer the question "What time is it now?" by applying a "look up" operation: by reading the digits on the clock, I will know the current time. However, it is not as well suited for me to answer the question "How much time is left in the exam?" , because this requires more than a simple look up – I have to remember that the exam is supposed to end at 11:00, and then proceed to subtract the current time from this to get my answer. In contrast, the hourglass is very well suited for me to answer the question "How much time is left in the exam?" ; all I need to do is look at how much sand is in its top. However, it is much more complicated to use this device to tell the current time – I would have to know the time at which the hourglass was turned, the rate of flow of its sand from top to bottom, the amount of sand that had accumulated in its bottom portion, and then perform the relevant computation.

The point of this example is to demonstrate that one can take the same kind of information and represent it in different symbolic formats. The choice of symbolic format determines the kinds of operations or manipulations that can be easily applied, and as a result determines which information-processing tasks can be performed quickly, and which tasks will take longer. The characteristics of the functional architecture thus have important influence over the tacit behavioral regularities of an information-processing system.

Cognitive scientists have been aware of this for a long time. After observing the behavior of the systems that they wish to explain, they become aware that certain tasks are easily performed, while others are not (e.g., they take longer, or produce more errors). Often times they attempt to explain differences in task difficulty by treating this as a tacit behavioral regularity that is a direct result of

Example Architecture	Representative Publication
brainstate-in-a-box	Anderson, Silverstein, Ritz, & Jones (1977)
Boltzman machine	Ackley, Hinton, & Sejnowski (1985)
CHARM	Eich (1982)
conceptual structure	Jackendoff (1983)
dual-coding theory	Paivio (1971)
feature maps	Treisman & Gelade (1980)
frames	Minsky (1975)
full primal sketch	Marr (1982)
geons	Biederman (1987)
generalized cylinders	Marr (1982)
Hopfield net	Hopfield (1982)
mental images	Kosslyn (1980) Shepard & Cooper (1982)
levels of processing	Craik & Lockhart (1972)
mental models	Johnson-Laird (1983)
metric spaces	Tourangeau & Sternberg (1981)
multilayer perceptron	Rumelhart, Hinton, & Williams (1986a)
production system	Newell & Simon (1972) Anderson (1983)
propositions	Pylyshyn (1973)
prototypes	Rosch & Mervis (1975)
scripts	Schank & Abelson (1977)
semantic features	Rips, Shoben, & Smith (1973)Tversky (1977)
semantic networks	Collins & Quillian (1969)
textons	Julesz (1981)
transformational grammar	Chomsky (1965)

Table 6.1 A sample of cognitive architectures that have been proposed for cognitive science, with citations to representative papers. Connectionist architectures are in italics.

the functional architecture. Specifically, they propose an architecture – a structure/process pairing – which is very well suited for the easy tasks, and is less well suited for those that are more difficult. The result of this is that there have been a large number of different proposals about what the functional architecture of cognition is like, not to mention vibrant debates concerning the merits of each proposal (e.g., VanLehn, 1991). Table 6.1 provides a sample of this diversity.

It is well beyond the scope of this book to describe the characteristics of the architectures proposed in table 6.1. I can only direct the interested reader to consult a survey text in cognitive psychology for an overview of the many structure/process pairings that have been proposed, or to delve further in the example references provided in the box. However, table 6.1 can be used to make some important points about functional architecture and cognitive science. First, the number and diversity of the proposed architectures attests to the fact that being required to identify the functional architecture does not limit the possible forms that this architecture could take. Second, the fact that these proposals can be described as structure/process pairings indicates the concern that cognitive scientists have with identifying the cognitive architecture, as is to be expected from the account of cognitive science that has been given in this book.

Functional Architecture and Strong Equivalence

In chapter 4, we introduced the notion that two different information-processing systems could have varying degrees of equivalence to one another. It was noted that the goal of cognitive science was to produce strongly equivalent models of cognitive processes; if two systems are strongly equivalent to one another, then they use the same method to solve the same information-processing problem. Now that we have introduced the functional architecture, the concept of "using the same method" can be spelled out in a less ambiguous fashion.

In order to explore the relationship between models and the phenomena that they model, Fodor (1968) compares a person speaking and a phonograph playing a recording of that speech. "Suppose we played a recording of precisely the set of sentences that constituted Smith's life history of utterances. In that case, the phonograph would have produced precisely the same sequences of speech sounds as Smith has produced" (p. 130). Fodor argues (and I think that we would agree) that this phonograph should not be viewed as explaining anything about what Smith has said, or why Smith said these things. What evidence can be used to make this case?

Fodor (1968) suggests that there are two fundamental flaws with the "phonograph model" of speech. First, while the phonograph generates exactly the same sounds as did Smith, it does not generate them in the same way. Because of this, while the phonograph does exactly what Smith did (in terms of the sounds that were generated), the phonograph cannot do what Smith *could* have done! Fodor notes that a proper account of Smith's verbal behavior involves describing it as a selection of utterances from the possible English sentences that could have been uttered. "What we are ultimately attempting to simulate when we build a psychological model is not the observed behavior of an organism but rather the behavioral repertoire from which the observed behavior is drawn" (p. 133). So, the problem with the phonograph is that even though it gives the same verbal performance as did Smith, it does not have Smith's competence.

For example, if we were able to take Smith back in time and change her environment slightly, she could generate a different verbal response than she did originally because of her linguistic competence. Imagine that Smith had a severe allergy to milk. At one time in her life she was in a coffee shop, and the proprietor asked her, "Would you like some cream in your coffee?" , to which she replied "No." If we took her back in time and had the proprietor ask her, "Do you take your coffee black?" , we would expect to change her reply to "Yes." In contrast, if we took the phonograph back in time and changed its environment in the same way, it would not generate a new verbal behavior, because it lacks Smith's linguistic competence. (Being a phonograph, it also lacks Smith's milk allergy, but you get the point!)

The question is this: if the goal of a psychological model is not only to simulate behavior that was observed, but is also to simulate behavior that would have been observed in a different setting, then how is this to be done? Fodor's (1968) view of psychological models as being models of competence points clearly to the answer to this question. In very general terms, the competence of an information processor defines the information-processing problems that it could (in principle) solve, as well as the problems that it could not (in principle) solve. This competence is defined by the functional architecture of the information processor – the set of problems that an information processor could solve is the set of programs that could be written using its primitive operations. So to ensure that our model has the same competence as the subject being modeled, we must ensure that both employ identical functional architectures.

However, while the condition that two systems have the same functional architecture ensures that they have the same competence, it does not (by itself) ensure that they have the same performance. For example, two identical computer architectures could be behaving very differently because they are running different programs. So, to guarantee that our model has both the same competence and the same performance as the subject being modeled, our model has to be using its architecture to run the same algorithm.

Everything is now in place to define the ultimate goal of cognitive science, which is the development of strongly equivalent models of cognition. Let us imagine that we are modeling a particular human cognitive phenomenon. A model is strongly equivalent if 1) it is solving the same information-processing problem as the person being modeled, as defined at the computational level; 2) it is using the same procedures to solve the problem as the person, as defined at the algorithmic level; and 3) the procedures being used by both the model and the person are based upon the same functional architecture. This notion of strong equivalence, and its relationship to the tri-level hypothesis, is illustrated in figure 6.5.

The Relevance of Implementation

An important point that figure 6.5 makes explicit is that strong equivalence depends (ultimately) upon the relationship between the functional architectures

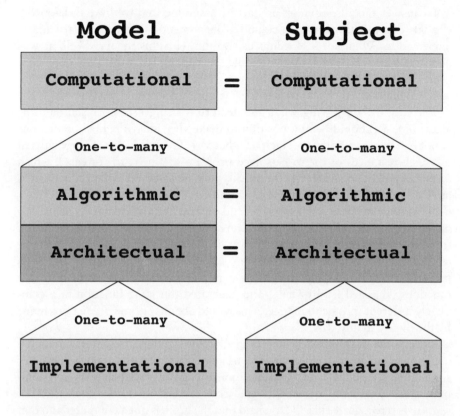

Figure 6.5 Strong equivalence and the tri-level hypothesis. The model is strongly equivalent to the modeled subject if it is identical to the subject in terms of the computational, the algorithmic, and the architectural descriptions.

of the model and of the person being modeled. It does not depend upon any physical equivalence between the two systems. This raises an important issue in regards to viewing strongly equivalent models as explanations of cognitive phenomena.

On the one hand, if strong equivalence can be defined in the absence of physical equivalence, and if the goal of cognitive science is to generate strongly equivalent models, then this suggests that implementational accounts are not needed in cognitive science. This would appear to be the status quo view within classical cognitive science. "The implementation, and all properties associated with the particular realization of the algorithm that the theorist happens to use in a particular case, is irrelevant to the psychological theory; only the algorithm and the representations on which it operates are intended as a psychological hypothesis" (Fodor & Pylyshyn, 1988). On the other hand, we have already noted in this chapter that implementational accounts are required for functional accounts to serve as explanations. How are we to reconcile this strange situation in which implementational accounts are both irrelevant and necessary?

To answer this question, let us start by assuming that we have developed a strongly equivalent theory of a cognitive phenomenon that we are particularly interested in. What sorts of things can we do with this theory? Well, as was noted in chapter 3, the theory should be capable of capturing important generalizations. In particular, by knowing what information-processing problem is being solved, by knowing what algorithm is being used to solve the problem, and by knowing what architecture is being used to instantiate the algorithm, we should be in a position to make very finely detailed predictions about behavioral regularities, tacit or otherwise. Our functional theory will tell us which instances of the to-be-solved problem will be hard (or easy), which instances will be solved slowly (or quickly), which instances will produce errors (and what kinds of errors will be produced), and so on.

Now, none of these predictions depend on how the architecture is physically implemented. All of these predictions can be derived from a theory derived from forward engineering; while the validity of the theory requires that an architecture be specified, the theory does not use the physical account of any of its primitives to make its predictions. For example, if we took one of the primitive functions, changed it physically, and generated the same function in a completely different (physical) manner, this would not change the predictions made by the theory in any way.

Indeed, the fact (already raised in chapter 2) that the same functional component can be realized in a wide variety of physical forms, makes computer simulation a valuable and plausible tool in cognitive science – though computers are physically quite different from brains. Certainly the critics of cognitivism recognize this: "I have said that the brain is not a computer and that the world is not so unequivocally specified that it could act as a set of instructions. Yet computers can be used to *simulate* parts of brains and even to help build perception machines based on selection rather than instruction" (Edelman, 1992, p. 189, his italics). Even Edelman uses computer simulation as a fundamental tool for understanding his (biological) theory of neuronal group selection (e.g., 1992, ch. 19)!

From this, if one of cognitive science's goals is to capture generalizations across a number of different people via strongly equivalent functional theories, then it would appear that this goal can be accomplished in the absence of an implementational account of what is going on. This is because while a strongly equivalent theory requires its primitive functions to be identified, it does not depend upon any specifics about how these functions are physically realized. Any old physical story will do, provided that the correct set of primitive functions is the result.

However, another of cognitive science's goals could be to explain how a particular functional theory is realized in an individual system. To accomplish this goal, a researcher is going to have to provide an account of how the primitive functions are physically realized in the to-be-explained system. Any other account would be empty – for example, it would not provide any reason to believe that Ryle's Regress had been avoided.

Now, it could be argued that the physical account required to "bottom out" the functional analysis of an individual system is orthogonal to the functional account that captures generalizations across individuals. Let's take a strong assumption from classical cognitive science that will be discussed in more detail in the next chapter: that there exists a single functional architecture for human cognition, and that we all have this architecture. The physical complexity of the brain makes it extremely unlikely that all of our brains would implement this architecture in exactly the same way (e.g., Edelman, 1988, p. 182). As a result, we would have to provide one physical account of how the architecture is implemented in my brain, a different physical account of how the architecture is implemented in your brain, and so on. By appealing to the architecture itself, we can ignore these complications, and still have enormous predictive power.

Nevertheless, to steadfastly believe in the "irrelevance" of these physical accounts to the functional theory is, in my view, a mistake. This is because I have difficulty believing that cognitive science will be able to provide strong evidence for the subsumption of primitives without appealing to the methods of neuroscience.

Consider a mature cognitive science in which there was a strong consensus regarding the (functional) nature of the architecture. This consensus could give cognitive neuroscientists some detailed ideas about the kind of implementational properties or regularities that they should be seeking in their studies of the brain. Imagine that these researchers began to report results in which Brain A had a set of physical properties that could be viewed as instantiating a particular architecture, Brain B had a different set of physical properties that could be interpreted as instantiating the same architecture, Brain C had yet another set of physical properties leading to the same architecture, and so on. Would classical cognitive scientists view this as irrelevant to their functional theory? Clearly not – instead, they would leap upon these results as providing the ultimate validation of their information-processing theories!

In short, the prevailing view that implementational accounts are irrelevant to cognitive theory is misleading. In the current state of the art, the functional theories of cognitive science and the biological theories of neuroscience are not mature enough to be synthesized. As these disciplines mature, we can hope that this situation will change. When it does, claims that biology is irrelevant to cognitive science will appear ludicrous.

The Cognitive Penetrability Criterion

We have seen that primitive functions have a role that can be described in completely algorithmic terms (i.e., as components of a functional analysis). We have also seen that an implementational account of primitive functions is viewed by some classical cognitive scientists as being unnecessary or irrelevant. These two points are related to one another in that they both raise an important methodological question: is it possible to only use algorithmic evidence to support or refute the claim that a particular component belongs to the architecture? Can a researcher state univocally that "This function is a primitive!" without appealing directly to physical measurements?

Interestingly, it appears that the empirical techniques described in the previous chapter can be used to investigate whether a particular functional proposal is primitive or not. This is because one does not require a physical description of how the function is instantiated to do this (although, of course, this kind of description would be a very powerful weapon for defending architectural claims). Instead, all one needs is strong evidence that the function cannot be further analyzed into subfunctions.

The rationale for "algorithmically" defending the claim that some function is primitive is related to a distinction that was noted earlier in the chapter: the programming description of an information processor can easily be changed by altering the data that it is representing, but the architectural description of this same information processor is much less malleable. To change the architectural description, you have to physically change the machine itself.

If human cognition is information processing, then this information processing is ultimately rooted in brain function. As we learn new information, our neural structure is changed, because there is a great deal of evidence to suggest that learning and experience modify patterns of connections in the brain (for an introduction, see Shepherd, 1988, ch. 29). However, there is no reason to believe that all aspects of brain function are equally plastic; for instance, Newell (1990) notes that "fixed structures" in the brain are those that change relatively slowly. "Such continuous plasticity does not invalidate the notion of an architecture as a *fixed* structure; it just makes the term fixed relative to the time scale" (p. 82, his italics). These fixed structures are used to instantiate the architecture, and are contrasted with other structures that change much more rapidly, and are used as memories to hold the data that the architecture is manipulating. In other words, cognitive scientists view some parts of the brain as being analogous to the tape head of a Turing machine, while other parts of the brain are viewed as being analogous to the tape.

An important consequence of having the architecture instantiated by (relatively) fixed brain structures is that these structures, like the architectural description of a Turing machine, will not change as new information is stored to memory. "An architecture provides a boundary that separates structure from content. Behavior is determined by variable content being processed according to the fixed processing structure, which is the architecture" (Newell, 1990, p. 82). As a result, we can test our hypothesis that a particular function is part of the architecture by changing the content of someone's representations in some way that is rationally related to the task at hand. If this change in content results in changes in our measures of the function's operation, then this indicates that the function is not part of the architecture. This is because if it is part of the architecture, then it is fixed, and isolated from content, and should not be affected by manipulations of content.

Pylyshyn (e.g., 1984) calls this the *cognitive penetrability criterion*. If the behavior of a function is changed by altering a subject's beliefs, then Pylyshyn describes the function as being cognitively penetrable, and not part of the functional architecture. If a wide variety of relevant content changes do not affect the behavior of the function, then Pylyshyn describes it as being cognitively impenetrable, which is consistent with claims that the function is part of the architecture. The penetrability criterion "allows us to drive a wedge between cognitive processes and the part of the cognitive system fixed with respect to cognitive or semantic influences" (Pylyshyn, 1984, p. 139).

To illustrate the cognitive penetrability criterion, examine the Müller–Lyer illusion illustrated in figure 6.6a. If you are like most observers, you will experience the two lines with arrowheads on them as being of different lengths. By probing your experience of this illusion, I am obtaining a pre-test measure of some aspects of your visual system. Now, to apply the cognitive penetrability criterion, I manipulate your beliefs about these lines in some fashion that can be rationally related to your experience of them. For example, in figure 6.6b, I have changed the arrowheads into flat lines, and thus demonstrated that the two lines are in fact equal in length. Clearly, this is a powerful manipulation of a belief that is very pertinent to the illusion! However, if you look back at figure 6.6a to see how you experience the display (this is my post-test measure of your visual system), you will still have the strong impression that the two lines are of different lengths – even though you know that this is not true. The fact that the processes that generate the illusion are not affected by my manipulations of your beliefs is consistent with the claim that early visual processing is part of the functional architecture.

Examples of Using the Cognitive Penetrability Criterion

The imagery debate represents one research area in which the cognitive penetrability criterion has played an important role. Mental images are "pictures in the head" that we often use to solve spatial problems. For instance, if I ask you to tell me how many windows there are in your house, you are very likely to answer this question by generating a visual image of your house in your mind, and by looking at this image (probably changing perspectives from one wall to another) to count the number of windows that you see in it. Through the 1970s and early 1980s, many experiments were performed to attempt to determine the basic properties of mental images (for details, see Kosslyn, 1980; Shepard & Cooper, 1982). The regularities that these experiments revealed suggested that mental images were spatial in nature; for instance, the time to rotate a mental image was a function of the amount of rotation that was required, and so on. The basic issue in this debate was this: are the spatial properties of mental images part of the functional architecture, or are mental images constructed from more primitive architectural components?

The imagery debate was one of the most fierce in cognitive science's history (for an introduction to its most important papers, see Block, 1981), and has (in my opinion) never been satisfactorily resolved. With this qualifier in mind,

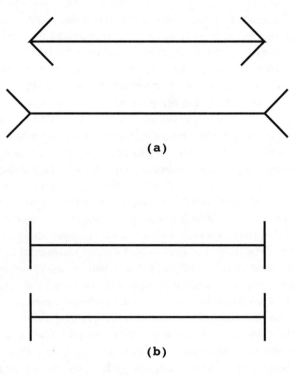

(a)

(b)

Figure 6.6 Cognitive impenetrability of the Müller–Lyer illusion. (a) If you experience the illusion, then you should see the top line as being shorter than the bottom. (b) The lines are actually the same length, as can be seen when the arrow heads are replaced with straight lines. However, this knowledge does not affect perceptions of (a).

experimental evidence suggests that mental imagery is cognitively penetrable, and as a result is not a part of the architecture.

For instance, scanning visual images was one of the key paradigms for studying mental imagery (e.g., Kosslyn, 1980, pp. 36–52). In a typical scanning experiment, subjects first memorized a picture of a map so well that they could easily generate its image in their minds. Then, they were called upon to use this image to solve certain problems. For example, they would start by focusing their attention at a named location in their imagined map. "A word was then presented that either did or did not name another location on the map. The subject was to scan to the object if it was on the map and push a button when he or she arrived, or was to examine the map and push another button if the named object could not be found" (Kosslyn, 1980, pp. 43–4). The independent measure is the distance between the two locations, the dependent measure is the time taken to complete the scan, and the basic finding is that reaction time is a linear function of distance.

If this linear effect is the result of an architectural property of mental imagery, then changing beliefs about the nature of the task should not alter this result.

However, the map scanning result does appear to be cognitively penetrable. For instance, in one condition of his doctoral experiment, Liam Bannon adopted the Kosslyn methodology, and replicated the basic image scanning result (e.g., Pylyshyn, 1981, pp. 242–3). However, Bannon hypothesized that these instructions led subjects to tacitly believe that image scanning should take time (e.g., because of instructions about pressing the button "when they arrived" at the second location). In a second condition, Bannon altered his instructions to prevent this belief from being communicated. "The instructions specified merely that subjects give the compass bearing of the second place – that is, to state whether the second place was north, northeast, east, southeast, and so on of the first" (p. 243). In this condition, there was no relation between distance and reaction time; this result has been replicated by other researchers (e.g., Finke & Pinker, 1982). This suggests that the map scanning results are not due to a primitive property of an imagery architecture, but are rather due to subjects' beliefs about the strategies that they should be using to answer the questions that are posed.

The imagery debate is not the only forum in which the cognitive penetrability criterion has appeared. It has also been used to investigate the basis for different kinds of motion perception. One major distinction made by perceptual psychologists is between real and apparent motion. Real motion is perceived when a physical object or element is viewed while being continuously displaced through space and time. The defining characteristic of real motion is that sensory receptors along the projected motion path are physically stimulated (e.g., Anstis, 1978; Gregory, 1966, pp. 94–7). As was described in chapter 3, apparent motion is an illusion perceived when, under appropriate viewing conditions, a dynamic percept is generated from successive glimpses of stationary elements. This stimulus-based distinction between two types of motion has led, in turn, to a process-based distinction between them. In this distinction, real motion is described as being detected by an architectural component: it is classified as a sensation mediated by physiological processes that detect the continuous path of activation of an object moving through space and time. In contrast, apparent motion is classified as an inference mediated by "high-level" processes that generate the impression of movement that is most likely to be seen, given the incomplete information at hand. For example, apparent motion can involve impossible or improbable impressions of movement in which the visual system is freely changing the shapes and colors of "moving" elements, even though such changes often appear to be unnecessary (e.g., Dawson, 1991; Farrell & Shepard, 1981; Kolers, 1972; Kolers & Pomerantz, 1971; Kolers & von Grunau, 1976). In considering such findings, Goodman (1978, p. 78) concluded that "plainly the visual system is persistent, inventive, and sometimes rather perverse in building a world according to its own lights." This perversity is to be expected if apparent motion is at the whim of general inferential processing – if it's detection is not built directly into the architecture.

However, a closer examination of the evidence reveals that the distinctions described above are not quite so clear cut. Specifically, some aspects of apparent motion appear to be cognitively impenetrable, and thus are indeed mediated by processes that are built directly into the architecture; however, other aspects of motion processing are cognitively penetrable, and are thus not primitive mechanisms (e.g., Dawson, 1990a; Dawson & Wright, 1989; Wright & Dawson, 1994).

To conclude this section, the cognitive penetrability criterion is a plausible algorithmic-level approach for falsifying claims about whether a function is part of the architecture. However, it has not been widely used by empirical cognitive scientists. One reason for this is that the criterion is very difficult to apply in practice. While the cognitive penetrability criterion has an important role to play within cognitive science, the defense of claims that certain functions comprise the architecture is likely to require alternative evidence. This evidence will in all likelihood be provided by neuroscientists interested in studying cognition at the implementational level that is introduced in the next chapter.

Part III   Reverse Engineering and the Functional Architecture

Up to this point in the chapter, we have been discussing the functional architecture from the perspective of classical cognitive science. Now let us change directions and discuss the functional architecture from the perspective of connectionism. As we have seen in earlier chapters, while classical cognitive scientists can be viewed as forward engineers or analytic psychologists, connectionists are better described as reverse engineers or synthetic psychologists. Connectionists do not decompose complex phenomena in search of a functional architecture. Instead, they propose a particular functional architecture, and then set out to discover what kinds of phenomena can be constructed from it.

The synthetic approach of connectionism does not imply, however, that the specification of the functional architecture is not an issue for this kind of cognitive science. It turns out that connectionists have to be just as concerned with the functional architecture as are their classical counterparts. In this part of the chapter, I will review the work of Dawson and Schopflocher (1992b), who analyzed a particular kind of memory network in order to make this point. I will use this review to raise the following issues: 1) Often times, connectionists adopt a functional architecture that is not powerful enough to do everything that they need. 2) Because of this problem, it is possible to view many connectionist networks as "dynamic symbols" that are completely consistent with classical cognitive science. 3) If connectionists really wish to distance themselves from classical cognitive science, then they will have to pay much more attention to detailing all of the required properties of their functional architecture.

Autonomy and the Structure/Process Distinction

In general, classical cognitive science makes a sharp qualitative distinction between two components of a complete information processor: it distinguishes structures or symbols that represent information from the processes or rules that are used to manipulate symbols. The Turing machine provides an excellent example of the structure/process distinction: the machine's tape holds the symbols that are being manipulated, while the machine's tape head is in essence the set of rules that are being used to do this manipulation. However, this structure/process distinction does not appear to exist for connectionist networks. In contrast to classical models, PDP networks are designed to "exhibit intelligent behavior without storing, retrieving, or otherwise operating on structured symbolic expressions" (Fodor & Pylyshyn, 1988, p. 5).

One way of characterizing this difference between classical and connectionist cognitive science is to examine the autonomy of their content-bearing entities. The "content-bearing entities" of an information processor are those components of the system that are used to represent information – the symbols or the data. If these components are themselves autonomous, then they can be let alone in some environment and can carry out the information processes that they are supposed to do. If these components are not autonomous, then they cannot do this without the aid of additional components which are not themselves used to represent information.

In a classical architecture, the content-bearing entities are the symbols that are to be manipulated. However, a set of symbols does not itself comprise an autonomous representational system, because full-fledged computation requires that symbols be manipulated by additional external processes. These external processes are the formal rules that are sensitive to symbolic structure. For example, Newell (1980, pp. 142–7) describes a paradigmatic symbol system in which symbolic expressions are stored in one physical device (memory), and are manipulated through the action of a central controller and ten different operators. In this system, the controller and operators are not components of the symbolic expressions – each exists as a physical device separate from the memory. Thus, symbols represent information, but do not simultaneously represent how this information can be transformed. Classical symbols are not autonomous because classical models embody a sharp distinction between structure and process.

This is not true of the PDP architecture as it is typically presented (e.g., Rumelhart, Hinton, & McClelland, 1986; Smolensky, 1988; for details, see below). In a PDP network, information is represented in terms of the pattern of connectivity among a set of processing units. However, this pattern also specifies the causal interactions between processing units, determining (for example) what happens to a network when a particular signal is presented to it. The state changes produced in a network as a function of signals being modified by the pattern of connectivity are analogous to symbol manipulations in a classical architecture, insofar as they occur when information is retrieved from, or when new information is added to, a network.

From this perspective, a PDP network can simultaneously represent and manipulate content. Thus, a PDP network is typically presumed to differ markedly from a classical symbol because the network does comprise an autonomous representational system – one need not appeal to external rules or processes to explain how the network functions. "Much of the allure of the connectionist approach is that many connectionist networks program themselves, that is, they have autonomous procedures for tuning their weights to eventually perform some specific computation" (Smolensky, 1988, p. 1).

The claim that a PDP model is autonomous amounts to the proposal that the basic "building blocks" defined in the PDP functional architecture are powerful enough to account for all of a network's capabilities. I will argue below that this is not true. Current PDP networks are not autonomous because their learning principles are not in fact directly realized in the network architecture. For example, networks governed by these principles require explicit signals from some external controller to determine when they will learn or when they will perform a learned task.

By showing that current PDP models are not autonomous – that an account of the capabilities of even the simplest PDP network requires an appeal to processes that are external to the network – a fundamental difference between classical and connectionist cognitive science is brought into question. If the current PDP architecture is not sufficiently powerful to instantiate autonomous networks, then PDP researchers are not providing architectural innovations different in kind from previous classical proposals that images, propositions, scripts, schemata, or prototypes are primitive symbolic structures. If PDP networks are not autonomous, then they are simply proposals for a different type of symbolic structure consistent with the assumptions of the classical architecture (see also Bechtel, 1988).

PDP Networks and Functional Architecture

As we noted earlier in this chapter, the functional architecture for an information-processing system defines primitive (i.e., physically realized) representational structures and processes, and restrictions on the flow of control from one process to another. Connectionist networks are information processors, and as a result of this connectionists are committed to specifying a functional architecture. If such an architecture is not specified, then connectionist cognitive science would succumb to Ryle's Regress.

The functional architecture for connectionism is the set of basic components of PDP networks that were introduced in chapter 3. Because they play a key role in the analysis to be provided below, it will do us no harm to refresh our memory about what these components are. First, connectionist networks are constructed from a set of processing units. A single processing unit in this generic architecture performs three basic functions, which are defined by its net input function, its activation function, and its output function. Second, processing units communicate with one another through weighted connections, which also belong to the generic architecture. Connections between units in the generic architecture are communication channels that transfer numeric signals from one unit to another. Third, an important property of connections in the generic architecture is that they are modifiable. This means that the current weights of any of a network's connections can be changed as a function of environmental input by applying a learning rule.

In the remainder of this chapter, a very simple memory network is examined. This network is consistent with the generic PDP architecture that was described in more detail in chapter 3. This memory network, if it were constructed, could be used to recall whatever information was stored in its connection weights. I will argue that the functional architecture of this network is incapable of autonomously modifying its connection strengths. This is because the learning principle that is used to modify connection strengths is not actually part of the network.

The Standard Pattern Associator

Some of the earliest research on parallel systems was concerned with the development of distributed memories capable of learning associations between pairs of input patterns (e.g. Steinbuch, 1961; Taylor, 1956), or of learning to associate an input pattern with a categorizing response (e.g., Rosenblatt, 1962; Selfridge, 1959; Widrow & Hoff, 1960). Many recent models have also dealt with this kind of problem. Of these models, some can be described in terms of basic matrix operations (e.g., Anderson, 1972; Kohonen, 1977; Willshaw, Buneman, & Longuet-Higgins, 1969), while others can be described in terms of the holographic operations of correlation and convolution (e.g., Eich, 1982; Murdock, 1982). Though the relative merits of these two approaches have been subject to debate (Murdock, 1985; Pike, 1984), they postulate similar general principles. These principles have also been extended to autoassociative networks for pattern classification and completion (e.g., Anderson, Silverstein, Ritz, & Jones, 1977; Hopfield, 1982, 1984).

Figure 6.7 depicts a PDP network designed to implement a distributed memory. This network is often used to introduce some of the basic properties of PDP connectionism, and has come to be called the *standard pattern associator* (e.g., McClelland, 1986). Versions of figure 6.7 have a long history (e.g., Kohonen, 1977, fig. 1.9; McClelland & Rumelhart, 1988, ch. 4, fig. 3; Rumelhart, McClelland, & the PDP Group, 1986, ch. 1, fig. 12, ch. 9, fig. 18, ch. 12, fig. 1, ch. 18, fig. 3; Schneider, 1987, fig. 1; Steinbuch, 1961, fig.2; Taylor, 1956, figs. 9 & 10). Physiological analogs of this figure have appeared in sources ranging from Anderson *et al.* (1977, fig. 1) to James (1890/1950, fig. 40).

The standard pattern associator is constructed from the processing units and modifiable connections defined in the PDP architecture. Thus, the processing units in this network (represented by the triangles in figure 6.7) and the

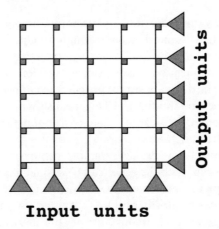

Input units

Figure 6.7 The standard pattern association network. Triangles represent processing units, lines represent connections, and the small squares represent the modifiable weight of a connection from an input unit to an output unit. The purpose of this network is to learn the association between two patterns of activity simultaneously placed in the input and output units.

modifiable connections in the network (represented by the small squares in figure 6.7) do not have any functional properties that are not specified in the "generic" PDP architecture described by Rumelhart, Hinton, and McClelland (1986); this same architecture was introduced in chapter 3.

The standard pattern association network consists of two sets of processing units; one is typically called the input set, the other the output set. Learning in this network, which is illustrated in figure 6.8, proceeds as follows: On each learning trial, the activation states of the input processing units are used to represent a cue pattern and the activation states of the output processing units are used to represent a to-be-recalled pattern. The connection weights are then modified in a manner governed by the "Hebb learning rule." This rule is based upon the following famous passage written by Canadian neuropsychologist Donald Hebb (1949, p. 62): "When an axon of a cell A is near enough to excite cell B or repeatedly or persistently takes part in firing it, some growth or metabolic change takes place in both cells such that A's efficiency, as one of the cells firing B, is increased."

Informally speaking, the Hebb rule is designed to strengthen the connection between two units if they are doing the same thing at the same time, and to weaken the connection between two units if they are doing different things at the same time. Usually, when the rule is used it is assumed that positive activation in a unit indicates that it is "ON," and negative activation in a unit indicates that it is "OFF." The Hebb works as follows: the activity of the input unit at one end of the connection, and the activity of the output unit at the other end of the connection, are multiplied together. The weight of the connection is then changed by adding this product (or some function of it) to the current weight. The logic of the rule is as follows: if both units are "ON," or if both

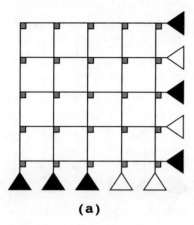
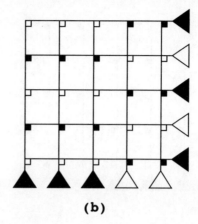

(a)　　　　　　　　　　　　　　(b)

Figure 6.8 Learning in the standard pattern associator. (a) Patterns are presented to the two banks of processing units by turning them "ON" (white triangles) or "OFF" (black triangles). The gray boxes indicate that some learning has already resulted in connection weights being assigned some values. (b) The Hebb rule is used to update connection weights. If the input and output unit are in the same state, the connection becomes more excitatory (white squares). If the input and output unit are in opposite states, the connection becomes more inhibitory (black squares).

units are "OFF," they are doing the same thing at the same time. The product of their activities will be a positive number, and when this is added to the connection weight, it will make the connection stronger (more excitatory). However, if one unit is "ON," and the other unit is "OFF," then they are doing different things at the same time. The product of their activities will be a negative number, and when this is added to the connection, it will make the connection weaker (more inhibitory). For the interested reader, more formal accounts of Hebb learning have been presented in greater detail in a number of different sources (e.g., Anderson & Hinton, 1981; Anderson *et al.*, 1977; Jordan, 1986; Knapp & Anderson, 1984; Kohonen, 1977, sec. 2.3.5; Pike, 1984).

Items are retrieved from the network by *only* activating the input processing units (i.e., by encoding the cue in these processing units), as is depicted in figure 6.9. This results in a signal being sent through the network to determine the activation state of each output unit. In networks that use Hebb learning, an output unit's activity is typically equal to its net input. In other words, during recall, an output unit will add up the weighted signals that are being sent to it from the input units to which it is connected, and its internal activity will be equal to this sum. The set of activation states of all of the output units represents the pattern recalled. Ideally, when this network is presented a particular cue, the pattern of activity that will be recalled in the output units will be the same pattern that was associated with the cue during learning. Jordan (1986) presents a very readable account of the mathematics of this recall process.

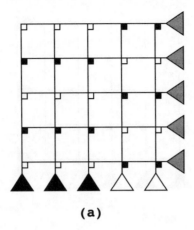
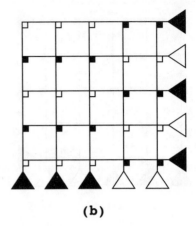

(a)   (b)

Figure 6.9 Recall in the standard pattern associator. (a) A pattern of activity is placed in the input units (black and white triangles); the gray triangles indicate that no pattern is presented to the output units at this time. (b) Signals travel from the input units, through the weighted connections, and result in activity in the output units. When the memory is functioning properly, the recalled pattern is the one that was associated with the input pattern during learning, as in figure 6.8.

The Standard Pattern Associator is Not Autonomous

We now know enough about the standard pattern associator to consider two limitations, originally described by Dawson and Schopflocher (1992b), of the figure 6.7 network. These limitations *prevent* the network from learning and recalling information *autonomously*. Specifically, if this standard pattern associator is only constructed from the building blocks defined by "generic" connectionism, then external processes or operators are required in order to change the network's states in accordance with the Hebb rule for learning and recall.

Limitation 1: Simultaneous learning and recall is not possible. Simulations of the standard pattern associator are usually described in terms of serial stages of control (e.g., Anderson & Rosenfeld, 1988, pp. xvii–xviii). Specifically, for some period of time the system is subject to a learning phase during which the distributed memory for specific associations is created. At a later time, a recall phase occurs during which the system's performance is examined.

This serial description of control affects the description of the output units in figure 6.7. During the learning phase these units are treated as a second bank of input units, and represent one of the patterns involved in changing connection strengths. During the recall phase these same units are treated as output units proper, and represent a recalled pattern.

However, there is no reason why the memory system could not be learning and recalling simultaneously. Indeed, this is required of an autonomously functioning system, because an autonomous network cannot be explicitly signaled that learning (or recall) should be occurring by some external controller. The problem that arises is that the architectural properties of the figure 6.7 network render it incapable of simultaneous learning and recall.

Consider the state of activation in the output units during the learning phase. On the one hand, these units must represent a to-be-recalled pattern being learned. On the other hand, these units must represent a pattern being recalled from the current memory – because a cue pattern is also being presented to the other set of processing units! As the two possible activation patterns in the output units will almost always be different, the network diagrammed in figure 6.7 is not capable of simultaneous learning and recall. Furthermore, there is no means realized within the network for individuating learning and recall phases, since there are no network components to signal how the output units are being used.

The network in figure 6.7 can be readily elaborated to include two sets of input units and one set of output units, as is usually done by researchers constructing neural memory networks (e.g., McNaughton, 1989, fig. 2). Presumably, the reason that this is not done in the standard model is simply a matter of convenience – in the very controlled environment of the computer simulation, it is possible for a programmer to combine input and output functions in the same units. At one point in the simulation, the controlling program uses the units one way; at a later point it uses them in another. However, there is much more than convenience at stake here. While the network is interpreted as being an autonomous system, in reality it is being manipulated as if it were a classical symbol – its state changes depend upon the explicit control of its learning/recall principles by external processes.

Limitation 2: The learning principle is not part of the network. My description of PDP connectionism indicated that single connections only represent a weighted "communication channel" from one processing unit to another. At any given time, a connection is characterized by a single number representing its weight or strength. However, the network depicted in figure 6.7 requires more sophisticated connections if its weights are to be modified autonomously.

A weighted connection in the distributed memory system must simultaneously provide three functional capabilities: (i) it must compute and represent the product of the current activations of an input unit and an output unit; (ii) it must represent the sum of any previous products of unit activations (i.e., memory of previous learning trials); and (iii) it must apply the learning rule to modify the "contents" of its "memory" on the basis of represented properties (i) and (ii).

The problem is to implement these three capabilities using a connection that is only characterized by a single number or weight. To update connection strengths in accordance with the Hebb rule – or with any more sophisticated learning rule – capabilities (i) and (ii) must be performed independently and simultaneously. This is clearly impossible if connections can only represent a single number (current product or previous sum) at any one time.

To see why this is impossible, consider a problem often encountered by students in their first course on computer programming: sorting a list of objects.

Let us say that during this operation, you need to swap the position of items x and y. A common beginning mistake is to move item x, and then write item y in its place. This is a mistake because when the student goes to write item x into the place that item y was, item x has disappeared, because it was "moved" to nonexistence! The proper way to perform the swap is to define another place (call it memory), write item x into memory, move item y from its place to item x's old place, and then move item x from memory to item y's old place. In short, to swap two items, you need some additional variables to hold items during the operation. Similarly, the modification of connection weights requires variables to hold *all* of the components involved in the calculation – that is, if the connection weight is to be updated autonomously. In other words, a single number won't do: we will need a number for the current weight as well as a number for the weight change.

These two limitations indicate that the standard pattern associator is not capable of autonomous learning, because the principles used to modify connection strengths are not physically realized within it. These principles are instead applied by some external agent – for instance, by the programmer controlling the network *in vitro*.

Importantly, the issues that I have raised above are not statements of principled limitations on the capabilities of PDP models. Instead, they are methodological criticisms of how PDP modelers deal with architectural issues in practice. The claim that I am making is that it is often the case that connectionists fail to completely specify the properties of their functional architecture, which can lead to the proposal of insufficient algorithms. With this in mind, it is appropriate to consider ways in which the limitations described above could be overcome. One approach, explored by Dawson and Schopflocher (1992b), is to specify an alternative functional architecture that is capable of creating an autonomous network.

An Autonomous Pattern Associator

One approach to overcoming the problems with the figure 6.7 network would be to treat it as a preliminary stage in a functional analysis. From this point of view, certain components in the figure (specifically, the "modifiable connections") would not be construed as representing primitive network capacities. Instead, these components would represent non-primitive properties that require further decomposition to describe how they are mediated by components that are part of the functional architecture (for examples realized in electronic components, see the proposals in Kohonen, 1984, sec. 3.4).

In order to demonstrate this strategy, Dawson and Schopflocher (1992b) developed a network that is capable of autonomous Hebb rule learning. This model represents an elaboration of figure 6.7 in two senses. First, the property "modifiable connection" was further analyzed into a circuit involving connections among three processing units. Second, additional kinds of units were proposed to instantiate certain computations. This was done to shift some of

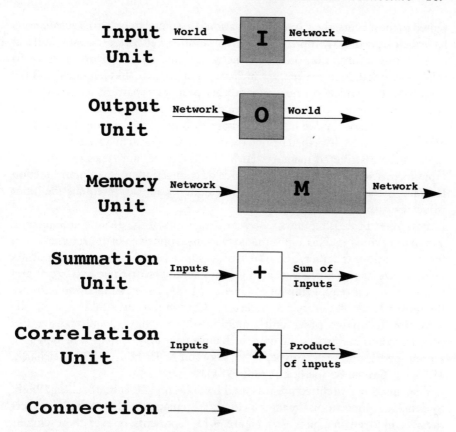

Figure 6.10 Notation for the elaborated functional architecture that Dawson and Schop-flocher (1992b) used to build an autonomous pattern associator.

the required computational burden from connections to units. However, it must be stressed that these elaborations were not intended as a strong proposal for a new PDP architecture. They were intended instead to illustrate the architectural directions that must be explored if autonomous PDP models are to be developed.

The functional architecture described below differs from that of generic PDP connectionism in two ways. First, connections between processing units are not assumed to vary in weight (i.e., they are "communication channels" with strength of 1.00). The only function of these connections is to transfer the current activation from one processing unit to another. Second, five different kinds of processing units are proposed, each performing a qualitatively different function in the network. Figure 6.10 provides a graphic notation for each component of this functional architecture.

Three of these processing unit types are similar to those employed by PDP connectionism. *Input units* have their states of activation determined by the environment, and then can have their states of activation transferred on to other (one or more) processing units. When no environmental information is presented to these units, their state of activation is assumed to be zero. *Output units* have their state of activation determined by another network processor, and can transfer this information out of the network (e.g., to the environment or to other networks). *Memory units*, which are analogous to "hidden units" in PDP networks (but which do not provide this particular pattern associator any additional computational power), have their state of activation determined by another processor, and transfer this state to other (one or more) processing units. In the model described below, these units are placed in a feedback loop to serve as the distributed memory. Each of these three unit types only receives input from a single environmental source or connection; the net input function for each is the identity function (i.e., the state of activation equals the input value), as is the output function.

Two other processing units represent extensions of the generic architecture. *Summation units* take as input the activations from two (or more) units, sum these activations together, and transfer this sum to another processing unit. As neurons are typically viewed as algebraic summers of their excitatory and inhibitory inputs (e.g., Feldman & Quenzer, 1984, ch. 4), summation units are the most neuron-like in our architecture. *Correlation units* take as input the activation from two other units, multiply these together, and transfer this product to another processing unit. Such units have long been used in models of motion perception (e.g., Anstis, 1980; Dawson & Di Lollo, 1990; Reichardt, 1961; van Santen & Sperling, 1984, 1985).

This functional architecture was used by Dawson and Schopflocher (1992b) to define a connectionist memory circuit to replace the "modifiable connections" employed in figure 6.7. Figure 6.11 represents one of these circuits receiving input from a pair of input units (one from Bank 1, the other from Bank 2). Each input unit is connected to a common correlation unit to determine the product of the input unit activations. This is required as part of Hebb rule learning. The product is then passed to a summation unit. The summation unit outputs to a memory unit, which in turn outputs back to the original summation unit. This feedback loop accomplishes two things.

First, when there is no learning occurring (i.e., when there is no pattern in one of the banks of units, as is the case during recall), the correlation unit in figure 6.11 outputs zero. The feedback loop between the summation and the memory units serves to maintain (remember) the current state of activation of the memory unit. Second, when learning does occur (i.e., when both Bank 1 and Bank 2 input units are active) the output of the correlation unit is added to the value of the memory unit. This serves to modify the activation of the memory unit in accordance with the Hebb learning rule. Thus the memory units in figure 6.10 represent the modifiable weights of figure 6.7. The circuitry of figure 6.11 indicates how these weights are modified and maintained.

A second circuit was required to define how stimulation of Bank 1 input units produces recall in the output units. Figure 6.12 illustrates one of these connections involving two input units and one output unit. Each input unit is connected to a correlation unit; the correlation unit also receives input from a

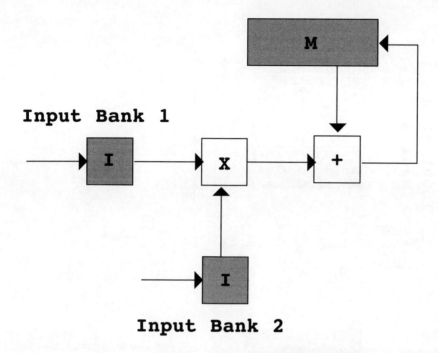

Figure 6.11 A memory circuit built from the Dawson and Schopflocher (1992b) architecture. The memory unit is analogous to a connection weight in figure 6.7. The feedback loop between the memory unit and the summation unit maintains the "weight" in memory. The weight will change only when the correlation unit sends a non-zero signal.

memory unit associated with the input unit (as in figure 6.11). The correlation unit is connected to a summation unit that also receives input from similar circuits involving different input unit/memory unit pairs. The summation unit can be described as summing the weighted activation values of the input units, which is required for recall of the type typically associated with networks that learn using the Hebb rule.

Figure 6.13 depicts a network, based upon the functional architecture described above, which is sufficient to implement the distributed associative memory system described earlier in the paper. The network is composed of two input unit banks and one output unit bank. The network is built by connecting pairs of input units from Banks 1 and 2 together with memory circuits like the one in figure 6.11, and by connecting input units from Bank 1 to appropriate output units with recall circuits like the one in figure 6.12. During the learning phase, to-be-associated patterns are presented to both sets of input units. If recall occurs at the same time, the result of the recall is represented as states of activation in the single bank of output units. During the recall phase, the desired cue is presented to Bank 1 of the input units. Bank 2 of the input units is connected in such a way that its pattern of activation cannot produce activation in the output units. For the sake of simplicity, the depicted network has only

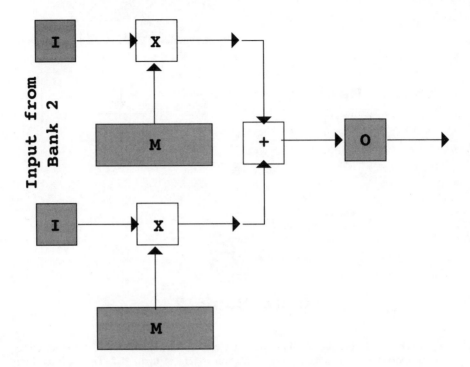

Figure 6.12 A recall circuit built from the Dawson and Schopflocher (1992b) architecture. The output unit receives the sum of two products in this example; each of these products is the value of an input unit multiplied by the "weight" value stored in a memory unit.

two units in its input and output banks. The general structure of the network can easily be expanded to accommodate larger patterns, as was the case in the simulation carried out by Dawson and Schopflocher (1992b). Clearly this network represents a marked elaboration of figure 6.7, but this does not result in an extension of computational capabilities. The network is still governed by the Hebb rule for learning and for recall.

A network of the type depicted in figure 6.7, but containing eight processing units in each input and output bank, was programmed by Dawson and Schopflocher (1992b). This was done to determine whether or not the system functioned in accordance with the Hebb rule, and to determine whether or not the system could learn autonomously. They found, as expected, that this network performed exactly as the mathematics of Hebb learning dictated. Furthermore, by watching the activity in each bank of units during every learning trial, they were able to show that the system was learning autonomously. In particular, the network was capable of simultaneous learning and recall, and only learned new information when both input unit banks were active.

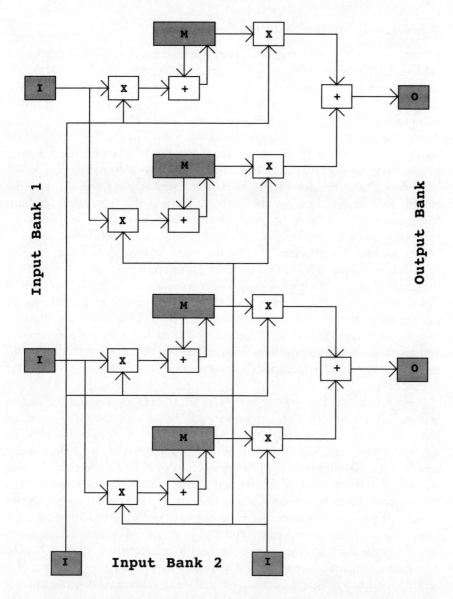

Figure 6.13 An autonomous pattern associator built from the Dawson and Schopflocher (1992b) architecture. The network is built from circuits of the type illustrated in figures 6.11 and 6.12. Note that this memory network is simpler than the one depicted in figure 6.7, in that it only has two processing units in each input bank. Dawson and Schopflocher created a computer simulation of this kind of network, but their simulation used eight processing units per input bank.

Are Networks Dynamic Symbols?

A diagram of a PDP network, like the example in figure 6.7, illustrates how a PDP model is constructed from the "generic" PDP architecture. But how should such a diagram be interpreted? One view, typically put forward by PDP researchers (e.g., Smolensky, 1988), is that such a diagram represents a realizable functional circuitry: If each diagram component was replaced by a physical device that instantiated a primitive function defined in the PDP architecture (i.e., an actual processing unit or an actual connection), then the result should be a working network, capable of autonomously performing a desired task. We have shown that this view cannot be correct. Networks constructed from the current PDP architecture are subject to limitations that prevent them from functioning autonomously. Diagrams like figure 6.7 do not represent all of the processing components that would be required to create a working system.

Dawson and Schopflocher (1992b), for example, have shown that autonomous learning is possible in PDP networks. However, if it is to be achieved, then the kinds of networks typically proposed by connectionists require substantial elaborations of the PDP architecture. This elaboration must be guided by an explicit statement of, and a strong commitment to, a functional architecture capable of solving the various control problems faced by an autonomous system. Without such a functional architecture, it is doubtful that connectionism can serve as a viable bridge between computational and physiological descriptions.

However, it could be argued that PDP researchers are not seeking such a bridge. Perhaps figure 6.7 only represents part of the architecture required for the standard pattern associating program – a data structure subject to the control of some external processor. Such a position has been adopted in the design of parallel computers. For example, Hillis's (1985) Connection Machine consists of a large number of processing/memory units that can be connected to one another via programmable software links. Processing/memory units are capable of performing computations on the basis of locally available information (e.g., input from other units to which they are connected). Processing/memory units that are connected together produce patterns called active data structures – in essence, dynamic symbols – capable of both representing and processing information. Nevertheless, active data structures in this machine are not autonomous networks. "The activities of these active data structures are directed from outside the Connection Machine by a conventional host computer. This host computer stores data structures on the Connection Machine in much the same way that a conventional machine stores them in a memory" (pp. 19–20). While active data structures are responsible for processing information, this processing is coordinated and controlled by the host machine. A similar approach was applied in Widrow's (1962) MADALINE system, as well as in more modern hybrid systems (such as the CAP2 architecture described by Schneider and Oliver, 1991) that attempt to get the best from both the classical and connectionist worlds.

Diagrams like figure 6.7 could represent the components of an active data structure for pattern association, and nothing else. Under this interpretation, the limitations described above – which are essentially problems of system control – are not relevant, because they would presumably be overcome by the operation of an external controller (i.e., a controller that is not part of the PDP network as typically described). This external controller would be responsible for programming or modifying connection strengths.

However, and as we have stressed above, treating PDP networks as active data structures leads to a major disappointment for those viewing connectionism as a potential "paradigm shift" in the study of psychology processes (a view proposed, for example, by Schneider, 1987). Classical cognitive science draws a sharp distinction between the structures and processes in a representational system, as noted by Fodor and Pylyshyn (1988, p. 61, italics theirs): "Data structures are the objects that the machine transforms, not the rules of transformation." Autonomy – the rejection of the structure/process distinction – is the characteristic that differentiates a PDP network from a classically defined symbol. "Knowledge is not directly accessible to interpretation by some separate processor, but it is built into the processor itself and directly determines the course of processing" (Rumelhart, Hinton, & McClelland, 1986, pp. 75–6). If PDP networks are not autonomous – if they are only active data structures – then PDP researchers are only proposing a new kind of classical symbol!

To put this in a slightly different light, we saw in chapter 3 that one approach to establishing the computational power of PDP networks was to assume that the network housed the mechanisms for manipulating external data. However, our consideration of the pattern associator turns this division of labor completely around. Now, instead of having the networks instantiate procedures for manipulating information, we are proposing that the networks may merely be some media which hold information, and which are manipulated by external rules. I don't think that this is much of a problem, although it might lead to some tough questions as researchers take another look at the computational power of networks. However, I do think that it makes connectionism look far less interesting than many of its proponents would like.

Let me emphasize that to say that connectionist networks are merely dynamic symbols is not to argue that there is a serious flaw in the PDP approach. On the contrary, statements like this raise interesting possibilities for integrating connectionist and traditional approaches in cognitive science. Both critics (e.g., Broadbent, 1985; Fodor & Pylyshyn, 1988) and supporters (e.g., Clark, 1989, ch. 7; Hawthorne, 1989; McClelland, Rumelhart, & Hinton, 1986; Smolensky, 1988; Rumelhart, Smolensky, McClelland, & Hinton, 1986) of connectionism have assumed that connectionist and classical approaches are qualitatively different. However, if PDP networks are properly viewed as active data structures, then it is false to assume this qualitative difference: networks like the one depicted in figure 6.7 become proposals for a specific kind of dynamic symbol no different in kind than other types of symbolic media proposed by classical researchers, including images, frames, schemata, and so on – the kinds of things that are listed in table 6.1 (see also Bechtel, 1988). The learning and retrieval principles described by PDP researchers define the regularities of "within-symbol" changes.

What remains to be specified in this "dynamic symbol" view of connectionism are the principles governing the interactions (or transformations) between dynamic symbols. And, contrary to some proposals advanced by PDP researchers (e.g., McClelland & Rumelhart, 1986, fig. 2; Schneider & Oliver, 1991), these interactions need not be governed by modifiable connections between networks (see also Clark, 1989). Interactions between dynamic symbols could in principle be controlled by rules of the sort espoused by the classical approach. These rules would be controlled by the same processing device required by current PDP models to determine whether a processor is being used to store or retrieve information, and to determine how a learning rule is to be employed to modify connection weights.

Part IV   The Functional Architecture and the Cognitive Sciences

We have now examined the importance of the functional architecture to both classical and connectionist cognitive science. Let us now bring this chapter to a close by comparing these two approaches at this level.

Previous chapters have indicated that classical and connectionist cognitive science are more similar than we might be led to believe after reading some of the current literature. At the computational level of analysis, we saw that classical architectures and PDP networks appear to have the same competence. At the algorithmic level of analysis, we saw that "obvious" differences between the two approaches started to disappear when, for instance, we analyzed the structure of a network to find out how it solved a problem, and extracted a very classical-looking algorithm.

More distinct differences between the two approaches do appear to be evident at the level of the functional architecture. In particular, if the structure/process distinction is true of classical architectures, but is not true of connectionist networks, then a fundamental difference between these two schools of thought has been revealed. Nevertheless, this is not a necessary distinction between the two; if classical researchers and connectionist researchers want to highlight the differences between their perspectives, then even more care must be given to specifying and identifying architectural properties.

As far as classical cognitive science is concerned, the use of functional analysis or forward engineering as a research methodology requires that a functional architecture be specified in order to escape Ryle's Regress. However, this does not rule out the distinct possibility that when the architecture is uncovered, it will have a distinctly connectionist appearance. Indeed, we have already had a glimpse of this possibility in chapter 5, when we saw that relatively abstract rules of logical inference could be translated into properties that emerge from a PDP network. Clearly, if classical researchers want to identify architectural properties that are distinct from connectionism, but are still rooted in brain processes, then they might be well advised to look for biological evidence of a distinction between biologically stored data and biologically instantiated rules.

As far as connectionism is concerned, networks are information processors. As a result of this, connectionists must also specify a functional architecture to prevent their brand of cognitive science from succumbing to Ryle's Regress. The components of the generic PDP architecture represent one attempt at doing this, and this attempt – insofar as it blurs the distinction between structure and process – offers an alternative to the classical view that markedly distinguishes symbols from the rules that manipulate them. However, this potential difference must be maintained by taking greater care with how the connectionist functional architecture is specified. Earlier in this chapter, we saw one example of this point with the Dawson and Schopflocher (1992b) analysis of the autonomy of distributed memories. If the functional architecture of connectionism is underdetermined to the extent that it can't be used to construct autonomous networks, then the networks themselves are best viewed as dynamic symbols. In this light, connectionism would become a relatively minor variation of classical cognitive science.

It is too early to tell whether the architectural differences between classical and connectionist cognitive science are real or imagined. The reason for this is that we simply do not know enough about human cognition to be able claim that we have identified its functional architecture. However, it is apparent that the search for the functional architecture is a major – if not *the* major – goal of cognitive science. Furthermore, it is almost certainly the case that neuroscience will have a major role to play in achieving this goal. When researchers explain how the architecture of cognition actually works, this explanation is going to have to provide a detailed account of how particular cognitive "programming instructions" are built into the brain. In the next chapter, let us turn our attention to the role of neuroscience within cognitive science by discussing the implementational level of analysis.

7

The Implementational Level

In previous chapters, we have seen that many important questions can be addressed at the computational level and at the algorithmic level (including the level of the functional architecture). Furthermore, the answers to these questions can indeed be pursued independently from neuroscience, physics, or engineering. As a result, it is sometimes hard to believe that cognitive scientists are fundamentally interested in brain function. "The mind can be studied independently from the brain. Psychology (the study of the programs) can be pursued independently from neurophysiology (the study of the machine and the machine code)" (Johnson-Laird, 1983, p.9).

In spite of these sorts of claims, though, it cannot be denied that implementational issues are crucial to cognitive science. Minsky (1985, p. 26) provided a nice sense of the situation: "Does this mean that psychology must reject the laws of physics and find its own? Of course not. It is not a matter of different laws, but of additional kinds of theories and principles that operate at higher levels of organization." In other words, functional theories – such as those that emerge from computational and algorithmic analyses – and implementational accounts must coexist. We already saw this in chapter 6, when we discussed the need for functional theories to be subsumed in physical causation.

Up to this point, much of this book has focused upon the additional theories and principles that Minsky (1985) alluded to. This chapter will change the focus by exploring some very general claims concerning the relationship between physical instantiation and cognitive theory. In the first half of the chapter I am going to describe how neuroscience can influence classical cognitive science by demonstrating how analyses at the implementational level are incorporated into methodological functionalism. In the second half of the chapter, I am going to investigate some relationships between neuroscience and connectionist cognitive science.

Part I   The Modularity of Mind

How does one go about relating implementational issues to classical cognitive science? One approach is to describe a problem at the computational level, and then to consider different ways in which this problem might be solved. Some of these solutions might agree quite nicely with what neuroscientists know about the brain. This section illustrates this approach. First, I will introduce the frame problem, which is one of the major difficulties facing classical cognitive scientists interested in higher-order cognition. Second, I will review Fodor's (1983) account of one way in which this problem might be solved. Third, I will outline how the evidence from neuroscience is related to Fodor's theory.

The Frame Problem

Dennett (1987) tells us the sad story of a robotics lab group that has developed the R1 robot, whose only goal is its own survival. In one test, R1 is told that its spare battery is in a room in which a time bomb is soon to explode. Desperate to save its energy supply, R1 finds its way into the room, where it locates its battery sitting on a wagon. R1 reasons that it can rescue the battery by pulling the wagon out of the room, and proceeds to do this. Shortly after, both the battery and R1 are destroyed by the exploding bomb, which (unfortunately for R1) was on the wagon as well. Dennett notes that R1 had failed to recognize that one obvious implication of its action was to change the location of the bomb.

The lab group next decides that the problem with R1 was that it failed to recognize not only the intended consequences of its planned actions, but also the unintended consequences of these actions. They design a new robot, R1D1, which deduces all of the consequences of its actions on the basis of its representation of the situation. However, R1D1 meets the same unhappy fate as R1: "It had just finished deducing that pulling the wagon out of the room would not change the color of the room's walls, and was embarking on a proof of the further implication that pulling the wagon out would cause its wheels to turn more revolutions than there were wheels on the wagon – when the bomb exploded" (Dennett, 1987, p. 42). R1D1 had paid the ultimate price for being as lost in thought as Tolman's rats.

Finally, the robotics group builds R2D1, which tags deductions as being either relevant or irrelevant, and then ignores the irrelevant ones. The results of the third site visit were devastating: "When they subjected R2D1 to the test that had so unequivocally selected its ancestors for extinction, they were surprised to see it sitting, Hamlet-like, outside the room containing the ticking bomb, the native hue of its resolution sicklied o'er with the pale case of thought, as Shakespeare (and more recently Fodor) has aptly put it. 'Do something!' they yelled at it. 'I am,' it retorted. 'I'm busily ignoring some thousands of implications I have determined to be irrelevant. Just as soon as I find an irrelevant implication, I put it on the list of those I must ignore, and . . . ' the bomb went off" (Dennett, 1987, p. 42).

All of the robots described by Dennett failed because they could not solve what has become known as the *frame problem*. The frame problem faces any system that has to represent a changing world. In order to represent a situation after some action has occurred, a system is not only faced with deducing what changes are produced by the action, but also must deduce what changes are not produced by the action. "In fact, very little of what from a purely logical point of view could happen as a result of an action, does happen. [. . .] The outcome is a problem solver sitting in the midst of a sea of axioms representing non-changes, endlessly calculating non-effects" (Janlert, 1987, p. 6).

One reason that a general reasoning system is confronted with the frame problem is that its set of beliefs is what Fodor (1983) calls *isotropic*. This means that the system may use any of its current beliefs to aid in establishing the truth or falsehood of some new belief. For example, when I was a child, I came home from school one day to find that my pet beagle was no longer there. My parents told me the soothing story that the dog (which was getting on in years) had been given to a farmer to run free on an acreage. Many years later, my mother inadvertently let the truth slip out – the dog was becoming aggressive towards the neighborhood kids, and had to be euthanized. What were the possible consequences of my new belief? Well, of course I had to update my specific memories of the dog. However, this could not be done without also considering changes in my other beliefs too. I had to consider changing the truth value of "I believe that my parents always tell me the truth." (Admittedly, finding out about Santa Claus when I was 8 had already severely challenged that belief!) Then, of course, I had to check the validity of beliefs based on other things that my parents had told me – what else had they lied about? Furthermore, lots of my other beliefs had depended on things that they had told me, even more of my beliefs depended on beliefs that depended on things that my parents had told me, and so on.

The advantage of an isotropic belief system is that you can bring any potentially relevant belief to bear on some problem that you are solving. One reason for this is that general reasoning often proceeds via the process of drawing analogies, and as a result may involve comparisons between ideas that don't appear to even be remotely related. One very nice fictional example of this is provided in Crichton's (1969, p. 271) *The Andromeda Strain*, when, after daydreaming about driving home on the Santa Monica Expressway, a researcher realizes that a lethal microorganism will only grow in a narrow range of pH. A very nice nonfictional example of this is provided by Hopfield's (1982) realization that the properties of a particular type of magnetic solid, a spin glass, could be used to create a mathematical model of a biological memory system. Of course, the disadvantage of an isotropic belief system is that it leads directly into the frame problem.

Our everyday experience of the world suggests that we can easily solve the frame problem for general reasoning; we don't get lost in thought. There is considerable debate among researchers about how humans solve this problem (for example, see the variety of papers in Pylyshyn, 1987). This debate won't concern us here. Instead, to move closer to the implementational level, let us consider Fodor's (e.g., 1983) hypothesis that some of our belief systems must act very quickly to aid in our survival, and as a result they are rescued from the frame problem by being isolated from the system that manipulates our general knowledge of the world.

Modularity and the Frame Problem

In the 1950s, an extremely cognitive approach to visual perception was enjoying wide popularity; it was called the "New Look," and was epitomized by Bruner's (1957) influential description of the approach in *Psychological Review*. According to New Look theorists, visual perception was equivalent to problem-solving, and as a result could be affected by a perceiver's beliefs or expectations.

Bruner's (1957) classic example of this was an experiment in which subjects were presented pictures of playing cards in which the colors were reversed (i.e., diamonds and hearts were black, and spades and clubs were red). Using a tachistoscope to control the viewing duration, Bruner reported that at short durations subjects did not notice the problem with the playing cards, and in fact reported seeing the expected colors of cards (e.g., seeing red diamonds even though the presented cards were black). Surprisingly long durations were required before subjects noticed that the cards were in fact "wrong." This result was so striking that it was adopted by Kuhn (1970) as an example of showing how a paradigm could affect the interpretation of data. For the New Look, seeing was indeed believing.

The New Look is no longer in fashion, although versions of it have been proposed in more recent times (e.g., Rock, 1983). The reason that the New Look has passed out of favor is because a perceptual system that is based completely on problem-solving, and which is affected completely by the top-down influences of beliefs, does not have much survival value. First, if you only see what you expect to see, you won't live long. After all, situations that unfold as you expect are rarely dangerous – it's environmental surprises that kill you! Second, if perception was full-blown problem-solving, then all aspects of perception would have to be part of an isotropic belief system. As a result, your vision would be subject to the frame problem, slowing it down for the same reasons that Dennett's (1987) robots could not work fast enough to escape the time bomb. A perceptual system that allowed you to infer that you were being attacked by a tiger wouldn't be much use if it didn't provide this information quickly enough for you to attempt escape.

Fodor (e.g., 1983, 1987; Fodor & Pylyshyn, 1981) has argued that both of these difficulties can be solved by isolating at least some early perceptual processes from general problem-solving; this amounts to an explicit rejection of the New Look. Fodor calls these isolated perceptual systems *modules*. According to Fodor (1983), the operations performed by modular systems are rapid, mandatory, and run to completion once they are initiated. Modules are also domain specific, designed to solve specific problems, and incapable of solving others. For example, a module might be able to solve the "what went where" correspondence problem for motion (see chapter 9), but be completely incapable of solving other problems associated with motion perception, or even of solving correspondence problems that occur in domains that do not involve motion.

Figure 7.1, adapted from Wright and Dawson (1994, fig. 5), illustrates the relationship between modular and nonmodular processing by describing perception as a three-stage process. The first stage of processing consists of a set of modules that serve the role of *transducers*. The purpose of the transducers is to convert sensed energy (e.g., photons of light) into symbolic codes that can be processed by later stages. This first stage of processing is completely data-driven, and is unaffected by the perceiver's beliefs, desires, or goals. The second stage of processing consists of a set of modules that operate on the representations output by Stage 1 modules. The purpose of these modules is to perform complex computations on transduced information. Wright and Dawson suggest that while the operations of Stage 2 modules are completely independent of beliefs and expectations, higher-order processes might be able to operate as a "key" that can start some of these modules to operate. In this sense, Stage 2 processes are akin to the intermediate visual processes that have been proposed by others (e.g., Pylyshyn, 1987; Ullman, 1986). The final stage of full-blown visual processing is general inference. General inference takes information computed by previous stages and relates it to general knowledge of the world. For example, it is at this point that a complex visual representation would be assigned to a semantic category.

Fodor (1985, p. 2) has suggested that while "perception is smart like cognition in that it is typically inferential, it is nevertheless dumb like reflexes in that it is typically encapsulated." Note that in the figure 7.1 model only Stage 3 is isotropic. In contrast, modular systems are said to be *informationally encapsulated*. That is, operations within a given module never have access to information outside the module. They only have access to the information that is input to them (which could be a complex data structure that has been compiled by an earlier module); they also have access to special-purpose information built into the module. This is Fodor's solution to the frame problem for vision: information encapsulation enables modular input systems to process complex data structures quickly without interacting with higher order, cognitive processes. In other words, modules are not faced with the task of updating every relevant chunk of knowledge in a belief system, because they are not "connected" to most of this knowledge.

How does the modularity proposal tie into the implementational level? The answer to this question comes from Fodor's (1983) consideration of how one can have fast, mandatory, informationally encapsulated systems as part of

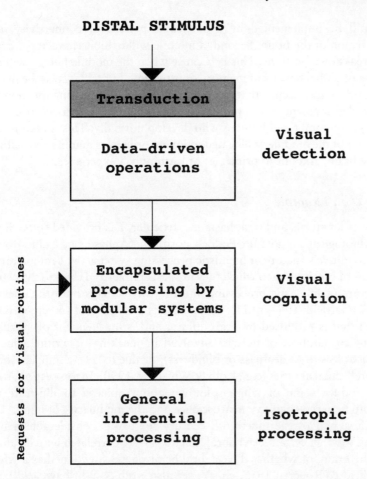

Figure 7.1 A three-stage model of perception, adapted from Wright and Dawson (1994). Transduction and data-driven operations are performed by modules in Fodor's (1983) strictest sense. Visual cognition is performed by visual routines, which are similar to modules in that they are encapsulated, but are not mandatory. Instead, they can be initiated (but not guided) by general inferential processing. Isotropic processing has the responsibility of attaching semantic labels to visual objects.

human cognition. Fodor argues that this is accomplished by associating each module with fixed neural architecture – modularity is physically built into the brain. The corollary of this position is that general inferential processing, which is by definition nonmodular, is *not* going to be associated with a fixed neural architecture. It is because of this that Fodor (p. 119) is not surprised that we have a neuroscience of sensory systems, but that we do not have a neuroscience of thought.

Given the hypothesis that modularity is accomplished by being built directly into "wetware," it is far from surprising that Fodor (1983) also proposes that modules will be associated with specific implementational properties. First, as noted above, modules will be associated with a fixed neural architecture – each module will be implemented by a particular pattern of connectivity in a localized region of the brain. Second, a module will exhibit characteristic and specific breakdown patterns. This is because when the module fails, it will not be because of global deficits in memory or attention, but will instead be due to deficits in the neural circuits that are specialized for implementing the module. Third, the development of the module will exhibit a characteristic pace and sequencing, common to all humans who develop normally. This is because the development of the module will be tied to innate principles guiding the maturation of the brain, and not to principles of learning via experience.

Aphasia as an Example

The study of language, and of aphasia in particular, has provided some of the strongest biological support for Fodor's position. "Aphasias give clues to the modular cognitive structure of linguistic processing systems (by demonstrating the patterns of breakdown to which they are susceptible) and clues to the neural infrastructure of linguistic processing and the way it maps onto the relevant processes" (Garfield, 1987, p. 11). An aphasia is a disorder of speech, writing, or reading that is produced by brain injury, and is independent of language deficits due to paralysis of muscles involved in speaking or writing, due to sensory disorders (e.g., deafness or blindness), or due to severe impairment in general intellectual abilities (e.g., Kolb & Whishaw, 1990). In this section, I will briefly introduce some of what is known about aphasia to illustrate the relationship between cognitive neuroscience and the modularity of mind.

In the first half of the nineteenth century there was considerable debate concerning whether certain behavioral functions were correlated with localized areas in the brain, or whether the cerebral hemispheres functioned as a whole (e.g., Penfield & Roberts, 1959, ch. IV; see also Kolb & Whishaw, 1990, pp. 568–9). While Bouillard, in search of clinical support for some of Gall's phrenology proposals, had proposed in 1825 that the left hemisphere played a key role in speech production, there was little supporting evidence for this claim. This state of affairs, however, changed dramatically in 1861.

At this time, Pierre Paul Broca described a patient named Leborgne who could understand language, but who had lost the ability to speak at the age of 30. "He was only able to say 'tan' and to curse, 'Sacre nom de D...'" (Penfield & Roberts, 1959, p. 57). For the remainder of Leborgne's life, there was a gradual progression of paralysis and blindness which eventually led to his being bedridden. (The history of the neurology of language was forever changed because his sheets were only changed once a week. As a result he developed cellulitis in his right leg, a condition which brought him into Broca's care and attention.) Leborgne died at the age of 61. An autopsy by Broca revealed damage to a region of his brain now called Broca's area (see figure 7.2). By 1864, Broca had completed a study of eight such patients, and was able to announce "one of the most famous principles of brain function: 'Nous parlons avec l'hémisphère gauche!'" (Kandel, 1991, p. 11).

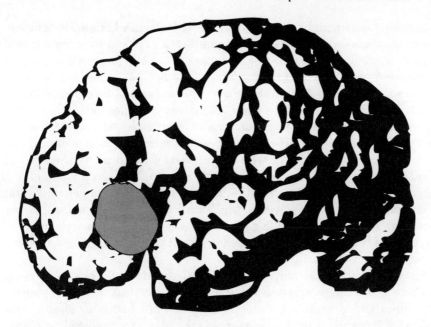

Figure 7.2 The gray patch in this silhouette of an adult human brain indicates the approximate location of Broca's area, which is the name given to the third frontal convolution on the left cerebral hemisphere.

Broca's aphasia typically results when the brain is damaged at or near Broca's area. Patients suffering from Broca's aphasia appear (at first glance) to have no difficulty understanding language that is presented to them, and also appear to have good understanding of what they are attempting to say, but have a great deal of difficulty speaking. Their speech is slow and deliberate, and uses a very simplified grammatical structure in which verbs are reduced to the infinitive or the participle, nouns are only expressed in singular form, and other parts of speech (conjunctions, adverbs, adjectives, articles) are missing (Kolb & Whishaw, 1990, p. 580). The latter characteristic is called *agrammatism*.

Detailed examinations of patients afflicted with Broca's aphasia also show comprehension deficits that appear to be closely tied to the grammatical structure of presented sentences. For instance, Goodglass, *et al.* (1979) have shown that Broca's aphasics can understand conjoined sentences, but cannot understand embedded sentences that convey the same meaning. So, a sentence like "The Montreal Canadiens won the Stanley Cup in 1993 and the Montreal Canadiens have won 24 Stanley Cups" would be understood, but the sentence "The Montreal Canadiens, who won the Stanley Cup in 1993, have won 24 Stanley Cups" would not be understood. A variety of other comprehension problems have been documented in Broca's aphasics; these generally appear to be due to problems processing the grammatical structure of stimulus sentences (for reviews, see Bradley, Garrett, & Zurif, 1980; Nass & Gazzaniga, 1987; Zurif, 1990).

Bradley, Garrett, and Zurif (1980) attempted to gain additional insight into the comprehension deficits associated with Broca's aphasia by using a lexical decision task. In this kind of task, a subject is visually presented a string of letters, and must press a key to indicate whether this string is a word or nonword. The dependent measure for a lexical decision task is response latency. The lexical decision task is of interest because response latency can be affected by a number of different independent variables. For instance, consider words that are called *open class*. These are generally content words, like nouns, that refer to things or events in the world. Open class words demonstrate a strong word frequency effect: the more frequently an open class word is found in a language, the faster is its identification as a word in a lexical decision task. This is in contrast to closed class words, which are generally not content words, but serve a grammatical function (e.g., the articles "a" and "the" are examples of closed class words). For normal subjects, closed class words do not exhibit a word frequency effect.

However, Bradley, Garrett, and Zurif (1980) found that Broca's aphasics did not provide these typical results in the lexical decision task. For these patients both open and closed class words revealed a word frequency effect . This indicated that while normal subjects could take advantage of special properties of closed class words and process them in a different (and more efficient) manner, agrammatic aphasics could not take advantage of these properties.

Kean (1980) has argued that the special properties of closed class words that Broca's aphasics are insensitive to are ultimately grounded in their phonological representation. In other words, there is evidence to suggest that Broca's area is responsible for a very specific task: performing the mapping between the phonological and the syntactic representations of a sentence. The fact that a localized area in the brain is associated with such a specific information processing task provides strong support for Fodor's (1983) argument that some cognitive processing is modular.

Other results from the neurology of language are also consistent with Fodor's (1983) position. Broca's research in the early 1860s paved the way for an intensive (and successful) search for cortical areas responsible for other functions. For example, in 1876 Carl Wernicke reported a different language deficit (now called *Wernicke's aphasia*) in which patients could speak, but not understand language. While a Wernicke's aphasic's articulation of words is quite fluent, the utterances are typically "word salads" that are devoid of meaning. For instance, when asked by an examiner to tell something about their problem, one patient replied: "Yes, I ugh can't hill all of my way. I can't talk all of the things I do, and part of the part I can go alright, but I can't tell from the other people. I usually most of my things. I know what can I talk and know what they are but I can't always come back even though I know they should be in, and I know should something eely I should know what I'm doing ... " (Akmajian, Demers, & Harnish, 1984, p. 511).

Wernicke demonstrated that this newly classified aphasia was associated with injury to a different area of the brain than that identified by Broca (see

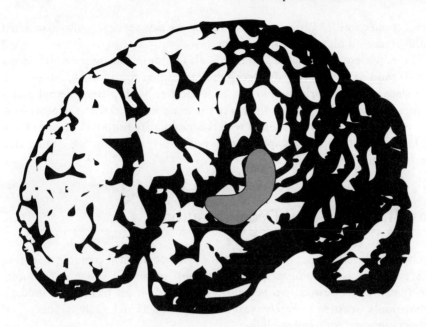

Figure 7.3 The gray patch indicates the approximate location of Wernicke's area in an adult human brain. This name is given to the first temporal convolution on the left cerebral hemisphere.

figure 7.3). On the basis of these observations, Wernicke proposed a modular, neurological theory of language processing. Wernicke suggested that Broca's area was responsible for controlling the motor programs involved in generating speech and writing, while the area that he had discovered on the left temporal lobe was responsible for the sensory (and semantic) aspects of language processing. This distinction is still commonly seen in the literature. For example, Akmajian, Demers, and Harnish (1984, p. 511) suggest that "the Sylvian fissure separating Broca's and Wernicke's areas may represent a neuroanatomical boundary separating the phonological from the syntactic and semantic components at the cortical level."

With modern advances in brain imaging and other techniques, new evidence is emerging that is changing our understanding of aphasia. For example, researchers now generally accept the view that the comprehension deficits associated with Wernicke's aphasia are not "semantic" *per se*, but are instead rooted in problems with processing phonetic information. "Comprehension fails not because, as has been traditionally believed, the posterior perisylvian sector is a center to store 'meanings' of words but rather because the normal acoustic analyses of the word-forms the patient hears are aborted at an early stage" (Damasio & Damasio, 1992, p. 93). From this perspective, Wernicke's area has the specialized function of determining the mapping between acoustic signals and phonetic representations. This makes a great deal of sense, given the close proximity of Wernicke's area to the primary auditory cortex, and given its direct connections to Broca's area, which (as we saw earlier) is also associated with specialized phonological functions.

This new view of Wernicke's aphasia is also far more consistent with Fodor's (1983) modularity hypothesis. Recall that according to this view, our general knowledge of the world should not be associated with a fixed neural architecture. The discovery of a small area of the brain involved with the processing of "meaning" would be in conflict with the modularity proposal. However, the updated view of Wernicke's aphasia does not involve the claim that a brain area for "meaning" has been localized.

Part II   Functional Decomposition

In chapter 4, we saw that one of the major tasks of classical cognitive scientists was the analysis of complex phenomena into organized systems of simpler functions. We reviewed two general types of empirical techniques used by behaviorally oriented researchers to perform a functional analysis: functional dissociation and protocol analysis.

The discussion of modularity in Part I of the current chapter should make clear that evidence from neuroscience can also play a great role in supporting functional analysis. Our confidence in functional accounts increases when neuroscience provides evidence which is consistent with them. Furthermore, these functional accounts could be dismissed if biological accounts weighed against them. In short, any neuropsychological evidence that can be used to support the modularity hypothesis can also be used to support functional decompositions.

However, there is a fly in this ointment. Fodor (1983) is quite explicit in claiming that modular systems are special, and that not all of cognition is modular. Higher-level processes such as thinking, problem-solving, and so on are presumed by Fodor to be carried out by central processes which must be isotropic. Unfortunately, "if central processes have the sorts of properties that I have ascribed to them, then they are bad candidates for scientific study" (p. 127). One reason for this pessimistic view is that the more isotropic cognition is, the less likely is the underlying neuroarchitecture to mirror the structure of the computations that it implements. As a result, Fodor believes that neuropsychological studies of higher-order cognitive phenomena will not be successful. "The limits of modularity are also likely to be the limits of what we are going to be able to understand about the mind" (p. 126).

However, the view that cognitive science will only provide scientific insight into those processes that turn out to be modular strikes me as being too extreme. By definition, modules are informationally encapsulated. But informationally encapsulated systems are not the only aspects of the cognitive architecture that might be associated with specific neural structures or deficits (e.g., Farah, 1994). For instance, Pylyshyn's (1984) description of the functional architecture does not only consist of primitive symbols and primitive rules for their manipulation. It also includes "such basic resources and constraints of the system, as a limited memory" (p. 30).

Memory is one cognitive capacity that would seem to be an important component of central processing (but see Moscovitch, 1992), and which might as a result be difficult to associate with fixed neural structures. Indeed, Lashley (1950) described 30 years of his own research which attempted to "find the locus of specific memory traces" (p. 455). His results? "I sometimes feel, in reviewing the evidence on the localization of the memory trace, that the necessary conclusion is that learning is just not possible" (p. 479). Other lines of argument also suggest that memory cannot be modular in Fodor's (1983) sense. First, it is hard to imagine how any thinking or problem-solving (using any possible information) could be done without the use of memory. Second, it seems implausible to view memory as being informationally encapsulated, because during a particular act of problem-solving, any relevant information might have to be retrieved, and held in a short-term store while being considered.

Since Lashley's (1950) seminal paper, though, there have been many dramatic results which have led some researchers (e.g., Mishkin & Appenzeller, 1990) to claim that it is possible to sketch the anatomy of memory. Furthermore, many of these results are very consistent with functional decompositions of memory based on behavioral studies. This shows that researchers performing functional analysis can turn to neuroscientists for support, even when the components that are being proposed are not clearly modular. The sections that follow illustrate some examples of validating functional analyses on the basis of implementational-level claims.

Short-term vs. Long-term Memory

In chapter 5, we saw that one of the best and earliest examples of functional analysis in cognitive psychology was the use of behavioral evidence to support the two-store memory model. The distinction between short- and long-term memory stores emerged in cognitive psychology in the late 1950s with the work of Brown (1958) and Peterson and Peterson (1959); the modal two-store model of memory did not come into widespread acceptance until approximately a decade later (Atkinson & Shiffrin, 1968; Waugh & Norman, 1965).

Ironically, strong evidence for the modal memory model had been available in the neuropsychological literature much earlier than this. In 1953, Dr William Scoville extracted approximately eight centimeters of tissue from the inside of both temporal lobes of a 27-year-old man suffering from escalating and debilitating epileptic seizures. The surgery resulted in the removal of all of his amygdala and much of his hippocampus, which are parts of the limbic system that underlies the cortex. Some cortical tissue in his temporal lobes was also taken. At the time, it was not known that these structures played a critical role in memory. This all changed after this operation, because it produced horrible memory problems in the most famous patient in clinical neuropsychology, known only as H.M.

After the operation, H.M. had above-normal intelligence, and his recollections of events in his life up until the operation were intact. However, H.M. suffered from severe anterograde amnesia – he appeared to be incapable of adding new memories. This is chillingly revealed in Ingram's (1994, ch. 15) samples of a 1992 conversation between H.M. and Dr Suzanne Corkin, an MIT researcher who has been studying H.M. for three decades:

SC: When you're not at MIT what do you do during a typical day?
HM: Uhh see that's ... I don't remember things.
SC: Do you remember what you did yesterday?
HM: No I don't.
SC: How about this morning?
HM: I don't even remember that.
SC: Could you tell me what you had for lunch today?
HM: I don't know ... to tell you the truth.

Ingram provides many more selections from this conversation, which in his words "provide a moving look into the life of a person who lives almost entirely in the present but who nonetheless tries to martial all his intellectual resources to cope with a crippling disability" (p. 162).

Scoville provided few hints to neurosurgeons that an operation of the type performed on H.M. could result in severe memory deficits; he even repeated the procedure on another patient eight months after H.M.'s treatment (Ingram, 1994, pp. 172–5). However, when detailed studies revealed memory problems in several of Scoville's patients who had hippocampal tissue removed from both hemispheres, it was recognized that the hippocampus plays a critical role in remembering. This was reported to the medical community (Scoville & Milner, 1957) in order to prevent further use of this operation.

Memory deficits like H.M.'s are associated with other disorders as well. For instance, Korsakoff's syndrome is a memory dysfunction that is the result of a thiamin deficiency brought about from prolonged alcohol abuse (e.g., Kolb & Whishaw, 1990). This vitamin deficiency is thought to produce damage to an interior part of the brain called the thalamus, which is near (and connected to) the hippocampus. Many of the symptoms of Korsakoff's syndrome are similar to those exhibited by H.M. For example, Sacks (1987, ch. 2) describes the patient "Jimmy G." , who was seen in 1975 but who apparently had no memories more recent than 1945. After performing an interview with this patient, Sacks left the room for a couple of minutes; when he returned, the patient had forgotten ever having met him! The existence of Korsakoff's patients has been important for the study of memory, because such patients are far more common than surgical patients like H.M.

Cognitive psychology was not keeping up with the medical literature, and as a result was unaware of the existence of H.M. for nearly a decade after his description by Scoville and Milner (1957). At this time, Milner (e.g., 1965, 1966) began publishing a series of papers concerning the relation between brain and memory as revealed from the behavior of neurosurgery patients. Milner's work brought H.M. and similar patients to the attention of a field that was undertaking intensive research on human memory, and which was in the process of fleshing out the modal, two-store model of memory (e.g., Waugh & Norman, 1965). Milner's articles revealed a new kind of evidence that could be used to support the modal model.

For instance, when a free recall task (see chapter 5) was used to examine a group of amnesiac patients (which included H.M.), it was discovered that their recency effect was normal, but that they exhibited a dramatically reduced primacy effect (Baddeley & Warrington, 1970). Similarly, Drachman and Arbit (1966) studied H.M. with an extended digit-span task. In this task, the researcher says a sequence of digits to the subject, who is then asked to repeat the sequence. If this is done correctly, then another string that is one digit longer is presented. If there is an error, then the string is corrected. Normal subjects will start by being able to handle 6 or 7 digits in a sequence, and can increase their digit span to up to 20 in this task. Drachman and Arbit found that this was not the case for H.M., who was unable to extend his span at all beyond 6. Similar results were obtained for four other amnesic patients. These results are samples from many studies that together indicated that patients like H.M. have normal short-term memory, but have dysfunctional long-term memory.

Neuropsychological support for the modal model is not complete without demonstrating that a double dissociation exists: it is imperative that evidence be found that someone can have a normal long-term memory, but suffer from an abnormal short-term store. Shallice and Warrington (1970) reported one such patient. K.F. had suffered a lesion in the brain near to the language areas described earlier in this chapter, but was not aphasic. Instead, K.F. had an extremely deficient verbal short-term store. For instance, in a free recall experiment, K.F. had no recency effect. With the Brown–Peterson paradigm, his performance with zero delay prior to recall was the same as his performance with a delay. This indicated that there was no real benefit to the zero delay condition, consistent with the hypothesis that K.F. had no STM. Shallice and Warrington had found, however, that K.F.'s long-term memory was normal. For instance, in the free recall task, K.F. exhibited a normal primacy effect. Similar results were reported by Basso, Spinnler, Vallar, and Zanobio (1982) in their study of another patient, P.V.

It would be difficult to underestimate the importance of these results from clinical neuropsychology to the cognitivism that emerged in the 1960s. At a very specific level, these results provided converging evidence, that had been derived by studying the behavior of normal subjects, for the functional dissociation of memory. "The findings from amnesia underscore and confirm the distinction between short-term and long-term memory. [...] Indeed, experimental psychologists have at times concluded that the findings from case H.M. provide the best evidence of all for their distinction" (Squire, 1987, p. 142). More generally, the biological support for the modal model gave cognitivism a strong, scientific aura – why else would the results from studying amnesiacs be singled out as providing "the best evidence of all?" By appealing to this evidence, cognitivists were able to show rather convincingly that their theories, under attack for being abstract descriptions which could not possibly be viewed as explanations, said something not only about how the mind was organized, but also about how this organization was reflected in the structure of the brain.

Cognitive Neuroscience and other Decompositions of Memory

As we saw in chapter 5, the modal model of memory is long out of date. As researchers became more and more sophisticated in their experimental methods, they found that they could functionally analyze memory into many specific components. These functional decompositions were not merely possible because "a new label [for a memory store] is added each time someone devises a different way of presenting new material, or testing its recall, or doing things in between presentation and recall" (Calvin & Ojemann, 1994, p. 111). Instead, these decompositions captured significant structural differences between qualitatively distinguishable memory types. Importantly, evidence from clinical neuroscience has been used to support these more modern analyses.

For example, an important distinction in the modern memory literature is between declarative and nondeclarative memories (e.g., Schacter, 1992; Squire, 1992). Declarative memory or explicit memory concerns facts and events that can be made conscious, so that the content of these memories can be declared. Nondeclarative memory or procedural memory concerns skills, abilities, and other kinds of knowledge that can be learned, but which cannot be declared, and often which cannot be made conscious. For example, I have a vivid declarative memory of where I was when I first learned to tie my shoelaces. However, even now I am unable to write down for you in any comprehensible form the method that I use to tie my shoelaces – this information is part of my nondeclarative memory.

The distinction between these kinds of memories was revealed when researchers discovered that H.M. could acquire new nondeclarative memories, even though he was unable to do this for declarative information. For instance, Milner (1965) demonstrated that with practice H.M. improved his performance on a particular motor skill – a challenging mirror drawing task, in which he traced a design while looking at the design in a mirror. H.M.'s performance on this task remained high for several days afterward, indicating that the required skills had been stored in some form of memory. At the same time, however, H.M. was unable to recall ever having performed the task previously. Similarly, Cohen, Eichenbaum, Deacedo, and Corkin (1985) demonstrated that H.M. could improve performance on the Tower of Hanoi puzzle. Anyone who has ever tried to solve this puzzle will be familiar with the feeling that after thinking about it for a while, the moves involved become automatic (and difficult to verbalize). H.M. was able to internalize the motor component of this task, but again could never recall ever having working on the puzzle.

Another important qualitative distinction between memory systems was proposed by Paivio (e.g., 1969, 1986) in his dual-code theory of imagery. Paivio's work paved the way for the cognitive study of phenomena that behaviorists argued could not be studied scientifically because they could not be directly observed. Painstakingly, Paivio employed the standard techniques of verbal learning theorists who, in essence, were using behaviorist research methods to study human memory. Paivio carefully controlled all of the variables that verbal learning theorists viewed as being critical, and demonstrated that, compared to these variables, the best predictor of the ability to remember a word were subjects' reports about how easily they could create a mental image to it. To account for these results, Paivio proposed two interconnected but functionally independent subsystems. One was a verbal system specialized for the processing of speech and visible language; the other was a nonverbal imagery system specialized for processing objects and events. Words associated with high mental imagery (e.g., "dog") could evoke processing in both systems, which led them to be better memorized than words that could not easily activate the nonverbal system (e.g., "economy").

Again, evidence from clinical neuropsychology is consistent with Paivio's (e.g., 1969) distinction between verbal and nonverbal memory systems. For example, Teuber, Milner, and Vaughan (1968) reported their studies of a patient called N.A., who turned at the wrong time while a roommate was playing with a fencing foil in the barracks of an airforce base, and was skewered through his nostril into the left side of his midbrain. In many respects, N.A. is very similar to H.M., in that new memories are very hard to acquire – his memories since 1960 (when the accident occurred) are very poor. However, it also appears that this deficit is limited to verbal information; N.A. can learn new nonverbal information. This suggests that Paivio's nonverbal store is associated with the right hemisphere, while the verbal store in dual-code theory is associated with the left hemisphere. Kolb and Whishaw (1990, pp. 544–5) summarize the results of 11 different studies which were concerned with patients who had tissue removed from either the left or the right hippocampus. The results of all of these studies are consistent with the claim that the left hippocampus is critical for the memory of verbal material, while the right hippocampus is specialized for the memory of visual and spatial information.

Another important distinction in the study of memory is Tulving's (e.g., 1983) decomposition of declarative memory into semantic memory and episodic memory. Semantic memory is comprised of our general or abstract knowledge of the world. In contrast, episodic memory is comprised of our knowledge of past events in our own lives. For example, imagine that I bring you into my lab for a memory experiment. As part of the experiment, I present a list of words that includes the word "magpie." Later on, I ask you to recall the members of the list. Let's pretend that you don't recall the word "magpie." This doesn't mean that you have no idea what a "magpie" is – the information can

214 The Implementational Level

still reside in your semantic memory. (If you live in western Canada, you know that a magpie is a striking-looking white and iridescent bird, related to blue jays, and mean enough to attack unwary cats.) What you have forgotten is a particular episode in your life, an event in which the word "magpie" was presented to you while you were participating in an experiment.

There is considerable debate among neuropsychologists concerning the relationship between amnesia and the semantic/episodic memory distinction (e.g., Squire, 1987, pp. 169–74). Many researchers have argued that amnesia affects episodic memory, but spares semantic memory; Squire himself argues that such a view is inaccurate. One case study does appear to support Tulving's distinction quite clearly, however. Damasio, Eslinger, Damasio, van Hoesen, and Cornell (1985) reported the case of a patient called D.R.B., who had been afflicted with herpes simplex encephalitis. This is a virus that attacks the hippocampus and the temporal lobes of the brain; in D.R.B. it destroyed tissue in the hippocampus, amygdala, the temporal lobes, and substantial areas of the frontal cortex adjacent to the temporal lobes. As a result, D.R.B. is similar to H.M. in being unable to acquire new memories. Interestingly, though, this problem appears to be related to episodic memory, and not to semantic memory. D.R.B. is unable to learn the association between new stimulus objects and a particular temporal context, but he can learn new general concepts.

All of the examples described above in this section illustrate the role of clinical neuropsychology in supporting modern functional decompositions of what was known in the 1960s as secondary memory. This kind of evidence has also been brought to bear on modern functional decompositions of primary memory.

As we also saw in chapter 5, Baddeley (e.g., 1986) has been prominent for his functional analysis of short-term memory, as well as for spurring on elaborations of the modal memory model that have produced the more modern notion of working memory and its functional subcomponents. Part of the motivation for Baddeley's refinement of the modal model came from considering results from clinical neuropsychology. In the previous section we cited the existence of a double dissociation between short- and long-term memory deficits, as evidenced by patients with perfectly normal long-term memories, but suffering from abnormal short-term retention (e.g., Basso, Spinnler, Vallar, & Zanobio, 1982; Shallice & Warrington, 1970). While this kind of evidence, particularly coupled with studies of patients like H.M., distinguished short- and long-term stores, it also weighed against the modal model. According to this model, information would first be held in a short-term storage before being transferred to secondary memory through the mechanism of elaborative rehearsal. But how then could patients like K.F. have normal secondary memories if the bottleneck to secondary memory (i.e., primary memory) was dysfunctional?

The solution to this puzzle was to assume that primary memory itself could be decomposed into an organized system of subfunctions (e.g., Baddeley, 1986; Baddeley & Hitch, 1974) – the components of working memory that we saw in chapter 5. Again, the functional analysis of the components of working memory, which was primarily accomplished by observing the effects on normal memory of different kinds of dual-task experiments, has also been supported by studying memory deficits in patients who have suffered brain damage.

For example, Vallar and Baddeley (1984) have intensively studied one patient called P.V., and argued that she was suffering from a dysfunctional phonological store. First, in a task in which presented words had to be shadowed, P.V. had a memory capacity of approximately four items for visually presented words (which would be processed by the visuospatial scratchpad), but only had a memory capacity of two items when the same words were presented auditorally. Second, phonological similarity disrupted memory when stimuli were spoken, but not when they were presented visually. Third, problems with phonological stimuli did not appear to be due to a dysfunctional articulatory loop (although P.V. rarely used rehearsal as a memory strategy). This was concluded after a number of tasks indicated that her articulatory skill was normal.

Baddeley (e.g., 1986) has also used neurological evidence to validate the existence of the central executive. In the working memory model, the central executive bears a strong resemblance to what cognitive psychologists would typically describe as attention, and is used to accomplish planning and decision-making, and to perform tasks involving sequences that have not yet been mastered by other subsystems. Baddeley has suggested that the frontal lobes of the cortex are responsible for instantiating the central executive, and that frontal lobe damage disrupts the central executive, producing dysexecutive syndrome.

One example of dysexecutive syndrome was the patient R.J., reported by Baddeley and Wilson (1986). He had suffered damage to both frontal lobes as the result of a car accident. This brain damage produced decreases in his IQ (particularly performance IQ), long-term learning, and semantic memory. His digit span was normal. A striking deficit was noted in his episodic memory, because he had forgotten important events in his life (such as his marriage), as well as elaborate descriptions of events that had never happened to him. R.J. was viewed as suffering from dysexecutive syndrome because of his difficulty in initiating and controlling activity.

For instance, when R.J. was asked to generate as many names of animals as possible in a minute, he produced a third of the number that would be expected from a healthy patient. However, this was not due to a deficit in semantic memory, because when this was probed by asking him specific questions about animal names (e.g., "give me an animal name beginning with the letter *k*") he showed no difficulty. "Provided that someone else can serve as their frontal lobes by initiating behavior, they can often perform surprisingly well" (Baddeley, 1986, p. 241). As well, R.J. exhibited very little flexibility in his behavior, which resulted in strong performance deficits. He had difficulty solving a very small child's jigsaw puzzle because he appeared unable to consider the shape of the puzzle piece and the part of the picture on the puzzle piece simultaneously.

This coordination of information would be one of the tasks of the central executive in Baddeley's working memory model.

Animal Studies and Memory Decomposition

All of the implementational evidence cited above for the functional decomposition of memory has been obtained from the study of clinical patients. However, this is not the only source of verification from neurobiology. In recent years, researchers have been involved in developing and testing animal models of memory processes. In general, this kind of research attempts to duplicate memory deficits of the type that we have been discussing above in a system that permits a more detailed and precise analysis of underlying mechanisms. This work is done in the hope that researchers "will be able to analyze higher mental functions in terms of the coordinated activation of neurons in various structures in the brain" (Goldman-Rakic, 1992, p. 111).

One example of developing animal models of memory is the work of Mishkin and his colleagues (for an introduction, see Mishkin & Appenzeller, 1990). One of the goals of this research was to gain a more detailed understanding of anterograde amnesia of the type that afflicted H.M. Macaque monkeys were studied using a delayed nonmatching-to-sample task. In this task, the animal is shown an unfamiliar object. After a delay, the animal is shown this object again, as well as another unfamiliar object. The animal is required to move the new object in order to obtain a reward; this requires it to remember the other object over the delay period. A normal monkey has no difficulty with this task. However, if the monkey has had the bilateral removal of both the amygdala and the hippocampus (a similar operation to that performed on H.M.), then deficits became apparent. While the lesioned animal can learn the task if the delay is very short, its performance falls to chance if the delay is increased to only one or two minutes. This was true for both visual and tactile presentations of stimuli, indicating that the amnesia produced by the surgery was global.

The foundation for the neuropsychological decomposition of memory was laid with the discovery that H.M.'s nondeclarative memory was not affected by his surgery. Similar dissociations have been observed in macaque monkeys. For instance, Mishkin, Malamut, and Bachevalier (1984) found that surgical removal of the amygdala and hippocampus did not prevent learning in an object discrimination task. In this procedure, the animal is presented a sequence of twenty different object pairs. A reward is consistently associated with one object in each pair. Once each day the animal is presented exactly the same sequence of objects; learning has reached criterion when the animal is capable of choosing the rewarded object in each pair. Mishkin, Malamut, and Bachevalier have found that the surgically treated monkeys perform as well on this task as do control animals, even though the treated monkeys are unable to learn the delayed nonmatching-to-sample task. Mishkin and Appenzeller (1990, p. 101) strongly hint that learning in the object discrimination task involves nondeclarative memory: "It is noncognitive: it is founded not on knowledge or even on memories (in the sense of independent mental entities) but on automatic connections between a stimulus and a response."

Dissociations between declarative and nondeclarative memories have also been studied in the rat (e.g., Eichenbaum, 1992). Eichenbaum performed an extensive review of the literature in search of an operational definition of this memory distinction, because the distinction as normally defined for humans presents "a formidable challenge for the study of animals" (p. 218). Eichenbaum concluded that declarative memory is primarily involved in the comparison among items, as well as when memory must be exploited in novel situations. In contrast, nondeclarative memory is viewed as being noncomparative and inflexible. In one example of the application of these operational definitions, Eichenbaum discusses the results of a study in which the effect of lesions to the fornix of the rat (which is part of its hippocampal system) affected odor discrimination learning. In one condition, two odors were presented simultaneously, and rats had to learn an appropriate discriminative response. Compared to control animals, fornix-lesioned rats were severely impaired in this task, which requires the comparison of the two odors. However, if the two odors were presented successively – hindering the comparative component of the task, and necessitating noncomparative strategies – the experimental animals were actually superior to normal animals.

Animal researchers have also attempted to gain insight into the mechanisms underlying working memory by studying the characteristics of the prefrontal cortex (for an introduction see Goldman-Rakic, 1992). One aspect of this research has been the use of single-cell recording techniques to reveal the biological reality of working memory (Funahashi, Bruce, & Goldman-Rakic, 1989). First, monkeys are trained to perform the following visual tracking task: The animal starts by fixating its gaze on a central display marker. During fixation, a target flashes on the screen and then disappears. After a delay of several seconds, the central display marker disappears, and the monkey moves its eyes to look at the location where the target had appeared. Once the animal is trained, electrodes are inserted into its prefrontal cortex to measure the activity of neurons there when the task is performed. Some of these neurons exhibit memory fields: they become highly active when the target disappears from view, and do not decrease activity until the animal shifts its gaze at the end of the trial. This strongly suggests that these neurons are instantiating the visuospatial scratchpad, representing the spatial position of the (absent) target until this position is responded to.

Part III   Can Connectionism Inform Neuroscience?

The previous two parts of this chapter have examined some of the relationships between classical cognitive science and neuroscience. In both parts, we have been emphasizing the fact that the when neuroscientists find evidence that particular functions are localized in the brain, this evidence can be used to support functional decompositions that have been based on behavioral studies. In this part of the paper, we continue our interest in the mapping of "localized" behaviors to localized brain areas, but do so from a connectionist perspective. In particular, we will consider how connectionism can inform neuroscience by providing a medium in which to test the soundness of certain methodological assumptions that cognitive neuroscientists frequently adopt.

Connectionism vs. Neuroscience

One reason for the current popularity of connectionism is the hope that PDP models can fill a "biological vacuum" that has been left by other approaches to modeling that cognitive scientists have endorsed (e.g., Clark, 1989). As we saw in chapter 3, this is because connectionist models are touted as being "neuronally inspired" – processing units are roughly equivalent to neurons, and connections between processors are roughly equivalent to synapses (see, for example, the visual analogy rendered in Rumelhart, Hinton, & McClelland, 1986, fig. 1).

In spite of the claims that connectionists make about the neuronal inspiration of their models, neuroscientists are quite skeptical about the biological plausibility of the PDP architecture. For instance, one can generate long lists of PDP architectural properties that are clearly not true of the brain (e.g., Crick & Asanuma, 1986; Smolensky, 1988, table 1). As a result, PDP models are often vilified as oversimplifications by neuroscientists; Douglas and Martin (1991, p. 292) refer to them as "stick and ball models." Reeke and Edelman (1988, p. 144) offer this blunt assessment of the neurophysiological relevance of PDP connectionism: "These new approaches, the misleading label 'neural network computing' notwithstanding, draw their inspiration from statistical physics and engineering, not from biology."

Neuroscientists' concerns about the relevance of PDP models to their discipline are justified if connectionists are claiming that these models bear a strong relationship to actual neural circuitry. However, other claims are possible, and can mediate a much more fruitful relationship between connectionism and neuroscience. Armony, Servan-Schreiber, Cohen, and LeDoux (1995, p. 247) make this point very nicely about their own connectionist research: "Although an important goal of our work is to develop neurally constrained models, we do not intend to reproduce the full complexity of the neurobiological system under study. Rather, our goal is to use computational models as a means of exploring the relationship between neurobiological findings and behavior. Through such explorations, we hope to discover whether certain basic principles can account for both a set of detailed neurobiological findings and, at the same time, patterns of behavior related to the functioning of this neurobiological system." In other words, one way to view the relationship between connectionism and neuroscience is to treat a PDP network as a medium in which general principles of interest to neuroscience can be explored. One recent example of this, in which PDP networks are used to examine the validity of a general methodological assumption of cognitive neuroscience, is described below.

Of course, Goldman-Rakic (1992) suggests that nonmechanistic approaches to cognition are not characteristic of good science. For example, she points out that "for the greater part of this century, neurobiologists often denied that [higher-order] functions were accessible to scientific analysis or declared that they belonged strictly to the domain of psychology or philosophy" (p. 111). Goldman-Rakic's implication is that cognitivism can now be viewed as being respectable now that the brain scientists have something to say about this. Of course, as was discussed in chapter 6, the issue is quite a bit more complicated than she lets on. However, she does raise an important issue: if empirical data from neuroscience and clinical neuropsychology can be used to support (and even motivate) decompositions of cognitive capacities, then why should we be considering cognition at any level more abstract than the implementational?

Behavioral Dissociations and the Locality Assumption

As we have already seen in this chapter, behavioral deficits associated with brain injury have served as the primary type of data used to make inferences about the underlying functional organization of the brain. In practice, cognitive neuroscientists generally find it useful to distinguish between qualitatively different types of behavioral deficits. A single dissociation consists of a patient performing task I extremely poorly and task II at normal level or at least very much better than task I. In contrast, a double dissociation occurs when one patient performs task I significantly poorer than task II, and another patient performs task II significantly poorer than task I (e.g. Shallice, 1988).

Cognitive neuroscientists have spent a great deal of time examining the logic underlying the kinds of valid inferences that can be drawn from dissociations (e.g., Caramazza, 1986; Shallice, 1988). As a result, these scientists are particularly interested in discovering double dissocations. For example, Shallice argues that there is no evidence that a double dissociation can be observed as the result of two different lesions to a "properly distributed network" (p. 257). The corollary of this view is that "the existence of a neuropsychological double dissociation signifies that at least part of an overall system is functionally specialized" (p. 258).

The view that dissociation data can be used to conclude that internal structures are functionally specialized or local in nature is strongly related to what Farah (1994) calls the *locality assumption*. The locality assumption is the view that when one component of the functional architecture is damaged, the effects of this damage will be exclusively local – the nondamaged components of the architecture will continue to function normally in the absence of the damaged component. As a result "the patient's behavior will therefore manifest the underlying impairment in a relatively direct and straightforward way" (1994, p. 43). Kosslyn and Van Kleeck (1990, p. 390) equate the locality assumption with the view that behavioral deficits directly mirror the structure of the underlying mechanism. "It as if when Humpty-Dumpty falls, the pieces separate in predetermined ways, and the whole can be understood by studying the pieces."

Recently, researchers have voiced strong concerns about the validity of the locality assumption. For example, Kosslyn and Van Kleeck (1990) argue that there are six different reasons to distrust the assumption. First, functional components cannot logically be identified with symptoms. Second, functional components need not be associated with spatially local brain structures, and can be associated with redundant mechanisms (see also Medler & Dawson, 1994). Third, the mapping from functions to behavioral deficits is not one-to-one. Fourth, behavior is determined by multiple components, and after brain injury the resulting behavior is likely to reflect the interactions of remaining components, and not necessarily the absence of a particular function (e.g., Kean, 1980). Fifth, after damage the system might dynamically adjust to compensate for difficulties. Sixth, the localization of a lesion does not necessarily localize the functional damage. After considering evidence in support of these arguments, Kosslyn and Van Kleeck note that "on the face of things, patterns of behavioral dysfunction following damage are no better than any other behavioral data" (p. 397).

Using PDP Networks to Examine the Locality Assumption

Farah (1994) has also argued against the locality assumption. Of interest to us in this chapter is the fact that her arguments against the assumption were framed in the context of connectionist networks. Farah hypothesized that the locality assumption may be unwarranted because it is possible that nonlocal or distributed architectures, such as PDP networks, could also produce single or double dissociations when they were lesioned. In other words, if behavioral dissociations were observed in a connectionist network, this would be evidence against adopting the locality assumptions, because by definition such networks are not supposed to have any internal, local structure.

Farah proceeded to consider PDP networks for three content areas (visual attention, semantic memory, and face recognition) in which neuropsychological dissociations had been previously used to make inferences about the underlying architecture via the locality assumption. For each of these content areas, Farah provided an alternative, interactive (nonlocal) architecture – a PDP network. For each of these models, local damage produced (local) behavioral deficits analogous to the neuropsychological dissociations at hand. In two of these cases she produced a single dissociation, while in a third she produced a double dissociation (but see Butterworth, 1994, regarding this latter claim). These data suggested to Farah that one cannot conclude that a specific behavioral deficit is associated with the loss of a local function. Moreover, because PDP models putatively embody theories that are more parsimonious, and more consistent with other information about brain structure and function, the strong conclusion to be drawn is that the locality assumption is unnecessary and false.

Farah's results raise an interesting question. If one can perform two different lesions to a single PDP model, and these lesions produce a double dissociation in the network's behavior, is this sufficient evidence to dismiss the locality assumption? The traditional PDP position (e.g., Farah, 1994) answers in the affirmative because networks constructed from the generic connectionist architecture are "by definition" interactive (and thus nonlocal). In contrast, Shallice's (1988) interpretation of this result would be that the network's behavior indicates the existence of internal functional specificity because only such specificity can mediate a double dissociation.

How can one adjudicate these quite different interpretations of the same effect? The answer is that it is an empirical issue. One must take the network, perform a detailed analysis of its internal structure, and then use this analysis to support one (and refute the other) interpretation of the double dissociation. In other words, before drawing conclusions from the network's behavior, one must independently determine whether the internal structure of the lesioned network is local or not. This is necessary because, as we saw in chapter 5, when one interprets a PDP network, one might find that it is actually far more functionally specialized than Farah assumes (e.g., Berkeley, Dawson, Medler, Schopflocher, & Hornsby, 1995).

Medler, Dawson, Kingstone, and Panasiuk (1998) attempted to further Farah's research program by lesioning networks, but combining these lesioning experiments with an interpretation of the internal structure of the network being damaged. The purpose of this was to determine whether or not any observed local deficits in network behavior were associated with the removal of local network components.

Medler *et al.* (1998) conducted their study on a network trained on Bechtel and Abrahamsen's (1991) logic problem, which was described earlier in chapter 5. They chose this problem because it was 1) psychologically interesting, 2) nontrivial in its level of difficulty, and 3) known to produce some local internal structure when it is learned by a network of value units. (This local structure is revealed by the banding analysis that was described in chapter 5.) They trained a value unit network with 10 hidden units to solve the problem successfully using the Dawson and Schopflocher (1992a) version of the generalized delta rule. They then used the Berkeley *et al.* (1995) banding analysis to analyze the functional role of each hidden unit. Finally, they created 10 different "patients" by taking the network and lesioning one of its hidden units. After lesioning the network, they examined its responses to the training set (recall that the network is trained to identify four different kinds of logic problems, and to indicate whether the problem is valid or invalid). Each "patient" network was created by ablating a different hidden unit from the complete network.

Medler *et al.* (1998) found that different lesions to the network produced very different kinds of effects on its responses to the logic problems. For instance, in some cases very clean double dissociations were identified. When Hidden Unit 3 was ablated from the network, it became completely unable to identify *modus ponens* and *modus tollens* problems, but had no difficulty identifying alternative syllogisms or disjunctive syllogisms. In contrast, when Hidden Unit 7 was ablated from the network, it became completely unable to identify disjunctive syllogisms, but was responded correctly to *modus ponens*, *modus tollens*, and alternate syllogisms. In other cases, lesioning the network had absolutely no effect whatsoever. For example, when Hidden Unit 4 was lesioned, the network responded normally to all four problem types.

Why did different lesions to the network have such different effects? A qualitative analysis of the network revealed that the extent of the deficit in network behavior was related to how local was the function of the ablated hidden unit. Medler *et al.* (1998) used the interpreted bands of the ablated hidden units to support this qualitative analysis. For example, the banding analysis revealed that Hidden Unit 3 had a very particular local function – its role was to detect the presence of the connective "IF ... THEN" in the input logic problem. As only *modus ponens* and *modus tollens* problems contain this connective, it is not surprising that when this unit was lesioned, only the performance on these two types of problems was affected. Similarly, the banding analysis of Hidden Unit 7 indicated that it also had a highly local functional role – its only purpose was to detect the connective "NOT BOTH ... AND." As this connective is only found in disjunctive syllogisms, it is not surprising that when this unit was ablated, only the performance on disjunctive syllogisms was affected. Finally, the analysis of Hidden Unit 4 indicated that it had no local structure at all – its jittered density plot did not band at all. Medler *et al.* argued that this absence of local structure might be responsible for the fact that when it was lesioned, no local behavioral deficits were observed at all.

The qualitative analysis above indicates the strong possibility that, in contrast to Farah's (1994) claim, local behavioral deficits in a PDP network are connected with the loss of local internal structure, where "local structure" in this particular case is revealed by the degree of banding of a jittered density plot. Medler *et al.* (1998) performed one additional quantitative analysis to support this possibility. They reasoned that Kaiser's (1958) use of variance to measure the "simple structure" of factor analytic solutions could also be used to measure the degree of banding of a jittered density plot: highly banded density plots will have high measures of variance, while density plots that are "smeared" will have very low variance. Using their 10 "patient" networks to provide the data, they correlated the variance of the density plot of the lesioned network with the locality of the behavioral deficit (i.e., with the total number of errors made by the lesioned network, or with the total number of different types of errors made by the network). They found an extremely high correlation (0.93) between the two measures. This result was consistent with Shallice's (1988) suggestion that highly local behavioral deficits are associated with the disruption of local brain mechanisms. This result was inconsistent with Farah's (1994) dismissal of the locality assumption on the basis of her connectionist experiments. Because Farah did not examine the internal structure of her networks, it is not clear that she produced local behavioral deficits by removing nonlocal structure.

Summary

The results above should not be taken as a definitive statement on the status of the locality assumption. The Medler *et al.* (1998) results merely indicate that just because one has trained a PDP network, its internal structure may not be as nonlocal as some might assume. It could very well be that Farah's (1994) main point is valid. All that it would take to establish this point would be to demonstrate that lesions to a nonlocal network can indeed produce highly specific behavioral deficits. The Medler *et al.* study merely emphasizes the fact that before this point can be established, network interpretation is required to verify the fact that the lesioned network is indeed nonlocal.

The more important point to be gleaned from the section above is the fact that one can fruitfully use connectionist networks as a medium in which to explore some of the basic methodological assumptions that cognitive neuroscientists adopt. In particular, researchers' confidence in the locality assumption can be strengthened (or undermined) on the basis of results that can be obtained by PDP researchers. In this sense, it is clearly the case that connectionism can inform neuroscience. In the next part of the chapter, let us turn to the reverse issue: to what extent can information from neuroscience be used to strengthen connectionist research?

Part IV   Can Connectionism be Informed by Neuroscience?

At the start of the previous part of the chapter, it was pointed out that neuroscientists are extremely sceptical about the biological plausibility of connectionist networks. However, these criticisms miss the mark. As we saw in both chapter 3 and chapter 6, PDP networks are designed to be extreme simplifications, glossing over many of the complex details true of neural systems (for an example, see Braham & Hamblen, 1990). This is because the PDP architecture is itself functionalist in nature. It attempts to capture just those properties of biological networks that are computationally relevant. The intent of this enterprise is to describe neural networks in a vocabulary that permits one to make rigorous claims about what they can do, or about why the brain might have the particular structure that it does. For example, claims about the competence of neural networks only arise when one abstracts over neurophysiological details, and describes important aspects of neuronal function either mathematically or logically (e.g., McCulloch & Pitts, 1943/1988). Furthermore, functional descriptions and computational analyses can often shed light on questions that one would imagine neuroscience has basic answers to, but in fact does not. For example, why do different functions appear to be localized in different regions of the brain? Ballard (1986) argues that this type of organization is to be expected of a connectionist system that evolves to solve the so-called packing problem: how to pack an enormous variety of functions into a network (like the brain) with a finite number of processors.

It is because of its functionalist approach to neuroscience that PDP research has the potential to build a strong bridge between neuroscience and cognitive theories. Furthermore, such a bridge – be it connectionist in nature or not – is required to provide explanatory force to cognitive theory, as we saw in chapter 6. However, there are many factors working against realizing connectionism's potential to subsume cognitive theory.

Dawson and Shamanski (1994) have argued that the design decisions governing connectionist theory are determined by engineering needs – generating the appropriate output – and not by cognitive or neurophysiological considerations. For example, at the implementational level connectionists often make design decisions about their architecture without justifying them as computationally relevant properties of neural circuits. It is perfectly reasonable to propose an architecture that ignores complex properties of neural substrate with the goal of making computationally relevant properties explicit. It is quite another to create an architecture that incorporates properties that make it work, independent of whether these properties bear any relation to neural substrates whatsoever.

In the sections below, I will briefly review some of the examples of connectionists adopting biologically undefended design decisions that were discussed by Dawson and Shamanski (1994). In each of these examples, I will also try to show how adopting additional constraining information from neuroscience can enhance connectionism's role within cognitive science.

Connectionists Adopt Monotonic Activation Functions

To a large extent, changes in conceptualizations of activation functions for processing units (see chapter 3) have been responsible for the evolution from less powerful, single-layer networks of the "old connectionism" to the more powerful multilayer networks of the "new connectionism." For example, in a perceptron (e.g., Rosenblatt, 1962), the activation function for the output unit is a linear threshold function (figure 3.5a): If the net input to the unit exceeds a threshold, then it assumes an activation of 1, otherwise it assumes an activation of 0. This kind of activation function is roughly analogous to the "all-or-none law" governing the generation of action potentials in neurons (e.g., Levitan & Kaczmarek, 1991, pp. 37–44). However, linear threshold functions are characterized by mathematical properties that make them difficult to work with.

The learning procedures developed within the new connectionism were made possible by approximating the linear threshold function with more tractable mathematical equations. For example, it has been quite common to adopt sigmoid-shaped "squashing" functions, like the logistic depicted in figure 3.5b. The mathematical limits of this nonlinear equation are functionally equivalent to the two discrete states of the linear threshold function. However, the function itself is continuous, and therefore has a derivative. Because of this property, one can use calculus to determine rules that will manipulate weights in such a way to perform a gradient descent in an error space (e.g., Rumelhart *et al.*, 1986b, pp. 322–7). In short, continuous activation functions permit one to derive powerful learning rules.

However, "squashing" functions have another mathematical property that makes these learning rules practical to apply. Such activation functions are monotonic – they are nondecreasing in relation to increases in net input. The derivation of the generalized delta rule (Rumelhart *et al.*, 1986b, p. 325), and the derivation of learning rules for stochastic autoassociative networks like Boltzman machines (e.g., Muller & Reinhardt, 1990, p. 37) stipulate that activation functions be monotonic. If they are not, then in practice they are not always guaranteed to work. For example, Dawson and Schopflocher (1992a) found that if processing units that had a particular nonmonotonic activation function (the Gaussian illustrated in figure 3.5c) were inserted into a network trained with the standard version of the generalized delta rule, then quite frequently the network settled into a local minimum in which it did not respond correctly to all inputs.

The assumption that activation functions are monotonic appears to be a practical requirement for learning procedures. However, adopting this assumption for this reason alone is dangerous practice, because monotonicity does not appear to be universally true of neural mechanisms. For instance, Ballard (1986) uses a relatively coarse behavioral criterion (i.e., the response of a cell as a function of a range of net inputs) to distinguish between *integration devices* – neurons whose behavior is well described with activation functions like the logistic in figure 3.5b – and *value units* – neurons whose behavior is well described with activation functions like the Gaussian in figure 3.5c.

Nonmonotonicity becomes even more apparent at a more detailed level of analysis. It should be apparent that the activation function for a connectionist processor is strongly related to the mechanisms that produce action potentials in neurons. A major component of these mechanisms are voltage gated ion channels in nerve membranes (for an introduction, see Levitan & Kaczmarek, 1991, pp. 51–124). These channels allow ionic currents to pass through them, and as a result affect a neuron's resting membrane potential. In turn, changes in membrane voltage affect the likelihood that these channels are open or closed. In some cases, such as the potassium channel considered by Levitan and Kaczmarek (1991, fig. 3.9) the relationship between this likelihood and membrane voltage is monotonic. In other important cases, it is decidedly nonmonotonic. For instance, as membrane voltage becomes positive, voltage gated sodium channels begin to open. As the voltage continues to increase, the channel becomes inactive. The nonmonotonic character of the sodium channel played an important role in Hodgkin and Huxley's (e.g., 1952) quantitative modeling of the action potential.

PDP learning rules are not limited in principle to monotonic activation functions. For instance, we have already seen that Dawson and Schopflocher (1992a) derived a modified version of the generalized delta rule that is capable of training networks of value units (i.e., processors with Gaussian activation functions). Radial basis function networks (e.g., Moody & Darken, 1989) also have units with nonmonotonic activation functions, although they use a net input function that in effect makes them behave monotonically (see Dawson & Schopflocher, 1992a, fig. 2c).

Furthermore, the move away from monotonic activation functions – inspired by biology – can lead to technical advances in connectionist models. For example, Dawson and Schopflocher (1992a) developed the value unit architecture with the sole intent of incorporating nonmonotonicity into the generic PDP architecture. They were surprised to find that the learning rule that they developed resulted in networks that could learn to solve many problems much faster than standard PDP networks. Furthermore, they had no idea that this modification of the architecture would eventually lead to a new method for interpreting networks, Berkeley *et al.*'s (1995) banding method. In other words, the value unit architecture is a case in point where our attempts to be better neuroscientists resulted in our being better computer scientists!

Connectionists Assume Modifiable Biases

A tenet of the PDP approach is that connection "weights are usually regarded as encoding the system's knowledge. In this sense, the connection strengths play the role of the program in a conventional computer" (Smolensky, 1988, p. 1). Thus the basic goal of a connectionist learning rule is to manipulate the pattern of connectivity in a network. This is in accordance with current understanding of actual neural circuits that are capable of learning. For example, experimental studies of the gill withdrawal reflex in the sea slug *Aplysia Californica* have indicated that learning alters the efficacy of synapses between neurons (for a review, see Dudai, 1989, ch. 4).

However, when networks are trained by supervised learning procedures like the generalized delta rule (e.g., Rumelhart, Hinton, & Williams, 1986a, 1986b), the pattern of connectivity in the network is not all that is changed. It is quite typical to also modify the *bias values* of the activation function as well. For a sigmoid "squashing" function like the logistic, the bias is a parameter that positions the activation function in net input space; changing bias is equivalent to translating the activation function along an axis representing net input. In other words, the bias of a processing unit is analogous to its threshold. Biases can be modified by construing them as connection weights emanating from a "bias processor" that is always on (e.g., Rumelhart *et al.*, 1986b, fn. 1). A processing unit's bias is manipulated by modifying the strength of the connection between it and its "bias processor." However, it is important to note that this is merely a description which permits unit bias to be learned. "Bias processors" are not presumed to exist in a network. Instead, modifying the bias of a unit's activation function is analogous to directly modifying a neuron's threshold for generating an action potential.

The assumption that bias can be modified violates the connectionist tenet that all that matters are patterns of connectivity. This in itself is not problematic. The problem arises in justifying this design decision – in defending the existence of modifiable biases in the connectionist architecture. In point of fact, there is little evidence that threshold membrane potentials in real neural networks are modifiable. For example, Kupfermann, Castellucci, Pinsker, and Kandel (1970) demonstrated that in the neural circuits that mediate the gill withdrawal reflex in *Aplysia*, the thresholds of motor neurons to constant external current did not change as a function of learning. It was concluded that learning only modified synaptic properties in this neural circuit. Similarly, neuroscientists concerned with learning in the mammalian brain have focused on a particular mechanism, the long-term potentiation of synapses (for reviews, see Cotman, Monaghan, & Ganong, 1988; Massicotte & Baudry, 1991). To our knowledge, neuroscientists do not believe that neuron thresholds are themselves plastic.

Why does PDP connectionism use modifiable bias terms, when this maneuver does not appear to be supported by extant neurophysiological evidence? The answer is that without modifiable biases, it is impossible for some PDP networks to learn how to solve a variety of problems. In other words, incorporating modifiable biases is an engineering decision. When biases are modifiable, networks can learn to solve many more problems than when they are not.

This is not to say that connectionist research in general is fundamentally flawed because it requires modifiable biases. Many architectures can use fixed thresholds in their processing units, including Hopfield nets (e.g., Hopfield, 1982), Boltzman machines (e.g., Ackley, Hinton, & Sejnowski, 1985), and value unit networks (e.g., Dawson *et al.*, 1992). The critical issue is that modifiable biases are adopted in some architectures without being neurophysiologically justified. If it is indeed the case that plastic neural circuits do not have directly modifiable thresholds, then such justification is important, because without it certain architectures – i.e., those that require modifiable biases in order to learn – may be deemed uninteresting to cognitive science.

Are there any advantages to working with networks in which biases are held constant during a network's training? One study performed by Dawson, Schopflocher, Kidd, and Shamanski (1992) demonstrated that holding bias constant can be a bad engineering decision, but might make good sense as far as cognitive science goes. They trained networks of value units on a data compression task called the *encoder problem* (see figure 7.4). In this problem, the network learns to reproduce its input unit activity on its output units, but must do so after sending the input signal through a "bottleneck" of a small number of hidden units. In one condition, biases were trained; in another condition, biases were held constant. Dawson *et al.* found that when biases were held constant, it took networks substantially longer to solve the problem. Thus holding biases constant is a practice that probably would not be encouraged from a computer science perspective. However, even though learning was slower, another unanticipated benefit was discovered. Dawson *et al.* found that when biases were not modified, there was a significant increase in the number of

Output units

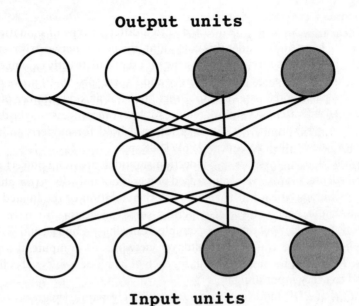

Input units

Figure 7.4 A network for the 4-2-4 encoder problem. In this network, whatever activity is placed in the input layer is supposed to be echoed in the output layer. In this figure, the pattern of activity in the input layer consists of two "ON" and two "OFF" processors. The network is generating this same pattern in its output units. To do so, however, the input pattern is compressed by a narrow "bottleneck" of two hidden units. Other versions of this problem can be created by increasing the number of input units, output units, and hidden units. Typically, if there are N input and output units, there will be $\log_2 N$ hidden units in an encoder network.

"dead" connections (i.e., connection weights whose absolute value was 0.01 or less). Thus, holding bias constant in the value unit architecture might lead to networks with significantly simpler structure (i.e., fewer connections).

Connectionists Adopt Massively Parallel Patterns of Connectivity

The history of connectionism can be presented in capsule form as follows: In the beginning, connectionist networks had no hidden units. Minsky and Papert (1969/1988) then proved that such networks had limited competence, and were thus not worthy of further study. The new connectionism was born when learning rules for networks with hidden units were discovered (e.g., Ackley, Hinton, & Sejnowski, 1985; Rumelhart *et al.*, 1986a). These rules provided researchers the ability to teach networks that were powerful enough to overcome the Minsky/Papert limitations. (Detailed versions of this history are provided in Hecht-Nielsen, 1987, pp. 14–19; Papert, 1988.)

What is interesting about this history is that it pins the blame for the limitations of networks created by old connectionism – perceptrons – on the number of processing layers. It neglects the fact that Minsky and Papert (1969/1988) were extremely concerned with a different type of limitation, the *limited-order constraint*. Under this constraint, the neural network is restricted to being local – there is no single processing unit that can directly examine every input unit's activity. For example, Minsky and Papert (pp. 56–9) prove that to compute the parity predicate (i.e., to assert "true" if an odd number of input units has been activated), a network requires at least one processor to be directly connected to every input unit. Such proofs still hold for modern multilayer perceptrons (see Minksy & Papert, 1969/1988, pp. 251–52).

There is no doubt that the new-connectionist models are more powerful than their antecedents. However, this increased power is not only due to the addition of layers of hidden units, but is also due to the violation of the limited-order constraint: these new models also permit some processors to have direct connections to every input unit. For example, Rumelhart, Hinton, and Williams (1986b, fig. 6) have trained a multilayer network to compute the parity predicate. However, the network requires each of its hidden units to be directly connected to every input unit.

The fact that PDP models permit such massively parallel patterns of connectivity between input units and hidden units is unfortunate. While it is true that this design decision will increase the network's competence, it does this at the expense of both biological and empirical plausibility. With respect to the former issue, there is no evidence to indicate that, in human sensory systems, massively parallel connections exist between receptor cells and the next layer of neurons. Indeed, computational modelers of visual processing attempt to increase the biological plausibility of their models by enforcing spatially local connections among processing units (e.g., Ullman, 1979). With respect to the latter issue, humans may indeed be subject to computational limits due to the limited-order constraint. For example, Minsky and Papert (1969/1988, p. 13) have used a small set of very simple figures to prove that a perceptron of limited order cannot determine whether all the parts of any geometric figure are connected to one another. Psychophysical experiments have shown that preattentive visual processes involved in texture perception (e.g., Julesz, 1981) and motion perception (Dawson, 1990a) are insensitive to this property as well. It is quite plausible to suppose that this insensitivity is related to the fact that the neural circuitry responsible for registering these figures is not massively parallel.

Indeed, the relationship between PDP models and biological networks can be strengthened by imposing the limited-order constraint. Moorhead, Haig, and Clement (1989) trained a PDP network to behave as a skeletal model of the early visual system. In their network, input units were analogous to retinal ganglion cells, output units were trained to behave as simple cells, and it was hypothesized that hidden units would evolve center-surround receptive fields analogous to the parvocellular neurons in the lateral geniculate nucleus. This hypothesis, though, was not supported. The receptive fields of the hidden units were quite unlike those of biological neurons. As a result, Moorhead, Haig, and

Clement concluded that there were substantial shortcomings in the use of connectionist networks to model the visual pathway.

However, one substantial problem with the Moorhead, Haig, and Clement (1989) simulation was that it failed to impose the limited-order constraint, because every hidden unit in the network had a connection to every input unit. In a follow-up study, Dawson, Kremer, and Gannon (1994) trained a network that was similar to the Moorhead *et al.* model, but manipulated the presence or absence of the limited-order constraint to determine whether this would affect the relationship between receptive fields in the network and those found in biological vision systems. In their study, they used an 11×11 array of input units that were analogous to retinal receptors, a 9×9 array of hidden units, and two output units that were analogous to complex cells in the primate visual system (see figure 7.5). One of the output units was trained to turn "ON" to a horizontal edge presented anywhere in the input array, while the other was trained to turn "ON" to a vertical edge presented anywhere in the input array. In one condition, the limited-order constraint was not imposed, and every hidden unit was connected to each of the 121 input units. In the other condition, a strong version of the limited-order constraint was imposed: each hidden unit was only connected to a small 3×3 "window" of input units.

Of interest to Dawson, Kremer, and Gannon (1994) was the nature of the receptive fields that would emerge in the hidden units. It was assumed that the hidden layer was analogous to a layer of simple cells, which have receptive fields tuned to detect short line segments oriented in a particular direction. In the condition where there was no limited-order constraint, no such receptive fields were found. In contrast, when the limited-order constraint was imposed, a significant number of "simple cell" receptive fields were observed. In short, the use of the limited-order constraint produced a network that was more biologically relevant. These results also raised the possibility that simple cell receptive fields might arise in biological systems because neurons in the early visual pathway are not fully connected to the retina.

Connectionists Assume Homogenous Processing Units

One of the interesting properties of PDP models is their homogeneity (for an exception, see the hybrid networks described by Dawson & Schopflocher, 1992a). It is typically the case that all of the units in PDP networks are of the same type, and that all of the changes that occur during learning in the network are governed by a single procedure. "The study of connectionist machines has led to a number of striking and unanticipated findings; it's surprising how much computing can be done with a uniform network of simple interconnected elements" (Fodor & Pylyshyn, 1988, p. 6).

In some sense, the homogenous structure of PDP networks can be construed as "neuronally inspired." At a macroscopic level, neurons themselves appear to be relatively homogenous; Kuffler, Nicholls, and Martin (1984, ch. 1) note that the nervous system uses only two basic types of signals, which are virtually

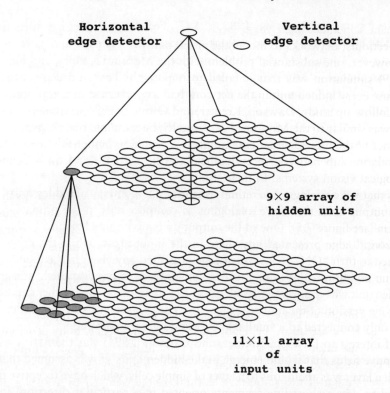

Horizontal
edge detector

Vertical
edge detector

9×9 array of
hidden units

11×11 array
of
input units

Figure 7.5 The limited-order constraint as imposed in the Dawson, Kremer, and Gannon (1994) network. The two output units are trained to detect either horizontal or vertical edges presented anywhere in the input layer. Each output unit is connected to every hidden unit. However, in Dawson *et al.*'s experimental condition, the connections from the hidden units to the input units were of limited order. As illustrated, each hidden unit was only connected to a small 3 × 3 window of input units in this condition.

identical in all neurons. Furthermore, these signals appear to be common to an enormous range of animal species; much of our molecular understanding of neuronal mechanisms comes from the study of invertebrate systems. "The brain, then, is an instrument, made of 10^{10} to 10^{12} components of rather uniform materials, that uses a few stereotyped signals. What seems so puzzling is how the proper assembly of the parts endows the instrument with the extraordinary properties that reside in the brain" (Kuffler, Nicholls, & Martin, p. 7). The answer to this puzzle, according to both neurophysiologists and connectionists, lies in understanding the complex and specific patterns of connectivity between these homogenous components. Getting (1989, p. 186) has noted that in the neuroscience of the late 1960s "the challenge of uncovering the secrets to brain function lay in the unravelling of neural connectivity."

However, a more microscopic analysis of relatively simple plastic neural circuits has revealed neural networks have properties that are far more diverse and complicated than was anticipated. "No longer can neural networks be viewed as the interconnection of many like elements by simple excitatory or inhibitory synapses" (Getting, 1989, p. 187). For example, Getting notes that there is an enormous variety of properties of neurons, synapses, and patterns of connectivity. These serve as the building blocks of neural circuits, and importantly can change as a function of both intracellular and extracellular contexts. As a result, a detailed mapping of the connectivity pattern in a neural network is not sufficient to understand its function. The functional connectivity in the network – the actual effects of one cell on another – can change as the properties of the network's "building blocks" are modulated, even though the anatomical connections in the network are fixed (see Getting, 1989, fig. 2 for a striking example).

Getting (p. 199) has painted quite a different picture of neural networks than would appear to be reflected in the PDP architecture: "The comparative study of neural networks has led to a picture of neural networks as dynamic entities, constrained by their anatomical connectivity but, within these limits, able to be organised and configured into several operational modes." The dynamic changes in biological networks would appear to be computationally relevant. Thus, if connectionism is to make good its promise to provide a more biologically feasible architecture than is found in classical systems, it would appear that the generic architecture must be elaborated extensively. The homogeneity-of-processors assumption must be abandoned, and in its place should be processing units and connections that have diverse and dynamic properties.

One advantage of the value unit learning rule developed by Dawson and Schopflocher (1992a) is that it can be used to take a small step towards the training of hybrid networks. The learning rule is capable of training PDP networks composed of both value units and integration devices. This is because the value unit learning rule only changes the way in which errors for output units are computed, and does not alter the general backpropagation of error algorithm.

Dawson and Schopflocher (1992a) exploited this property to provide a nicely controlled test of their learning rule's ability (figure 7.6). In a control condition, a standard network of integration devices (i.e., a network of units that used the logistic activation function) was trained to solve different versions of the encoder problem. In an experimental condition, the same sized network was used, and the hidden units were still integration devices, but the output units were changed into value units. Dawson and Schopflocher found that the hybrid networks learned to solve the encoder problem significantly faster than did the homogenous networks in the control condition. They also found that this advantage grew as the size of the encoder problem (i.e., the number of input and output units used to define the problem) was increased. While the intent of this network was to raise the biological relevance of the PDP architecture by using a hybrid model, it raised an interesting technological possibility: one might be able to speed up the learning of standard pattern classification networks by simply replacing their output units with value units, and training the entire network with the elaborated version of the generalized delta rule. Again, this is

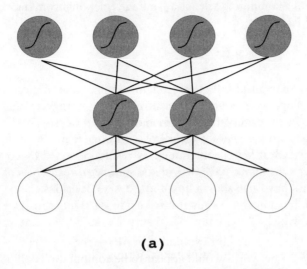

(a)

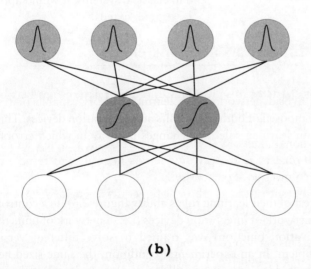

(b)

Figure 7.6 (a) A homogenous network designed for solving the 4-2-4 encoder problem. Note that all of the output and hidden units are integration devices that use the logistic activation function. (b) A hybrid network for solving the same problem. In this network, the output units are value units that use the Gaussian activation function. The hidden units are integration devices. The hybrid network learns solutions to the encoder problem much faster than does the network illustrated in (a).

an instance of a computing science advantage emerging from the exploration of a biological issue.

Summary

Dawson and Shamanski (1994) have claimed that while connectionist technology is flourishing, connectionist cognitive science is languishing. Their reason for this claim is the observation that in many cases the design decisions made by connectionists are driven by technical concerns (e.g., building a working network) instead of being constrained by results obtained by cognitive scientists. The sections above have provided a number of examples of such design decisions, and have also shown how these design decisions can be informed or constrained by implementational-level evidence. One consequence of such constraints, which should not be a surprise at all, is that the biological plausibility of PDP networks can be enhanced. A second, and more surprising, consequence is that in many cases incorporating a biologically motivated design feature into a network can actually lead to improvements that an engineer or computer scientist would be pleased to see.

Part V   Innateness and Universals

The first two parts of this chapter focused on relationships between classical cognitive science and implementational analyses. The next two parts of this chapter focused on relationships between connectionist cognitive science and implementational analyses. In this final part of the chapter, let us turn to an implementational issue that in my view is neutral with respect to anyone's classical or connectionist persuasion.

It might be surprising to those who criticize cognitivism because of its functionalist leanings (e.g., Edelman, 1992) to find out that cognitivism was responsible for reinvigorating the study of brain/behavior relations within psychology. This is because leading cognitivists, such as Piaget, Kohlberg, and Chomsky, were responsible for the resurgence of nativism in the study of psychological processes (e.g., Flanagan, 1984). In the form that it takes within cognitive science, nativism amounts to the view that "certain aspects of our knowledge and understanding are innate, part of our biological endowment, genetically determined, on a par with the elements of our common nature that cause us to grow arms and legs rather than wings" (Chomsky, 1988, p. 4).

Why does nativism emerge in cognitive science? One reason is the commitment that cognitive scientists have to the existence of the functional architecture. In computer science "it is customary to say ... that the architecture is the *fixed* structure and to talk about the architecture as genuinely immutable" (Newell, 1990, p. 81). While Newell goes on to point out that it is unlikely that the functional architecture of human cognition is completely static, he also argues that relative to other human cognitive changes (e.g., changes in knowledge or the acquisition of skills), the architecture is relatively fixed. If the functional architecture is at least relatively fixed in nature, then where does it come from? Cognitive scientists adopt nativism to answer this question, and argue that it is an innate property of the brain that is the product of human (cognitive) evolution.

A second reason for the emergence of nativism in cognitive science comes from our realization that in order to solve many different kinds of information-processing problems, we must exploit knowledge that preexists within us. Consider language acquisition, which we discussed in detail in chapter 4. Jackendoff (1994, p. 26) describes the "paradox of language acquisition" as follows: "an entire community of highly trained professionals [linguists], bringing to bear years of conscious attention and sharing of information, has been unable to duplicate the feat that every normal child accomplishes by the age of ten or so, unconsciously and unaided." Nativism is invoked to explain this paradox. "*Children have a head start on linguists*: children's unconscious strategies for language learning include some substantial hints about how a mental grammar ought to be considered" (p. 26).

An exact parallel to this paradox occurs in the study of vision (for more details, see chapter 9, below). In many cases, the visual information encoded in our retinal receptors is not by itself sufficient for us to generate a unique and accurate experience of the visual world around us (e.g., Marr, 1982). As a result, researchers believe that the visual system encodes or exploits additional assumptions about the nature of the world, and that this additional information is used to disambiguate retinal stimulation. Again, the question that arises is where does this additional information come from? And again, nativism provides the answer: it is assumed that the visual system has evolved in such a way that it encodes just those aspects of the world that have proven to be invaluable in solving visual information-processing problems. Evolution is the glue that holds together the two notions of an intrinsically structured world and of neural substrates that exploit such intrinsic structure. A usually implicit assumption underlying the natural computation approach is that the visual system has a particular format because it has evolved in a world that is characterized by structure (or, in Gibson's (1979) terms, characterized by invariants). An organism whose visual system was so structured to be able to take advantage of such invariants would be more competitive, in terms of natural selection, than an organism whose visual system could not take advantage of this information. In short, for a natural computation researcher, the anatomy of the visual system is a direct consequence of countless generations of evolution in a structured visual world. Furthermore, this advantageous anatomy is going to be encoded as part of the human genome.

Of course, one consequence of the view that human cognition comes innately equipped with particular resources that are used to solve information-processing problems is that strong implementational predictions are made. In particular, cognitive scientists not only make the claim that certain aspects of cognition are innate, but they also make the claim that these components of cognition are universal to all humans. These claims are implementational in the sense that any component of human cognition that is innate and universal must be strongly tied to specific brain structures. In the sections that follow, let us briefly review some examples of claims about innateness and universality that have arisen in cognitive science.

Proposing an Innate Language Faculty

In his book *Aspects of the Theory of Syntax*, Chomsky (1965) spearheaded the resurgence of nativism in cognitive science by arguing that language learning requires that a child enters a linguistic environment armed with a set of innate, tacit assumptions about human language. "The child approaches the data with the presumption that they are drawn from a language of a certain antecedently well-defined type, his problem being to determine which of the (humanly) possible languages is that of the community in which he is placed" (p. 27). Chomsky called this tacit knowledge about language the *universal grammar*.

In chapter 4 we discussed at length the motivation for assuming the existence of a universal grammar; let us merely review the key points here. Language learning, when described formally, is a process of generating hypotheses about the structure of a to-be-learned language after being presented examples of it (e.g., Gold, 1967). In text learning, only valid examples of a language are presented. Studies indicate quite clearly that children acquire natural languages via text learning (e.g., Pinker, 1979). However, text learning on its own should be unable to account for the acquisition of human languages. This is because Gold proved that text learning could only be used to teach very simple grammars (i.e., finite cardinality languages), and was unable to teach languages whose complexity begins to approach that of natural languages (e.g., context-sensitive and context-free grammars). The conclusion to be drawn from this is that text learning of human language is only possible for children because they come equipped with pre-existing knowledge that permits them to escape the limitations established by Gold. "Language learning would be impossible unless this were the case" (Chomsky, 1965, p. 27).

Given the Chomskian position, a major task for linguistics is identifying the components of the universal grammar. Chomsky (1965) distinguishes between two different types of universals. Substantive universals represent a fixed set of items from which the basic items in any language must be drawn. For example, certain syntactic categories (e.g., noun, verb) are presumed to be substantive universals that provide the underlying syntactic structure of any language. Chomsky also points out that there is a basic set of phonemes from which the phonological sounds in any human language appear to be drawn. If phonemes are substantive universals, then it should be possible to show that prelinguistic children have tacit abilities specialized for speech perception.

Eimas, Miller, and Jusczyk (1987) reviewed literature on speech perception in infants. They considered two general methodologies. In one, the formation of phonemic equivalence classes is studied using a discriminative head-turning response. The infant learns to turn his or her head when a target phoneme briefly interrupts a background sound (i.e., another phoneme). This is accomplished by turning on a noisy, moving toy when the stimulus sound changes; infants quickly learn to turn their heads when they hear a new sound because they are anticipating the appearance of a toy. A researcher can determine whether two sounds fall into different phonemic classes by observing whether one elicits the response against the background context of the other.

In the other paradigm reviewed by Eimas, Miller, and Jusczyk (1987), the presentation of a synthetic speech sound occurs when the infant sucks a soother that is wired up to both initiate stimuli and to measure sucking responses. In this situation, infants initially suck at a higher frequency, and then sucking frequency decreases when the infant habituates to the stimulus. At this point, a new stimulus is presented. If it re-initiates higher sucking frequency, this indicates that it is classified by the infant as a novel stimulus (i.e., it falls into a different phonemic category than does the initial sound).

Both of these types of studies have indicated that even very young infants are sensitive to the broad range of articulatory features that adults are sensitive to when phonemic categories are perceived. These include vowel quality, voice-onset time, place of articulation, manner of articulation, oral/nasal distinctions, and distinctions between the glides /r/ and /l/. "Nature has generously endowed human infants with a sufficiently complex perceptual system so that their initial efforts at language acquisition can be directed toward discovering how the outputs of this system are to be used linguistically" (Eimas, Miller, & Jusczyk, 1987, p. 170).

The case for phonemes as substantive universals can be made even stronger. In one landmark study, Werker and Tees (1984) used two consonant sounds that are distinguished by Salish speakers (Salish is a native language spoken in south-central British Columbia), but which are indistinguishable to English speakers. Twelve infants, with an average age of approximately 7 months, were tested using the head-turning paradigm described earlier to see whether or not they could distinguish these sounds. These infants were being raised in English-speaking households. As measured by this paradigm, the infants could discriminate the two phonemes almost as well as Salish-speaking adults; both of these groups significantly outperformed English-speaking adults, who performed abysmally. A second study showed, however, that this ability was essentially gone by the time infants are 12 months old. Together, these results are consistent with the claim that regardless of the linguistic community into which they are born, human infants come equipped with the innate ability to discriminate any of the phonemes that could occur in a linguistic environment. After a year's exposure to a particular linguistic environment, though, this discriminative ability deteriorates, and the children can only discriminate the phonemes used in their linguistic community.

The other kind of universal proposed by Chomsky (1965) is a formal universal. Formal universals are abstract properties that the grammar of every language must meet. Chomsky suggests that the claim that the grammar of any human language contains transformational rules is a formal universal, as is the claim that the phonological component of a grammar is rule governed (e.g., Kenstowicz, 1994).

The specification of both substantive and formal universals is extremely challenging, because linguists must balance the need to posit language properties common to all humans with the need to specify a system flexible enough to instantiate any human language. One proposal that appears to meet these competing needs is the view that language learning involves setting parameters made available in a universal grammar, a view that we already discussed in more detail in chapter 4.

I personally find the work of Bickerton (1981) to provide the most intriguing evidence concerning innateness and parameters in the universal grammar. In the 1870s, there was an enormous expansion of the sugar plantations in Hawaii. The owners of the sugar plantations fueled this expansion by using slaves from Puerto Rico, Portugal, the Philippines, and various places in the Orient. In order to prevent the planning of subversive activities, these workers were placed in a community in which there was no common language. While in their homes the slaves could speak their own language, in the plantation community a pidgin English developed, and was in wide use by the early 1900s. In general, pidgin languages are extremely simple – they have crude syntax, no grammatical morphemes, and no embedded clauses. While their parents worked the plantation, children were tended to by caretakers who would only communicate to them in pidgin English.

One issue of interest to Bickerton (1981) was the nature of the language of children raised in this pidgin-speaking environment. Interestingly, these children developed a completely new language, called Hawaiian Creole. Unlike pidgin English, Hawaiian Creole has a definite syntax that is uniform from speaker to speaker. The language has a predominate word order (subject-verb-object), permits subordinate clauses, and includes a system of functional words (e.g., such as articles). Clearly, Bickerton was documenting a grammatical language that emerged out of an essentially agrammatical linguistic environment.

Creole languages have also emerged in other parts of the world, when conditions like the "natural experiment" in Hawaii were duplicated. It is important to note that each of these Creoles developed independently, when children were raised in an essentially agrammatic linguistic environment. In comparing the structure of these different Creoles, Bickerton (1981) found many striking similarities. Furthermore, Bickerton noted that some of the syntactic constructions common to these Creoles are also characteristic in the early language of children raised in more typical linguistic environments. Bickerton uses this evidence to claim that the grammar of Creole is determined by an innate "bioprogram." In short, for Bickerton, Creole grammar is identical to Chomsky's (e.g., 1965) universal grammar. Because of the impoverished linguistic environment, the parameter settings in Creole grammar can be described as the default settings in universal grammar!

A Proposal for an Innate Semantics

Another contentious argument for innateness was offered by Fodor (1975), who argued for the existence of innate concepts (i.e., innate meanings). Fodor began by considering what he called a truth definition for some natural language L. This amounts to a theory that associates a truth value with each of the (infinitely many) statements or predicates that could be expressed in L. Now, to account for learning a language that can produce infinitely many statements, Fodor took a step that should be familiar to us: he distinguished the primitive predicates in L from the complex predicates in L. With this move of Fodor's, the truth definition of L only requires a list of the meanings of its primitive predicates, as well as a set of rules for combining primitive predicates together to create truthful or meaningful complex predicates.

For Fodor (1975), learning a language L involved at the very least learning its truth definition. This would appear to involve using mental representations to express hypotheses about the truth conditions associated with L's predicates, and then to involve manipulating these mental representations to confirm or disconfirm these hypotheses. But Fodor demonstrated that when such hypothesis testing activity is expressed in a very general formal notation, it is very clear that learning a truth definition requires using mental representations which are already powerful enough to capture the semantic distinctions (i.e., the primitive predicates) of L. "The upshot would appear to be that one can learn L only if one already knows some language rich enough to express the extension of any predicate of L. To put it tendentiously, one can learn what the semantic properties of a term are only if one already knows a language which contains a term having the same semantic properties" (p. 80). In short, Fodor's position was that learning the meanings of a first language requires pre-existing or innate meanings and concepts!

In part because of Fodor's (1975) tendentious presentation, the idea that there existed a set of innate meanings was extremely controversial, and was the subject of a vigorous debate. Let us ignore this debate for the time being, and simply consider a basic question: does there exist any empirical evidence that is consistent with this extreme position?

One plausible place for someone like Fodor (1975) to look for innate meanings would be in the outputs of transducers (e.g., Fodor & Pylyshyn, 1981). As was noted earlier in this chapter, transducers are modules that are designed to convert energy into representations that can then be subject to additional processing. Given that transducers are presumed to be associated with fixed neural architecture, and that as such are likely to be biologically determined, it would seem reasonable to supposed that transducers could be the source of meanings that are universal (i.e., constant both within and between cultures). For example, there is no evidence that the "wetware" involved in color perception is not essentially the same for every normal-seeing human. Could this result in "color meanings" being universal?

At first glance, this does not seem to be the case, because there is quite a bit of

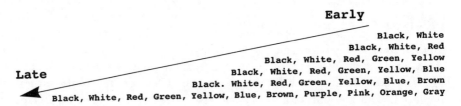

Figure 7.7 Berlin–Kay sequence of color word emergence in the evolution of language. This sequence is thought to be universal.

variation between cultures with respect to the color terms used in language. For instance, English nomenclature for colors is hierarchically structured and very refined, permitting many terms to be used to distinguish different colors (e.g., "magenta" vs. "purple"). In contrast, the Dani from the central highlands of western New Guinea have only a pair of color terms, one for light and the other for dark (e.g., Heider, 1972). However, careful study has not only shown a wide degree of agreement between cultures in color judgments, but has also revealed systematic constraints on the use of color terms in any language.

Berlin and Kay (1969) studied color concepts in speakers from twenty different languages. They used a set of 320 color chips from the Munsell representation of color that were all at maximum saturation, but varied in terms of hue and brightness. They asked speakers to trace out the boundaries of different colors by sorting the color chips into groups, with each group corresponding to a color term used in the speaker's language. They also asked their subjects to choose the best example of each color term. Within languages, there was little agreement between speakers about the boundaries between color terms. However, there was remarkable agreement between speakers regarding the best example of each color, and this agreement held to a large degree across all of the languages that were studied. This indicated that there exist universal prototypes for different colors. Berlin and Kay argued, on the basis of their results, that eleven such prototypes existed.

Berlin and Kay (1969) also argued that the eleven color prototypes provided powerful constraints on how color terms are included in a language. Their point was that while different languages may employ different numbers of color terms, the order in which these terms emerge in the history of the language is invariant and universal. This sequence of the color term emergence is illustrated in figure 7.7. Ratliff (1976) argues that the universality of this sequence may be due to innate factors; specifically, the maturation of the human color perception system. Interestingly, the Berlin and Kay sequence is also reflected in language production; McManus (1983) has shown that in color-word usage by prominent English poets, words appearing early in the sequence are used more frequently than words appearing later in the sequence.

Conclusion

If cognitive science were completely mature, then a strong proposal about the components of the functional architecture would have been put forward. Under these circumstances, the task of an implementational-level analysis would be to explain how each of these components worked. For instance, imagine for a moment that connectionists are correct in assuming that neurons comprise the primitive level of a functional analysis of cognition. The implementational level would be responsible for providing a detailed account of how individual neurons work, perhaps focusing upon the properties of membrane channels in nerve membranes (e.g., Hille, 1990). Of course, other proposals for functional primitives might turn out to be correct (see table 6.1). The task of an implementational-level analysis would be the same for these proposals – the explanation of how the primitives are instantiated in the brain.

However, cognitive science has not currently achieved a level of maturity where it can confidently argue that a particular proposal for the functional architecture is worthy of detailed study at the implementational level. This does not mean, though, that it is either appropriate or necessary to ignore implementational issues at this stage of cognitive science's development. One can begin to generate preliminary proposals about the brain's relation to cognition, just as one can generate preliminary computational and algorithmic accounts of cognitive processing. Furthermore, hypotheses generated at one level of analysis can be used to guide those generated at another.

For example, Kosslyn and Van Kleeck (1990) are in favor of an interactive methodology in which information-processing theories are subject to both anatomical constraints and information-processing constraints. On the one hand, anatomical information is used to ensure that cognitive theories are consistent with what is known about the structure of the brain. On the other hand, computational and algorithmic analyses provide information about major qualitative distinctions between information processes, which are thus likely to be reflected in brain structure. This provides a general framework to guide an implementational-level analysis; "such constraints provide a skeleton for Humpty-Dumpty, offering hope that after his fall we might be able to put him back together again" (Kosslyn & Van Kleeck, 1990, p. 400).

In this chapter, we have seen several examples of how such interactive approaches can be used to incorporate implementational-level information into a predominately functionalist cognitive science. We have seen how a solution to the frame problem, which is formulated at the computational level of analysis, can be related to our knowledge about the localization of brain structure. We have seen how cognitive neuroscience can provide evidence to support the functional analysis of cognitive processing. We have seen how PDP networks can be used as a medium in which methodological assumptions used by neuroscientists can be put to the test. We have seen how PDP models can be informed by the results from neuroscience, generating new architectures that are more biologically plausible, and in some cases more interesting from an engineering point of view. We have seen how claims about the innateness and universality of cognitive processes can lead to strong predictions about cognitive processes that can be tested by studying cognitive development and cross-cultural cognition. Newell (1990, p. 42) pointed out that "theories of human cognition are ultimately theories of physical, biological systems." Hopefully, this chapter has given you the sense of how functionalist theories – both classical and connectionist – can move towards this ultimate level.

8

A Case Study in Cognitive Science

The preceding chapters of this book have described how the tri-level hypothesis affects or guides the research of both classical and connectionist cognitive scientists. To this point, though, the book has emphasized the relative independence of each of these levels. For example, we have considered each level of analysis in its own chapter. Furthermore, we have not emphasized the relationships between research questions asked at each level of analysis by considering a single phenomenon at each level.

The purpose of this chapter is to correct this notion. We will consider a single phenomenon, the motion correspondence problem, at each level of analysis. The main reason for doing this is to show how results obtained at one level of analysis can in turn influence research done at another level of analysis. That this can occur provides a strong reason for cognitive scientists interested in particular levels of analysis to maintain lines of communication with other cognitive scientists who study the same phenomenon, but at different levels.

The chapter proceeds as follows: First, I introduce the notion of a problem of underdetermination in vision, and describe one view – Marr's (1982) natural computation approach – of how such problems can be solved. Second, I introduce a specific problem of underdetermination found in the perception of apparent motion, called the motion correspondence problem. Third, I describe computational, algorithmic, and implementational approaches to explaining how the human visual system solves the motion correspondence problem. One theme that emerges from these descriptions is that research questions that are raised at one level of analysis can affect the research questions that are raised at another level.

Part I   Problems of Underdetermination in Vision

What is So Hard About Seeing?

For most people, visual perception is extremely easy: we just look at something and see it. The whole process is so natural, so direct, and so fast, that we usually take it for granted. Because of this, the pioneers of artificial intelligence research had no reason to suspect that building computer simulations of visual processes would pose any great problem. Marvin Minsky has admitted that he assigned computer vision to a student as a summer programming project (Horgan, 1993).

However, when serious research was directed towards programming a machine to see, astonishing difficulties arose. It became painfully obvious that underlying the process of seeing was a set of enormously complicated information-processing problems that the human visual system was solving effortlessly in real time. Identifying the nature of these problems, let alone solving them, became a staggering challenge for vision researchers.

What is it about vision that has made it such a challenge to AI researchers? Many have described the goal of visual perception as the construction of useful representations about the world (e.g., Horn, 1986; Marr, 1976, 1982; Ullman, 1979). These representations are derived by interpreting the information projected from a three-dimensional visual world (called the distal stimulus) onto an essentially two-dimensional surface of light receptors in our eyes. The identification of the distal stimulus must be determined from the resulting pattern of retinal stimulation (called the proximal stimulus).

However, the information represented in the proximal stimulus cannot, by itself, be used to completely determine the nature of the distal stimulus. One reason for this is because the proximal stimulus does not preserve the full dimensionality of the physical world. The mapping from three-dimensional patterns to two-dimensional patterns is not uniquely invertible (c.f., Gregory, 1970; Horn, 1986; Marr, 1982; Richards, 1988). This means that given a rich description of a scene, someone well versed in the laws of optics as well as the optical properties of the eyes could potentially give an exact description of the proximal stimulus that the distal stimulus would produce. However, the reverse would not be true: given an exact description of the proximal stimulus, the laws of optics cannot be used to give a precise description of the scene out there in the world. Retinal stimulation geometrically underdetermines interpretations of the physical world.

There is another, less obvious, reason that the proximal stimulus cannot, by itself, be used to completely determine the nature of the distal stimulus. This has to do with the fact that the neural circuitry underlying visual perception is of "limited order" (c.f. Minsky & Papert, 1969/1988). What this means is that each cell that processes the proximal stimulus actually only has access to a small

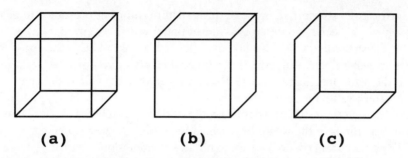

(a)   **(b)**   **(c)**

Figure 8.1 Underdetermination means ambiguity. To illustrate this, consider the Necker cube (a). After looking at this diagram for a while, one sees that it changes appearance. Sometimes it looks like the cube illustrated in (b), while other times it looks like the cube illustrated in (c). In other words, the line drawing in (a) is consistent with more than one interpretation.

part of it. Our global percept – our interpretation of the proximal stimulus – must therefore be created by combining many different local measurements together. However, it turns out that there are many different global interpretations that are consistent with a single set of local measurements. As a result, the local measurements by themselves cannot completely determine the global percept that we experience.

Figure 8.1 attempts to provide the reader with some intuitions about what a problem of underdetermination in vision is like. Figure 8.1a is the classic Necker cube illusion. When you look at it, you will likely experience it as a three-dimensional figure. If you look at it long enough, you will see that its three dimensional structure changes. Sometimes it will look like the cube illustrated in figure 8.1b. At other times it will look like the cube illustrated in figure 8.1c. If you consider figure 8.1a to be analogous to a proximal stimulus, then you will now realize that it is consistent with at least three different interpretations (the two cubes already discussed, as well as an arrangement of lines on a flat surface – which, of course, is the correct interpretation!) At any one time, why is one interpretation preferred over another? An answer to this question is a solution to a problem of underdetermination.

The problem facing computer vision researchers is to come up with answers to problems of underdetermination for general scenes. As a result, they cannot take advantage of special properties of a single display like the Necker cube. Furthermore, they typically are dealing with situations in which a potentially infinite number of different possible interpretations could be assigned to a proximal stimulus. Finally, their solution must be something that could in principle be arrived at very quickly, because in practice vision is very fast.

Using Constraints to Solve Problems of Underdetermination

The natural computation approach to vision, which Marr (e.g., 1977, 1982) founded, attacks problems of underdetermination by adopting naive realism. Specifically, a natural computation researcher presupposes that the visual world is intrinsically structured. Some of this structure is further presumed to be true of any visual scene. Finally, it is assumed that a visual system that has evolved in such a structured world would have taken advantage of any visual properties that are generally true of any scene. "If you look attentively at a fish you can see that the water has shaped it. The fish is not merely in the water: the qualities of the water itself have called the fish into being" (Horwood, 1987, p. 35). In a very real sense, the aim of a natural computation researcher is to show how the visible qualities of the world have called the visual system into being.

The visual properties of interest to natural computation researchers are called *natural constraints*. A natural constraint is a property of the visual world (it is not a psychological property) that is almost always going to be true of any location in any scene. For example, a great many visual properties of three-dimensional scenes (depth, texture, color, shading, motion) vary smoothly. This means that two points very near one another in a scene are very likely to have very similar values for any of these properties. Points that are not close together in a scene will not necessarily have similar values for any of these properties.

Natural constraints can be used to solve visual problems of underdetermination by imposing restrictions on scene interpretations. Figure 8.2 provides a visual metaphor to illustrate how this is so. In figure 8.2a, the visual system has a very weak constraint placed upon it: it must simply select an interpretation that is consistent with the proximal stimulus. However, because of the problem of underdetermination, this means that many different interpretations are possible; unfortunately, the visual system will not be able to distinguish the correct interpretation from all that are possible. In figure 8.2b, natural constraints are exploited: the visual system must choose an interpretation that 1) is consistent with the proximal stimulus, and 2) is also consistent with one or more natural constraints. With appropriate natural constraints, only a single interpretation will meet both of these criteria (for many examples, see Marr, 1982). A major research goal for those who endorse the natural computation approach to vision is to identify natural constraints that filter out correct interpretations from all the other (incorrect) possibilities.

An Example Problem of Underdetermination

The human visual system can produce *apparent motion* from a rapid succession of static images (see figure 8.3). For example, a motion picture is in reality a long string of still photographs (frames). When each of these photographs is presented for a very brief period of time, we do not experience them as being stationary. Instead, our visual system fills in an illusion of movement between each frame. This illusion is so powerful that we often cannot distinguish it from real motion, and never experience the intrinsically static nature of the film. Apparent motion is found throughout our technologically advanced society, providing the strong sense of movement in such important things as television, video arcade games, and the electric signs that beckon us into movie theaters and used car lots.

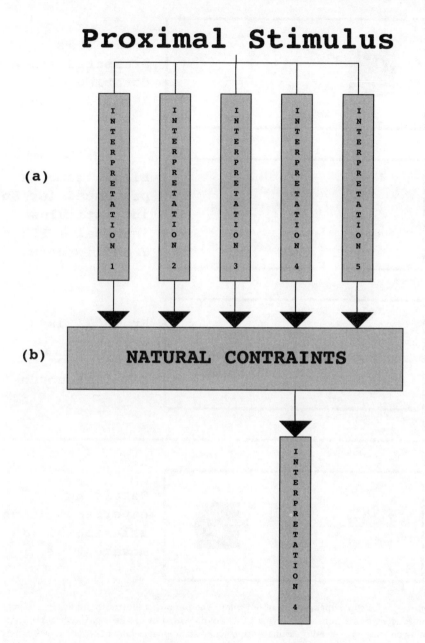

Figure 8.2 Using natural constraints to solve problems of underdetermination. (a) Without natural constraints, a single proximal stimulus can give rise to many different interpretations, only one of which will be correct. There is not enough information in the proximal stimulus to determine which interpretation is correct. By adding natural constraints (b), the goal is to filter out the incorrect interpretation, so that the only interpretation that is arrived at is the correct one.

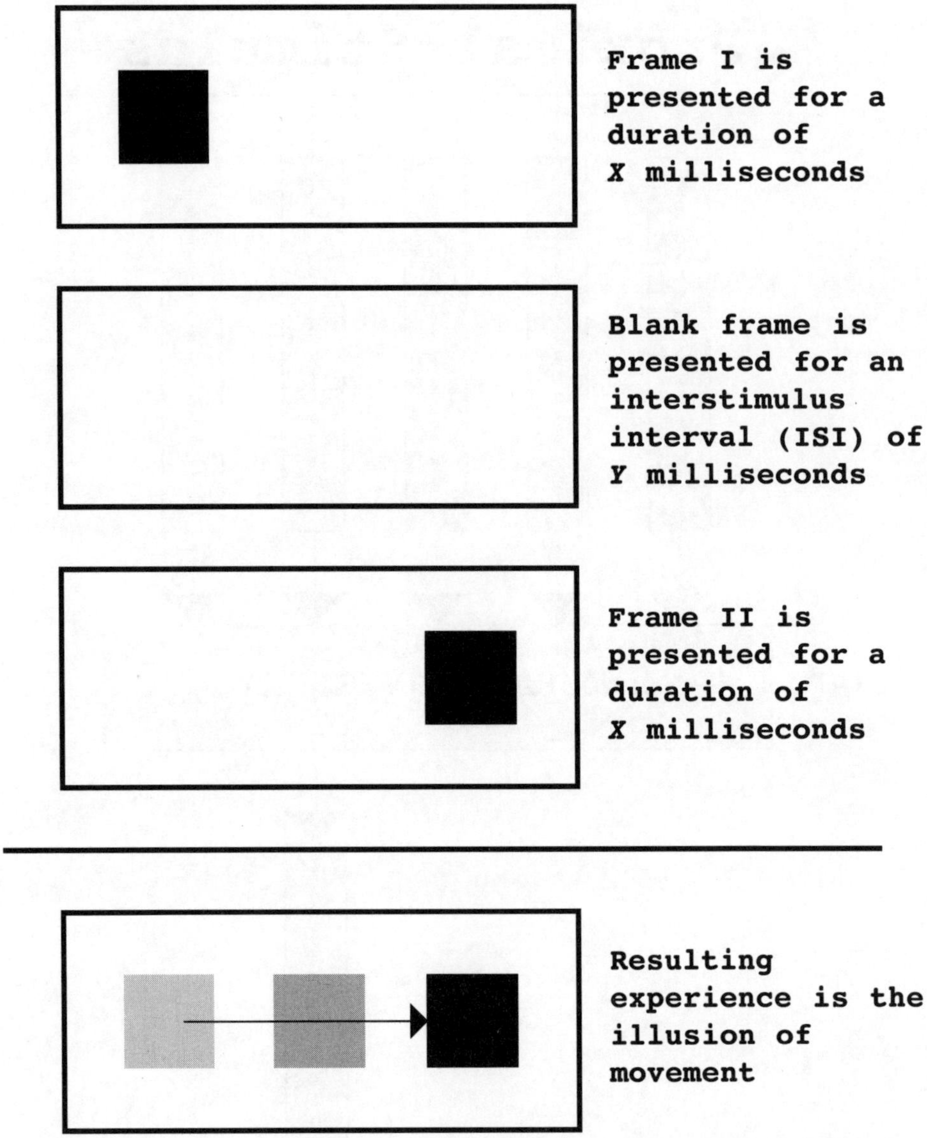

Frame I is presented for a duration of X milliseconds

Blank frame is presented for an interstimulus interval (ISI) of Y milliseconds

Frame II is presented for a duration of X milliseconds

Resulting experience is the illusion of movement

Figure 8.3 A simple apparent motion display. The top of the illustration indicates different frames of view (different static images) that are presented in a sequence. Under appropriate timing conditions, instead of seeing a sequence of static images human observers will report the strong illusion of motion illustrated at the bottom of the figure.

The phenomenon of apparent motion was discovered by Sigmund Exner in 1888, and has since played an important role in a number of psychological worldviews (e.g., Cutting, 1986; Koffka, 1935; Kolers, 1972; Rock, 1983), not to mention philosophical arguments (e.g., Goodman, 1978). Psychological research into apparent motion has often been concerned with identifying principles that could explain why people would see particular patterns of motion, and not others (e.g., Attneave, 1974; more on this below). Ullman's (1979) seminal contribution to the field was his translation of this problem into the precise vocabulary of information processing.

Some forms of apparent motion are presumed to be detected by the so-called long-range motion system (e.g., Anstis, 1978, 1980; Braddick, 1973, 1974, 1980; Petersik, 1989; Ullman, 1981). This system is capable of detecting movement that occurs over relatively long spatial and temporal intervals, and begins processing after some primitive figural properties have already been extracted from the proximal stimulus. These figural properties will be called elements, and an element will be generically defined as an individuated component of the proximal stimulus. In other words, an element is a visual "thing" : some aspect of the proximal stimulus that can be referred to by a unique symbolic code (e.g., a token, or a FINST in the sense of Pylyshyn, 1989). Ullman (1979, ch. 2) presents evidence suggesting that these tokens could represent components such as oriented parts of edges, corners, and terminators (i.e., the type of information available in the primal sketch of Marr, 1982).

As was noted earlier, to generate apparent motion, the long-range system must identify an element in a position in one image (Frame I) and another element in a different position in the next image (Frame II) as constituting different glimpses of the same moving thing. A motion correspondence match between a Frame I element and a Frame II element is such an identification. The basic idea here is that the long-range system first tracks the location of an element from Frame I to Frame II; a motion correspondence match represents the result of this tracking. Then, the long-range system fills in the illusion of movement that occurs from the first location to the second.

Interestingly, one kind of information that does not appear to be used to track elements is appearance (e.g., element shape, color, topology).There are at least two kinds of arguments that support this claim. First, we will see later in this chapter that physiological evidence supports the existence of at least two predominately independent anatomical pathways in the visual system, one of which is sensitive to movement but not to form (e.g., Botez, 1975; Livingstone & Hubel, 1988; Maunsell & Newsome, 1987; Ungerleider & Mishkin, 1982). Second, we will also see later that while human observers are very sensitive to manipulations of element positions in apparent motion displays, they are much less sensitive to manipulations of figural properties such as shape, color, or spatial frequency (e.g., Baro & Levinson, 1988; Burt & Sperling, 1981; Cavanagh, Arguin, & von Grunau, 1989; Dawson, 1990a; Kolers, 1972; Kolers & Green, 1984; Kolers & Pomerantz, 1971; Kolers & von Grunau, 1976; Krumhansl, 1984; Navon, 1976; Ullman, 1979, ch. 2; Victor & Conte, 1990).

If it doesn't use element appearance, then what kinds of information does the long-range system use to track elements? Human observers can easily experience apparent motion for displays in which all elements are of identical appearance (e.g., all are dots, or lines, etc.). For such displays, the assignment of motion correspondence matches can only be based upon measurements of element positions. This indicates that the long-range system tracks elements by only paying attention to where elements are in the respective frames of view. In other words, the long-range system processes the locations of elements, and essentially ignores element appearances.

However, measurements of Frame I and Frame II element positions under-determine the motion correspondence matches that can be assigned to an apparent motion display. Several different sets of motion correspondence matches are consistent with the same set of positions. This is illustrated in figure 8.4. In general, if there are N elements in Frames I and II, and if one assumes a one-to-one mapping between frames of view, then there are $N!$ different sets of correspondence matches that are consistent with the proximal stimulus (Ullman, 1979). If a one-to-one mapping between frames of view is not assumed, then the number of possible solutions increases to 2^N. In order to solve the motion correspondence problem, one set of motion correspondence matches (a "global interpretation") must be selected from the many consistent with the position measurements.

Since measurements of element locations are not sufficient to solve the motion correspondence problem, additional rules or principles must be exploi-ted. The discovery of the principles used by the human visual system to solve this problem of underdetermination has been an important goal of apparent motion research (e.g., Attneave, 1974; Dawson, 1991; Petersik, 1989; Rama-chandran & Anstis, 1986a; Ternus, 1938; Ullman, 1979). The next part of the chapter describes computational-level work on the motion correspondence problem, which is charged with the responsibility of identifying potential natural constraints that can be used to solve this particular problem of under-determination.

Part II   Computational Analysis of the Motion Correspondence Problem

As we saw earlier in this book, Marr (1977, 1982), described a theory of a computation as an account of what is being computed, and why. For Marr, an answer to the question "what is being computed?" must specify what information-processing problem is being solved. In vision, this would mean providing a description of a particular problem of underdetermination. For instance, in the example introduced above, the answer to this question would be "a solution to the motion correspondence problem" ; this answer would be stated in as precise a vocabulary as possible (e.g., in some formal expression).

An answer to the question "why is this being computed?" should specify why the system was solving a particular information-processing problem, and not some other problem. In a theory of vision, such an answer would detail the set of constraints that were being placed on the potential operations of a visual system. The idea would be to specify a set of constraints that 1) would be

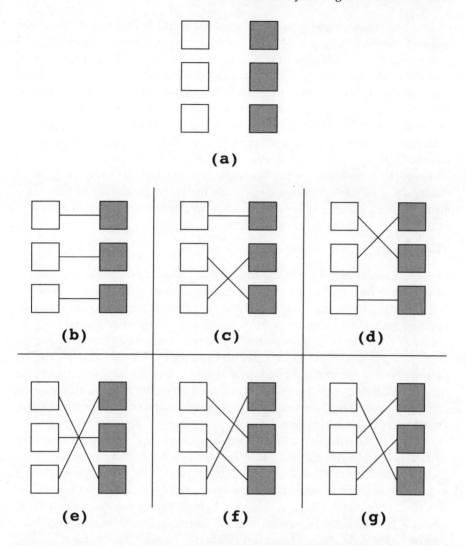

Figure 8.4 Underdetermination of motion correspondence matches. (a) A simple apparent motion display consisting of three Frame I elements and three Frame II elements. In an actual display, all of these elements would be of the same colour. In this figure, colour is used to indicate which frame (white for Frame I, grey for Frame II) an element appears in. (b–g) Assuming one-to-one matches between elements in different frames, there are six different possible sets of motion correspondence matches that could be assigned to the display depicted in (a). Only one of these solutions (b) is generated by the human visual system. What principles are used to assert that (b) is a correct solution, and that the other five solutions are incorrect?

sufficient to solve a particular problem, and 2) would identify a system uniquely as one that is solving the problem. "In the theory of visual processes, the underlying task is to reliably derive properties of the world from images of it; the business of isolating constraints that are both powerful enough to allow a process to be defined and generally true of the world is a central theme of our inquiry" (Marr, 1982).

Importantly, the identification of the constraints on visual problems of underdetermination is typically a task that is done at the computational level of analysis. This is because it is at this level that one might go about proving, for instance, that a particular set of constraints will lead to a unique solution to the problem at hand. Similarly, one must also be prepared to argue that a particular constraint is natural (e.g., a property that is generally going to be true of the world). Often this kind of argument is defended at the computational level. To illustrate this aspect of the study of computational vision, let us now turn to an examination of three different constraints that Dawson (1991) incorporated into a particular theory of how the motion correspondence problem is solved.

The Nearest Neighbor Principle

An experimental technique called the *motion competition paradigm* has been used to study how the human visual system solves the correspondence problem (e.g., Ullman, 1979, ch. 2). In the simplest motion competition display, two opposing paths of apparent motion (i.e., two opposing motion correspondence matches) compete with one another for assignment. In Frame I of such a display, a single element is presented in the center. In Frame II, the Frame I element has disappeared and two lateral elements are now displayed, one to the right of center, the other to the left (see figure 8.5). Under appropriate temporal conditions, the Frame I element is seen to move either to the left or to the right. Of interest are the factors that determine the perceived direction of motion.

In a competition display, a very strong predictor of the perceived direction of motion is element displacement (i.e., the distance between a Frame I element and a potentially corresponding element in Frame II). The visual system prefers to assign correspondence matches that represent short element displacements (e.g., Burt & Sperling, 1981; Ullman, 1979, ch. 2). For example, if motion to the left in a competition display involves a shorter element displacement than motion to the right, then motion to the left will be preferred (figure 8.5). This suggests that one constraint that the visual system uses to solve the motion correspondence problem is a *nearest neighbor principle*, in which motion correspondence matches are created between Frame I elements and their nearest neighbors in Frame II.

One role of a computational-level analysis is to make the case that something like the nearest neighbor principle is a natural constraint. Ullman (1979, pp. 114–18) has done this by showing that the nearest neighbor principle is consistent with the geometry of the typical viewing conditions for motion. When movement in a three-dimensional world is projected onto a two-dimensional surface (e.g., the retina), its depth component is lost. As a result, slower movements occur with much higher probability on the retina than do faster movements. This suggests one principle that the visual system could use to solve the motion correspondence problem: choose the set of matches that

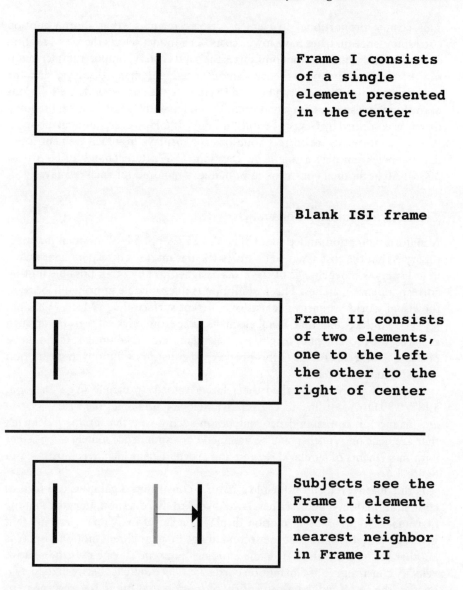

Figure 8.5 The static images that are used to create a simple motion competition display, which is typically used to study the effect of the nearest neighbor principle.

represent the slowest overall movement. It turns out that the nearest neighbor principle defines this set of matches, because a short correspondence match represents slow motion, while a long correspondence match represents fast motion.

The nearest neighbor principle is employed in Ullman's (1979) minimal mapping theory of motion correspondence processing. In minimal mapping theory, a cost is associated with each possible motion correspondence match.

This cost is proportional to element displacement, so that shorter motion correspondence matches have lower costs. The model selects the set of motion correspondence matches that minimizes the total cost. A computer implementation of minimal mapping theory demonstrated, for many displays, that the nearest neighbor principle can be used to emulate the correspondence solutions of the human visual system (an alternative implementation of minimal mapping theory is described by Gryzwacz and Yuille, 1988). However, minimal mapping theory cannot generate correct solutions for displays in which element interdependencies can play a role (e.g., Dawson, 1987; Ramachandran & Anstis, 1985). An additional constraining principle is required for such displays.

The Relative Velocity Constraint

A major assumption underlying Ullman's (1979, pp. 84–6) minimal mapping theory is that the cost assigned to any particular motion correspondence match in a display is independent of the costs assigned to any other possible motion correspondence matches. This assumption is questionable in principle because the visual world primarily consists of coherent surfaces (e.g., Marr, 1982, pp. 44–51). To the extent that visual elements arise from physical features on such surfaces, the movement of neighboring elements should be similar. It should be possible to take advantage of this property to constrain solutions to the motion correspondence problem.

One such property is called the relative velocity principle (e.g., Dawson, 1987, 1991). According to the relative velocity principle, the visual system assigns motion correspondence matches in such a way that Frame I elements that are near one another will be assigned correspondence matches consistent with movements of similar direction and speed. This principle is illustrated in figure 8.6.

Is the relative velocity principle a natural constraint? Again, we can turn to computational-level analyses to answer "yes" to this question. Imagine that the first image in an apparent motion display is a set of individual elements that define a "pattern," and that the second image in an apparent motion display is another set of elements that define another "pattern." If one uses the relative velocity constraint to assign motion correspondence matches between these two images, the result will be a perception of motion that minimizes the apparent distortion as the first pattern changes into ("morphs" into) the second.

Yuille (1983) has performed mathematical analyses of transformations that minimize the distortion of moving figures. He proved that such movements maximize a property called *motion smoothness* (Hildreth, 1983; Horn & Schunk, 1981). Motion is smoothest when neighboring points on a contour have nearly identical velocities. Furthermore, Hildreth (1983) has proven that coherent objects moving arbitrarily in three-dimensional space produce unique, smooth patterns of retinal movement. In other words, motion smoothness is a natural constraint. This means that if the relative velocity principle minimizes figural distortions during movement, and if transformations that minimize such

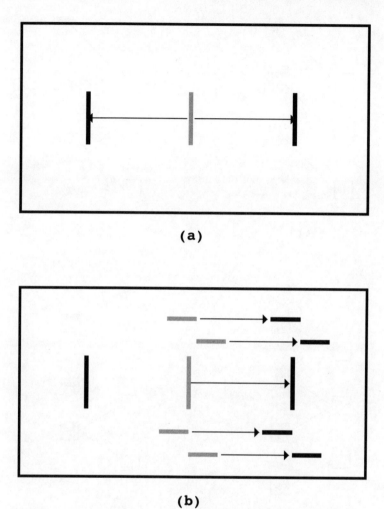

(a)

(b)

Figure 8.6 Evidence for the relative velocity principle. (a) An ambiguous display, in which the central Frame I element (drawn here in gray) will be seen to split into two directions, because it has two nearest neighbors in Frame II. (b) When other context elements are added to Frames I and II, the ambiguity of the central display (which is the same as in (a)) disappears. The visual system assigns matches in such a way that the central element is seen to move with the context, which is consistent with the relative velocity principle.

distortions are equivalent to transformations that generate the smoothest movement, then the relative velocity principle must be a natural constraint too.

The Element Integrity Principle

Experimental studies of motion perception suggest that the human visual system prefers one-to-one mappings between elements in different frames of

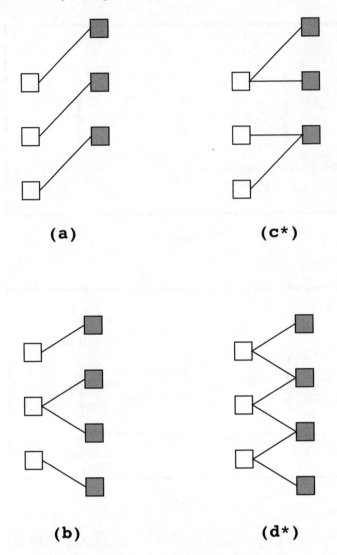

Figure 8.7 The element integrity principle. Humans generate the motion correspondence matches illustrated in (a) and (b). Motion correspondence models that do not use the element integrity constraint generate incorrect solutions for these displays, illustrated in (c) and (d).

view. Figures 8.7a and 8.7b illustrate two examples of this. These displays can pose problems for motion correspondence models based upon the two principles described above. Figure 8.7c depicts an incorrect solution for 8.7a that is generated by minimal mapping theory (Ullman, 1979, p. 99). Figure 8.7d depicts an incorrect solution for 8.7b generated by the relative velocity principle (Dawson, 1986, fig. 5.9).

The two incorrect solutions depicted in figure 8.7 show, for some displays, that the nearest neighbor principle and the relative velocity principle, when applied to the motion correspondence problem, include motion correspondence matches that are discarded by the human visual system. To deal with this problem, Ullman (1979, pp. 97–101) modified his theory of motion correspondence processing to include an *element integrity principle*. According to this principle, the splitting of one element into parts during movement, or the fusing together of different elements into one, should be penalized. Ullman incorporated these penalties into the nearest neighbor cost function, and as a result extended the range of problems solved by minimal mapping theory.

Is the element integrity principle a natural constraint? It is consistent with general assumptions about the physical nature of moving surfaces (see also Marr's discussion of stereopsis, 1982, pp. 111–14). Specifically, proximal stimulus elements are assumed to correspond to parts of coherent, physical stimuli, such as edge segments, physical markings, and so on (cf. Ullman, 1979, ch. 2). The physical coherence of surfaces (and therefore surface parts) suggests that the splitting or fusing of visual elements is very unlikely. As well, one-to-one mappings between elements over time will be correct everywhere except at surface discontinuities (e.g., at an occluding edge where different elements may be suddenly appearing or disappearing). However, discontinuities make up a very small proportion of scenes and images, and as a result the element integrity principle is likely to be true over most of an image.

Nevertheless, element integrity by itself is a very weak constraining principle. For instance, each of the possible motion correspondence solutions illustrated in figure 8.4 is consistent with the element integrity principle. Therefore this principle alone will not generate unique solutions to the correspondence problem. The utility of this principle, illustrated in Ullman's (1979) modified minimal mapping theory, is that it may select one solution from a set that cannot be differentiated by other constraints, as in figure 8.7.

Part III   Algorithmic Issues and Motion Correspondence

In the preceding part of the paper, we considered one role of computational analyses in the study of motion correspondence processing. In this part of the paper, we briefly consider two examples of algorithmic analyses of solutions to the motion correspondence problem. Two different algorithmic approaches are briefly reviewed. One is the use of the results of psychophysical studies of human motion perception to defend design decisions made when creating a theory of motion correspondence processing. The other is the creation of a working computer simulation that exploits the three constraints that we have been discussing, and as a result is capable of solving a variety of motion correspondence problems.

Experimental Studies Of Motion Correspondence

In the previous part of the chapter, we described three different properties that could, in principle, serve as natural constraints on the motion correspondence problem. However, just because these constraints could be used in principle to solve the problem does not mean that they are actually used by the human visual system. Computational analyses simply do not address this kind of issue. In order to support the claim that the human visual system exploits a particular property to solve the motion correspondence problem, we have to perform experimental studies of human perceptions of apparent motion. In this section, we will consider three different examples of this approach.

For example, we saw earlier that Ullman (1979) argued that the assignment of one motion correspondence match to a display was independent of the assignment of any other correspondence match. If this was true of human motion perception, then it would be inappropriate to incorporate the relative velocity constraint in any model of human motion correspondence processing. However, Dawson (1987) was able to provide empirical support for the relative velocity principle; this empirical support shows that the independence assumption in Ullman's minimal mapping theory is incorrect. Human observers were presented competition displays embedded in the context of a moving configuration (similar to figure 8.6b). The presence of a moving context had a pronounced effect on the perceived direction of the Frame I element, when compared to control displays with no contexts. There was a strong tendency to see the central element and the context move in the same direction. This demonstrates that element interdependencies are important determinants of motion correspondence matches. This result is also consistent with several others showing that the human visual system minimizes patterns of relative motion for various discrete element displays (e.g., Cutting & Proffitt, 1982; Gogel, 1974; Johansson, 1950; Proffitt & Cutting, 1979, 1980; Ramachandran & Anstis, 1985, 1986a).

Another example of an issue that emerges at the algorithmic level concerns the assumption that the human visual system is essentially blind to the appearance of elements when the correspondence problem is solved. What empirical evidence is there that the human visual system solves the motion correspondence problem using, for the most part, information about element locations and not information about element shapes and colors? It turns out that many psychophysical experiments have shown that while human observers are very sensitive to manipulations of element positions in apparent motion displays, they are much less sensitive to manipulations of figural properties such as shape, color, or spatial frequency (e.g., Baro & Levinson, 1988; Burt & Sperling, 1981; Cavanagh, Arguin, & von Grunau, 1989; Dawson, 1990a; Kolers, 1972; Kolers & Green, 1984; Kolers & Pomerantz, 1971; Kolers & von Grunau, 1976; Krumhansl, 1984; Navon, 1976; Ullman, 1979, ch. 2; Victor & Conte, 1990).

Results of this type frequently come from the use of motion competition displays. In these experiments, two versions of the motion correspondence display are created. In one, all of the elements have the identical appearance, and their position is manipulated to measure the strength of the nearest neighbor principle. In the other, one of the Frame II elements has the same appearance as the central Frame I element, while the other Frame II element has a different appearance (see figure 8.8). If element appearance has a strong effect on motion correspondence processing, then it would be expected that the visual system would have a preference to violate the nearest neighbor principle by making a longer correspondence match than is necessary, provided that this longer match preserves the appearance of the object as it "moves" from Frame I to Frame II. However, this effect is rarely found – responses to the two types of displays are identical, indicating that element appearance is essentially ignored, and instead the nearest neighbor principle accounts for how motion correspondence matches are assigned.

Let us consider a final example of a motion correspondence issue that can be studied at the algorithmic level of analysis. The evidence cited above suggests that element locations provide the primary "raw data" that the visual system uses to solve the motion correspondence problem. However, what is the nature of these locations? In particular, are they the positions of elements in a two-dimensional space (e.g., position on the retina), or are they instead the positions of elements in the three-dimensional space of the distal world?

Dawson and Wright (1989) addressed this question using the motion competition paradigm. They created cardboard displays of a textured corridor that provided a strong sense of depth, particularly when viewed monocularly through a long tube. They presented motion competition displays in a "window" cut out of the cardboard. In one condition, this window was rectangular in shape, and appeared to be floating in the corridor perpendicular to the viewer's line of sight. In another condition, this window was trapezoidal in shape, and appeared to be rotated back in depth away from the viewer. The question was whether the perceived three-dimensional nature of the window would affect perceptions of distance in the display, and as a result affect the manner in which the nearest neighbor principle manifested itself. However, Dawson and Wright found that for the competition display, there was no effect of the apparent depth of the display. They concluded that motion correspondence is computed using the positions of elements in a two-dimensional space, and is not affected by the apparent three-dimensional locations of objects in the world.

An Algorithm to Solve the Correspondence Problem

As we have already seen in this chapter, computational analyses can be used to identify potential constraints on the motion correspondence problem. Furthermore, the likelihood that the human visual system uses these constraints can be established through the use of psychophysical experiments. However, to take a step towards developing a strongly equivalent theory of motion correspond-

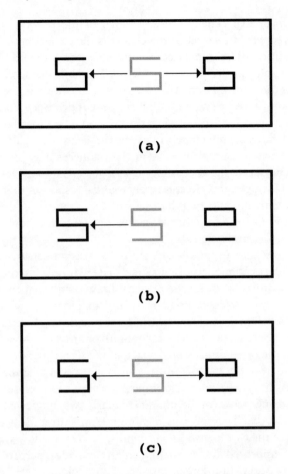

Figure 8.8 Competition displays used to determine whether the figural property of "connectedness" affects motion correspondence processing. (a) An ambiguous display, in which figural information and the nearest neighbor principle cannot be used to choose between the two motion correspondence matches illustrated with the arrows. (b) If element connectedness affects correspondence processing, this display should not be ambiguous – the connected figure in Frame I should be matched to the connected figure in Frame II. (c) However, human observers do not generate the solution illustrated in (b). For them, the display is still ambiguous, indicating that the human visual system is insensitive to this particular figural property.

ence processing, we need to build a computer simulation that incorporates all of the constraints of interest, as well as the design decisions that have been experimentally supported. There are two advantages of creating this kind of model. The first is that its performance on a number of "benchmark" displays can be studied to determine whether this model generates the same motion correspondence solutions as does the human visual system under a wide variety of conditions. The second is that its performance can be used to motivate new experimental studies of motion correspondence processing. For example, if it is discovered that the model generates interesting and surprising correspondence solutions to some displays, it is natural to ask whether human observers will do the same.

Dawson (1991) has proposed a model which, when one inputs the two images of an apparent motion display, assigns motion correspondence matches between the elements in these two images. This particular algorithm chooses the set of motion correspondence matches that best satisfies the three natural constraints that were described in the previous part of the chapter: the nearest neighbor principle, the relative velocity principle, and the element integrity principle.

Dawson's (1991) model is a connectionist network. In this network, each processing unit represents a possible correspondence match for an input display (see figure 8.9). Every processing unit has a weighted connection to every other processing unit in the network, as well as a recurrent connection to itself. The set of connection weights in the network implements the three natural constraints used to assign correspondence matches. The specific equations used to assign these weights in accordance with these constraints are not relevant to our discussion in this chapter; the interested reader can find them in Dawson (1991, pp. 574–6). For our present purposes, it can be simply stated that if two different motion correspondence matches are highly compatible with each other in terms of the three constraints, then the two processors that represent these matches will have mutually excitatory connection weights. If the two matches are highly incompatible, then the two processors will have mutually inhibitory connections.

Dawson's (1991) motion correspondence model is an autoassociative network. This means that the activation levels of the processors are modified via an iterative feedback loop: processors send their activity through network connections; in turn, the signals transmitted through the connections produce changes in processor activities. This iterative processing continues until the network converges to a stable state, which will not change with additional processing. This stable state represents a solution to the motion correspondence problem that was presented to the model. In this stable state, processing units with activities higher than a preset threshold represent matches that should be assigned to the display. All other processing units will be "OFF," and will represent motion correspondence matches that are not assigned to the display. In general, when the network converges to a stable state, the processing units that remain "ON" represent the set of matches that are most compatible with the constraints that are embodied in the network's connection weights.

When developing a model of motion correspondence processing, it is difficult to specify an optimal procedure to test its capabilities. There are an infinite number of potential displays that the model could process. The problem is to choose an interesting and informative subset of these potential tests. The strategy adopted to test Dawson's (1991) model was to choose a set of "benchmark" displays to investigate the capabilities of the model. For the most part, these benchmark displays were quite simple, primarily because the qualitative nature of human motion correspondence solutions is only known for

(a)   **(b)**

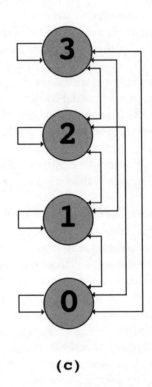

(c)

Figure 8.9 Dawson's (1991) motion correspondence network. (a) A simple apparent motion display, consisting of two Frame I and two Frame II elements. (b) This simple display has four possible correspondence matches that could be assigned to it. (c) A network constructed for this particular display. Each processing unit (gray circle) represents a particular motion correspondence match in (b). Lines and arrows represent connections between processing units; the weights of these connections are set to reflect the nearest neighbor principle, the relative velocity principle, and the element integrity principle. At the end of processing, some of the processing units will be "ON," while others will be "OFF," indicating which correspondence matches should be assigned to the display. For this particular example, units 3 and 0 would be on, and units 1 and 2 would be off when the network converged to a solution.

relatively simple displays (see, for instance, the many examples in Kolers, 1972). The particular "benchmarks" tested were selected for a variety of reasons. Some of the displays tested the utility of a particular constraint, or posed potential challenges because they violated a constraint exploited by the model. Still others were selected to differentiate the current model from those developed by other researchers.

The benchmark displays included stimuli in which (a) a single element translated to a new position in Frame II; (b) multiple elements translated to new positions in Frame II; (c) multiple elements rotated about an origin from Frame I to Frame II; (d) nearest neighbor sensitivity was required; (e) context sensitivity (with respect to the relative velocity principle) was required; (f) elements "sheared" in opposite directions; and (g) elements did not move from Frame I to Frame II. For all of these benchmark displays, Dawson (1991, fig. 7) found that the model's solutions were qualitatively identical to those generated by the human visual system. In addition, Dawson found that when one or more of the constraints was excluded from the model, it failed to generate human-like solutions for at least some of the benchmark displays. From this performance of the model, Dawson concluded that the three natural constraints incorporated into it provided a reasonable account of the human visual system's ability to solve the motion correspondence problem.

The tests of the model that were described above were designed to determine whether the computer simulation was capable of solving motion correspondence problems that it was designed to solve. However, this is not the only kind of test that one can perform on the computer simulation. One can also use the model to determine the extent to which the constraining principles built into it account for phenomena not originally considered when the model was designed. Indeed, one measure of a model's strength is its ability to account for a wider range of phenomena than was originally intended. Dawson (1991) discovered several examples of his motion correspondence providing an account of apparent motion displays that it was not originally intended to deal with. Let us consider one of these here, the ability of the model to generate motion correspondence matches that represent "least energy transformations" of moving objects.

In some cases, there is more than one set of *physically plausible* motion correspondence matches that can be assigned to a display. Consider the two different apparent motion displays illustrated in figure 8.10. Both of these could be geometrically described, and plausibly perceived, as a rigid clockwise rotation of three points about the marked origin. The motion correspondence matches associated with this interpretation of these two displays are given in figures 8.10b and 8.10 a.

However, human observers do *not* generate these sets of motion correspondence matches. For the first display, humans generate the set of matches illustrated in figure 8.10a. This solution is consistent with the perception of the three elements translating downwards, accompanied by a 45 degree clockwise rotation about the middle point. For the second display, humans generate the

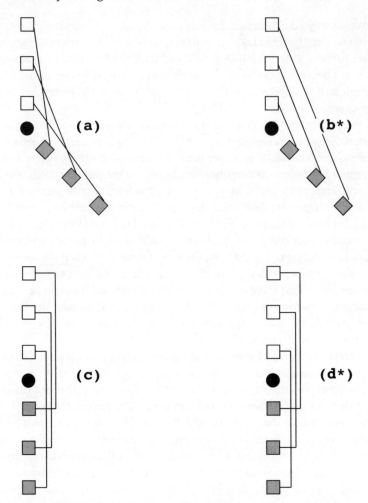

Figure 8.10 Rotations of three elements about a central origin. If humans saw these apparent motion displays as rigid rotations, they would generate the (physically plausible) correspondence matches illustrated in (b) and (d). However, they instead see "least energy" transformations, and generate the matches illustrated in (a) and (c).

set of matches in figure 8.10c. This solution is consistent with the perception of the three elements translating downwards. These two "alternative" solutions are generated because they produce lower total element displacement and relative velocity than the matches consistent with a rigid clockwise rotation. Thus, when the model is faced with choosing between two physically plausible interpretations (i.e., figure 8.10a vs. figure 8.10b, or figure 8.10c vs. figure 8.10d), it selects that interpretation that represents a "least energy" transformation: the interpretation that produces the least cost with respect to the three applied constraints.

When this performance of the model was discovered, a natural question emerged: would human observers also see this least change transformation, or would they see the other physically plausible interpretation of the motion (i.e., rigid rotation). Dawson and Pylyshyn (1988) conducted an experiment to answer this question, and found that human observers almost always generated the same set of motion correspondence displays as did the model. This is one example of how having a working computer simulation can point researchers towards obtaining new experimental evidence from human subjects.

It turns out that a preference for "least energy" movement is characteristic of the human visual system (e.g., Farrell & Shepard, 1981; Shepard & Judd, 1976). This has led some researchers to propose models of apparent motion perception that apply explicit principles of least energy transformations (e.g., Caelli & Dodwell, 1980; Foster, 1978; Mori, 1982; Restle, 1979; Shepard, 1982, 1984). Of interest is that Dawson's (1991) motion correspondence model generates such solutions "for free" – that is, without ever being intended to do this. It is possible that the preference for "least energy" movement identified by other researchers is a property that emerges from a visual system that is designed to solve lower-level problems of underdetermination (i.e., the motion correspondence problem) by applying other constraints that are not necessarily related to the notion of "least energy."

Part IV   From the Algorithmic to the Computational

Why should cognitive scientists who are interested in the same phenomenon, but who study the phenomenon at different levels of analysis, still maintain contact with one another? One reason is that advances at one level of analysis can affect the kinds of questions that are asked at another level of analysis. In this part of the paper, we will consider two examples of how algorithmic studies of the motion correspondence problem resulted in new issues being raised at the computational level.

Algorithmic Influences on Computational Research

Dawson's (1991) model of motion correspondence processing is cast into a particular mathematical framework. First, it is an autoassociative network, and is strongly related to other such networks, including Anderson, Silverstein, Ritz, and Jones's (1977) "brainstate-in-a-box" and Hopfield's (e.g., 1982) network. The mathematical regularities of such networks are well understood. Second, Dawson's model can easily be described in the mathematical language of linear algebra – in fact, the network can be correctly described as a vector (i.e., processing unit activities), which at each iteration of processing is rotated by a matrix (i.e., the connection weights) and then which is normalized to unit length. Because Dawson's network can be described mathematically, one can take this particular algorithm and answer specific computational questions about it.

For instance, for any model that uses iterative processing, it is important to know whether or not the model will actually converge to a solution for every problem that it is presented. Dawson (1991) was able to prove that this was the case. He showed that the iterative processing of the network could be described as a single operation in which the matrix of connection weights was multiplied by itself many times, and the result of this was used to multiply the processing weights. This is equivalent to what has been called the "power method" for extracting the most dominant eigenvector of a matrix (e.g., Hall, 1963, pp. 63–6). The power method is guaranteed to converge for symmetric matrices, because with each multiplication of a symmetric matrix with itself, the other components (i.e., eigenvectors) of the matrix become weaker and weaker, and finally vanish. Because the connection matrix of Dawson's network was symmetric, he was able to use its relationship to the power method to guarantee that it would converge to a solution.

Another computational question about this algorithm was whether it would converge to a unique solution. After all, this is what is of interest when problems of underdetermination are solved. If the network converged to a solution, but converged to different solutions for the same display on different times, then it would not be of particular interest to us. However, Dawson's (1991) demonstration that the model would converge to the most dominant eigenvector (which he was able to do by relating his algorithm to the power method) indicated that for most displays, uniqueness was guaranteed. This is because most matrices have only one eigenvector that is dominant, and Dawson's algorithm was guaranteed to converge on this one solution. The only time for which uniqueness was not guaranteed was for matrices that had two dominant eigenvectors (i.e., the first and second eigenvector associated with identical eigenvalues). However, this situation should only occur in exceptional cases, and thus would not in general cause a problem for Dawson's algorithm. Furthermore, the discovery of such a display for the model would immediately lead to the prediction that the same display would lead to two qualitatively different experiences for human observers. In other words, rather than posing a problem for Dawson's network, this kind of display would lead to an interesting experiment that could be used to provide stronger support for it.

Finally, given that in most cases the network will converge to a unique solution, can it be said that this solution is indeed the most consistent with the constraints that are embodied in the network? Dawson (1991) was able to prove that this was so by relating his model to an autoassociative network proposed by Hopfield (1982). Hopfield defined a cost function for his network, and was able to show that the processing of this network was guaranteed to change the states of the network's processors to the pattern that produced minimum cost – or, in other words, was most consistent with the connectivity of the network. Dawson was able to translate Hopfield's cost function into a related cost function for the motion correspondence network. He was then able to prove that the global minimum for this cost function was the most dominant eigenvector of the connection matrix. In other words, when the network converges to a unique solution, this solution will be the one that is most consistent with the constraints that are represented in the network's connection weights!

Experimental Influences on Computational Research

The apparent motion display in figure 8.11a is known as the *Ternus configuration*, and has played an important role in current theorizing about human motion perception. This is because it is multistable – changes in temporal parameters produce qualitative changes in the display's appearance. Group motion (figure 8.11b) is seen when frame duration and ISI are both long. However, with long frame duration and short ISI, quite a different percept is experienced: two elements in the middle of the display remain stationary, while a third element moves back and forth around them (figure 8.11c). This is called *element motion*. The empirical distinction between group motion and element motion has played a central role in the debate about the existence of qualitatively different motion perception mechanisms (e.g., Braddick, 1980; Breitmeyer & Ritter, 1986; Petersik, 1989).

The Ternus configuration was of particular interest to Dawson (1991) because it turned out that minor manipulations of element positions for this display caused Dawson's motion correspondence model to generate different solutions to it. In particular, when elements in the display were close together, the motion correspondence model generated the set of matches consistent with group motion. In contrast, when the elements in the display were further apart from one another, the model generated the set of matches consistent with group motion. This finding was significant for two different reasons. First, the model was not designed with the Ternus configuration in mind, so it was particularly interesting to find that the model could generate either group or element motion solutions. Second, the fact that the motion correspondence model could generate both solutions indicated that a single theory might account for how the human visual system interprets the display, in contrast to those researchers who have argued that the Ternus configuration is evidence for there being two different motion perception mechanisms in humans (e.g., Braddick, 1980; Petersik, 1989).

Because of the surprising ability of Dawson's (1991) model to generate two different sets of motion correspondence matches to the Ternus configuration, Dawson and his colleagues started to perform some new experimental studies of how humans perceive the display. Importantly, these results pointed to the fact that one of the assumptions underlying the model was not completely accurate. As a result, a fourth natural constraint had to be included in more recent versions of Dawson's original model.

In particular, Dawson, Nevin-Meadows, and Wright (1994) explored a variety of techniques to see whether or not the relative frequencies of seeing element motion or group motion could be affected by changing the appearance of elements in the display. Specifically, they manipulated the contrast polarity of

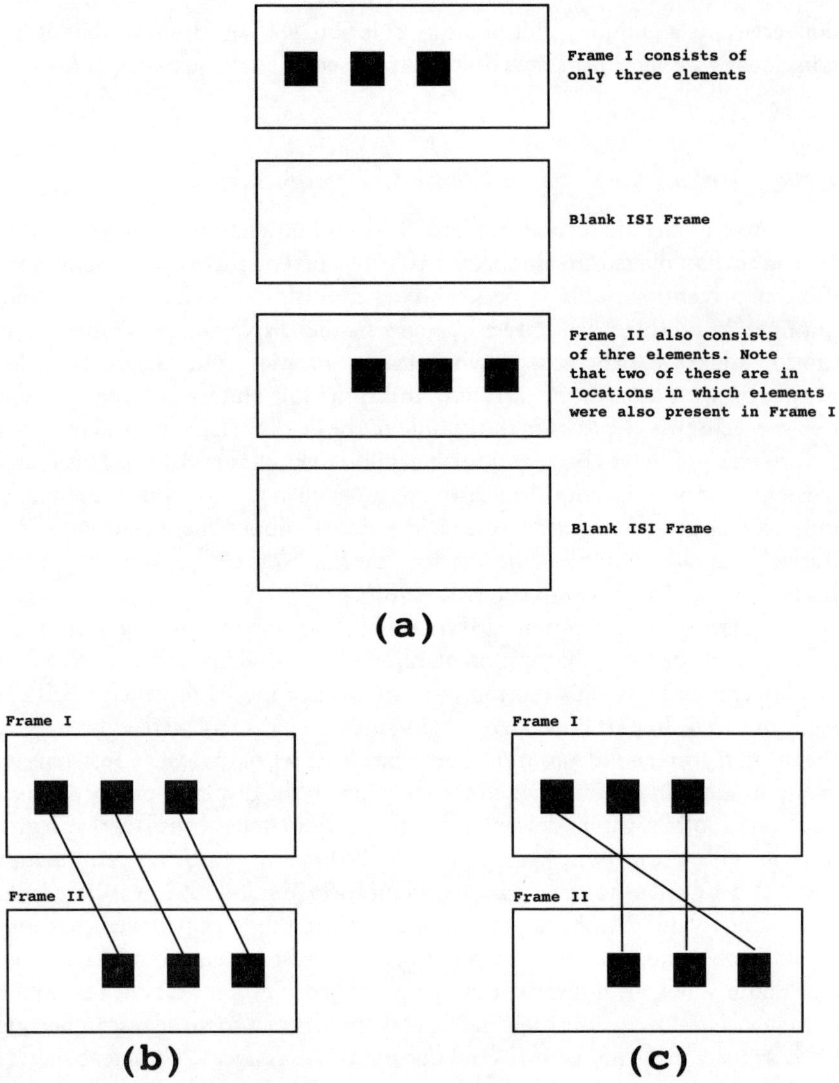

(a)

(b)   **(c)**

Figure 8.11 The Ternus configuration. (a) The four static images that are used to create this display. A second ISI frame is included because one typically "cycles" this display over and over again to generate the illusion of back-and-forth motion. (b) The set of correspondence matches from Frame I to Frame II that are consistent with group motion. (c) The set of correspondence matches from Frame I to Frame II that are consistent with element motion. For this display, subjects will see group motion or element motion depending on a number of factors, including the duration of Frames I and II as well as the duration of the blank ISI frames.

display elements – whether the elements were brighter or darker than a neutral grey background. In control displays, elements had all the same contrast polarity (as in figure 8.11). In experimental displays, contrast polarity was manipulated in a fashion that could bias one perception of the display over

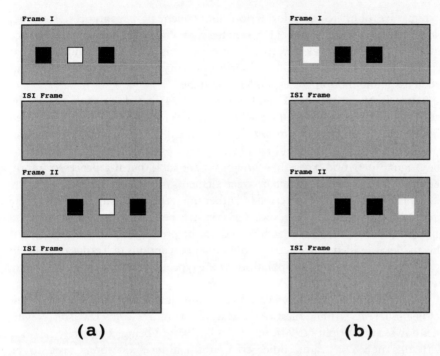

Figure 8.12 Contrast polarity manipulations of the Ternus configuration. (a) If contrast polarity affects motion correspondence matching, then this pattern of dark and light elements will have a tendency to produce perceptions of group motion. (b) If contrast polarity affects motion correspondence matching, then this pattern of dark and light elements will have a tendency to produce perceptions of element motion.

another. For example, in figure 8.12a the appearance of the elements is such that if the visual system preferred to make correspondence matches between elements of the same contrast polarity, then group motion should be seen more frequently for this display than for a control display. Similarly, figure 8.12b is a display in which element motion would be seen more frequently than in a control condition if contrast polarity matching was used by the visual system.

Now, as we have already seen, one of the major assumptions of Dawson's (1991) motion correspondence model is that element appearances should not affect motion perception. Similar assumptions have been made in other models (e.g., Grossberg & Rudd, 1989, 1992; Ullman, 1979). All of these models would predict that the manipulation that is illustrated in figure 8.12 should not affect perceptions of the Ternus display. However, Dawson, Nevin-Meadows, and Wright (1994) found that this manipulation had a small but significant effect on the perception of the Ternus configuration, particularly for displays in which Frame I and Frame II were presented for longer durations.

One implication of this finding was that models such as Dawson's (1991) motion correspondence network and Grossberg and Rudd's (1989, 1992) motion-oriented contrast filter do not provide an adequate account of motion perception, because they are based on the assumption that motion perception systems are blind to *all* information about element appearances. Dawson, Nevin-Meadows, and Wright (1994) noted that while most element appearance information may be irrelevant to motion processing, their results indicated that a particular type of information – contrast polarity – appeared to be important when assigning motion correspondence matches.

Dawson, Nevin-Meadows, and Wright (1994) acted on their results by building a fourth constraint into the Dawson (1991) network, which they called the *polarity matching constraint*. They defined a new set of (symmetric) connection weights that could be added to the connection weights defined by the original network. These new weights were such that if a processor represented a correspondence match between elements of the same contrast polarity, then the match would be preferred (all other things being equal). Similarly, if the processor represented a correspondence match between elements of opposite contrast polarity, then the match would not be preferred. The performance of this model provided a nice account of human perceptions of Ternus displays in which contrast polarity manipulations of the type illustrated in figure 8.12 were performed.

It is important to note, however, that the introduction of this new constraint to the model raises other questions that were not addressed by Dawson, Nevin-Meadows, and Wright (1994). In particular, before being completely satisfied with this new constraint, other computational-level questions need to be answered about it. In particular, is there any reason to believe that this constraint is actually natural? Furthermore, is there any computational proof that would indicate why this kind of figural property has a stronger effect on motion correspondence processing than do other figural properties? Finally, is there any argument that could be made as to why this property is less important to motion correspondence processing than are the other three constraints that are built into the model? Currently, we do not have any answers to these questions. Of importance to the current chapter, however, is the fact that new computational-level questions can be raised (and should be investigated) if one pays attention to developments that occur as the result of algorithmic-level research.

Part V   The Implementation of Motion Correspondence Processes

In previous parts of this chapter, we have seen how the motion correspondence problem can be studied at both the computational and the algorithmic level. We have also seen how results at one of these levels can affect the kinds of questions that emerge at the other. In this part of the chapter, we now turn to issues that arise when motion correspondence processing is dealt with at the implementational level. One advantage of using vision as a test case for the methodology of cognitive science is that we do have a great deal of knowledge about how visual processing is instantiated in the brain. In this part of the chapter, I will review a number of implementational results that have an important bearing on the motion correspondence problem. In the next part of the chapter, I will discuss how these implementational results can affect questions that arise at the computational and algorithmic levels.

The Motion Pathway in Vision

Evidence from anatomy, physiology, and clinical neuroscience has led many researchers to suggest that there exist parallel physiological pathways in the human visual system (e.g., Livingstone & Hubel, 1988; Maunsell & Newsome, 1987; Ungerleider & Mishkin, 1982). Each pathway is argued to be responsible for the processing of different kinds of visual information. In particular, one major pathway appears to be specialized for the processing of visual form (i.e., specifying what an object is), while a second major pathway appears to be specialized for the processing of visual motion (i.e., specifying where an object is). These two pathways are typically assumed to be distinct and independent, suggesting that the perception of motion is mediated by physiological processes independent of those that mediate the perception of form. While such an extreme view is unlikely to be completely correct (see DeYoe & van Essen, 1988), Livingstone and Hubel demonstrate that it is a powerful heuristic for uniting many results in physiology and psychology.

The existence of a distinct pathway for the processing of visual motion is supported by a variety of findings. First, it has been discovered that certain kinds of damage to the human brain produce severe deficits in the perception of motion, but have little effect on the perception of form (e.g., Hess, Baker, & Zihl, 1989; Zihl, von Cramon, & Mai, 1983; see Botez, 1975 for examples of lesions that affect form perception but do not affect motion perception). Second, physiological recordings of cell responses to stimuli have revealed many neurons that are highly sensitive to stimulus movement, but are not affected by the color, size, or shape of stimuli (e.g., Albright, 1984; Albright, Desimone, & Gross, 1984; Dubner & Zeki, 1971; Maunsell & van Essen, 1983c; Rodman & Albright, 1987; Zeki, 1974). Third, anatomical evidence reveals patterns of neural connectivity that appear to define an anatomical pathway for processing motion. Specifically, there exist rich interconnections between cell regions that are highly sensitive to motion, while rich interconnections do not exist between such cell regions and those that are highly sensitive to other stimulus properties, such as color (e.g., Livingstone & Hubel, 1988).

Figure 8.13 depicts the major components of the motion pathway, and illustrates their direct interconnections. Note that this figure is highly simplified: there likely exist many additional connections between this network and other physiological components of the visual system (Desimone & Ungerleider, 1986; DeYoe & van Essen, 1988; Maunsell & van Essen, 1983b). As well, actual patterns of connectivity are much more complicated than illustrated, for in most cases direct connections between components are reciprocal (e.g., Maunsell &

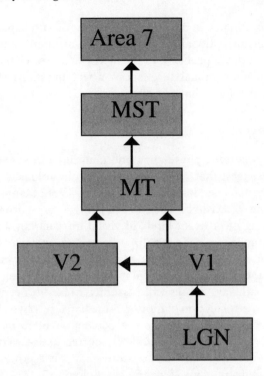

Figure 8.13 Functional architecture for the motion pathway in vision. LGN = the magnocellular laminae of the lateral geniculate nucleus. V1 = the striate visual cortex, of which only two layers are included in the motion pathway. V2 = Area 2 of the visual cortex, of which only the thick stripes are part of the motion pathway. MT = the middle temporal visual area, located within the superior temporal sulcus. Note that this component of the pathway receives input from both V1 and V2. MST = the medial superior temporal area, also located within the superior temporal sulcus. Area 7 = part of the parietal association cortex. It is argued in the text that motion correspondence matches are assigned by this component of the pathway, on the basis of stimulus properties detected by MT and MST.

Newsome, 1987). Nevertheless, figure 8.13 captures the basic structure of what physiologists describe as a pathway for the processing of motion.

Where in the Motion Pathway is Correspondence Computed?

The perception of motion serves as the foundation for many different functions, including the segregation of figure and ground, the perception of depth, the coordination of eye movements, and locomotion through space (e.g., Gibson, 1966; Lisberger, Morris, & Tychsen, 1987; Nakayama, 1985; Regan, 1986). Each of these functions also requires different kinds of motion measurements or computations (e.g., Ullman, 1981). That the motion pathway is likely to mediate many (if not all) of these measurements suggests that each component of the pathway is probably responsible in part for many different functions. In this section it is argued that one of the several functions likely to be carried out by area 7 of the posterior parietal cortex is the assignment of correspondence matches. It is also argued that these matches are assigned on the basis of motion measurements that are not coded until relatively late in the pathway (i.e., coded in MT and MST). These points are made by considering the properties required of a neural substrate if it were to implement correspondence processing of the type described in Part III above.

1) *The neural substrate must be sensitive to individuated elements.* It has been argued (e.g., Dawson, 1991) that motion correspondence matches are assigned *after* the to-be-tracked moving elements have been individuated as figures against a background (e.g., Anstis, 1980; Ramachandran & Anstis, 1986b). In the motion pathway, discrete elements are probably not individuated until MT, indicating that MT marks the earliest point in the motion pathway at which correspondence processing could occur. There are two general types of evidence for this claim.

First, Allman, Miezin, and McGuinness (1985) have found that MT is characterized by very large directionally selective receptive fields that have an antagonistic organization. Thus, a cell in MT will respond vigorously when a small central region of its receptive field is being stimulated by movement in one direction and at the same time the remaining part of the receptive field is being stimulated by coherent movement in a different direction. If the entire receptive field is stimulated by coherent motion in a single direction, the cell will not respond. It appears that one major function of cells in MT is to individuate elements from their background on the basis of motion information. It has been shown that elements defined in terms of relative motion can serve as inputs to human motion correspondence processes (e.g., Pantle & Picciano, 1976; Prazdny, 1986). In the primate visual system, such elements do not appear to be defined prior to MT.

Second, Chubb and Sperling (1988) have shown that the Reichardt class of detector often used to model early motion perception (e.g., Dawson & Di Lollo, 1990; Reichardt, 1961; van Santen & Sperling, 1984, 1985) is incapable of detecting the coherent, global movement of certain figural patterns (e.g., the plaid pattern produced by superimposing two drifting sinusoid gratings). However, human observers can easily detect such motion (e.g., Chubb & Sperling, 1988; Lelkens & Koenderink, 1984; Victor & Conte, 1990). Movshon, Adelson, Gizzi, and Newsome (1984) have shown that neurons in MT respond to pattern motion. Furthermore, Movshon *et al.* show that cells located earlier in the motion pathway (i.e., in striate cortex) are not sensitive to the motion of global patterns. On the basis of his own physiological studies of MT, Albright (1984) has proposed a network for the detection of pattern motion. Albright's model works by tracking small unoriented subunits of the moving stimulus – thus his mechanism for pattern motion detection in MT requires that parts of a moving stimulus be individuated.

2) *The neural substrate must be sensitive to element locations.* A second important property of motion correspondence processing, defended on both empirical and theoretical grounds earlier in this chapter, is that motion correspondence matches are assigned primarily on the basis of element locations.

Physiological evidence indicates that the parietal cortex of the human brain is primarily involved in the representation of spatial locations. For example, damage to the posterior parietal lobe produces severe deficits in the ability to accurately reach towards a visual target (e.g., Damasio & Benton, 1979; Ratcliff & Davies-Jones, 1972), and can also produce severe deficits in the ability to perceive motion (e.g., Hess, Baker, & Zihl, 1989; Newsome & Pare, 1988; Zihl, von Cramon, & Mai, 1983). However, damage localized in the parietal cortex appears to have little effect on the processing of visual form. The latter parts of the motion pathway, beginning with MT, are near or in parietal cortex, and are thus located in a region of the brain that appears to be responsible for representing and processing location information. For instance, MT is a small area on the posterior bank of the superior temporal sulcus (e.g., Maunsell & Newsome, 1987, fig. 2). This portion of the superior temporal sulcus is surrounded by the angular gyrus of the inferior parietal lobule (Barr, 1974, p. 211). MST lies immediately adjacent to MT in the medial part of the superior temporal sulcus. Area 7 is itself located in the posterior part of the parietal lobe.

In addition, of course, the physiological evidence used to defend the notion of distinct pathways for processing motion and form emphasizes the role of stimulus location. Specifically, many neurons in MT (e.g., Albright, 1984; Albright, Desimone, & Gross, 1984; Dubner & Zeki, 1971; Maunsell & van Essen, 1983c; Rodman & Albright, 1987; Zeki, 1974) and in MST (e.g., Saito *et al.*, 1986; Tanaka *et al.*, 1986) are insensitive to the figural appearances of stimuli. These neurons respond to element motion, and not to element size, color or shape.

3) *The neural substrate must have very large receptive fields.* Under the traditionally assumed two-process distinction that has guided motion perception research over the last two decades, the motion correspondence problem is assumed to be solved by the long-range process. This is because "classical" apparent motion can be perceived between elements separated by several degrees of visual angle in the visual field; the short-range process is assumed to be unable to detect motion over these large distances. The physiological implications of this view are quite straightforward: the neural substrate involved in assigning motion correspondence matches must have very large receptive fields.

Cavanagh and Mather (1989) have argued that the so-called long-range motion system should not be interpreted as being responsible for element tracking, because there is no physiological evidence for receptive fields large enough to accomplish this task throughout the visual field. However, recent experiments show that this view is incorrect. Allman, Miezin, and McGuinness (1985) have shown that classical techniques used to map out receptive field sizes (i.e., the use of small bars or spots as stimuli) vastly underestimate the effective receptive field size of cells in MT. This is because these classical techniques do not stimulate the peripheral components of the receptive fields in such a way as to generate maximal responses from the cells (i.e., classical stimuli do not stimulate the antagonistically organized receptive fields of these cells). When stimuli designed to more adequately stimulate the peripheral parts of the receptive field are used, the size of the receptive field of most MT cells appears to be 50 to 100 times as large as revealed using classical stimuli. Furthermore, in terms of absolute size the techniques of Allman *et al.* reveal that these MT receptive fields are enormous. Allman *et al.* estimated that the smallest receptive field size that they observed was $1,200^{o2}$; the largest was estimated to be between $4,900^{o2}$ and $7,000^{o2}$. Noting that the total visual field for the animals studied was approximately $20,000^{o2}$, this suggests that the receptive field of a single MT cell could cover between 6 and 35 percent of the entire visual field (for similar estimates, see Saito *et al.*, 1986; Tanaka *et al.*, 1986). Noting that it is commonly assumed that the receptive fields of cells late in visual pathways are constructed by synthesizing or combining receptive fields from cells earlier in the pathway (e.g., Kuffler, Nicholls, & Martin, 1984, pp. 64–7), this implies that the receptive field size of cells located in MST or in area 7 are even larger than those found in MT. Indeed, Robinson, Goldberg, and Stanton (1978, p. 922) report that the receptive fields of neurons in area 7 frequently cover one or two quadrants of the visual field; on occasion receptive fields have been found covering the entire visual field (see also Motter & Mountcastle, 1981).

4) *The neural substrate must be involved in tracking objects.* To convincingly argue that some particular neural substrate is responsible for assigning correspondence matches, one must clearly demonstrate that it is responsible for object tracking. Evidence concerning this "object tracking criterion" places correspondence processing later in the motion pathway than in MT, as is shown below.

In examining the functional properties of area 7, many researchers have observed cells that appear to mediate object tracking (e.g., Hyvarinen & Poranen, 1974; Goldberg & Bruce, 1985; Lynch, Mountcastle, Talbot, & Yin, 1977; Motter & Mountcastle, 1981; Robinson, Goldberg, & Stanton, 1978; Sakata, Shibutani, Kawano, & Harrington, 1985); such cells are not evident earlier in the motion pathway. Visual fixation neurons produce sustained responses when a target is fixated; some of these cells only respond when the target occupies a preferred spatial location. Visual tracking neurons respond when a moving stimulus is tracked by smooth-pursuit eye movements. Visual tracking neurons will also respond when a stationary object is fixated while another object moves, but will not respond with stationary fixations alone (e.g., Robinson, Goldberg, & Stanton, 1978). Many visual tracking neurons exhibit a preferred direction of object motion. Saccade neurons respond up to 150 milliseconds prior to a saccadic eye movement to a designated target. Saccade neurons do not respond during stationary fixations, object tracking, or prior to spontaneous saccades to non-target elements.

5) *The neural substrate must track elements defined in different sensory modalities.* The "object tracking criterion" can be elaborated to place additional constraints on localizing motion correspondence processing in a particular physiological structure. Dawson (e.g., 1991) has argued that motion

correspondence processing is responsible for the primitive tag-assignment function in Pylyshyn's (1989) model of spatial indexing. One consequence of this argument is that the principles governing correspondence processing in the visual modality should also govern object tracking in other sensory modalities (i.e., to track the identities of visual FINSTs and of haptic ANCHORS). Physiologically speaking, this implies that the neural substrate responsible for visual tracking must also be responsible for other kinds of tracking (e.g., tracking of haptic objects). This hypothesis is supported by experimental studies of area 7. For example, Robinson, Goldberg, and Stanton (1978) describe the properties of *hand projection neurons*. These neurons respond to targets to which hand movements are to be directed. Hand projection neurons do not respond to the reaching movement in the absence of a visual stimulus. Hyvarinen and Poranen (1974) also observed many area 7 cells that responded during manual reaching, tracking, or manipulation, and noted that many of these cells had a preferred direction of reaching. It is likely that damage to these types of cells are responsible for deficits in visual localization (i.e., accurate reaching towards visual targets) observed in humans with parietal lobe lesions (e.g., Damasio & Benton, 1979; Ratcliff & Davies-Jones, 1972).

6) *The neural substrate must mediate attentional processing of tracked elements.* One further implication of the putative relationship between motion correspondence and tag-assignment processing concerns the involvement of visual attention. Pylyshyn and Storm (1988) have shown that human observers are capable of simultaneously tracking several target elements individuated from distractors by attention alone. Dawson (e.g., 1991) has argued that this tracking must be mediated by motion correspondence processes. Therefore, the neural substrate responsible for such processing must be capable of distinguishing attended from nonattended objects, even if both are equally visible. Again, area 7 exhibits this capability. Without exception, researchers who examine the properties of neurons in area 7 note that they are governed by strong extraretinal influences (e.g., Hyvarinen & Poranen, 1974; Goldberg & Bruce, 1985; Lynch, Mountcastle, Talbot & Yin, 1977; Robinson, Goldberg, & Stanton, 1978; Sakata, Shibutani, Kawano, & Harrington, 1985). Specifically, strong responses in all of the different types of area 7 neurons only occur when the object stimulating their receptive fields is being attended to, or is of some interest to the observing animal. If the object is not being attended to, the area 7 neurons will have very weak responses (for a striking example, see Robinson, Goldberg, & Stanton, 1978, fig. 17).

Summary. This evidence concerning the tracking of attended objects clearly indicates that area 7 in the posterior parietal lobe is the major locus for motion correspondence processing. However, this does not also indicate that other parts of the motion pathway are not also critically important for the assignment of motion correspondence matches. For instance, Lisberger, Morris, and Tychsen (1987, pp. 108–9) note that oculomotor pursuit depends on the kind of information represented in MT, even though the evidence above would indicate that pursuit processing itself occurs later in the motion pathway. This suggests that motion correspondence matches are assigned by neural mechanisms in area 7, but this assignment depends upon measurements performed earlier in the motion pathway, particularly in MT and MST.

Neural Measurements for Motion Correspondence Processing

The preceding section argued that correspondence matches are assigned in area 7 by considering very general characteristics of motion correspondence processing – characteristics that should be true of any correspondence model. In this section, the biological plausibility of the Dawson (1991) model is explored by determining whether there is any evidence that the specific motion measurements that it requires are made in MT or MST.

The nearest neighbor principle. Both Dawson's (1991) model and Ullman's (1979) minimal mapping theory incorporate the assumption that the nearest neighbor principle is required to assign motion correspondence matches. As we saw earlier, the nearest neighbor principle amounts to the claims that the visual prefers slow element velocities. Physiological evidence indicates that the stimulus measurements represented by cells in MT are well suited for implementing the nearest neighbor principle.

Cells in MT appear to encode the velocity of moving elements. Many experiments have shown that cells in MT have both a preferred direction and a preferred speed of stimulus motion (e.g., Albright, 1984; Dubner & Zeki, 1971; Maunsell & van Essen, 1983c; Mikami, Newsome, & Wurtz, 1986; Rodman & Albright, 1987). The extent of speeds preferred by these velocity-sensitive neurons is rather broad, ranging from 2 to 256°/sec (e.g., Maunsell and van Essen, 1983c, p. 1137).

At first glance, the broad range of preferred speeds for MT neurons seems inconsistent with the nearest neighbor principle, as is evidence that MT allows faster velocities to be coded than do directionally selective cells in area V1 (e.g., Mikami, Newsome, & Wurtz, 1986; Newsome, Mikami, & Wurtz, 1986). However, a closer examination of the distribution of speed preferences in MT is consistent with a preference for slow velocities. While directionally selective MT cells code a broad range of speeds, most prefer slow or intermediate speeds. For example, all of the 70 cells studied by Dubner and Zeki (1971) had preferred speeds ranging from 1 to 5°/sec. Similarly, over half of the 109 cells examined by Maunsell and van Essen (1983c, fig. 7a) had preferred speeds of 32°/sec or less. Zeki (1974) estimated that the preferred speeds for a population of MT cells ranged between 5 and 50°/sec, although his methods limited the accuracy of this estimate. In sum, the evidence indicates that while MT can encode many different stimulus velocities, slow velocities are much more likely to elicit responses in MT then are fast velocities.

An additional assumption in the current model is that the nearest neighbor principle is defined using two-dimensional coordinates; motion correspondence matches are not assigned in three-space. Again, the characteristics of neural responses in MT are consistent with this assumption. As can be seen in figure

8.13, MT receives direct input from area V2 in the visual cortex, which encodes information about the binocular disparity of stimuli (e.g., Livingstone & Hubel, 1988). Thus, in principle, MT could represent the three-dimensional velocities of elements. However, this does not appear to be done in practice. Instead, MT neurons appear to encode the two-dimensional velocity of elements at fixed horizontal disparities (i.e., elements moving in fixed frontoparallel planes). For example, Maunsell and van Essen (1983a) report that some MT neurons code the velocity of an element moving in a plane that is far from the observer, while others code the velocity of an element moving in a plane that is near to the observer. "To our surprise, no neurons in our sample from MT were truly selective for motion in depth in the sense of responding maximally to stimuli that simulated movement with components toward or away from the animal" (p. 1149). This property, though surprising to Maunsell and van Essen, is assumed in both Dawson's (1991) model and in minimal mapping theory (e.g., Ullman, 1979), and is consistent with psychophysical evidence suggesting that the human visual system does not assign correspondence matches in three-space (e.g., Dawson & Wright, 1989; Ullman, 1978).

The relative velocity principle. Dawson's (1991) motion correspondence model can be differentiated from Ullman's (1979) minimal mapping theory in exploiting a relative velocity principle, which encourages the assignment of similar motion correspondence matches (or, equivalently, similar velocities) to elements near one another in Frame I. With respect to establishing the biological plausibility of the relative velocity principle, two questions must be considered: First, do there exist neurons that are explicitly sensitive to relative velocity information? Second, is there any evidence that measurements of relative velocity are integrated by physiological structures in such a way that the relative velocity principle is directly implemented?

With respect to the first question, cells sensitive to the relative movements of stimuli have been found in many areas of the brain, including the superior colliculus (Mandl, 1985), the striate cortex or area V1 (Bridgeman, 1972; Hammond, Ahmed, & Smith, 1986; Hammond, Pomfrett, & Ahmed, 1989; Hammond & Smith, 1984; Kaji & Kawabata, 1985; Orban, Gulyas, & Vogels, 1987), area V2 (Orban, Gulyas, & Spileers, 1988), MT (e.g., Allman, Miezin, & McGuinness, 1985), MST (Saito *et al.*, 1986; Tanaka *et al.*, 1986), and area 7 (e.g., Motter & Mountcastle, 1981; Sakata, Shibutani, & Tsurugai, 1986). The seemingly ubiquitous presence of such detectors is consistent with the importance of relative motion information for many visual functions (for reviews, see Nakayama, 1985; Regan, 1986) and with the results of many psychophysical experiments showing that human observers are highly sensitive to such motion (e.g., Cutting & Proffitt, 1982; Dawson, 1987; Gogel, 1974; Johansson, 1950; Proffitt & Cutting, 1979, 1980; Ramachandran & Anstis, 1985, 1986a).

With respect to the second question, it must be determined whether relative velocity measurements are integrated in a manner consistent with the relative velocity principle – do there exist any cells which have a preference for several elements moving with similar velocities (i.e., cells that prefer small relative velocities)? As it was argued above that MT, MST, and area 7 were most likely sites for motion correspondence processing, in considering this issue we will restrict our attention to these locations.

The relative velocity measurements instantiated in MT do *not* appear to be consistent with the relative velocity principle. Allman, Miezin, and McGuinness (1985) have shown that directionally selective neurons in MT have an antagonistic organization to their receptive fields (see also Tanaka *et al.*, 1986). These cells have a strong preference for stimuli in which a small central region is moving in one direction, and in which the background is moving coherently in some other direction. These cells do *not* respond when the entire receptive field is stimulated by coherent motion in a single direction. Thus these cells prefer nonzero relative velocities, in contrast to the processing units in Dawson's (1991) computer simulation.

However, there is evidence indicating that some of the directionally selective neurons in MST behave in a manner consistent with the relative velocity principle. Tanaka *et al.* (1986) examined 519 neurons in MST, of which the majority (285) were classified as being directionally selective. These directionally selective cells were assigned to three different categories: *figure cells* had strong responses to antagonistic patterns of motion and to the motion of single elements, but did not respond to the coherent motion of entire fields. *Nonselective cells* had equally strong responses to the motion of single elements and to field motion, provided that the motion was in a preferred direction. *Field cells* had strong responses to the motion of coherent fields, but did not respond to the motion of single elements. It is the behavior of field cells that is consistent with the relative velocity principle – these cells show little response to a single element moving in a preferred direction, but show a strong response when several elements move in this direction. Furthermore, these cells are relatively common. As the ratio of occurrence of the three types of cells is 2:3:2 respectively, it can be estimated that field cells comprise over 15 percent of the entire population of MST neurons. In addition, field neurons are unique to MST – they are not found in MT.

While the existence of field neurons in MST is consistent with the relative velocity principle, their behavior does not provide conclusive evidence for the principle's implementation. This is because it is unclear as to whether field cells are responding strongly to the small relative velocities of several individuated elements, or are instead merely responding to a coherent flow of motion which does not require any individuation of elements at all. Weak arguments can be made in favor of the former case. First, sensitivity to pattern motion exists at this later stage in the motion pathway (Movshon *et al.*, 1985), and this sensitivity may depend upon the individuation of pattern parts (Albright, 1984). Second, Tanaka *et al.* (1986, p. 141) report that there is some tendency for field cells to prefer patterns composed of large dots (2–4° in diameter), suggesting that these cells are sensitive to the component elements of the pattern, and not just the unindividuated luminance profile of the pattern.

The element integrity principle. Both Dawson's (1991) model and Ullman's (1979) modified minimal mapping theory (see also Grzywacz & Yuille, 1988) apply an element integrity constraint to the assignment of motion correspondence matches. This constraint is used to prevent the splitting or fusing of moving elements, causing the computer simulations to prefer one-to-one matches between frames of view.

One method for implementing this constraint is to abandon the *cover principle* used in minimal mapping theory (Ullman, 1979). The cover principle is the restriction that every Frame I element, and every Frame II element, must be "covered" by a motion correspondence match. In essence, the cover principle prevents elements from being interpreted as suddenly appearing or disappearing. Dawson (1991) argued that the cover principle is not appropriate for models of motion correspondence processing, and suggested that one advantage that his model had over Ullman's was the fact that it did not need a cover principle in order to generate solutions to correspondence problems.

If a physiological substrate solves the motion correspondence using rules that do not require the cover principle (i.e., by applying rules as specified in Dawson's 1991 model), then it should be able to respond to the sudden appearance or disappearance of elements instead of only being able to respond to element motion. Motter and Mountcastle (1981) observed some cells in area 7 that respond in this fashion. In 357 light-sensitive neurons that they studied, 52 percent produced a transient response following the sudden appearance of a stationary stimulus, 17 percent produced sustained responses to its appearance, and a small number of cells (12) generated a transient response at both the stimulus's sudden appearance and disappearance. Thus many cells in area 7 – the likely site for the actual assignment of identity matches – can clearly signal that a new element has been added to the display.

Unfortunately, there is very little additional physiological evidence supporting or disconfirming the implementation of the element integrity principle in any other manner, such as the inhibitory connections used in the current model. In my view, this is because element splitting or fusing is not an important property of motion perception in general, but is specifically related to element tracking, which physiologists have not considered as an important function served by the motion pathway. As a result, stimuli specifically designed to test the element integrity principle (e.g., motion competition displays, moving elements that actually break into two) have simply not been studied in physiological experiments. This points to the need for using multiple element displays to increase our understanding of the physiological processes responsible for the assignment of correspondence matches.

Part VI   Implementational Influences on Other Levels

The preceding part of the chapter suggested that area 7 in the parietal cortex is a plausible candidate for the physiological site of motion correspondence processing. As well, the types of motion measurements coded by areas in the motion pathway just prior to area 7 are consistent with the constraints exploited by the current model. While it is clear that further experimentation is required to gain a more complete understanding of the neural mechanisms underlying the assignment of motion correspondence matches, the evidence cited above indicates that the major assumptions underlying Dawson's (1991) network are biologically plausible.

Nevertheless, some attributes of Dawson's (1991) network are clearly *not* biologically plausible. This is because specific characteristics of the model were not designed to be consistent with neural circuitry, but were rather designed to provide a convenient medium in which to test the utility of the three constraining principles. In this section, some of these implausible characteristics are briefly considered. Proposals for altering the network's structure to eliminate these characteristics – without changing the nature of the network's computations – are also described. These proposals illustrate the fact that information gleaned at the implementational level can influence studies conducted at the algorithmic level.

Designing a Fixed Processing Network

A major problem with the biological plausibility of Dawson's (1991) model is that it does not use a fixed architecture. Instead, a new network is constructed for each problem presented to the model. A physiological implementation of the model would require the design of a fixed network (i.e., a set of processing units with fixed patterns of interconnectivity) capable of dealing with any presented problem.

A fixed motion correspondence network is possible in principle, and could be constructed in such a way that it performed the same computations as Dawson's (1991) model. A fixed network would have a set of input units (i.e., a two-dimensional retina) that coded the location of elements. Temporal filtering, resulting in the decay of these inputs over time, would be used to differentiate Frame I elements from Frame II elements (i.e., the processors coding the location of Frame I elements would have less activation because of the temporal decay of activation). These input units would be connected to a layer of "match processors" that would represent possible motion correspondence matches. Each match processor would be connected to only two of the input units, one representing the starting position of the match in Frame I, the other representing the end of the match in Frame II. A match processors would only become active, and thus would only become available for assignment, when both of its input units were activated. The physical connections between match processors would be as defined in the equations in Part II, and would thus implement the three constraining properties. The weights of these connections can be defined in advance, and thus "hardwired" into the system, because they depend only upon the start and end locations of a particular motion correspondence match, which in turn are fixed by the connections to the processors in the input array.

A fixed network of this type may indeed be instantiated in the brain. Albright, Desimone, & Gross (1984) have demonstrated that MT exhibits a columnar organization of directionally selective cells. Each column of cells detects motion for a particular region of the visual field. Within each column exist cells sensitive to different directions of motion (and presumably different speeds as well). As motion correspondence matches can be translated into element velocities, the cells within each MT column may be serving a function similar to the match processors in the fixed network described above.

Abandoning Vector Normalization

A second biologically implausible property of Dawson's (1991) algorithm involves how processing unit activities are normalized during each iterative pass of the network. In the model, as signals pass from the processors through the connections and back into the processors, there is a problem of processor activities becoming increasingly large. This is essentially the same as the jarring feedback effect that one often hears when someone brings a microphone too close to a speaker that it is sending a signal too. In order to prevent "jarring feedback" from occurring in his network, after each processing pass the vector of processing unit activities was scaled so that this vector always had a length of one unit. (In essence, this is done by dividing each processor's activity by a function of the length of the vector of processor activities, so that everything is scaled back down to size.) Because of this normalization procedure, Dawson called his network the "brainstate-in-a-sphere." In a very real sense, one could view the network as a model in which a vector of constant length (i.e., the processors) was rotated in multidimensional space (i.e., by the connection matrix) until it pointed in a stable direction.

However, normalizing the vector of processors is implausible for two reasons. First, the neural circuitry required to implement such a normalization is unlikely to be feasible, because it would involve massively parallel connections between processors (see below). Second, physiological evidence concerning similar systems suggests that normalization is not performed. For instance, Georgopoulos, Lurito, Petrides, Schwartz, & Massey (1989) describe how a population of neurons (i.e., a "neuronal vector") in the motor cortex represents an upcoming movement in space. In a task requiring the mental rotation of a planned movement, it was discovered that activation levels in the neuronal vector changed as well, and could be interpreted as representing the mental rotation. With respect to the current issue, though, in addition to changing direction, the neuronal vector also changed length. Its length was not normalized to a constant value.

Vector normalization is not required for Dawson's (1991) model to assign motion correspondence matches. For instance, Dawson (1988) has shown that it can be replaced with a "brainstate-in-a-box" restriction on processing (e.g., Anderson, Silverstein, Ritz, & Jones, 1977) in which individual processors are driven by processing to either a maximum or minimum activation level. This latter type of processing is clearly more biologically plausible, because the maximum or minimum activation level of a processor can easily be interpreted in terms of the maximum or minimum spike frequency of a neuron.

It is important to note, however, that replacing the "brainstate-in-a-sphere" model with a "brainstate-in-a-box" model may result in slight (but empirically significant) changes in what the network is actually computing. Dawson's (1991) model was formulated as a "brainstate-in-a-sphere" because this allowed a proof to be derived that the network would converge to a uniquely definable "least energy" state (see earlier in this chapter). This same proof cannot be generated for the "brainstate-in-a-box" model. Thus in some cases, the two networks may converge to very different solutions, and for some displays, it is possible (though unlikely) that the "brainstate-in-a-box" will fail to converge at all. In this case, the price of increasing biological plausibility may be a less certain computational understanding of what the model is doing.

Eliminating Massively Parallel Connections

A third biologically implausible characteristic of Dawson's (1991) model is that it is massively parallel. In other words, every processor in the network is connected to every other processor. This type of interconnectivity is not characteristic of human cortex (e.g., Crick & Asanuma, 1986, p. 370).

However, the massive parallelism in the model is pure convenience. This type of connectivity speeds up processing considerably (see Grzywacz & Yuille, 1988). Massive parallelism also permits the modeling of the mutual influence of stimuli relatively far apart in the visual field on each other's processing. The large size of the receptive fields in MT, MST, and area 7 indicates that such "distant influences" need to be modeled. However, this modeling can be done without massive parallelism, for the rather small cost of slowing down processing. In a biologically plausible network, two processors need not be directly connected to affect each other's performance. They can instead affect each other via indirect connections with intermediate processors.

Massive parallelism can easily be eliminated from the network by placing some restrictions on which processors can be connected to one another. For instance, if two possible motion correspondence matches were beyond some critical distance apart, then a connection between them would not be established. This would not affect the formal properties of the network (i.e., the convergence proof that was described earlier). One could represent the fact that two processors weren't connected by creating a connection between them with zero weight. As a result, a symmetric connection matrix for the network could still be defined, and the conditions required for proving that the network will converge would still remain.

Adding Temporal Characteristics to the Model

One characteristic of biological vision systems is that their temporal properties are not exact. For instance, when a biological transducer detects a stimulus, it does not respond immediately – a short period of time is required for the transducer's response to build up to a maximum value. Similarly, when the stimulus disappears, the transducer's response may remain, because it will take some time for the response to decay back to a minimum value. This tendency for the perceptual effects of a stimulus to persist after the stimulus has itself disappeared is called *visible persistence* (e.g., Coltheart, 1980).

Visible persistence is strongly affected by temporal manipulations. In particular, it appears to be governed by the so-called *inverse duration effect*. This is because the strength of visible persistence decreases as stimulus duration increases. This effect is typically attributed to a process of decay over time which begins at stimulus onset (e.g., Di Lollo, 1980). Thus, strictly speaking, it is not a "duration" effect at all; in multiple frame displays the strength of visible persistence is a function of stimulus onset asynchrony (SOA). SOA is the difference in time between the onset of Frame I and the onset of Frame II of an apparent motion display. Thus, it is equal to the duration in time of Frame I, plus the duration of the interstimulus interval (ISI), which is the period of time that a blank screen (i.e., neither Frame I nor Frame II) is presented after Frame I and before Frame II. According to the inverse duration effect, for a given apparent motion display one could produce the same decrease in the persistence of Frame I by increasing the duration of this frame by 50 milliseconds, or by increasing the subsequent ISI by 50 milliseconds.

Visible persistence is assumed to be a property that emerges from the mechanics of a biological visual system – it exists because neurons are slow to turn on and turn off. Recently, visible persistence has become involved in accounts of human perceptions of apparent motion displays. For example, Breitmeyer and Ritter (e.g., 1986a, 1986b) have argued that the appearance of the Ternus configuration (see above) is determined primarily by the visible persistence of its elements. Specifically, they operationalize "stationary elements" as "elements with strong visible persistence." According to Breitmeyer and Ritter, when there is strong visible persistence of the "interior elements" of the Ternus display, the result should be element motion. Group motion should only be seen when the visible persistence of these "interior elements" is at a much lower level.

The visible persistence account of the Ternus configuration has been supported in a series of recent experiments (Breitmeyer, May, & Ritter, 1988; Breitmeyer & Ritter, 1986a, 1986b; Casco, 1990; Ritter & Breitmeyer, 1989).

These experiments have taken advantage of the fact that in addition to the inverse duration effect, visible persistence can be affected by retinal eccentricity, stimulus size, spatial frequency, and stimulus contrast. In all of these experiments conditions that favored increases in visible persistence produced increased reports of element motion, and conditions that favored decreases in visible persistence produced increased reports of group motion.

Given that visible persistence is a phenomenon that is both tightly related to our understanding of the biology of transducing visual signals, and has been invoked as being important in our understanding of how human observers experience particular apparent motion displays, it would seem that one important step towards improving the biological plausibility of the Dawson (1991) motion correspondence model would be to add visible persistence to it. In a recent paper, Dawson and Wright (1994) took this step.

Dawson and Wright (1994) increased the plausibility of Dawson's (1991) original model with two separate temporal modifications. The first was the addition of a stimulus-onset dependent decay function for visual elements. This function resulted in Frame I elements decaying over time; if the SOA between Frames I and II was short enough, some Frame I elements could persist enough to be included as additional elements in Frame II.

The second modification performed by Dawson and Wright (1994) was the addition of what Ullman (1979, ch. 2) called the *principle of ISI equation*. According to this principle, when there is a short ISI separating the two frames of view in an apparent motion display, the visual system has a very strong preference for short correspondence matches over long correspondence matches. In contrast, when the ISI is longer, the preference for short matches over long matches is mitigated. The "increase in the ISI has the effect of making the affinities more uniform, thereby masking correspondence preferences" (p. 52). Ullman argued that the principle of ISI equation accounts for the difference between group and element motion in the Ternus configuration (pp. 55–60).

In order to test their model, Dawson and Wright (1994) presented the Ternus display to it, using a variety of durations for Frames I and II, as well as a number of different ISIs. These simulations indicated a number of interesting findings. First, the model generated three different motion correspondence solutions to the display: group motion, element motion, and *simultaneity*. Simultaneity was a set of correspondence matches that was consistent with an observer seeing four stationary elements (i.e., the three elements from Frame I overlapping in space with the three elements of Frame II). Second, the solutions generated by the model were systematically related to frame duration and ISI. When both ISI and duration were short, the model generated the set of correspondence matches consistent with simultaneity. When duration was long and ISI was short, the model generated the set of correspondence matches consistent with element motion. As both duration and ISI were increased, there was an increased tendency for the model to generate the set of correspondence matches consistent with group motion.

Dawson and Wright (1994) also studied human responses to the Ternus configuration as a function to temporal manipulations. Unlike previous researchers, they not only asked subjects to indicate whether group motion or element motion was seen, but also asked subjects to indicate when they saw simultaneity. One of their major results was that the relationship between the three percepts of the Ternus configuration and the manipulated temporal parameters was qualitatively similar to that of the model. With respect to Breitmeyer and Ritter's (e.g., 1986a) visible persistence theory of the display, Dawson and Wright found some support: SOA was indeed a significant predictor of each of the three types of motion judgments. However, Dawson and Wright also found that there was a significant interaction between duration and ISI that was an important predictor of both simultaneity and element motion judgments. Together, these findings indicated that visible persistence is very important, but cannot by itself account for all aspects of the Ternus configuration. Dawson and Wright argued that the similarity between the judgments of human observers and the performance of the model indicated that the principle of ISI equation and the SOA law governing persistence – in combination with Dawson's (1991) original three natural constraints – are required to provide a full account of the Ternus configuration.

Conclusion

This chapter has presented a single case study of a research topic in cognitive science, the motion correspondence problem. One of the main points to take home from this chapter is that cognitive scientists can indeed take a single phenomenon and study it in detail at each level of the tri-level hypothesis. For example, in this chapter we have seen how computational analyses can be used to propose natural constraints on the motion correspondence problem. We have also seen how computer simulation and psychophysical experiments can be used to gain a further understanding of motion correspondence processing at the algorithmic level. Finally, we have several examples of how one can use the results of neuroscience to improve our knowledge about human motion correspondence processing. No doubt that there are a great many facts still to be learned about how the human visual system assigns motion correspondence matches. However, it should be clear from this chapter that the general approach of cognitive science – the tri-level hypothesis – has been extremely fruitful for this particular research topic.

Importantly, a second main point of this chapter was to show that results at one level of analysis have important implications for research conducted at other levels of analysis. For instance, we have seen how new experimental results about motion correspondence, and new computer simulations of correspondence processing, can lead to advances at the computational level. We have also seen how issues raised at the implementational level of analysis can impact the algorithmic and the computational levels of analysis. In other words, it is important for researchers who primarily study a phenomenon at one level of analysis to pay attention to the results of those who study the same phenomenon at another level of analysis. In my opinion, one of the great benefits of the tri-level hypothesis is that it provides a clean framework in which such attention can be comfortably paid. This topic, as well as some other concluding thoughts, are dealt with in the next (and final) chapter of this book.

9

The Tri-Level Hypothesis and Cognitive Science

The preceding chapters introduced the foundations of classical cognitive science. The major theme of these chapters was that cognitive science is characterized by a set of basic assumptions that let researchers from many different disciplines communicate with one another as they work towards a common goal. This goal is to try to gain a further understanding of cognition in general, and of human cognition in particular.

The foundations of cognitive science are rooted in the information-processing assumption, which in turn leads to what we have called the tri-level hypothesis. Let us take a moment to review this position:

1   Cognitive scientists assume that cognition is information processing.
2   A direct implication of (1) is that some aspects of cognition are best captured at the computational level, where researchers ask "What information-processing problem is the system solving?"
3   A direct implication of (1) is that some other aspects of cognition are best captured at the algorithmic level, where researchers ask "What method is the system using to solve this information-processing problem?"
4   A direct implication of (1) is that still other aspects of cognition are best captured at the implementational level, where researchers ask "What physical properties are used to implement the (functional) method that the system uses to solve this information-processing problem?"
5   Because each of these levels of analysis is assumed to capture different kinds of generalizations about cognition, a complete explanation of a particular cognitive phenomenon requires analyses at each of the three levels, as well as an account of the relationship between these different analyses.

The purpose of this chapter is to briefly consider the status of the tri-level hypothesis in cognitive science. First, I will describe some of the major advantages that I see in adopting the tri-level hypothesis. Second, I will use the tri-level hypothesis to consider for one final time potential similarities and differences between classical and connectionist cognitive science.

Part I Why Adopt the Tri-Level Hypothesis?

In this part of the chapter, I would like to discuss what I believe are three of the major advantages to adopting the tri-level hypothesis. The first is that the tri-level hypothesis provides a medium in which an appropriate balance can be struck between theory and method. The second is that it provides a framework that permits diverse research methods to be used to achieve a common goal. The third is that it offers the opportunity for constructive communication among researchers from different disciplines.

Balancing Theoretical Relevance and Methodological Correctness

Bruner (1990, p. 1) has argued that modern cognitive psychology has lost interest in the kinds of theory that cognitivists were supposed to create to fill the void left by behaviorism. Cognitive psychologists developed a large number of experimental techniques for studying cognitive phenomena. Unfortunately, the price for this was a corresponding inattention to the "big picture" questions or theories that the methodologies were supposed to be informing. "The new cognitive science, the child of the revolution, has gained its technical successes at the price of dehumanizing the very concept of mind it had sought to reestablish in psychology, and that it has thereby estranged much of psychology from the other human sciences and the humanities."

This is not a new critique of cognitive psychology. For example, Newell (1973a) characterized cognitive psychology as a flurry of activity in which combinatorial variations of manipulations were exhaustively explored to study newly discovered phenomena. "Those phenomena form a veritable horn of plenty for our experimental life – the spiral of the horn itself growing all the while it pours forth the requirements for secondary experiments" (pp. 285–6). Unfortunately, in Newell's opinion this experimental activity was viewed as being explicitly distanced from the asking of general theoretical questions: "Indeed, psychology with its penchant for being explicit about its methodology has created special terms, such as 'orienting attitudes' and 'pretheoretical dispositions,' to convey the large distance that separates the highest levels of theory from the immediate decisions of day to day science" (p. 287).

One problem with cognitive psychology's methodological fixation – and dismissal of its theoretical foundations as being "nonexperimental" – is that this leads to a theoretical vacuum in which the importance of empirical results cannot be established. In particular, by isolating itself in the algorithmic level, cognitive psychology appears to have forgotten the criteria required to distinguish a cognitive explanation from a cognitive description. One example of this is Kosslyn and Pomerantz's (1977, pp. 64–5) response to Pylyshyn's (1973) argument that mental images are not part of the functional architecture: "It seems likely that imagery can be described in terms of more basic processes, perhaps including propositional representations . . . But will this exercise increase our understanding of mental phenomena or merely cloud over important distinctions?" Another example is the interesting fact that none of the following terms have entries in The *Blackwell Dictionary of Cognitive Psychology* (Eysenck, 1994b): "architecture," "functionalism," "functional analysis," "instantiation," "primitive," or "subsumption." With such inattention paid to what can convert a cognitive description into a cognitive explanation, is it any wonder that Newell (e.g., 1973a, 1990) was concerned about the status of cognitive theory?

Fortunately, the tri-level hypothesis offers an approach to cognitivism in which method and theory are each given an appropriate emphasis. This is because when research is conducted within the context of the tri-level hypothesis, it is impossible to dismiss nonalgorithmic issues as being "nonexperimental." Instead, these issues provide a context in which experimental or algorithmic discoveries can be better understood. In particular, nonalgorithmic issues make it clear why particular empirical results are important. For instance, it is in the context of the tri-level hypothesis that we understand that cognitive explanations require the identification of primitives. Similarly, it is in the context of the tri-level hypothesis that we can gain an appreciation that theories can be equivalent to varying degrees, and that as a result we should be searching for evidence of strong equivalence. When empirical evidence is obtained by considering the algorithmic level alone, we simply wind up with a set of data. It is the tri-level hypothesis that lets us understand why this set of data might actually be important.

From a personal perspective, this unifying context was one of the most powerful messages that I saw when I first was introduced to cognitive science as a student. During my training, I had become acquainted with a disparate set of methodologies used by cognitive psychologists, and I had become familiar with the results obtained from these paradigms. However, I had not arrived at any understanding of the relationship between these methods or results and the fundamental issues that cognitive psychology needed to address. When I first was exposed to the tri-level hypothesis, I finally started to see why the results from specific experiments could have important implications for "big picture" theories of cognition.

Expanding Methodologies

Langer (1942, p. 4) wrote that "a philosophy is characterized more by the formulation of its problems than by its solution of them. Its answers establish an edifice of facts; but its questions make the frame in which its picture of facts is plotted." If a discipline is defined by the questions that it asks, then it follows that an interesting discipline is one that asks interesting questions. Furthermore, the kinds of questions that a discipline can ask, depend crucially upon the methods that are available to it. However, it is not enough to merely have a diversity of applicable research methods at hand. In addition, all of these methods must be related in the sense that they are being used to accomplish a common goal. In other words, a new discipline (like cognitive science was in the 1970s) is defined not only be the content area that it studies, but also by the systematically related set of methodologies used by the discipline to investigate this area.

One of the great attractions of cognitive science is its use of a great number of qualitatively different research tools. These include the formal methods used to develop computational proofs, the programming techniques of computer science, the experimental practices of psychology and psycholinguistics, and a variety of paradigms (such as brain imaging techniques and single-cell recording) of neuroscience. Importantly, this diversity of research instruments is systematically linked by the tri-level hypothesis. It is the tri-level hypothesis that provides the theoretical context in which it is apparent that all of these diverse tools are being used to shed light on common issues.

Some researchers suggest that the algorithmic methods like those used by cognitive psychology are central to cognitive science (e.g., Fodor, in his interview with Baumgartner and Payr, 1995). Other researchers declare that computer simulation methods characterize cognitive science, and differentiate it from (say) cognitive psychology (e.g., Gardner, 1984; Johnson-Laird, 1983). Some researchers point out that computational methods give cognitive scientists the opportunity to generate proofs that have the same scope, power, and longevity of the proofs developed by mathematicians and physicists (e.g., Marr, 1982). Other researchers claim that an understanding of cognition requires cognitive science to be guided by the methods and results of neuroscience (e.g., Churchland & Sejnowski, 1990; Edelman, 1992; Searle, 1992). However, according to the tri-level hypothesis, a complete understanding of cognition will require explication at the computational level, the algorithmic level, and the implementational level. This suggests that all of these different approaches are necessary if cognitive science is to flourish. In other words, the tri-level hypothesis does not merely provide a context in which the use of diverse methodologies is *plausible*. When one endorses the tri-level hypothesis, one must recognize that the use of these diverse tools is *mandatory*.

Conversations and Cognitive Science

Simon (1980, p. 33) defines cognitive science as "a recognition of a fundamental set of common concerns shared by the disciplines of psychology, computer science, linguistics, economics, epistemology, and the social sciences generally." The common concerns of cognitive scientists are rooted in the shared belief that cognition is information processing. As we have seen throughout this book, this shared belief can be elaborated to take the form of the tri-level hypothesis. From this perspective, the tri-level hypothesis not only provides a skeletal framework in which diverse methodologies can be fit, but also provides a theoretical context in which researchers from different disciplines can have meaningful conversations.

Such conversations can have important consequences. In many cases, they have been instrumental in leading researchers into careers in cognitive science. For example, Baumgartner and Payr (1995) have published a set of interviews with twenty eminent cognitive scientists. In many of these interviews, one finds mention of interest in cognitive science emerging upon an individual's realization that people trained in other disciplines have something to contribute to the study of cognition. For instance, philosopher (and noted AI critic) Hubert Dreyfus recalls his visit to the Rand Corporation in 1965 as follows: "What I discovered was that far from being antiphilosophy – and far from what I had suspected – these people were indeed working on the very problems that philosophers had worked on, and they were in some way – even if they weren't making much progress – at least turning these problems into a research program in which one could make progress" (p. 71).

The interdisciplinary nature of cognitive science is a major strength, but also can lead to some interesting problems. For example, in order to do cognitive science, must "everyone become everyone, each person an expert in all disciplines, all issues?" (Norman, 1980, p. 28). Norman went on to argue that this was not likely a strategy that would lead to productive individuals, or a productive discipline. Instead, he suggested that researchers tackle specific problems, requiring cognitive science to be decomposed into smaller, tractable issues. Norman also noted that for this approach to succeed, specialists must have enough general knowledge to reflect on general issues in cognitive science, and to use this reflection to choose promising and interesting research domains. I would add to this the need to be enough of a generalist to be able to communicate with specialists in other fields, because these specialists are also going to be actively involved in cognitive science. My suspicion is that an understanding of the tri-level hypothesis and its implications might be sufficient for such communication to succeed.

Part II   Comparing the Classical and Connectionist Approaches

As we have already seen, many researchers are now of the opinion that the classical approach is ill-suited to provide explanations of cognition. For instance, Horgan and Tienson (1996, p. 178) point out that "our quarrel with the classical paradigm is that we do not think it can give us an adequate understanding of the mind." Dreyfus and Dreyfus (1988, p. 33) call the classical approach "a degenerating research program," while Garson (1994, p. 36) has characterized it as "a dying paradigm."

Connectionism's reemergence over the past 10 to 15 years has been largely fueled by the view that it offers solutions to the problems that have been associated with classical cognitive science. To many, connectionism represents a much-needed paradigm shift for cognitive science (e.g., Horgan & Tienson, 1996; Schneider, 1987). To what extent does connectionism *really* represent an alternative to the classical approach? There is a growing body of work that suggests that though these two views of cognitive science exhibit interesting differences, they are in fact highly similar (for example, see many of the papers in Ramsey, Stich, & Rumelhart, 1991). These similarities are rooted in the fact that connectionists have not abandoned the foundational assumption that cognition is information processing. As a result, the tri-level hypothesis can be just as fruitfully applied to connectionism as it can be to classical cognitive science (see also Horgan & Tienson, 1996). Indeed, by using the tri-level hypothesis to focus the issues, we can get a more sophisticated sense of potential similarities and differences between these two approaches.

Computational Level

At the computational level, we ask the question "What information-processing problem is being solved by a system of interest?" With respect to comparing the two views of cognitive science at this level, some classical researchers have argued that the connectionist architecture does not have the computational power to solve the same kind of problems as the classical architecture (e.g., Fodor & Pylyshyn, 1988; Lachter & Bever, 1988).

For example, Fodor and Pylyshyn (1988) have emphasized the fact that language demonstrates certain systematic relationships. They noted that you won't find someone who can understand the sentence "John loves the girl," but who cannot understand the sentence "The girl loves John." Underlying this systematicity is the principle of compositionality, which is the claim that the constituents of a sentence make approximately the same semantic contribution to whatever sentence they occur in. This principle can be exploited to great advantage in a language that is characterized by a combinatorial syntax and semantics. For instance, sentences can be understood by parsing them into their constituents.

Systematicity and compositionality characterize the operation of classical architectures like the Turing machine, and in fact are responsible for the enormous computational power of these systems. Fodor and Pylyshyn's (1988) point, though, is that systematicity and compositionality do not characterize connectionist architectures, because connectionist networks are not sensitive to systematic relationships among constituents of inputs. This stands as a computational argument against the adoption of connectionism in cognitive science (see also Fodor & McLaughlin, 1990).

Recent developments have taken some of the bite out of this argument, however. In a series of papers, Hadley (1994a, 1994b, 1997) has argued that Fodor and Pylyshyn's (1988) notion of systematicity glosses over several important distinctions, and has proposed a more sophisticated notion in which systematicity can be exhibited to different degrees. This reformulation is strongly tied to the ability of a system to generalize – to correctly respond to new stimuli – and defines degrees of systematicity in terms of varying degrees of generalization. Hadley has shown that many connectionist networks (Elman, 1990; Chalmers, 1990; McClelland & Kawamoto, 1986; Pollack, 1990; Smolensky, 1990; St John & McClelland, 1990) achieve sufficient degrees of systematicity to serve as counterexamples to Fodor and Pylyshyn's claim. Furthermore, Hadley and Hayward (1997) have recently described a connectionist network that demonstrates Hadley's strongest degree of systematicity. In short, the empirical evidence stands against Fodor and Pylyshyn's computational criticism.

That this is the case should not be surprising. In chapter 4, we reviewed a number of results pertaining to the computational power of connectionist architectures in general. connectionist models have the power to be arbitrary pattern classifiers, universal function approximators, and – importantly – Universal Turing Machines. In other words, a computational-level comparison of the two views of cognitive science reveals no differences between them in principle.

Algorithmic Level

An alternative approach to comparing classical and connectionist architectures is to examine them in terms of their general characteristics as computers, as is done by Von Eckardt (1993, pp. 125–41). She concludes that if one considers the "high-level" representations in PDP models (i.e., patterns of activity, instead of the properties of individual processing units), then connectionist networks can be viewed as computers analogous to those brought to mind when one thinks of classical architectures. This is because connectionist networks have the capacity to input and output, store, and manipulate represented information.

However, even if we grant that connectionist and classical architectures both define "computers," this ignores a further important detail – the progams that such computers actually execute. Many of the proponents of connectionism would argue that it is to be preferred over classical cognitive science because connectionist computers are capable of "running" more appropriate "programs" than classical computers. Comparing the two views of cognitive science in this light involves examining them at the algorithmic level of analysis, where we determine the kinds of procedures that are being used to solve an information-processing problem of interest.

A casual glance at a PDP network gives the strong impression that the connectionist architecture executes algorithms that are extremely different in nature than those of classical machines. Connectionist networks do not appear to have a central executive that is analogous to the machine head of a Turing machine. Connectionist networks do not appear to make a sharp distinction between rules and the symbols that these rules manipulate (e.g., Dawson & Schopflocher, 1992b). Connectionist networks, with their extremely distributed nature, do not appear to encode discrete symbols that are characteristic of classical theories. Connectionist networks appear to be extremely well suited to solving information processing by applying soft constraints (e.g., Horgan & Tienson, 1996; see also chapter 8, above). Indeed, it is largely because of these observations that there has been a strong tendency to view connectionism as offering a qualitatively different alternative to classical modeling in cognitive science. "Among their other merits, at least some connectionist models show how a system might convert a meaningful input into a meaningful output without any rules, principles, inferences, or other sorts of meaningful phenomena in between" (Searle, 1992, p. 246).

However, the problem with making a strong case about the difference between classical and connectionist networks using such casual observations is that they do not depend upon a technical specification of the kinds of procedures that PDP models actually use. We saw in chapter 5 that one of the major problems facing connectionist cognitive science is the need to articulate them at the algorithmic level – the need to say precisely how a trained network actually solves a problem. When algorithms are extracted from networks, the differences between classical and connectionist theories becomes blurred. In chapter 5, we saw one example of this when we reviewed Berkeley *et al.*'s (1995) extraction of traditional logical rules from a network trained to identify and validate syllogisms.

In addition to blurring the distinction between the two approaches, such discoveries raise interesting issues at the algorithmic level. Take the Berkeley *et al.* (1995) results as an example. Are the rules that were extracted from the network truly "classical" ? Or are they instead emergent or epiphenomenal regularities that are mere approximations of the underlying "subsymbolic" regularities embodied in the network's connections (c.f. Smolensky, 1989)? To answer these kinds of questions, one needs to take a very sophisticated look at the properties of the extracted rules in order to determine whether they satisfy all of the criteria of being classical in nature. However, as soon as this research project is begun, it becomes evident that many of the characteristics of classical rules and tokens are not particularly well understood (e.g., Searle, 1992, ch. 9; Von Eckardt, 1993, ch. 3).

In other words, though it would not be surprising to find out that classical and connectionist algorithms exhibit fundamental differences, it is premature to spell out these differences at the current time. In fact, in the long run it might turn out that principled differences between these two types of algorithms do not exit. Clearly, this is one area that requires a lot of future research. Furthermore, it is a research area that reveals a growing need for a more technical account of the fundamental nature of both classical and connectionist information processing.

Architecture

Algorithmic comparisons between classical and connectionist cognitive science will ultimately be grounded in comparisons of functional architectures. While we saw in chapter 6 that cognitive science requires that the functional architecture of cognition be specified, there is no indication that this goal will be achieved in the near future. While classical cognitive science has proposed a large number of possible architectures, the existing empirical evidence is not sufficient to make a strong case for one over another. While connectionist cognitive science has made strong proposals about the nature of the functional architecture (e.g., the generic PDP architecture that was introduced in chapter 3), there are reasons to believe that this proposal is not yet complete, nor is it sufficiently distinct from classical proposals (Dawson & Schopflocher, 1992b; see also chapter 6 above).

Such comparisons are further limited by the need for a more detailed and technical account of what the properties of a classical functional architecture are, and of what characteristics might differentiate it from some other proposal (e.g., connectionism). We saw in chapter 6 that a wide variety of classical architectures have been proposed. Some researchers have noted that within this class of architectures, there are enormous differences from proposal to proposal. Nevertheless, these differences do not prevent us from viewing all of these proposals as classical. What is it about the differences between (for example) production systems and PDP networks that indicates that these are radically different architectures, while at the same time the differences between (for instance) production systems and mental images are not large enough to prevent us from viewing both as being classical? When considering this kind of question, Cummins (1991) concludes that there are not enough qualitative differences between classical and connectionist architectures to plausibly argue that they represent completely different approaches to cognitive modeling.

In summary, it is clearly far too early to make meaningful architectural comparisons between classical and connectionist cognitive science. However, there are some interesting differences that emerge between these two approaches with respect to the way in which architecture is approached. Classical cognitive science is predominately an analytic discipline, in which complex phenomena are decomposed into functional subcomponents as part of the search for functional primitives (e.g., Cummins, 1983). In contrast, connectionist cognitive science is predominately a synthetic discipline (in the sense of Braitenberg, 1984), in which basic components of an architecture are first hypothesized, followed by an attempt to determine the kinds of phenomena that can be constructed from these primitives (e.g., Seidenberg, 1993). The use of the term "predominately" here is intentional, because it would not be fair to say that either approach is purely analytic or synthetic. For instance, Newell's (1973b) classical model of Sternberg's (1969) memory scanning results is prototypical synthetic psychology. Similarly, when connectionists interpret the internal structure of their networks (e.g., Hanson & Burr, 1990), they are obviously adopting an analytic approach. This suggests that the analytic/ synthetic distinction might only have heuristic value in distinguishing classical and connectionist cognitive science.

Implementational Level

One compelling difference between classical and connectionist cognitive science is the extent to which biological plausibility is a critical issue. It is clearly the case that connectionist researchers have been largely responsible for an increasing interest in the relationship between cognition and the brain. In fact, classical researchers have argued that connectionism should not be properly viewed as being cognitive science, because PDP networks are only implementational descriptions (e.g., Broadbent, 1985; Fodor & Pylyshyn, 1988). However, while this implementational emphasis is indeed characteristic of connectionism, it cannot be used to cleanly segregate it from classical cognitive science.

First, it is important to remember that the generic PDP architecture is itself functionalist in nature. Its components are functional descriptions of the "simplifying features of the brain" that have been discovered by neuroscientists, and which appear to be relevant to describing those aspects of brain function that are relevant to information processing (see chapter 3). The functionalism inherent in this approach is apparent when one realizes that connectionist networks are in fact simulated by digital computers.

Second, connectionist networks cannot be dismissed as mere implementations, because they can generate theories that are described in a cognitive vocabulary, as opposed to an implementational vocabulary (e.g., Dawson, Medler, & Berkeley, 1997; see also chapter 7 above). For example, we saw that when the internal structure of a network trained on a logic problem was extracted, this led to some proposals of how humans might solve similar problems (e.g., the "default rules" of table 5.4). These proposals could be tested with the methods of cognitive psychology, because they were cognitive in nature. They were not implementational proposals to be tested with the methods of neuroscience.

Third, the functionalist nature of connectionist networks has led researchers to question the degree to which they actually inform neuroscience (see chapter 7 above). Many neuroscientists dismiss connectionism as being too simplistic to capture the complex kinds of information processing that are carried out by the brain. In fact, it has been argued that many of the design decisions that go into connectionist networks have not been motivated by "neuronal inspiration," but instead have been driven by (biologically implausible) engineering decisions (e.g., Dawson & Shamanski, 1994; see also chapter 7). We saw in chapter 7 that a variety of design decisions could be explored to make connectionist networks more biologically relevant.

Conclusion

Connectionism has been championed as being a paradigm shift away from classical cognitive science (e.g., Schneider, 1987). While there certainly are potential (and interesting) differences between these two approaches, it is not clear that a compelling argument can be made that such a paradigm shift has occurred. This chapter has shown that when using the tri-level hypothesis to focus our comparison of these two approaches, we find many similarities between them. Indeed, the fact that the two can be compared in this way at all indicates a commitment to a common paradigm – an endorsement of the foundational assumption of cognitive science: cognition is information processing.

References

Ackley, D. H., Hinton, G. E. & Sejnowski, T. J. (1985). A Learning Algorithm for Boltzman Machines. *Cognitive Science*, 9, 147–69.

Adler, I. (1961). *Thinking Machines*. New York: Signet Science Library.

Akmajian, A., Demers, R. A. & Harnish, R. M. (1984). *Linguistics: An Introduction to Language and Communication*. Cambridge, Mass.: MIT Press.

Albert, M. S. & Lafleche, G. (1991). Neuroimaging in Alzheimer's Disease. *The Psychiatric Clinics of North America*, 14, 443–59.

Albright, T. D. (1984). Direction and Orientation Selectivity of Neurons in Visual Area MT of the Macaque. *Journal of Neurophysiology*, 52, 1106–30.

Albright, T. D., Desimone, R. & Gross, C. G. (1984). Columnar Organization of Directionally Selective Cells in Visual Area MT of the Macaque. *Journal of Neurophysiology*, 51, 16–31.

Alkon, D. L. (1987). *Memory Traces in the Brain*. Cambridge: Cambridge University Press.

Allman, J., Miezin, F. & Mcguinness, E. (1985). Direction- and Velocity-specific Responses from Beyond the Classical Receptive Field in the Middle Temporal Visual Area (MT). *Perception*, 14, 105–26.

Amit, D. J. (1989). *Modeling Brain Function: the World of Attractor Neural Networks*. Cambridge, Mass.: Cambridge University Press.

Anderson, J. A. (1972). A Simple Neural Network Generating an Interactive Memory. *Mathematical Biosciences*, 14, 197–220.

Anderson, J. A. & Hinton, G. E. (1981). Models of Information Processing in the Brain. In Hinton & Anderson (eds) *Parallel Models of Associative Memory*. Hillsdale, NJ: Lawrence Erlbaum Associates.

Anderson, J. A. & Rosenfeld, E. (1988). *Neurocomputing: Foundations of Research*. Cambridge, Mass.: MIT Press.

Anderson, J. A., Silverstein, J. W., Ritz, S. A. & Jones, R. S. (1977). Distinctive Features, Categorical Perception and Probability Learning: Some Applications of a Neural Model. *Psychological Review*, 84, 413–51.

Anderson, J. R. (1983). *The Architecture of Cognition*. Cambridge, Mass.: Harvard University Press.

Anderson, J. R. (1985). *Cognitive Psychology and its Implications*, 2nd edn. New York: W. H. Freeman.

Anderson, J. R. & Bower, G. H. (1973). *Human Associative Memory*. Hillsdale, NJ: Lawrence Erlbaum Associates.

Anstis, S. M. (1978). Apparent Movement. In R. Held, H. W. Leibwitz & H. L. Teuber (eds) *Handbook of Sensory Physiology*. New York: Springer-Verlag.

Anstis, S. M. (1980). The Perception of Apparent Movement. *Philosophical Transactions of the Royal Society of London*, 290b, 153–68.

Antrobus, J. (1991). Dreaming: Cognitive Processes During Cortical Activation and High Afferent Thresholds. *Psychological Review*, 98, 96–121.

Arbib, M. A. (1972). *The Metaphorical Brain*. New York: John Wiley & Sons.

Armony, J. L., Servan-Schreiber, D., Cohen, J. D. & Ledoux, J. E. (1995). An Anatomically Constrained Neural Network Model of Fear Conditioning. *Behavioral Neuroscience*, 109, 246–57.

Ashcraft, M. H. (1989). *Human Memory and Cognition*. Glenview, Ill.: Scott, Foresman and Co.

Atkinson, R. C. & Shiffrin, R. M. (1968). Human Memory: A Proposed System and its Control Processes. In K. W. Spence (ed.) *The Psychology of Learning and Motivation: Advances in Research and Theory*, vol. 2. New York: Academic Press.

Attneave, F. (1974). Apparent Movement and the What–Where Connection. *Psychologia*, 17, 108-20.

Baddeley, A. (1986). *Working Memory*. Oxford: Oxford University Press.

Baddeley, A. (1990). *Human Memory: Theory and Practice*. Needham Heights, Mass.: Allyn & Bacon.

Baddeley, A. D. & Hitch, G. (1974). Working Memory. In G. A. Bower (ed.) *The Psychology of Learning and Memory*, vol. 8. New York: Academic Press.

Baddeley, A. D. & Warrington, E. K. (1970). Amnesia and the Distinction Between Long- and Short-term Memory. *Journal of Verbal Learning and Verbal Behavior*, 9, 176–89.

Baddeley, A. D. & Wilson, B. (1986). Amnesia, Autobiographical Memory and Confabulation. In D. Rubin (ed.) *Autobiographical Memory*. New York: Cambridge University Press.

Ballard, D. (1986). Cortical Structures and Parallel Processing: Structure and Function. *The Behavioral and Brain Sciences*, 9, 67–120.

Barlow, H. B. (1972). Single Units and Sensation: A Neuron Doctrine for Perceptual Psychology? *Perception*, 1, 371–94.

Barnard, E. & Casasent, D. (1989). A Comparison Between Criterion Functions for Linear Classifiers, with an Application to Neural Nets. *IEEE Transactions on Systems, Man, and Cybernetics*, 19, 834–46.

Baro, J. A. & Levinson, E. (1988). Apparent Motion Can Be Perceived Between Patterns with Dissimilar Spatial Frequencies. *Vision Research*, 28, 1311–13.

Barr, M. L. (1974). *The Human Nervous System*, 2nd edn. New York: Harper & Row.

Barto, A. G., Sutton, R. S. & Anderson, C. W. (1983). Neuronlike Adaptive Elements that Can Solve Difficult Learning Control Problems. *IEEE Transactions on Systems, Man & Cybernetics*, 13, 835–46.

Basso, A., Spinnler, H., Vallar, G. & Zanobio, E. (1982). Left Hemisphere Damage and Selected Impairment of Auditory Verbal Short-term Memory: A Case Study. *Neuropsychologia*, 20, 263–74.

Baumgartner, P. & Payr, S. (1995). *Speaking Minds: Interviews with Twenty Eminent Cognitive Scientists*. Princeton, NJ: Princeton University Press.

Bechtel, W. (1985). Contemporary Connectionism: Are the New Parallel Distributed Processing Models Cognitive or Associationist? *Behaviorism*, 13, 53–61.

Bechtel, W. (1988). Connectionism and Rules and Representation Systems: Are They Compatible? *Philosophical Psychology*, 1, 5–16.

Bechtel, W. (1994). Natural Deduction in Connectionist Systems. *Synthese*, 101, 433–63.

Bechtel, W. & Abrahamsen, A. (1991). *Connectionism and the Mind*. Cambridge, Mass.: Blackwell.

Bengio, Y. & De Mori, R. (1989). Use of Multilayer Networks for the Recognition of Phonetic Features and Phonemes. *Computational Intelligence*, 5, 134–41.

Benjafield, J. G. (1997). *Cognition*. Englewood Cliffs, NJ: Prentice-Hall.

Bergmann, M., Moor, J. & Nelson, J. (1990). *The Logic Book*. New York: McGraw Hill.

Berkeley, I. S. N., Dawson, M. R. W., Medler, D. A., Schopflocher, D. P. & Hornsby, L. (1995). Density Plots of Hidden Value Unit Activations Reveal Interpretable Bands. *Connection Science*, 7, 167–86.

Berlin, B. & Kay, P. (1969). *Basic Color Terms*. Berkeley, Calif.: University of California Press.

Best, J. B. (1995). *Cognitive Psychology*. St. Paul, Minn.: West Publishing.

Bever, T. G., Fodor, J. A. & Garrett, M. (1968). A Formal Limitation of Associationism. In T. R. Dixon and D. L. Horton (eds) *Verbal Behavior and General Behavior Theory*. Englewood Cliffs, NJ: Prentice-Hall.

Bickerton, D. (1981). *The Roots of Language*. Ann Arbor, Mich.: Karoma Publishers.

Biederman, I. (1987). Recognition by Components: A Theory of Human Image Understanding. *Psychological Review*, 94, 115-47.

Block, N. (1981). *Imagery*. Cambridge, Mass.: MIT Press.

Boden, M. A. (1981). *Minds and Mechanisms*. Ithaca, NY: Cornell University Press.

Borges, J. L. (1962). Avatars of the Tortoise. In D. A. Yates & J. E. Irby (eds) *Labyrinths: Selected Stories and Other Writings by Jorge Luis Borges*. New York: New Directions Publishing.

Boring, E. G. (1942). *Sensation and Perception in the History of Experimental Psychology*. New York: Appleton-Century-Crofts.

Born, R. (1987). *Artificial Intelligence: the Case Against*. London: Croom Helm.

Botez, M. I. (1975). Two Visual Systems in Clinical Neurology: Readaptive Role of the Primitive System in Visual Agnosis Patients. *European Neurology*, 13, 101-22.

Boylestad, R. L. (1990). *Introductory Circuit Analysis*, 6th edn. New York: Macmillan Publishing.

Bower, G. H. & Clapper, J. P. (1989). Experimental Methods in Cognitive Science. In M. I. Posner (ed.) *Foundations of Cognitive Science*. Cambridge, Mass.: MIT Press.

Braddick, O. J. (1973). The Masking of Apparent Motion in Random-dot Patterns. *Vision Research*, 13, 355–69.

Braddick, O. J. (1974). A Short Range Process in Apparent Movement. *Vision Research*, 14, 519-28.

Braddick, O. J. (1980). Low-level and High-level Processes in Apparent Motion. *Philosophical Transactions of the Royal Society of London*, 290b, 137-51.

Bradley, D. C., Garrett, M. F. & Zurif, E. B. (1980). Syntactic Deficits in Broca's Aphasia. In D. Caplan (ed.) *Biological Studies of Mental Processes*. Cambridge, Mass.: MIT Press.

Braham, R. & Hamblen, J. O. (1990). The Design of a Neural Network with a Biologically Motivated Architecture. *IEEE Transactions on Neural Networks*, 1, 251-62.

Braitenberg, V. (1984). *Vehicles: Explorations in Synthetic Psychology*. Cambridge, Mass.: MIT Press.

Bratko, I., Tancig, P. & Tancig, S. (1986). Detection of Positional Patterns in Chess. In D. F. Beal (ed.) *Advances in Computer Chess 4*. Oxford: Pergamon Press.

Breitmeyer, B. G., May, J. G. & Williams, M. C. (1988). Spatial Frequency and Contrast Effects on Percepts of Bistable Stroboscopic Motion. *Perception & Psychophysics*, 44, 525-31.

Breitmeyer, B. G. & Ritter, A. (1986a). Visual Persistence and the Effect of Eccentric Viewing, Element Size, and Frame Duration on Bistable Stroboscopic Motion Percepts. *Perception & Psychophysics*, 39, 275-80.

Breitmeyer, B. G. & Ritter, A. (1986b). The Role of Visual Pattern Persistence in Bistable Stroboscopic Motion. *Vision Research*, 26, 1801-6.

Bridgeman, B. (1972). Visual Receptive Fields Sensitive to Absolute and Relative Motion During Tracking. *Science*, 178, 1106-8.

Broadbent, D. (1985). A Question of Levels: Comment on McClelland and Rumelhart. *Journal of Experimental Psychology: General*, 114, 189-92.

Brooks, R. A. (1989). A Robot That Walks; Emergent Behaviours from a Carefully Evolved Network. *Neural Computation*, 1, 253-62.

Brown, J. (1958). Some Tests of the Decay Theory of Immediate Memory. *Quarterly Journal of Experimental Psychology*, 10, 41-2.

Bruner, J. S. (1957). On Perceptual Readiness. *Psychological Review*, 64, 123-52.

Bruner, J. S., Goodnow, J. & Austin, G. A. (1956) *A Study of Thinking*. New York: John Wiley & Sons.

Burt, P. & Sperling, G. (1981). Time, Distance and Feature Trade-offs in Visual Apparent Motion. *Psychological Review*, 88, 137-51.

Butterworth, B. (1994). Regional Specialities. *Behavioral and Brain Sciences*, 17, 63.

Caelli, T. & Dodwell, P. (1980). On the Contours of Apparent Motion: A New Perspective on Visual Space–Time. *Biological Cybernetics*, 39, 27–35.

Calvin, W. H. & Ojemann, G. A. (1994). *Conversations with Neil's Brain*. Reading, Mass.: Addison-Wesley.

Caramazza, A. (1986). On Drawing Inferences about the Structure of Normal Cognitive Systems from the Analysis of Patterns of Impaired Performance: the Case for Single-patient Studies. *Brain and Cognition*, 5, 41-66.

Carpenter, G. A. (1989). Neural Network Models for Pattern Recognition and Associative Memory. *Neural Networks*, 2, 243-57.

Casco, C. (1990). The Relationship Between Visual Persistence and Event Perception in Bistable Motion Display. *Perception*, 19, 437-45.

Caudill, M. & Butler, B. (1992a). *Understanding Neural Networks*, vol. 1. Cambridge, Mass.: MIT Press.

Caudill, M. & Butler, B. (1992b). *Understanding Neural Networks*, vol. 2. Cambridge, Mass.: MIT Press.

Cavanagh, P., Arguin, M. & Von Grunau, M. (1989). Interattribute Apparent Motion. *Vision Research*, 29, 1197-1204.

Cavanagh, P. & Mather, G. (1989). Motion: the Long and Short of It. *Spatial Vision*, 4, 103-29.

Chalmers, D. (1990). Why Fodor and Pylyshyn Were Wrong: the Simplest Refutation. *Proceedings of the Twelfth Annual Conference of the Cognitive Science Society*, Cambridge, Mass.

Chalmers, D. (1996). *The Conscious Mind: in Search of a Fundamental Theory*. New York: Oxford University Press.

Chambers, J. M., Cleveland, W. S., Kleiner, B. & Tukey, P. A. (1983). *Graphical Methods for Data Analysis*. Belmont, Calif.: Wadsworth International Group.

Chase, W. G. & Simon, H. A. (1973). The Mind's Eye in Chess. In W. G. Chase (ed.) *Visual Information Processing*. New York: Academic Press.

Chesterton, G. K. (1951). The Paradise of Thieves. In *The Father Brown Omnibus*. New York: Dodd, Mead & Company.

Chomsky, N. (1959). Review of B. F. Skinner, *Verbal Behavior* (1957). *Language*, 35, 26-58.

Chomsky, N. (1965). *Aspects of the Theory of Syntax*. Cambridge, Mass.: MIT Press.

Chomsky, N. (1988). *Language and Problems of Knowledge*. Cambridge, Mass.: MIT Press.

Chomsky, N. (1993). On the Nature, Use, and Acqusition of Language. In A. I. Goldman (ed.) *Readings in Philosophy and Cognitive Science*. Cambridge, Mass.: MIT Press.

Chomsky, N. (1995). *The Minimalist Program*. Cambridge, Mass.: MIT Press.

Chubb, C. & Sperling, G. (1988). Drift-balanced Random Stimuli: A General Basis for Studying Non-(91)Fourier Motion Perception. *Journal of the Optical Society of America*, 5a, 1986-2007.

Churchland, P. M. (1988). *Matter and Consciousness*, rev. edn. Cambridge, Mass.: MIT Press.

Churchland, P. M. (1992). *A Neurocomputational Perspective: the Nature of Mind and the Structure of Science*. Cambridge, Mass.: MIT Press.

Churchland, P. M. & Churchland, P. S. (1990). Could a Machine Think? *Scientific American*, 262(1), 32–7.

Churchland, P. S., Koch, C. & Sejnowski, T. J. (1990). What is Computational Neuroscience? In E. L. Schwartz (ed.) *Computational Neuroscience*. Cambridge, Mass.: MIT Press.

Churchland, P. S. & Sejnowski, T. (1989). Neural Representation and Neural Computation. In L. Nadel, L. A. Cooper, P. Culicover & R. M. Harnish (eds) *Neural Connections, Mental Computation*. Cambridge, Mass.: MIT Press.

Churchland, P. S. & Sejnowski, T. J. (1992). *The Computational Brain*. Cambridge, Mass.: MIT Press.

Clark, R. W. (1977). *Edison: the Man Who Made the Future*. New York: G. P. Putnam's Sons.

Cohen, N. J., Eichenbaum, H., Deacedo, B. S. & Corkin, S. (1985). Different Memory Systems Underlying Acquisition of Procedural and Declarative Knowledge. *Annals of the New York Academy of Sciences*, 444, 54–71.

Collins, A. (1977). Why Cognitive Science. *Cognitive Science*, 1, 1–2.

Collins, A. M. & Quillian, M. R. (1969). Retrieval Time From Semantic Memory. *Journal of Verbal Learning and Verbal Behavior*, 8, 240-7.

Coltheart, M. (1980). Iconic Memory and Visible Persistence. *Perception & Psychophysics*, 27, 183–228.

Conrad, R. (1964). Information, Acoustic Confusion, and Memory Span. *British Journal of Psychology*, 55, 429–432.

Cook, V. J. & Newson, M. (1996). *Chomsky's Universal Grammar: An Introduction*, 2nd edn. Oxford: Blackwell.

Cotman, C. W., Monaghan, D. T. & Ganong, A. H. (1988). Excitatory Amino Acid Neurotransmission: Nmda Receptors and Hebb-type Synaptic Plasticity. *Annual Review of Neuroscience*, 11, 61–80.

Cotter, N. E. (1990). The Stone-Weierstrass Theorem and its Application to Neural Networks. *IEEE Transactions on Neural Networks*, 1, 290–5.

Craik, F. I. M. & Lockhart, R. S. (1972). Levels of Processing: A Framework for Memory Research. *Journal of Verbal Learning and Verbal Behavior*, 11, 671–84.

Craik, K. J. M. (1943). *The Nature of Explanation*. Cambridge: Cambridge University Press.

Crichton, M. (1969). *The Andromeda Strain*. New York: Dell Publishing.

Crick, F. (1994). *The Astonishing Hypothesis*. London: Simon & Schuster.

Crick, F. & Asanuma, C. (1986). Certain Aspects of the Anatomy and Physiology of the Cerebral Cortex. In J. McClelland, D. Rumelhart & the PDP Group (eds) *Parallel Distributed Processing*, vol. 2. Cambridge, Mass.: MIT Press.

Cummins, R. (1975). Functional Analysis. *Journal of Philosophy*, 72, 741–60.

Cummins, R. (1983). *The Nature of Psychological Explanation*. Cambridge, Mass.: MIT Press.

Cummins, R. (1989). *Meaning and Mental Representation*. Cambridge, Mass.: MIT Press.

Cummins, R. (1991). The Role of Representation in Connectionist Explanations of Cognitive Capacities. In Ramsey, W., Stich, S. P. & Rumelhart, D. E. (eds) *Philosophy and Connectionist Theory*. Hillsdale, NJ: Lawrence Erlbaum Associates.

Cutting, J. E. (1986). *Perception with an Eye for Motion*. Cambridge, Mass.: MIT Press.

Cutting, J. E. & Proffitt, D. (1982). The Minimum Principle and the Perception of Absolute, Common, and Relative Motions. *Cognitive Psychology*, 14, 211–46.

Cybenko, G. (1989). Approximation by Superpositions of a Sigmoidal Function. *Mathematics of Control, Signals, and Systems*, 2, 303–14.

Damasio, A. R. & Benton, A. L. (1979). Impairments of Hand Movements Under Visual Guidance. *Neurology*, 29, 170–8.

Damasio, A. R. & Damasio, H. (1992). Brain and Language. *Scientific American*, 267(3), 88–95.

Damasio, A. R., Eslinger, P. J., Damasio, H., Van Hoesen, G. W. & Cornell, S. (1985). Multimodal Amnesic Syndrome Following Bilateral Temporal and Basal Forebrain Damage. *Archives of Neurology*, 42, 252–9.

Dartnall, H. J. A., Bowmaker, J. K. & Molino, J. D. (1983). Human Visual Pigments: Microspectrophotometric Results from the Eyes of Seven Persons. *Proceedings of the Royal Society of London*, B 220, 115–30.

Dawson, M. R. W. (1986). Using Relative Velocity as a Natural Constraint for the Motion Correspondence Problem. Ph.D. thesis, University of Western Ontario. (Available As University of Western Ontario Centre for Cognitive Science Cogmem no. 27.)

Dawson, M. R. W. (1987). Moving Contexts Do Affect the Perceived Direction of Apparent Motion in Motion Competition Displays. *Vision Research*, 27, 799–809.

Dawson, M. R. W. (1988). The Cooperative Application of Multiple Natural Constraints to the Motion Correspondence Problem. *Proceedings of the Seventh Canadian Conference on Artificial Intelligence*.

Dawson, M. R. W. (1990a). Apparent Motion and Element Connectedness. *Spatial Vision*, 4, 241–51.

Dawson, M. R. W. (1990b). Empirical Issues in Theoretical Psychology: Comment on Kukla. *American Psychologist*, 45, 778–80.

Dawson, M. R. W. (1991). The How and Why of What Went Where in Apparent Motion: Modeling Solutions to the Motion Correspondence Problem. *Psychological Review*, 98, 569–603.

Dawson, M. R. W. & Di Lollo, V. (1990). Effects of Adapting Luminance and Stimulus Contrast on the Temporal and Spatial Limits of Short-range Motion. *Vision Research*, 30, 415–29.

Dawson, M. R. W., Dobbs, A., Hooper, H. R., Mcewan, A. J. B., Triscott, J. & Cooney,

J. (1994). Artificial Neural Networks that Use Single-photon Emission Tomography to Identify Patients with Probably Alzheimer's Disease. *European Journal of Nuclear Medicine*, 21, 1303–11.

Dawson, M. R. W., Kremer, S. & Gannon, T. (1994). Identifying the Trigger Features for Hidden Units in a PDP Model of the Early Visual Pathway. In R. Elio (ed.) *Proceedings of the Tenth Canadian Conference on Artificial Intelligence*. Palo Alto, Calif.: Morgan Kaufman.

Dawson, M. R. W. & Medler, D. A. (1996). Of Mushrooms and Machine Learning: Identifying Algorithms in a PDP Network. *Canadian Artificial Intelligence*, Winter, 14–17.

Dawson, M. R. W., Medler, D. A. & Berkeley, I. S. N. (1997) PDP Networks Can Provide Models that are not Mere Implementations of Classical Theories. *Philosophical Psychology*, in press.

Dawson, M. R. W., Nevin-Meadows, N. & Wright, R. D. (1994). Polarity Matching in the Ternus Configuration. *Vision Research*, 34, 3347–59.

Dawson, M. R. W. & Pylyshyn, Z. W. (1988). Natural Constraints on Apparent Motion. In Z. Pylyshyn (ed.) *Computational Processes in Human Vision*. Norwood, NJ: Ablex.

Dawson, M. R. W. & Schopflocher, D. P. (1992a). Modifying the Generalized Delta Rule to Brrain Networks of Non-monotonic Processors for Pattern Classification. *Connection Science*, 4, 19–31.

Dawson, M. R. W. & Schopflocher, D. P. (1992b). Autonomous Processing in PDP Networks. *Philosophical Psychology*, 5, 199–219.

Dawson, M. R. W., Schopflocher, D. P., Kidd, J. & Shamanski, K. S. (1992). Training Networks of Value Units. *Proceedings of the Ninth Canadian Artificial Intelligence Conference*, pp. 244–50.

Dawson, M. R. W. & Shamanski, K. S. (1994). Connectionism, Confusion, and Cognitive Science. *Journal of Intelligent Systems*, 4, 215–62.

Dawson, M. R. W. & Wright, R. D. (1989). The Consistency of Element Transformations Affects the Visibility but not the Direction of Illusory Motion. *Spatial Vision*, 4, 17–29.

Dawson, M. R. W. & Wright, R. D. (1994). Simultaneity in the Ternus Configuration: Psychophysical Data and A Computer Model. *Vision Research*, 34, 397–407.

Dennett, D. (1978). *Brainstorms*. Cambridge, Mass.: MIT Press.

Dennett, D. (1987) Cognitive Wheels: the Frame Problem of AI. In Z. W. Pylyshyn (ed.) *The Robot's Dilemma*. Norwood, NJ: Ablex Publishing.

Dennett, D. (1991a). Mother Nature versus the Walking Encyclopedia: A Western Drama. In Ramsey, W., Stich, S. P. & Rumelhart, D. E. (eds) *Philosophy and Connectionist Theory*. Hillsdale, NJ: Lawrence Erlbaum Associates.

Dennett, D. (1991b). *Consciousness Explained*. Boston: Little, Brown.

Dennett, D. (1995). *Darwin's Dangerous Idea*. New York: Simon & Schuster.

Dennett, D. (1996). *Kinds of Minds*. New York: HarperCollins.

Desimone, R. & Underleider, L. G. (1986). Multiple Visual Areas in the Caudal Superior Temporal Sulcus of the Macaque. *The Journal of Comparative Neurology*, 248, 164–89.

Deyoe, E. A. & Van Essen, D. C. (1988). Concurrent Processing Streams in Monkey Visual Cortex. *Trends in Neuroscience*, 11, 219–26.

Di Lollo, V. (1980). Temporal Integration in Visual Memory. *Journal of Experimental Psychology: General*, 109, 75–97.

Douglas, R. J. & Martin, K. A. C. (1991). Opening the Grey Box. *Trends in Neuroscience*, 14, 286–93.

306   *References*

Drachman, D. A. & Arbit, J. (1966). Memory and the Hippocampal Complex. II. Is Memory a Multiple Process? *Archives of Neurology*, 15, 52–61.

Dreyfus, H. L. (1992). *What Computers Still Can't Do*. Cambridge, Mass.: MIT Press.

Dreyfus, H. L. & Dreyfus, S. E. (1988). Making a Mind versus Modeling the Brain. Artificial Intelligence Back at a Branchpoint. In S. Graubard (ed.) *The Artificial Intelligence Debate*. Cambridge, Mass.: MIT Press.

Dubner, R. & Zeki, S. M. (1971). Response Properties and Receptive Fields of Cells in an Anatomically Defined Region of the Superior Temporal Sulcus in the Monkey. *Brain Research*, 35, 528–32.

Dudai, Y. (1989). *The Neurobiology of Memory*. New York: Oxford University Press.

Dutton, J. M. & Briggs, W. G. (1971). Simulation Model Construction. In Dutton, J. M. & Starbuck, W. H. (eds) *Computer Simulation of Human Behavior*. New York: John Wiley & Sons.

Dutton, J. M. & Starbuck, W. H. (1971). *Computer Simulation of Human Behavior*. New York: John Wiley & Sons.

Edelman, G. M. (1987). *Neural Darwinism*. New York: Basic Books.

Edelman, G. M. (1988). *Topobiology*. New York: Basic Books.

Edelman, G. M. (1989). *The Remembered Present*. New York: Basic Books.

Edelman, G. M. (1992). *Bright Air, Brilliant Fire*. New York: Basic Books.

Edison, T. A. (1948). *The Diary and Sundry Observations of Thomas Alva Edison*. Ed. D. D. Runes. New York: Philosophical Library.

Eich, J. M. (1982). A Composite Holographic Associative Recall Model. *Psychological Review*, 89, 627–61.

Eichenbaum, H. (1992). The Hippocampal System and Declarative Memory in Animals. *Journal of Cognitive Neuroscience*, 4, 217–31.

Eimas, P. D., Miller, J. L. & Jusczyk, P. W. (1987). On Infant Speech Perception and the Acquisition of Language. In S. Harnad (ed.) *Categorical Perception*. New York: Cambridge University Press.

Elman, J. (1990). Finding Structure in Time. *Cognitive Science*, 14, 179–211.

Ericsson, K. A. & Simon, H. A. (1984). *Protocol Analysis: Verbal Reports as Data*. Cambridge, Mass.: MIT Press.

Eysenck, M. W. (1994). Cognitive Psychology, History of. In M. W. Eysenck, A. Ellis, E. Hunt & P. Johnson-Laird (eds) *The Blackwell Dictionary of Cognitive Psychology*. Cambridge, Mass.: Blackwell.

Eysenck, M. W. (1994). *The Blackwell Dictionary of Cognitive Psychology*. Oxford: Blackwell.

Fahlman, S. E. & Lebiere, C. (1990). *The Cascade-Correlation Learning Architecture*. Technical Report CMU-CS-90-100, School of Computer Science, Carnegie Mellon University.

Farah, M. J. (1994). Neuropsychological Evidence with An Interactive Brain: A Critique of the 'Locality' Assumption. *Behavioral and Brain Sciences*, 17, 43–104.

Farrell, J. E. & Shepard, R. N. (1981). Shape, Orientation, and Apparent Rotational Motion. *Journal of Experimental Psychology: Human Perception and Performance*, 7, 477–486.

Feigenbaum, A. & Feldman, J. (1995). *Computers and Thought*. Cambridge, Mass.: MIT Press.

Feigenbaum, E. A. & Mccorduck, P. (1983). *The Fifth Generation*. Reading, Mass.: Addison-Wesley.

Feldman, J. A. & Ballard, D. H. (1982). Connectionist Models and Their Properties. *Cognitive Science*, 6, 205–54.

Feldman, R. S. & Quenzer, L. F. (1984). *Fundamentals of Neuropsychopharmacology*. Sunderland, Mass.: Sinauer Associates.

Finke, R. A. & Pinker, S. (1982). Spontaneous Imagery Scanning in Mental Extrapolation. *Journal of Experimental Psychology: Learning, Memory, and Cognition*, 8, 142–7.

Flanagan, O. J. (1984). *The Science of the Mind*. Cambridge, Mass.: MIT Press.

Flanagan, O. J. (1992). *Consciousness Reconsidered*. Cambridge, Mass.: MIT Press.

Fodor, J. A. (1968). *Psychological Explanation: An Introduction to the Philosophy of Psychology*. New York: Random House.

Fodor, J. A. (1975). *The Language of Thought*. Cambridge, Mass.: Harvard University Press.

Fodor, J. A. (1983). *The Modularity of Mind*. Cambridge, Mass.: MIT Press.

Fodor, J. A. (1985). Précis of the Modularity of Mind, *The Behavioral and Brain Sciences*, 8, 1–42.

Fodor, J. A. (1987). Modules, Frames, Fridgeons, Sleeping Dogs, and the Music of the Spheres. In Z. W. Pylyshyn (ed.) *The Robot's Dilemma*. Norwood, NJ: Ablex Publishing.

Fodor, J. A. & McLaughlin, B. P. (1990). Connectionism and the Problem of Systematicity: Why Smolensky's Solution Doesn't Work. *Cognition*, 35, 183–204.

Fodor, J. A. & Pylyshyn, Z. W. (1981). How Direct is Visual Perception? Some Reflections on Gibson's "Ecological Approach" , *Cognition*, 9, 139–96.

Fodor, J. A. & Pylyshyn, Z. W. (1988). Connectionism and Cognitive Architecture. *Cognition*, 28, 3–71.

Foster, D. H. (1978). Visual Apparent Motion and the Calculus of Variations. In E. L. J. Leeuwenberg & H. F. J. M Buffart (eds) *Formal Theories of Visual Perception*. New York: Wiley.

Fu, L. (1994). Rule Generation From Neural Networks. *IEEE Transactions on Neural Networks*, 24, 1114–24.

Funahashi, K. (1989). On the Approximate Realization of Continuous Mappings by Neural Networks. *Neural Networks*, 2, 183–92.

Funahashi, S., Bruce, C. J. & Goldman-Rakic, P. S. (1989). Mnemonic Coding of Visual Space in the Monkey's Dorsolateral Prefrontal Cortex. *Journal of Neurophysiology*, 61, 331–49.

Gallant, S. I. (1993). *Neural Network Learning and Expert Systems*. Cambridge, Mass.: MIT Press.

Gallistel, C. R. (1996). The Replacement of General-purpose Theories with Adaptive Specializations. In M. S. Gazzaniga (ed.) *The Cognitive Neurosciences*. Cambridge, Mass.: MIT Press.

Gardner, H. (1984). *The Mind's New Science*. New York: Basic Books.

Gardner, M. (1982). *Logic Machines and Diagrams*, 2nd edn. Chicago: the University of Chicago Press.

Garfield, J. L. (1987). Introduction: Carving the Mind at its Joints. In J. L. Garfield (ed.) *Modularity in Knowledge Representation and Natural-language Understanding*. Cambridge, Mass.: MIT Press.

Garson, J. W. (1994). No Representations Without Rules: the Prospects for a Compromise Between Paradigms in Cognitive Science. *Mind and Language*, 9, 25–37.

Gazzaniga, M. (1978). *The Integrated Mind*. New York: Plenum Press.

Gazzaniga, M. (1992). *Nature's Mind*. New York: Basic Books.

Gazzaniga, M., Bogen, J. E. & Sperry, R. W. (1962). Some Functional Effects of Sectioning the Cerebral Commissures in Man. *National Academy of Sciences of the United States of America. Proceedings. Biological Sciences*, 48, 1765–9.

Georgopoulos, A. P., Lurito, J. T., Petrides, M., Schwartz, A. B. & Massey, J. T. (1989). Mental Rotation of the Neuronal Population Vector. *Science*, 243, 234–6.

Getting, P. A. (1989). Emerging Principles Governing the Operation of Neural Networks. *Annual Review of Neuroscience*, 12, 185–204.

Gibson, J. J. (1966) *The Senses Considered as Perceptual Systems*. Boston: Houghton Mifflin.

Gibson, J. J. (1979). *The Ecological Approach to Visual Perception*. Boston: Houghton Mifflin.

Giles, C. L., Miller, C. B., Chen, D., Chen, H. H., Sun, G. Z. & Lee, Y. C. (1992). Learning and Extracting Finite State Automata with Second-order Recurrent Neural Network. *Neural Computation*, 4, 393–405.

Girosi, F. & Poggio, T. (1990). Networks and the Best Approximation Property. *Biological Cybernetics*, 63, 169–76.

Glanzer, M. (1972). Storage Mechanisms in Free Recall. In G. H. Bower (ed.) *The Psychology of Learning and Motivation: Advances in Research and Theory*, vol. 5. New York: Academic Press.

Glanzer, M. & Cunitz, A. R. (1966). Two Storage Mechanisms in Free Recall. *Journal of Verbal Learning and Verbal Behavior*, 5, 351–60.

Gleick, J. (1992). *Genius*. New York: Pantheon Books.

Gogel, W. (1974). The Adjacency Principle in Visual Perception. *Quarterly Journal of Experimental Psychology*, 26, 425–37.

Gold, E. M. (1967). Language Identification in the Limit. *Information and Control*, 10, 447–74.

Goldberg, M. E. & Bruce, C. J. (1985). Cerebral Cortical Activity Associated with the Orientation of Visual Attention in the Rhesus Monkey. *Vision Research*, 25, 471–81.

Goldman-Rakic, P. S. (1992). Working Memory and the Mind. *Scientific American*, 267(3), 110–17.

Goodglass, H., Blumstein, S. E., Gleason, J. B., Hyde, M. R., Green, E. & Statlender, S. (1979). The Effect of Syntactic Encoding on Sentence Comprehension in Aphasia. *Brain and Language*, 7, 201–9.

Goodman, N. (1978). *Ways of Worldmaking*. Indianapolis, Ind.: Hacket Publishing.

Graubard, S. (1988). *The Artificial Intelligence Debate*. Cambridge, Mass.: MIT Press.

Green, D. W. (1996). *Cognitive Science: An Introduction*. Oxford: Blackwell.

Gregory, R. (1961). The Brain as an Engineering Problem. In W. H. Thorpe & O. L. Zangwill (eds) *Current Problems in Animal Behaviour*. Cambridge: Cambridge University Press.

Gregory, R. (1966). *Eye and Brain: the Psychology of Seeing*. New York: McGraw-Hill.

Gregory, R. (1970). *The Intelligent Eye*. London: Weidenfeld & Nicolson.

Grimson, E. (1981). *From Images to Surfaces*. Cambridge, Mass.: MIT Press.

Grossberg, S. (1980). How Does the Brain Build a Cognitive Code? *Psychological Review*, 87, 1–51.

Grossberg, S. (1987). Competitive Learning: From Interactive Activation to Adaptive Resonance. *Cognitive Science*, 11, 23–63.

Grossberg, S. & Rudd, M. E. (1989). A Neural Architecture for Visual Motion Perception: Group and Element Apparent Motion. *Neural Networks*, 2, 421–50.

Grossberg, S. & Rudd, M. E. (1992). Cortical Dynamics of Visual Motion Perception: Short-range and Long-range Apparent Motion. *Psychological Review*, 99, 78–121.

Gryzwacz, N. M. & Yuille, A. L. (1988). Massively Parallel Implementations of Theories for Apparent Motion. *Spatial Vision*, 3, 15–44.

Guthrie, E. R. (1935). *The Psychology of Learning*. New York: Harper.

Haberlandt, K. (1994). *Cognitive Psychology*. Boston, Mass.: Allyn and Bacon.

Hadley, R. F. (1994a). Systematicity in Connectionist Language Learning. *Minds and Machines*, 3, 183–200.

Hadley, R. F. (1994b). Systematicity Revisited: Reply to Christiansen and Chater and Niclasson and Van Gelder. *Mind and Language*, 9, 431–44.

Hadley, R. F. (1997). Cognition, Systematicity, and Nomic Necessity. *Mind and Language*, in press.

Hadley, R. F. & Hayward, M. B. (1997). Strong Semantic Systematicity from Hebbian Connectionist Learning. *Minds and Machines*, in press.

Hall, G. G. (1963). *Matrices and Tensors*. New York: Pergamon Press.

Hammond, P., Ahmed, B. & Smith, A. T. (1986). Relative Motion Sensitivity in Cat Cortex as a Function of Stimulus Direction. *Brain Research*, 386, 93–104.

Hammond, P., Pomfrett, C. J. D. & Ahmed, B. (1989). Neural Motion Aftereffects in the Cat's Striate Cortex: Orientation Selectivity. *Vision Research*, 29, 1671–83.

Hammond, P. & Smith, A. T. (1984). Sensitivity of Complex Cells in Cat Striate Cortex to Relative Motion. *Brain Research*, 301, 287–98.

Hanson, S. J. & Burr, D. J. (1990). What Connectionist Models Learn: Learning and Representation in Connectionist Networks. *Behavioral and Brain Sciences*, 13, 471–518.

Hanson, S. J. & Olson, C. R. (1991). Neural Networks and Natural Intelligence: Notes from Mudville. *Connection Science*, 3, 332–5.

Hartman, E., Keeler, J. D. & Kowalski, J. M. (1989). Layered Neural Networks with Gaussian Hidden Units as Universal Approximation. *Neural Computation*, 2, 210–15.

Haugeland, J. (1985). *Artificial Intelligence: the Very Idea*. Cambridge, Mass.: MIT Press.

Hawkins, R. D. & Bower, G. H. (1989). *Computational Models of Learning in Simple Neural Systems*. San Diego: Academic Press.

Hawthorne, J. (1989). On the Compatibility of Connectionist and Classical Models. *Philosophical Psychology*, 2, 5–15.

Hebb, D. O. (1949). *The Organization of Behaviour*. New York: Wiley.

Hecht-Nielsen, R. (1987). *Neurocomputing*. Reading, Mass.: Addison-Wesley.

Heider, E. R. (1972). Universals in Color Naming and Meaning. *Journal of Experimental Psychology*, 93, 10–20.

Helmholtz, H. V. (1968). The Recent Progress of the Theory of Vision. In R. M. Warren & R. P. Warren (eds) *Helmholtz on Perception: Its Physiology and Development*. New York: John Wiley & Sons.

Henle, M. (1974). The Snail Beneath the Shell. In S. Rosner & L. E. Abt (eds) *Essays in Creativity*. Croton-on-Hudson, NY: North River Press.

Henle, M. (1975). Fishing for Ideas. *American Psychologist*, 30, 795–9.

Hertz, J., Krogh, A. & Palmer, R. (1991). *Introduction to the Theory of Neural Computation*. Redwood City, Calif.: Addison-Wesley.

Hess, R. H., Baker, C. L. & Zihl, J. (1989). The "Motion-blind" Patient: Low-level Spatial and Temporal Filters. *The Journal of Neuroscience*, 9, 1628–40.

Hildreth, E. C. (1983). *The Measurement of Visual Motion*. Cambridge, Mass.: MIT Press.

Hille, B. (1990). *Ionic Channels of Excitable Membranes*. Sunderland, Mass.: Sinauer.

Hillis, W. D. (1985). *The Connection Machine*. Cambridge, Mass.: MIT Press.

Hillis, W. D. (1988). Intelligence as Emergent Behaviour, Or, the Songs of Eden. In S. R. Graubard (ed.) *The Artificial Intelligence Debate*. Cambridge, Mass.: MIT Press.

Hinton, G. E. (1986). Learning Distributed Representations of Concepts. *Proceedings of the Eighth Annual Meeting of the Cognitive Science Society*. Hillsdale, NJ: Lawrence Erlbaum Associates.

Hodges, A. (1983). *Alan Turing: the Enigma of Intelligence*. London: Unwin Paperbacks.

Hodgkin, A. L. & Huxley, A. F. (1952). A Quantitative Description of Membrane Current and its Application to Conduction and Excitation in Nerve. *Journal of Physiology*, 117, 500–44.

Hopcroft, J. E. & Ullman, J. D. (1979). *Introduction to Automata Theory, Languages, and Computation*. Reading, Mass.: Addison-Wesley.

Hopfield, J. J. (1982). Neural Networks and Physical Systems with Emergent Collective Computational Abilities. *Proceedings of the National Academy of Sciences*, 79, 2554–8.

Hopfield, J. J. (1984). Neurons with Graded Response have Collective Computational Properties Like Those of Two-state Neurons. *Proceedings of the National Academy of Sciences, USA*, 81, 3008–92.

Horgan, J. (1993). The Mastermind of Artificial Intelligence. *Scientific American*, 269(5), 35–8.

Horgan, J. (1994). Can Science Explain Consciousness? *Scientific American*, 271(1), 88–94.

Horgan, T. & Tienson, J. (1996). *Connectionism and the Philosophy of Psychology*. Cambridge, Mass.: MIT Press.

Horn, B. K. P. (1986). *Robot Vision*. Cambridge, Mass.: MIT Press.

Horn, B. K. P. & Schunk, B. (1981). Determining Optical Flow. *Artificial Intelligence*, 17, 185–203.

Hornik, M., Sinchcombe, M. & White, H. (1989). Multilayer Feedforward Networks are Universal Approximators. *Neural Networks*, 2, 359–66.

Horwood, H. (1987). *Dancing on the Shore*. Toronto: McClelland and Stewart.

Hsu, F., Anantharaman, T., Campbell, M. & Nowatzyk, A. (1990). A Grandmaster Chess Machine. *Scientific American*, 263(4), 44–50.

Hubel, D. H. & Wiesel, T. N. (1959). Receptive Fields of Single Neurones in the Cat's Striate Cortex. *Journal of Physiology*, 148, 574–91.

Hubel, D. H. & Wiesel, T. N. (1962). Receptive Fields, Binocular Interaction and Functional Architecture in the Cat's Visual Cortex. *Journal of Physiology*, 160, 106–54.

Hull, C. L. (1935). The Conflicting Psychologies of Learning – A Way Out. *Psychological Review*, 42, 491–516.

Hurlbert, A. & Poggio, T. (1988). Making Machines (and Artificial Intelligence) See. In S. Graubard (ed.) *The Artificial Intelligence Debate*. Cambridge, Mass.: MIT Press.

Hyvarinen, J. & Poranen, A. (1974). Function of Parietal Associative Area 7 as Revealed from Cellular Discharges in Alert Monkeys. *Brain*, 97, 673–92.

Ingram, J. (1994). *The Burning House*. Toronto: Viking Penguin.

Jackendoff, R. (1983). *Semantics and Cognition*. Cambridge, Mass.: MIT Press.

Jackendoff, R. (1987). *Consciousness and the Computational Mind*. Cambridge, Mass.: MIT Press.

Jackendoff, R. (1990). *Semantic Structures*. Cambridge, Mass.: MIT Press.

Jackendoff, R. (1994). *Patterns in the Mind*. New York: Basic Books.

Jain, A. N. (1991). Parsing Complex Sentences with Structured Connectionist Networks. *Neural Computation*, 3, 110–20.

James, W. ([1890] 1950). *The Principles of Psychology*, vol. 1. New York: Dover Publications.

Janlert, L.-E. (1987). Modeling Change – the Frame Problem. In Z. W. Pylyshyn (ed.) *The Robot's Dilemma*. Norwood, NJ: Ablex Publishing.

Johansson, G. (1950). *Configurations in Event Perception*. Uppsala, Sweden: Almqvist and Wiksell.

Johnson-Laird, P. N. (1983). *Mental Models*. Cambridge, Mass.: Harvard University Press.

Jordan, M. I. (1986). An Introduction to Linear Algebra in Parallel Distributed Processing. In D. Rumelhart, J. McClelland & the PDP Group (eds) *Parallel Distributed Processing*, vol. 1. Cambridge, Mass.: MIT Press.

Josephson, M. (1961). *Edison*. New York: McGraw-Hill.

Julesz, B. (1981). Textons, the Elements of Texture Perception. *Nature*, 290, 91–7.

Kaiser, H. R. (1958). The Varimax Criterion for Analytic Rotation in Factor Analysis. *Psychometrika*, 23, 187–200.

Kaji, S. & Kawabata, N. (1985). Neural Interactions of Two Moving Patterns in the Direction and Orientation Domain in the Complex Cells of Cat's Visual Cortex. *Vision Research*, 25, 749–53.

Kandel, E. R. (1991). Brain and Behavior. In E. R. Kandel, J. H. Schwartz & T. M. Jessell (eds) *Principles of Neural Science*, 3rd edn. New York: Elsevier.

Kandel, E. R., Schwartz, J. H. & Jessell, T. M. (1991). *Principles of Neural Science*, 3rd edn. New York: Elsevier

Katz, J. J. (1964). Mentalism in Linguistics. *Language*, 40, 124–37.

Kean, M. (1980). Grammatical Representation and the Description of Language Processing. In D. Caplan (ed.) *Biological Studies of Mental Processes*. Cambridge, Mass.: MIT Press.

Kehoe, E. J. (1988). A Layered Network Model of Associative Learning: Learning to Learn and Configuration. *Psychological Review*, 95, 411–33.

Kenstowicz, M. (1994). *Phonology in Generative Grammar*. Cambridge, Mass.: Blackwell.

Keynes, G. (1966). *The Life of William Harvey*. London: Oxford University Press.

Kidder, T. (1981). *The Soul of a New Machine*. New York: Avon Books.

Kilian, J. & Siegelmann, H. T. (1993). On the Power of Sigmoid Neural Networks. *Proceedings of the Sixth ACM Workshop on Computational Learning Theory*, pp. 137–43.

Kintsch, W. & Buschke, H. (1969). Homophones and Synonyms in Short-term Memory. *Journal of Experimental Psychology*, 80, 403–7.

Knapp, A. & Anderson, J. A. (1984). A Signal Averaging Model for Concept Formation. *Journal of Experimental Psychology: Learning, Memory and Cognition*, 10, 616–37.

Koch, S. (1976). Language Communities, Search Cells, and the Psychological Studies. In W. J. Arnold (ed.) *Nebraska Symposium on Motivation*, 23. Lincoln: University of Nebraska Press, pp. 477–559.

Koffka, K. (1935). *Principles of Gestalt Psychology*. New York: Harcourt, Brace & World.

Kohler, W. ([1947] 1975). *Gestalt Psychology*. New York: New American Library.

Kohonen, T. (1972). Correlation Matrix Memories. *IEEE Transactions on Computers*, 21, 353–9.

Kohonen, T. (1977). *Associative Memory: A System-theoretical Approach*. New York: Springer-Verlag.

Kohonen, T. (1984). *Self-organization and Associative Memory*. New York: Springer-Verlag.

Kolb, B. & Whishaw, I. Q. (1990). *Fundamentals of Human Neuropsychology*, 3rd edn. New York: W. H. Freeman & Co.

Kolers, P. (1972). *Aspects of Motion Perception*. New York: Pergamon Press.

Kolers, P. & Green, M. (1984). Color Logic of Apparent Motion. *Perception*, 13, 149–54.

Kolers, P. & Pomerantz, J. R. (1971). Figural Change in Apparent Motion. *Journal of Experimental Psychology*, 87, 99–108.

Kolers, P. & Von Grunau, M. (1976). Shape and Colour in Apparent Motion. *Vision Research*, 16, 329–35.

Kosslyn, S. M. (1980). *Image and Mind*. Cambridge, Mass.: Harvard University Press.

Kosslyn, S. M. & Pomerantz,, J. R. (1977). Imagery, Propositions, and the Form of Internal Representations. *Cognitive Psychology*, 9, 52–76.

Kosslyn, S. M. & Van Kleeck, M. (1990). Broken Brains and Normal Minds: Why Humpty-Dumpty Needs a Skeleton. In E. L. Schwartz (ed.) *Computational Neuroscience*. Cambridge, Mass.: MIT Press.

Kremer, S. C. (1995a). On the Computational Powers of Elman-style Recurrent Networks. *IEEE Transactions on Neural Networks*, 6, 1000–4.

Kremer, S. C. (1995b). A Theory of Grammatical Induction in the Connectionist Paradigm. Ph.D. thesis, University of Alberta.

Krumhansl, C. L. (1984). Independent Processing of Visual Form and Motion. *Perception*, 13, 535–46.

Kruschke, J. K. (1990). How Connectionist Models Learn: the Course of Learning in Connectionist Networks. *Behavioural and Brain Sciences*, 13, 498–9.

Kuffler, S. W., Nicholls, J. G. & Martin, A. R. (1984). *From Neuron to Brain*, 2nd edn. Sunderland, Mass.: Sinauer Associates.

Kuhn, T. S. (1970). *The Structure of Scientific Revolutions*, 2nd edn, enlarged. Chicago: University of Chicago Press.

Kupfermann, I., Castellucci, U., Pinsker, H. & Kandel, E. R. (1970). Neuronal Correlates of Habitutation and Dishabituation of the Gill-withdrawal Reflex in Aplysia. *Science*, 167, 1743–5.

Kurzweil, R. (1990). *The Age of Intelligent Machines*. Cambridge, Mass.: MIT Press.

Lachman, R., Lachman, J. L. & Butterfield, E. C. (1979). *Cognitive Psychology and Information Processing*. Hillsdale, NJ: Lawrence Erlbaum Associates.

Lachter, J. & Bever, T. G. (1988). The Relation Between Linguistic Structure and Associative Theories of Language Learning – A Constructive Critique of Some Connectionist Learning Models. *Cognition*, 28, 195–247.

Langer, S. K. (1942). *Philosophy in a New Key*. Cambridge, Mass.: Harvard University Press.

Lashley, K. S. (1950). In Search of the Engram. *Symposium of the Society for Experimental Biology*, 4, 454–82.

Lasker, E. (1947). *Lasker's Manual of Chess*. New York: Dover Publications.

Leahey, T. H. (1987). *A History of Psychology*, 2nd edn. Englewood Cliffs, NJ: Prentice-Hall.

Lelkins, A. & Koenderink, J. J. (1984). Illusory Motion in Visual Displays. *Vision Research*, 24, 1083–90.

Levitan, I. B. & Kaczmarek, L. K. (1991). *The Neuron: Cell and Molecular Biology*. New York: Oxford University Press.

Lewandowsky, S. (1993). The Rewards and Hazards of Computer Simulations. *Psychological Science*, 4, 236–43.

Lincoff, G. H. (1981). *National Audubon Society Field Guide to North American Mushrooms*. New York: Alfred A. Knopf Publishers.

Lippmann, R. P. (1987). An Introduction to Computing with Neural Nets. *IEEE ASSP Magazine*, April, 4–22.

Lippmann, R. P. (1989). Pattern Classification Using Neural Networks. *IEEE Communications Magazine*, November, 47–64.

Lisberger, S., Morris, E. J. & Tychsen, L. (1987). Visual Motion Processing and Sensory-motor Integration for Smooth Pursuit Eye Movements. *Annual Review of Neuroscience*, 10, 97–129.

Livingstone, M. & Hubel, D. (1988). Segregation of Form, Color, Movement and Depth: Anatomy, Physiology, and Perception. *Science*, 240, 740–50.

Lockhart, R. S. (1991). Varieties of Theoretical Perspectives. In W. E. Hockley and S. Lewandowsky (eds) *Relating Theory and Data: Essays on Human Memory in Honor of Bennet B. Murdock*. Hillsdale, NJ: Lawrence Erlbaum Associates.

Longoni, A. M., Richardson, J. T. W. & Aiello, A. (1993). Articulatory Rehearsal and Phonological Storage in Working Memory. *Memory & Cognition*, 21, 11–22.

Lorber, J. (1968). The Results of Early Treatment of Extreme Hydrocephalus. *Developmental Medicine and Child Neurology Supplement*, 16, 21–9.

Lovecraft, H. P. (1963). The Dreams in the Witch-House. In A. Derleth (ed.) *The Best of H. P. Lovecraft*. New York: Balantine Books.

Lucas, S. M. & Damper, R. I. (1990). Syntactic Neural Networks. *Connection Science*, 2, 195–221.

Lynch, G. (1986). *Synapses, Circuits, and the Beginnings of Memory*. Cambridge, Mass.: MIT Press.

Lynch, J. C., Mountcastle, V. B., Talbot, W. H. & Yin, T. C. T. (1977). Parietal Lobe Mechanisms for Directed Visual Attention. *Journal of Neurophysiology*, 40, 362–89.

Mandl, G. (1985). Responses of Visual Cells in Cat Superior Coliculus to Relative Pattern Movement. *Vision Research*, 25, 267–81.

Marcus, G. F. (1993). Negative Evidence in Language Acquisition. *Cognition*, 46, 53–85.

Marr, D. (1976). Early Processing of Visual Information. *Philosophical Transactions of the Royal Society of London*, 275, 483–524.

Marr, D. (1977). Artificial Intelligence – A Personal View. *Artificial Intelligence*, 9, 37–48.

Marr, D. (1982). *Vision*. San Francisco, Calif. : W. H. Freeman.

Marr, D. & Hildreth, E. (1980). Theory of Edge Detection. *Proceedings of the Royal Society of London*, B207, 187–217.

Marr, D. & Ullman, S. (1981). Directional Selectivity and its Use in Early Visual Processing. *Proceedings of the Royal Society of London*, B211, 151–80.

Massicotte, G. & Baudry, M. (1991). Triggers and Substrates of Hippocampal Synaptic Plasticity. *Neuroscience and Biobehavioral Reviews*, 15, 415–23.

Matlin, M. W. (1994). *Cognition*. Fort Worth, Tex.: Harcourt Brace.

Maunsell, J. H. R. & Newsome, W. T. (1987). Visual Processing in Monkey Extrastriate Cortex. *Annual Review of Neuroscience*, 10, 363–401.

Maunsell, J. H. R. & Van Essen, D. C. (1983a). Functional Properties of Neurons in Middle Temporal Visual Area of the Macaque Monkey. I. Selectivity for Stimulus Direction, Speed and Orientation. *Journal of Neurophysiology*, 49, 1127–47.

Maunsell, J. H. R. & Van Essen, D. C. (1983b). Functional Properties of Neurons in Middle Temporal Visual Area of the Macaque Monkey. II. Binocular Interactions and Sensitivity to Binocular Disparity. *Journal of Neurophysiology*, 49, 1148–67.

Maunsell, J. H. R. & Van Essen, D. C. (1983c). The Connections of the Middle

Temporal Visual Area (MT) and their Relationship to a Cortical Hierarchy in the Macaque Monkey. *Journal of Neuroscience*, 3, 2563–86.

Mayeux, R. & Kandel, E. R. (1991). Disorders of Language: the Aphasias. In E. R. Kandel, J. H. Schwartz & T. R. Jessell (eds) *Principles of Neural Science*, 3rd edn. New York: Elsevier.

McClelland, J. L. (1986). Resource Requirements of Standard and Programmable Nets. In D. Rumelhart, J. McClelland & the PDP Group (eds) *Parallel Distributed Processing*, vol. 1. Cambridge, Mass.: MIT Press.

McClelland, J. L. & Kawamoto, A. H. (1986). Mechanisms of Sentence Processing: Assigning Roles to Constituents of Sentences. In J. McClelland, D. Rumelhart & the PDP Group (eds) *Parallel Distributed Processing*, vol. 2. Cambridge, Mass.: MIT Press.

McClelland, J. L. & Rumelhart, D. E. (1986). A Distributed Model of Human Learning and Memory. In J. McClelland, D. Rumelhart & the PDP Group (eds) *Parallel Distributed Processing*, vol. 2. Cambridge, Mass.: MIT Press.

McClelland, J. L. & Rumelhart, D. E. (1988). *Explorations in Parallel Distributed Processing*. Cambridge, Mass.: MIT Press.

McClelland, J. L., Rumelhart, D. E. & Hinton, G. E. (1986). The Appeal of Parallel Distributed Processing. In D. Rumelhart, J. McClelland & the PDP Group (eds) *Parallel Distributed Processing*, vol. 1. Cambridge, Mass.: MIT Press.

McClelland, J. L., Rumelhart, D. E. & the PDP Group (1986). *Parallel Distributed Processing*, vol. 2. Cambridge, Mass.: MIT Press.

McCloskey, M. (1991). Networks and Theories: the Place of Connectionism in Cognitive Science. *Psychological Science*, 2, 387–95.

McCorduck, P. (1979). *Machines Who Think: A Personal Inquiry Into the History and Prospects of Artificial Intelligence*. San Francisco: W. H. Freeman.

McCulloch, W. S. & Pitts, W. ([1943] 1988). A Logical Calculus of the Ideas Immanent in Nervous Activity. In J. A. Anderson & E. Rosenfeld (eds) *Neurocomputing: Foundations of Research*. Cambridge, Mass.: MIT Press.

McGeer, P. L., Eccles, J. C. & Mcgeer, E. G. (1987). *Molecular Neurobiology of the Mammalian Brain*, 2nd edn. New York: Plenum Press.

McGuigan, F. J. (1994). *Biological Psychology: A Cybernetic Science*. Englewood-Cliffs, NJ: Prentice-Hall.

McManus, I. C. (1983). Basic Colour Terms in Literature. *Language and Speech*, 26, 247–52.

McNaughton, B. L. (1989). Neuronal Mechanisms for Spatial Computation and Information Storage. In L. Nadel, L. A. Cooper, P. Culicover & R. M. Harnish (eds) *Neural Connections, Mental Computation*. Cambridge, Mass.: MIT Press.

Medler, D. A. & Dawson, M. R. W. (1994). Training Redundant Artificial Networks: Imposing Biology on Technology. *Psychological Research*, 57, 54–62.

Medler, D. A., Dawson, M. R. W., Kingstone, A. & Panasiuk, L. (1998). The Locality Assumption Revisited: the Relationship Between Internal Structure and Behavioral Dissociations. *Journal of Cognitive Neuroscience*, under editorial review.

Melville, H. ([1851] 1930). *Moby Dick*. New York: the Modern Library.

Mettler, F. A. & Guiberteau, M. J. (1991). *Essentials of Nuclear Medicine Imaging*, 3rd edn. Philadelphia: W. B. Saunders.

Mikami, A., Newsome, W. T. & Wurtz, R. H. (1986). Motion Selectivity in Macaque Visual Cortex. II. Spatiotemporal Range of Directional Interactions in MT and V1. *Journal of Neurophysiology*, 55, 1328–39.

Miller, G. A., Galanter, E. & Pribram, K. H. (1960). *Plans and the Structure of Behavior*. New York: Henry Holt & Co.

Milner, B. (1965). Memory Disturbance after Bilateral Hippocampal Lesions. In P. Milner & S. Glickman (eds) *Cognitive Processes and the Brain*. Princeton, NJ: Van Nostrand.

Milner, B. (1966). Amnesia following Operation on the Temporal Lobes. In C. W. M. Whitty & O. L. Zangwill (eds) *Amnesia*. London: Butterworths.

Minsky, M. (1972). *Computation: Finite and Infinite Machines*. London: Prentice-Hall International.

Minsky, M. (1975). A Framework for Representing Knowledge. In P. H. Winston (ed.) *the Psychology of Computer Vision*. New York: McGraw-Hill.

Minsky, M. (1985). *The Society of Mind*. New York: Simon & Schuster.

Minsky, M. & Papert, S. ([1969] 1988). *Perceptrons*, 3rd edn. Cambridge, Mass.: MIT Press.

Mishkin, M. & Appenzeller, T. (1990). The Anatomy of Memory. In R. R. Llinas (ed.) *the Workings of the Brain: Development, Memory and Perception*. New York: W. H. Freeman & Co.

Mishkin, M., Malamut, B. & Bachevalier, J. (1984). Memories and Habits: Two Neural Systems. In G. Lynch, J. L. Mcgaugh & N. M. Weinberger (eds) *Neurobiology of Learning and Memory*. New York: the Guilford Press.

Mollon, J. D. (1982). Colour Vision and Colour Blindness. In H. B. Barlow & J. D. Mollon (eds) *The Senses*. Cambridge, Mass.: Cambridge University Press.

Moody, J. & Darken, C. J. (1989). Fast Learning in Networks of Locally-tuned Processing Units. *Neural Computation*, 1, 281–94.

Moorhead, I. R., Haig, N. D. & Clement, R. A. (1989). An Investigation of Trained Neural Networks From a Neurophysiological Perspective. *Perception*, 18, 793–803.

Mori, T. (1982). Apparent Motion Path Composed of a Serial Concatenation of Translations and Rotations. *Biological Cybernetics*, 44, 31–4.

Moscovitch, M. (1992). Memory and Working-with-memory: A Component Process Model Based on Modules and Central Systems. *Journal of Cognitive Neuroscience*, 4, 257–67.

Motter, B. C. & Mountcastle, V. B. (1981). The Functional Properties of the Light-sensitive Neurons of the Posterior Parietal Cortex Studied in Waking Monkeys: Foveal Sparing and Opponent Vector Organization. *The Journal of Neuroscience*, 1, 3–26.

Movshon, J. A., Adelson, E. H., Gizzi, M. S. & Newsome, W. T. (1985). The Analysis of Moving Visual Patterns. In C. Chagas, R. Gattas & C. G. Gross (eds) *Pattern Recognition Mechanisms*. Rome: Vatican Press.

Mozer, M. C. & Smolensky, P. (1989). Using Relevance to Reduce Network Size Automatically. *Connection Science*, 1, 3–16.

Müller, B. & Reinhardt, J. (1990). *Neural Networks*. Berline: Springer-Verlag.

Murdock, B. B. (1982). A Theory for the Storage and Retrieval of Item and Associative Information. *Psychological Review*, 89, 609–26.

Murdock, B. B. (1985). Convolution and Matrix Systems: A Reply to Pike. *Psychological Review*, 92, 130–2.

Nakayama, K. (1985). Biological Image Motion Processing: A Review. *Vision Research*, 25, 625–60.

Nass, R. D. & Gazzaniga, M. S. (1987). Cerebral Lateralization and Specialization in Human Central Nervous System. In F. Plum (ed.) *Handbook of Physiology*. Bethesda, Md.: American Physiological Society.

Navon, D. (1976). Irrelevance of Figural Identity for Resolving Ambiguities in Apparent Motion. *Journal of Experimental Psychology: Human Perception and Performance*, 2, 130–8.

Newell, A. (1973a). You Can't Play 20 Questions with Nature and Win: Projective

Comments on the Papers of this Symposium. In W. G. Chase (ed.) *Visual Information Processing*. New York: Academic Press.

Newell, A. (1973b). Production Systems: Models of Control Structures. In W. G. Chase (ed.) *Visual Information Processing*. New York: Academic Press.

Newell, A. (1980). Physical Symbol Systems. *Cognitive Science*, 4, 135–83.

Newell, A. (1990). *Unified Theories of Cognition*. Cambridge, Mass.: Harvard University Press.

Newell, A., Shaw, J. C. & Simon, H. A. (1958). Elements of a Theory of Human Problem Solving. *Psychological Review*, 65, 151–66.

Newell, A. & Simon, H. A. (1972). *Human Problem Solving*. Englewood Cliffs, NJ: Prentice-Hall.

Newport, E. L., Gleitman, H. & Gleitman, L. R. (1977). Mother, I'd Rather Do it Myself: Some Effects and Noneffects of Maternal Speech Style. In C. Snow and C. Ferguson (eds) *Talking to Children: Language Input and Acquisition*. Cambridge, Mass.: Cambridge University Press.

Newsome, W. T., Mikami, A. & Wurtz, R. H. (1986). Motion Selectivity in Macaque Visual Cortex. III. Psychophysics and Physiology of Apparent Motion. *Journal of Neurophysiology*, 55, 1340–51.

Newsome, W. T. & Pare, E. B. (1988). A Selective Impairment of Motion Processing Following Lesions of the Middle Temporal Visual Area (MT). *Journal of Neuroscience*, 8, 2201–11.

Nicholls, J. G., Martin, A. R. & Wallace, B. G. (1992). *From Neuron to Brain*, 3rd edn. Sunderland, Mass.: Sinauer Associates.

Norman, D. A. (1980). Twelve Issues for Cognitive Science. *Cognitive Science*, 4, 1–32.

Omlin, C. W. & Giles, C. L. (1996). Extraction of Rules from Discrete-time Recurrent Neural Networks. *Neural Networks*, 9, 41–52.

Orban, G. A., Gulyas, B. & Spileers, W. (1988). Influence of Moving Textured Backgrounds on Responses of Cat Area 18 Cells to Moving Bars. *Progress in Brain Research*, 75, 137–45.

Orban, B. A., Gulyas, B. & Vogels, R. (1987). Influence of a Moving Textured Background on Directional Selectivity of Cat Striate Neurons. *Journal of Neurophysiology*, 57, 1792–1812.

Osherson, D. N. (1995). *An Invitation to Cognitive Science*, 2nd edn. Cambridge, Mass.: MIT Press, 3 vols.

Osherson, D. N., Stob, M. & Weinstein, S. (1986). *Systems that Learn*. Cambridge, Mass.: MIT Press.

Paivio, A. (1969). Mental Imagery in Associative Learning and Memory. *Psychological Review*, 76, 241–263.

Paivio, A. (1971). *Imagery and Verbal Processes*. New York: Holt, Rinehart & Winston.

Paivio, A. (1986). *Mental Representations: A Dual-coding Approach*. New York: Oxford University Press.

Pantle, A. & Picciano, L. (1976). A Multistable Movement Display: Evidence for Two Separate Motion Systems in Human Vision. *Science*, 193, 500–2.

Papert, S. (1988). One AI or Many? In S. Graubard (ed.) *The Artificial Intelligence Debate*. Cambridge, Mass.: MIT Press.

Penfield, W. & Roberts, L. (1959). *Speech and Brain-mechanisms*. Princeton: Princeton University Press.

Penrose, R. (1989). *The Emperor's New Mind*. London: Oxford University Press.

Petersik, J. T. (1989). The Two-process Distinction in Apparent Motion. *Psychological Bulletin*, 106, 107–27.

Peterson, L. R. & Peterson, M. J. (1959). Short-term Retention of Individual Verbal Items. *Journal of Experimental Psychology*, 58, 193–8

Pike, R. (1984). Comparison of Convolution and Matrix Distributed Memory Systems for Associative Recall and Recognition. *Psychological Review*, 91, 281–94.

Pinker, S. (1979). Formal Models of Language Learning. *Cognition*, 7, 217–83.

Pinker, S. (1990). Language Acquisition. In D. N. Osherson & H. Lasnik (eds) *An Invitation to Cognitive Science*, vol. 1: *Language*. Cambridge, Mass.: MIT Press.

Pinker, S. (1994). *The Language Instinct*. New York: Morrow.

Pinker, S. & Prince, A. (1988). On Language and Connectionism: Analysis of a Parallel Distributed Processing Model of Language Acquisition. *Cognition*, 28, 73–193.

Poggio, T. & Girosi, F. (1989). A Theory of Networks for Approximation and Learning. *MIT AI Lab Memo No. 1140*.

Poggio, T. & Girosi, F. (1990). Regularization Algorithms for Learning that are Equivalent to Multilayer Networks. *Science*, 247, 978–82.

Pollack, J. B. (1990). Recursive Distributed Representations. *Artificial Intelligence*, 46, 77–105.

Pomerleau, D. A. (1991). Efficient Training of Artificial Neural Networks for Autonomous Navigation. *Neural Computation*, 3, 88–97.

Posner, M. (1978). *Chronometric Explorations of Mind*. Hillsdale, NJ: Lawrence Erlbaum Associates.

Posner, M. (1991). *Foundations of Cognitive Science*. Cambridge, Mass.: MIT Press.

Postman, L. & Phillips, L. W. (1965). Short-term Temporal Changes in Free Recall. *Quarterly Journal of Experimental Psychology*, 17, 132–8.

Power, D'arcy. (1897). *William Harvey*. London: T. Fisher Unwin.

Prazdny, K. (1986). What Variables Control (Long-range) Apparent Motion? *Perception*, 15, 37-40.

Prior, M. E. (1962). *Science and the Humanities*. Evanston, Ill.: Northwestern University Press.

Proffitt, D. & Cutting, J. E. (1979). Perceiving the Centroid of Configurations on a Rolling Wheel. *Perception & Psychophysics*, 25, 389–98.

Proffitt, D. & Cutting, J. E. (1980). An Invariant for Wheel-generated Motions and the Logic of its Determination. *Perception*, 9, 435–49.

Pylyshyn, Z. W. (1973). What the Mind's Eye Tells the Mind's Brain: A Critique of Mental Imagery. *Psychological Bulletin*, 80, 1–24.

Pylyshyn, Z. W. (1979). Metaphorical Imprecision and the "Top-down" Research Strategy. In A. Ortony (ed.) *Metaphor and Thought*. Cambridge, Mass.: Cambridge University Press.

Pylyshyn, Z. W. (1980). Computation and Cognition: Issues in the Foundations of Cognitive Science. *Behavioral and Brain Sciences*, 3, 111–69.

Pylyshyn, Z. W. (1981). Complexity and the Study of Artificial and Human Intelligence. In J. Haugeland (ed.) *Mind Design*. Cambridge, Mass.: MIT Press.

Pylyshyn, Z. W. (1984). *Computation and Cognition*. Cambridge, Mass.: MIT Press.

Pylyshyn, Z. W. (1987). Here and There in the Visual Field. In Z. Pylyshyn (ed.) *Computational Processes in Human Vision*. Norwood, NJ: Ablex.

Pylyshyn, Z. W. (1989). The Role of Location Indexes in Spatial Perception: A Sketch of the Finst Spatial-index Model. *Cognition*, 32, 65-97.

Pylyshyn, Z. W. (1991). The Role of Cognitive Architecture in Theories of Cognition. In K. Vanlehn (ed.) *Architectures for Intelligence*. Hillsdale, NJ: Lawrence Erlbaum Associates.

Pylyshyn, Z. W. & Storm, R. (1988). Tracking of Multiple Independent Targets: Evidence for a Parallel Tracking Mechanism. *Spatial Vision*, 3, 1–19.

Rager, J. & Berg, G. (1990). A Connectionist Model of Motion and Government in Chomsky's Government-binding Theory. *Connection Science*, 2, 35–52.

Ramachandran, V. S. & Anstis, S. M. (1985). Perceptual Organization in Multistable Apparent Motion. *Perception*, 14, 135–43.

Ramachandran, V. S. & Anstis, S. M. (1986a). The Perception of Apparent Motion. *Scientific American*, 254(6), 102–9.

Ramachandran, V. S. & Anstis, S. M. (1986b). Figure–Ground Segregation Modulates Apparent Motion. *Vision Research*, 26, 1969–75.

Ramsey, W., Stich, S. P. & Garon, J. (1991). Connectionism, Eliminativism, and the Future of Folk Psychology. In Ramsey, W., Stich, S. P. & Rumelhart, D. E. (eds) *Philosophy and Connectionist Theory*. Hillsdale, NJ: Lawrence Erlbaum Associates.

Ramsey, W., Stich, S. P. & Rumelhart, D. E. (1991). *Philosophy and Connectionist Theory*. Hillsdale, NJ: Lawrence Erlbaum Associates.

Ratliff, F. (1976). On the Psychophysiological Bases of Universal Color Terms. *Proceedings of the American Philosophical Society*, 120, 311–30.

Ratcliff, G. & Davies-Jones, G. A. B. (1972). Defective Visual Localization in Focal Brain Wounds. *Brain*, 95, 49–60.

Reed, S. K. (1996). *Cognition: Theory and Applications*. Belmont, Calif.: Wadsworth Publishing.

Reeke, G. N. & Edelman, G. M. (1988). Real Brains and Artificial Intelligence. In S. Graubard (ed.) *The Artificial Intelligence Debate*. Cambridge, Mass.: MIT Press.

Regan, D. (1986). Visual Processing of Four Kinds of Relative Motion. *Vision Research*, 26, 127–45.

Reichardt, W. (1961). Autocorrelation, a Principle for the Evaluation of Sensory Information. In W. A. Rosenblith (ed.) *Sensory Communication*. Cambridge, Mass.: MIT Press.

Reitman, W. B. (1965). *Cognition and Thought*. New York: Wiley

Renals, S. (1989). Radial Basis Function Network for Speech Pattern Classification. *Electronics Letters*, 25, 437–9.

Restle, F. (1979). Coding Theory of Motion Configurations. *Psychological Review*, 86, 1–24.

Richards, W. (1988). The Approach. In W. Richards (ed.) *Natural Computation*. Cambridge, Mass.: MIT Press.

Richmond, B. J. & Optican, L. M. (1992). The Structure and Interpretation of Neuronal Codes in the Visual System. In H. Wechsler (ed.) *Neural Networks for Perception*, vol. 1. Boston: Academic Press.

Rips, L. J. (1994). *The Psychology of Proof*. Cambridge, Mass.: MIT Press.

Rips, L., Shoben, E. J. & Smith, E. E. (1973). Semantic Distance and Verification of Semantic Relations. *Journal of Verbal Learning and Verbal Behavior*, 12, 1–20.

Ritter, A. D. & Breitmeyer, B. G. (1989). The Effects of Dichoptic and Binocular Viewing on Bistable Motion Percepts. *Vision Research*, 29, 1215–19.

Robinson, D. L., Goldberg, M. E. & Stanton, G. B. (1978). Parietal Association Cortex in the Primate: Sensory Mechanisms and Behavioural Modulations. *Journal of Neurophysiology*, 41, 910–32.

Rock, I. (1983). *The Logic of Perception*. Cambridge, Mass.: MIT Press.

Rodman, H. R. & Albright, T. D. (1987). Coding of Visual Stimulus Velocity in Area MT of the Macaque. *Vision Research*, 27, 2035–48.

Rogers, C. (1961). *On Becoming a Person*. Boston: Houghton-Mifflin.

Rosch, E. & Mervis, C. B. (1975). Family Resemblances: Studies in the Internal Structure of Categories. *Cognitive Psychology*, 7, 573–605.

Rosen, S. (1980). *The Limits of Analysis*. New York: Basic Books.

Rosenblatt, F. (1962). *Principles of Neurodynamics*. Washington: Spartan Books.

Royce, J. R. (1970). The Present Situation in Theoretical Psychology. In J. R. Royce (ed.) *Toward Unification in Psychology*. Toronto: University of Toronto Press.

Rumelhart, D. E., Hinton, G. E. & McClelland, J. L. (1986). A General Framework for Parallel Distributed Processing. In Rumelhart, Mcclelland & the PDP Group (eds) *Parallel Distributed Processing*, vol. 1. Cambridge, Mass.: MIT Press.

Rumelhart, D. E., Hinton, G. E. & Williams, R. J. (1986a). Learning Representations by Back-propagating Errors. *Nature*, 323, 533–6.

Rumelhart, D. E., Hinton, G. E. & Williams, R. J. (1986b). Learning Internal Representations by Error Backpropagation. In Rumelhart, J. McClelland and the PDP Group (eds) *Parallel Distributed Processing*, vol. 1. Cambridge, Mass.: MIT Press.

Rumelhart, D. E. & McClelland, J. L. (1985). Levels Indeed! A Response to Broadbent. *Journal of Experimental Psychology: General*, 114, 193–7.

Rumelhart, D. E. & McClelland, J. (1986). PDP Models and General Issues in Cognitive Science. In Rumelhart, McClelland & the PDP Group (eds) *Parallel Distributed Processing*, vol. 1. Cambridge, Mass.: MIT Press.

Rumelhart, D. E., McClelland, J. L. & the PDP Group. (1986). *Parallel Distributed Processing*, vol. 1. Cambridge, Mass.: MIT Press.

Ryle, G. (1949). *The Concept of Mind*. London: Hutchinson & Company.

Sacks, O. (1987). *The Man Who Mistook His Wife for A Hat*. New York: HarperPerrenial.

Saito, H., Yukie, M., Tanaka, K., Hikosaka, K., Fukada, Y. & Iwai, E. (1986). Integration of Direction Signals of Image Motion in the Superior Temporal Sulcus of the Macaque Monkey. *The Journal of Neuroscience*, 6, 145–57.

Sakata, H., Shibutani, H., Kawano, K. & Harrington, T. L. (1985). Neural Mechanisms of Space Vision in the Parietal Association Cortex of the Monkey. *Vision Research*, 25, 453–63.

Sakata, H., Shibutani, H. & Tsurugai, K. (1986). Parietal Cortical Neurons Responding to Rotary Movement of Visual Stimulus in Space. *Experimental Brain Research*, 61, 658–63.

Schacter, D. L. (1992). Priming and Multiple Memory Systems: Perceptual Mechanisms of Implicit Memory. *Journal of Cognitive Neuroscience*, 4, 244–56.

Schank, R. C. & Abelson, R. (1977). *Scripts, Plans, Goals and Understanding*. Hillsdale, NJ: Lawrence Erlbaum Associates.

Schlimmer, J. S. (1987). Concept Acquisition through Representational Adjustment (Technical Report 87-19). Doctoral dissertation, Dept of Information and Computer Science, University of California Irvine.

Schnapf, J. L., Nunn, B. J., Meister, M. & Baylor, D. A. (1990). Visual Transductions in Cones of the Monkey Macaca Fascicularis. *Journal of Physiology*, 427, 681–713.

Schneider, W. (1987). Connectionism: Is it a Paradigm Shift for Psychology? *Behavior Research Methods, Instruments & Computers*, 19, 73–83.

Schneider, W. & Oliver, W. L. (1991). An Instructable Connectionist/Control Architecture: Using Rule-based Instructions to Accomplish Connectionist Learning in a Human Time Scale. In K. Vanlehn (ed.) *Architectures for Intelligence*. Hillsdale, NJ: Lawrence Erlbaum Associates.

Schwartz, E. L. (1990). *Computational Neuroscience*. Cambridge, Mass.: MIT Press.

Scoville, W. B. & Milner, B. (1957). Loss of Recent Memory after Bilateral Hippocampal Lesions. *Journal of Neurology, Neurosurgery and Psychiatry*, 20, 11–21.

Searle, J. R. (1980). Minds, Brains, and Programs. *Behavioral and Brain Sciences*, 3, 417–24.

Searle, J. R. (1984). *Minds, Brains and Science*. Cambridge, Mass.: Harvard University Press.

Searle, J. R. (1990). Is the Brain's Mind a Computer Program? *Scientific American*, 262(1), 26–31.

Searle, J. R. (1992). *The Rediscovery of the Mind*. Cambridge, Mass.: MIT Press.

Seidenberg, M. (1993). Connectionist Models and Cognitive Theory. *Psychological Science*, 4, 228–35.

Seidenberg, M. & McClelland, J. (1989). A Distributed, Developmental Model of Word Recognition and Naming. *Psychological Review*, 97, 447–52.

Shallice, T. (1988). *From Neuropsychology to Mental Structure*. New York: Cambridge University Press.

Shallice, T. & Warrington, E. K. (1970). Independent Functioning of Verbal Memory Stores: A Neuropsychological Study. *Quarterly Journal of Experimental Psychology*, 37a, 507–32.

Shamanski, K. S. & Dawson, M. R. W. (1994). Problem Type by Network Type Interactions in the Speed and Transfer of Connectionist Learning. In B. Macdonald, R. Holte & C. Ling (eds) *Proceedings of the Machine Learning Workshop at AI/GI/VI'94*. University of Calgary Dept of Computer Science Research Report no. 94/539/08.

Shepard, R. N. (1982). Perceptual and Analogical Bases of Cognition. In J. Mehler, E. Walker & M. Garrett (eds) *Perspectives on Mental Representation*. Hillsdale, NJ: Lawrence Erlbaum Associates.

Shepard, R. N. (1984). Ecological Constraints on Internal Representation: Resonant Kinematics of Perceiving, Imagining, Thinking, and Dreaming. *Psychological Review*, 91, 417–47.

Shepard, R. N. & Cooper, L. A. (1982). *Mental Images and Their Transformations*. Cambridge, Mass.: MIT Press.

Shepard, R. N. & Judd, S. A. (1976). Perceptual Illusion of Rotation of Three-dimensional Objects. *Science*, 191, 952–4.

Shepherd, G. M. (1988). *Neurobiology*, 2nd edn. New York: Oxford University Press.

Siegelman, H. T. & Sontag, E. D. (1991). Turing Computability with Neural Nets. *Applied Mathematics Letters*, 4, 77–80.

Siegelman, H. T. & Sontag, E. D. (1992). On the Computational Power of Neural Nets. *Proceedings of the Fifth ACM Workshop on Computational Learning Theory*. New York: ACM, pp. 440–9.

Simon, H. A. (1979). *Models of Thought*. New Haven: Yale University Press.

Simon, H. A. (1980). Cognitive Science: the Newest Science of the Artificial. *Cognitive Science*, 4, 33–46.

Simon, H. A. (1989). *Models of Thought*, vol. 2. New Haven: Yale University Press.

Simon, H. A. (1996). *The Sciences of the Artificial*, 3rd edn. Cambridge, Mass.: MIT Press.

Simon, H. A. & Newell, A. (1958). Heuristic Problem Solving: the Next Advance in Operations Research. *Operation Research*, 6, 1–10.

Smolensky, P. (1988). On the Proper Treatment of Connectionism. *Behavioural and Brain Sciences*, 11, 1–74.

Smolensky, P. (1990). Tensor Product Variable Binding and the Representation of Symbolic Structures in Connectionist Systems. *Artificial Intelligence*, 46, 159–216.

Solso, R. L. (1995). *Cognitive Psychology*, 4th edn. Boston: Allyn and Bacon.

Sperry, R. W. (1958). Physiological Plasticity and Brain Circuit Theory. In H. F. Harlow

& C. F. Woolsey (eds) *Biological and Biochemical Bases of Behavior*. Madison: University of Wisconsin Press.

Squire, L. R. (1987). *Memory and Brain*. New York: Oxford University Press.

Squire, L. R. (1992). Declarative and Nondeclarative Memory: Multiple Brain Systems Supporting Learning and Memory. *Journal of Cognitive Neuroscience*, 4, 232–43.

St. John, M. F. & McClelland, J. L. (1990). Learning and Applying Contextual Constraints in Sentence Comprehension. *Artificial Intelligence*, 46, 217–57.

Steinbuch, K. (1961). Die Lernmatrix. *Kybernetik*, 1, 36–45.

Sternberg, R. J. (1996). *Cognitive Psychology*. Fort Worth, Tex.: Harcourt Brace College Publishers.

Sternberg, S. (1969). Memory-scanning: Mental Processes Revealed by Reaction-time Experiments. *American Scientist*, 4, 421–57.

Stewart, I. (1994). A Subway Named Turing. *Scientific American*, 271(3), 104–7.

Stich, S. (1990). *The Fragmentation of Reason*. Cambridge, Mass.: MIT Press.

Stillings, N., Feinstein, M. H., Garfield, J. L., Rissland, E. L., Rosenbaum, D. A., Weisler, S. E. & Baker-Ward, L. (1987). *Cognitive Science: an Introduction*. Cambridge, Mass.: MIT Press.

Stix, G. (1994). Bad Apple Picker: Can a Neural Network Help Find Problem Cops? *Scientific American*, 271(6), 44–6.

Swade, D. D. (1993). Redeeming Charles Babbage's Mechanical Computer. *Scientific American*, 268(2), 86–91.

Tanaka, K., Hikosaka, K., Saito, H., Yukie, M., Fukada, Y. & Iwai, E. (1986). Analysis of Local and Wide-field Movements in the Superior Temporal Visual Areas of the Macaque Monkey. *The Journal of Neuroscience*, 6, 134–44.

Taylor, W. K. (1956). Electrical Simulation of some Nervous System Functional Activities. In C. Cherry (ed.) *Information Theory*. London: Butterworths Scientific.

Ternus, J. (1938). The Problem of Phenomenal Identity. In W. D. Ellis (ed.) *A Sourcebook of Gestalt Psychology*. New York: Humanities Press.

Teuber, H.-L., Milner, B. & Vaughan, H. G. (1968). Persistent Anterograde Amnesia after Stab Wound of the Basal Brain. *Neuropsychologia*, 6, 267–82.

Tolman, E. C. (1932). *Purposive Behavior in Animals and Men*. New York: Century Books.

Tolman, E. C. (1948). Cognitive Maps in Rats and Men. *Psychological Review*, 55, 189–208.

Tourangeau, R. & Sternberg, R. J. (1981). Aptness in Metaphor. *Cognitive Psychology*, 13, 27–55.

Treisman, A. M. & Gelade, G. (1980). A Feature Integration Theory of Attention. *Cognitive Psychology*, 12, 97–136.

Tulving, E. (1983). *Elements of Episodic Memory*. Oxford: Oxford University Press.

Turing, A. M. (1936). On Computable Numbers, with an Application to the *Entscheidungsproblem*. *Proceedings of the London Mathematical Society*, Series 2, 42, 230–65.

Turing, A. M. (1950). Computing Machinery and Intelligence. *Mind*, 59, 433–60.

Ullman, S. (1978). Two-dimensionality of the Correspondence Process in Apparent Motion. *Perception*, 7, 683–93.

Ullman, S. (1979). *The Interpretation of Visual Motion*. Cambridge, Mass.: MIT Press.

Ullman, S. (1981). Analysis of Visual Motion by Biological and Computer Systems. *IEEE Computer*, August, 57–69.

Ungerleider, L. G. & Mishkin, M. (1982). Two Cortical Visual Systems. In D. J. Ingle,

M. A. Goodale & R. J. W. Mansfield (eds) *Analysis of Visual Behavior*. Cambridge, Mass.: MIT Press.

Vallar, G. & Baddeley, A. D. (1984). Fractionation of Working Memory: Neuropsychological Evidence for a Phonological Short-term Store. *Journal of Verbal Learning and Verbal Behavior*, 23, 151–61.

Vanlehn, K. (1991). *Architectures for Intelligence*. Hillsdale, NJ: Lawrence Erlbaum Associates.

Van Santen, J. P. H. & Sperling, G. (1984). A Temporal Covariance Model of Motion Perception. *Journal of the Optical Society of America*, 1a, 451–73.

Van Santen, J. P. H. & Sperling, G. (1985). Elaborated Reichardt Detectors. *Journal of the Optical Society of America*, 2a, 300–20.

Victor, J. D. & Conte, M. M. (1990). Motion Mechanisms have only Limited Access to Form Information. *Vision Research*, 30, 289–301.

Von Eckardt, B. (1993). *What is Cognitive Science?* Cambridge, Mass.: MIT Press.

Von Neumann, J. (1958). *The Computer and the Brain*. New Haven: Yale University Press.

Wallach, H. & O'Connell, D. N. (1953). The Kinetic Depth Effect. *Journal of Experimental Psychology*, 45, 205–17.

Wasserman, G. S. (1978). *Color Vision: An Historical Introduction*. New York: John Wiley & Sons.

Wasserman, P. D. (1989). *Neurocomputing: Theory and Practice*. New York: Van Norstrand Reinhold.

Watrous, R. L. & Kuhn, G. M. (1992). Induction of Finite-state Languages Using Second-order Recurrent Networks. *Neural Computation*, 2, 406–14.

Waugh, N. C. & Norman, D. A. (1965). Primary Memory. *Psychological Review*, 72, 89–104.

Weizenbaum, J. (1976). *Computer Power and Human Reason*. San Francisco: W. H. Freeman.

Werker, J. F. & Tees, R. C. (1984). Cross-language Speech Perception: Evidence for Perceptual Reorganization During the First Year of Life. *Infant Behavior and Development*, 7, 49–63.

Wexler, K. & Culicover, P. W. (1980). *Formal Principles of Language Acquisition*. Cambridge, Mass.: MIT Press.

White, P. (1991). *The Idea Factory*. New York: Plume Books.

Widrow, B. (1962). Generalization and Information Storage in Networks of Adaline "Neurons" . In M. Yovits, G. Jacobi & G. Goldstein (eds) *Self-Organizing Systems*. Washington, DC: Spartan Books.

Widrow, B. & Hoff, M. E. (1960). Adaptive Switching Circuits. *Institute of Radio Engineers, Western Electronic Show and Convention, Convention Record*, Part 4, 96–104.

Wiener, N. (1948). *Cybernetics*. New York: John Wiley & Sons.

Williams, R. & Zipser, D. (1989). A Learning Algorithm for Continually Running Fully Recurrent Neural Networks. *Neural Computation*, 1, 270–80.

Willshaw, D. J., Buneman, O. P. & Longuet-Higgins, H. C. (1969). Non-Holographic Associative Memory. *Nature*, 222, 960–2.

Winograd, T. & Flores, F. (1987). *Understanding Computers and Cognition*. New York: Addison-Wesley.

Wright, R. D. & Dawson, M. R. W. (1994). To What Extent do Beliefs Affect Apparent Motion? *Philosophical Psychology*, 7, 471–91.

Yuille, A. L. (1983). The Smoothest Velocity Field and Token Matching Schemes. *MIT AI Memo no. 724*.

Zeki, S. M. (1974). Functional Organization of a Visual Area in the Posterior Bank of the Superior Temporal Sulcus of the Rhesus Monkey. *Journal of Physiology*, 236, 549–73.

Zihl, J., Von Cramon, D. & Mai, N. (1983). Selective Disturbance of Movement Vision after Bilateral Brain Damage. *Brain*, 106, 313–40.

Zurada, J. M. (1992). *Introduction to Artificial Neural Systems*. St. Paul, Minn.: West.

Zurif, E. B. (1990). Language and the Brain. In D. N. Osherson & H. Lasnik (eds) *An Invitation to Cognitive Science*, vol. 1: *Language*. Cambridge, Mass.: MIT Press.

Name Index

Subject Index